SHADOW MEN

AN ENCYCLOPEDIA OF MIND CONTROL

By

Dr. Anthony Napoleon, Ph.D. © 2015

"Shadow Men – An Encyclopedia of Mind Control," by Dr. Anthony Napoleon, Ph.D. ISBN 978-1-62137-728-3 (softcover); 978-1-62137-729-0 (casebound).

Published by Virtualbookworm.com Publishing Inc., P.O. Box 9949, College Station, Texas, 77842, US.

TABLE OF CONTENTS

DEDICATION

To the men and women who will no longer tolerate the evil that lives and works in the shadows, this book is dedicated to you and your loved ones.

PREFACE

The path of the righteous man is beset on all sides by the inequities of the selfish and the tyranny of evil men. Blessed is he who, in the name of charity and good will, shepherds the weak through the valley of darkness, for he is truly his brother's keeper and the finder of lost children. And I will strike down upon thee with great vengeance and furious anger those who attempt to poison and destroy my brothers. And you will know my name is the Lord when I lay my vengeance upon you! ...Ezekiel 25:17.

In 1948 George Orwell provided Aldous Huxley a complementary copy of his new book, "*1984.*" Huxley wrote the following to Orwell after reading his groundbreaking book:

Within the next generation I believe that the world's rulers will discover that infant conditioning and narco-hypnosis are more efficient, as instruments of government, than clubs and prisons, and that the lust for power can be just as completely satisfied by suggesting people into loving their servitude as by flogging and kicking them into obedience. In other words, I feel that the nightmare of Nineteen Eighty-Four is destined to modulate into the nightmare of a world having more resemblance to that which I imagined in Brave New World. The change will be brought about as a result of a felt need for increased efficiency. Meanwhile, of course, there may be a large scale biological and atomic war — in which case we shall have nightmares of other and scarcely imaginable kinds.

Thank you once again for the book.

Yours sincerely,
Aldous Huxley

Shadow Men represents my latest effort to add dimension and clarity to the devious and highly sophisticated psychological operations (PSYOPs) erasing man's free will and transforming him into a more supplicant and controllable life form. In modern warfare and social engineering, PSYOPs are no longer limited to modifying the central nervous system (CNS) directly, but now involve the bio-psycho-social engineering of man's very nature. The vast majority of PSYOPs operate without their victim's awareness. They function exactly like unknown pathogens, that create visible disease but for which the cause remains shrouded in mystery.

I will teach you about the mind control technology shadow men's agents and proxies use on each and every one of us each and everyday of our lives. I will then equip you with the tools that will empower you to boost your immunity to these highly sophisticated PSYOPs that are designed to deny you your natural right to free will and freedom. Awareness, itself, is a powerful antidote to the insidious effects of mind control.

It is also my intent to provide to my readers insight into the motivations of the shadow men molding your nature. You will come to understand what motivates these men who live and practice their social engineering dark arts in the shadows. In order to accomplish these ambitious goals, I will explore how shadow men came into existence and spread throughout the world. I will profile their cognitive, emotional and behavioral characteristics.

For those of you who may have decided to read this book in order to consciously or unconsciously confirm your particular political ideology or religious beliefs, be advised that you will likely be disappointed, and here is why. You will learn that mind control technology, and those who use it as a weapon of mass control, are not dedicated members of any particular political ideology or religion, as their station in life is above all that which the masses have been led to believe is important, including political and/or religious affiliations, ideologies and national identity.

Shadow men rely upon their agents and proxies to carry out their will. These agents of the shadow elite head important institutions, enterprises and governmental posts. The proxies for shadow men who man their political operations serve in the roles of politician and bureaucrat at all levels of government. The agents of shadow men may work on-stage or, like their overseers, live and work in the shadows.

Regardless of where their agents fit into shadow men's organizational matrix, they are kindred spirits of their overseers. As a whole, they are obsessed with accumulating more power and are in love with control. Enough is never enough when it comes to shadow men and their agent's insatiable thirst for power. Power's utilitarian value derives from how its exercise controls thoughts, emotions and behavior. Power also serves as the cudgel by which shadow men can, and often do, vanquish their intramural competitors and enemies.

In order for shadow men to pursue their life's passion of absolute dominance over everyone and everything, they must exercise control over the masses and other competing shadow men within their elite group. Shadow men believe the masses possess only one power worthy of their attention, and that is the power of large numbers. Shadow men view the masses as a commodity to exploit, harvest, use for fun and experiment upon. Despite their power over the masses, shadow men fear them.

Shadow men's insatiable appetite for power and dominance necessitates that their surrogate institutions tasked with population management retain the services of mind control researchers, experts and operational agents who design, then employ, various mind control strategies and tactics.

Shadow men's matrix of power is self-perpetuating because of the following sobering realities. Legacy power transfers from one generation to another with each succeeding generation virtually guaranteed to leverage their great power over others who are either dupes, complicit or agents. Consider that only a very few among the masses will ever develop a *meaningful* understanding of shadow men. Of those very few, even fewer among the masses would dare challenge a power matrix that is, for all intents and purposes, functionally invisible to those who, presumably, would be interested in rising up to challenge shadow men.

If a member of the masses poses a viable threat to shadow men, then that very rare person may be seduced, if not ignored, by agents of shadow men and encouraged to join a branch of their matrix of power. Sex, power, wealth and possessing a pseudo-elite identity can be very seductive to a person who would otherwise be a champion for the masses; masses that have nothing to offer their potential savior in return. Not only do the masses have little or nothing to give back, saviors invariably have to deal with the masses' denial and psychological resistance to efforts to help them. The seduction of viable threats to shadow men is a well-practiced art among the agents of shadow men when ignoring the threat is unsuccessful. In the very rare instance that a viable threat successfully runs the gauntlet, that person's threat is terminated; never to be revealed, as anything other than an unfortunate accident, a regretful loss to disease or victim of random violence. If history is any guide, when brave champions of the masses are terminated, the masses cower in fear, use denial, rationalization and soon put the entire matter out of their limited awareness.

Consider also that no matter how talented or courageous the person who would rise up against shadow men, who is this brave person going to persuade to join him in what will be understood by other rare knowing persons to be a suicide mission? Is he going to persuade the masses that are emotionally and psychologically incapable of even accepting the existence of a mysterious hidden matrix of elite to join him? Is he going to pry the masses away from their reality TV and Twitter or Facebook digital world long enough to get them to take action? Can any viable threat to shadow men rise up to compete with legacy elites without first garnering the dedication and assistance, such that it is, of those same hapless, afraid and denial ridden masses who are struggling financially just to survive? Notwithstanding all of these daunting challenges, there is hope for those among the masses who will be content saving themselves and their loved ones; but first, you must come to understand why the matrix operates as it does and how it has been so successful. If you are willing to engage the fight, then read on.

CHAPTER 1: A PRIMER OF THE MIND

Shadow men, their agents and surrogate institutions control their victims by manipulating human nature. Shadow men's agents and surrogates are eugenicists who are intent upon bio-psycho-socially engineering a more supplicant and submissive human species. This includes modifying the breeding habits and customs of the masses. Man's central nervous system (CNS) is their central focus because it is the control center that, if modified then controlled, can immediately and sometimes permanently alter thoughts, emotions and behaviors. PSYOPs can target man's CNS like a sniper's bullet or they may be akin to blanket bombings. Control can be effectuated over man's CNS directly or indirectly.

Mechanisms of control can originate from external sources or they can originate from within the target's CNS. PSYOPs have been devised that transform external sources of control into internal control mechanisms. These locus of control modulators were developed because internal control mechanisms have any number of advantages over external methods of control, not the least of which is that internal control is often mistaken as the exercise of free will or democratic rule.

Internal control mechanisms have many advantages over external methods of control. Internal control requires less maintenance and manpower in order to insure it is working as designed. Internal controls are often thought of in the intelligence community as low or maintenance free PSYOPs. What follows is just one example of how an external control measure can be made to morph into a low maintenance internal control mechanism.

Have you ever paid attention to the fact that fully grown elephants are not infrequently held captive by a rather small sisal rope tied around one of the elephant's legs? You might ponder: how can a single strand of off-the-shelf rope hold an elephant captive, a creature that can easily uproot huge trees and move boulders weighting tons?

When the elephant was a baby its controllers attached a huge metal chain securely shackled around one of its legs. The chain was firmly staked deep into the ground. In response to the shackle the baby elephant made instinctually driven and repeated attempts to free itself. The baby elephant tried as he might but eventually became exhausted, often times ending up with a bruised and bloodied chained leg. At some point, the elephant became conditioned to believe that no matter what it did or how hard it pulled, it was trapped and could not free itself. Once external control, which took the form of the chain and long stake, were internalized by the baby elephant, the controller could then substitute the internal control of the sisal rope for the chain and stake because the elephant's instinctual quest for freedom had been subverted.

Could the elephant break the rope if he tried? Of course, in an instant the rope would snap and the elephant would be free. Will the elephant try to break free? No, he will not. From the outside looking in, ill-informed observers conclude that the elephant must be content because he stays tethered by only a rope. Similarly, outside observers conclude that the elephant's handlers are nice and must treat the elephant well; otherwise, the elephant would try to break free. Both conclusions are erroneous. The situation involving the masses is not much different from the fate of the captive elephant.

Individuals or groups can bring about external control. Individuals generally have much less influence over large segments of the population when compared to groups. Peer pressure, group norms, modeling, and mob-enforced conformity are all examples of how group psychology is used to effectuate control over the masses.

External control can be exercised directly or indirectly. For example, direct control occurs when a person is handcuffed and put in jail. The *threat* of jail time would constitute indirect control. Indirect control can be generated using cognitive mechanisms or may be effectuated by playing upon the emotion of the target. An example of cognitive control is a red light. The red light means "stop" and the threat of non-compliance means a traffic ticket, which translates into higher insurance-rates or "points" on one's driving record. Also, stopping at a red light is an act of conformity and doing the right thing, all of which controls the subject.

An example of emotionally mediated control involves the promotion of fear. The mere threat of a calamity, either personal or to one's environment is a very effective tactic that insures the victim's acquiescence to the controller's will. Primitive fears related to the weather, acts of terror or threats to one's family or health trigger primitive emotional responses in the victim. All that is required for any of these fear-based PSYOPs to work is for the mind controller to provide a to-do-list to his intended victims that will reduce their fear. PSYOPs that exploit engineered fear typically encourage a waxing and waning of the level of fear in order to maintain control. Thus, compliance is almost always assured when the victim is never allowed to feel totally comfortable.

Direct, indirect, external, internal, physical and psychological methods of control have an equally fascinating and inglorious provenance. Control first manifested as brute physical force. Clubbing to death a competitor, for example, inadvertently created the first mind control effect. This occurred when witnesses to the clubbing miraculously modified their behavior to become more deferential and submissive in their relationship to the person who had carried out the clubbing.

This crowd response was undoubtedly unanticipated but welcomed by both the clubber and would-be clubbers. Aggressors soon learned that they could control the behavior of their peers/competitors with one solitary display of violence. 30,000 years later this primitive mind control strategy is still employed in various parts of the world and takes the form of public executions.

What followed on the heels of brute force as a mechanism of control were *symbolic displays* of the threat of physical violence. Symbolically displaying the means to impart violence, for example, displaying a club on one's belt, by someone who is judged to be capable of inflicting violence, is generally enough to garner control. We see this ploy used in today's world when police agencies park unmanned police cars along roadways or warn drivers with road signs that aircraft are monitoring their speed. These symbolic displays of threat require less energy and effort than actually stopping and ticketing people for speeding. The reason symbolic displays work is because man is a natural symbol monger and trader.

Man carries in his head a symbolic representation of the world he lives in. Once internalized, symbols take on a life all their own. These internalized symbols of the *real* world become a *virtual* reality. Your brain responds similarly to the **symbols** of external reality as it does to actual reality. You will experience the joys, sorrows, pain, pleasure, arousal, hunger, thirst, fear, hope or any other thought or feeling in response to symbolic displays of reality similarly to the way you will respond to objective reality. Despite symbols near equivalency with reality, objective reality remains the dominant reality because man is an objective entity that exists in an objective world. Man is not merely as an avatar or social construct that exists in a virtual reality. Mankind's belief that virtual reality is equal or dominant to objective reality is a cognitive delusion caused by what I have named, "The Progressive Virus."

For those of you who have read the book: *The Progressive Virus*, you learned the details of how man has all but conflated virtual reality with objective reality, erroneously concluding that the virtual reality in his head *is* objective reality. Thus, modern man erroneously and dangerously concludes that he is the ruler of and creates objective reality.

Permit me to give you a few examples of how man can easily conflate virtual reality with objective reality. Keep in mind that we are delving into this issue in some detail because this phenomenon is the reason why human beings are genetically predisposed to be vulnerable to mind control PSYOPs. Shadow men and their agents were the first to discover this Achilles' heel in mankind's CNS and wasted little time putting it to use for their benefit.

There exist several billion-dollar businesses that rely upon your brain's responses to symbolic displays of real things. I'll focus on just a couple of these businesses to illustrate my point. The first industry I will focus upon is a part of the sex industry and is commonly referred to as phone sex. Phone sex is nothing more than the manipulation of sexual arousal using auditory symbols, i.e., words.

Speech is comprised of these symbols we have named words. Your brain responds to words similarly to the way it responds to the physical entities and acts that are represented by those same words. Your brain, in turn, regulates your body. It regulates such things as heart rate, vasodilatation/vasoconstriction, breathing rate, adrenaline and testosterone levels, pupil size and hundreds of thousands of other central and peripheral somatic processes, including the sexual arousal response. The fact that human beings can be sexually aroused and have a sexual experience by merely talking on the phone is proof positive of how the brain confuses symbolic displays of sex with the real thing.

Another example that virtually all people have experienced is related to how thoughts, feelings and behaviors can be modified by exposing the senses to mere images paired with accompanying sounds. I have termed the business that engages in exposing human beings to images/symbolic content and sounds the *media-entertainment complex*. Movie makers, content producers of all stripes and colors, music makers and producers, writers, scribes and on-air talent, along with their digital devices and delivery technologies, comprise the media-entertainment complex.

When a patron enters a movie theater, she knows with absolute certainty that the images she sees and the dialogue and sound track she hears are merely recreations of real things or fabricated from whole cloth. She knows that she is not looking at an actual person on the movie screen but a projected image of a real person. Nevertheless, as she sits comfortably in her movie theater seat, knowing full well that what she is seeing and hearing is not objective reality, she responds as though she is immersed in an objectively real environment. [1]

For example, if a movie patron is shown a first person point of view roller coaster scene, she will likely experience vestibular disequilibrium and may, in fact, become sick to her stomach and could vomit. Her CNS has reacted to virtual reality and in turn modifies any number of somatic processes existent in the objective world. She feels almost exactly *as if* she is actually riding on a real roller coaster. Flight simulators cue sensory systems using changes in orientation, gravity and movement that mirrors the visual and auditory images displayed to the pilot or patron. When somatic and sensory cues are synchronized with sounds and images, the effect can be a virtual reality that rivals the real thing.

---

[1] To visualize this phenomenon, access this YouTube video of children emotionally reacting to a puppet show: https://www.youtube.com/watch?v=HR5IJ7XRpRQ

People cry, scream, become enraged, fearful, happy, sad, sexually aroused in addition to a myriad of other thoughts, feelings and behaviors, while merely watching and hearing a movie, TV show/news, video, stream, digital media, any and all of it whether animated, acted or simply written. Thus, ALL media in ALL of its various forms and iterations can and do alter man's CNS which, in turn, changes man's virtual reality. This cognitive and perceptual dynamic creates a feedback loop between virtual and objective reality. As technology advances to the point where holographic images of living or once living people can appear on stage or interact with audience members, the ever-narrowing perceptual distinction between virtual and objective reality will become even closer.

The tendency to conflate virtual with objective reality has a neurological basis. Perceiving others engaging in some act or behavior can create the same underlying neurological behavior as if you were engaging in the act yourself. The elemental unit in the brain that is responsible for this is called: "The Mirror Neuron." Here is a formal definition of The Mirror Neuron:

"A mirror neuron is a neuron that fires both when an animal acts and when the animal observes the same action performed by another. Thus, the neuron "mirrors" the behavior of the other, as though the observer was engaged in the action himself. Such neurons have been directly observed in primate species. Birds have been shown to have imitative resonance behaviors and neurological evidence suggests the presence of some form of mirroring system. In humans, brain activity consistent with that of mirror neurons has been found in the premotor cortex, the supplementary motor area, the primary somatosensory cortex and the inferior parietal cortex."[2]

The final domino to fall in the PSYOP matrix characterized by this feedback loop between virtual and objective reality occurs when man unconsciously relies upon the virtual reality that resides in his CNS to filter his perceptions, feelings and ultimately change his behavior toward and in response to the objective world. We are very close to experiencing that last domino to fall as of 2015.

You may now have learned enough to comprehend what motivated social engineers to encourage, promote and ultimately brainwash the minds of the masses, for the past 60 years, to believe that their virtual reality is no different than actual reality. In fact, it has been widely taught to at least three generations of Americans that,

There is no such thing as objective reality, as what has been termed objective reality is merely a perception of man, a social construct.

The unnerving truth is this: Virtual reality is, in large measure, actively managed and under the control of shadow men and their agents, while objective reality resists direct manipulation and control from anyone or any force. Therefore, shadow men and their agents concluded that brainwashing the public to believe that virtual and objective reality are one and the same is the first

---

[2] Rizzolatti, Giacomo; Craighero, Laila (2004), "The mirror-neuron system" (PDF). Annual Review of Neuroscience 27 (1): 169–192. doi:10.1146/annurev.neuro.27.070203.144230. PMID 15217330.
-Keysers, Christian (2010), "Mirror Neurons" (PDF). Current Biology 19 (21): R971–973. doi:10.1016/j.cub.2009.08.026. PMID 19922849.
- Keysers, Christian (2011-06-23), The Empathic Brain. Kindle.
- Rizzolatti, Giacomo; Fadiga, Luciano (1999), "Resonance Behaviors and Mirror Neurons". Italiennes de Biologie 137: 85–100.
-Akins, Chana; Klein, Edward (2002), "Imitative Learning in Japanese Quail using Bidirectional Control Procedure". Animal Learning and Behavior 30 (3): 275–281. doi:10.3758/bf03192836. PMID 12391793.
- Molenberghs P, Cunnington R, Mattingley J (July 2009), "Is the mirror neuron system involved in imitation? A short review and meta-analysis." Neuroscience & Biobehavioral Reviews 33 (1): 975–980. doi:10.1016/j.neubiorev.2009.03.010.

step that had to be taken before shadow men and their agents could control the masses. In fact, **the deconstruction of both virtual and actual reality is the dual mandate of mind control agents.**

The people who comprise the demographic known as "Digital Natives" were raised in a world where the boundary line between the virtual and objective world was purposefully and with malice aforethought conflated and blurred. Keep in mind that the virtual world was no less attractive to earlier generations, though earlier generations, along with shadow men and their agents, did not have access to the technology that would so easily allow them to blur the differences between the virtual and objective world.

Smart phones have made it possible to carry around your virtual "friends," networks and associations 24/7. Futurists have wondered whether or not we will one day substitute our virtual address for our physical address. Society has already reached the point where our virtual "friends" comprise our virtual community. That community may function as a virtual support group, confidants and sexual liaisons, in addition to child/parent, mentor/protégé or any number of other virtual relationships.

The virtual world competes with the real world everywhere there is cellular or WI-FI service. Watch people interact at dinner and you will likely see at least one person leave objective reality to enter their virtual reality.

A Digital Native Leaves the Objective World to Visit Her Virtual World

The virtual world exists in a zero sum relationship with the real world. So when a dinner companion checks in with her virtual companions, she must leave her real-world community. Competition between the virtual and real world will require at some point in the not too distant future the formal creation of social norms that will serve as rules that will guide the transition between engaging with one's virtual "friends" and our real friends. That process has already begun. At some point in the future, as technology evolves, the distinction I make here, denoted by my use of quotation marks around the word friends, may functionally disappear.

If one wants proof that man easily blurs the boundary between the virtual and the real world and often conflates the two, study the perils and pitfalls of interacting in the virtual world. You can have sex in your virtual world, you can make "friends," have arguments, be stalked, be harassed, be supported, be brought to tears and be made to laugh. Exploring the ins and outs of man's virtual world is important to understanding the methods of shadow men.

We have invented terms for people who behave badly in the virtual world, e.g., "Troll." A troll is a person who overhears a conversation had in your virtual world and then inserts him or herself into the conversation, usually marked by a rude, snide and/or cryptic comment. If one dares to engage the troll, you soon learn that the underlying motivation of the troll is to ensnare an unwitting avatar into a faux "fight" without ever being physically harmed. In that regard, trolls take advantage of the virtual world's emphasis upon anonymity.

Because the vast majority of people using social media never actually meet their virtual friends, and most never even talk to them using voice communication, you ONLY know what you THINK you know about your virtual friends. People can and often do lie about their gender, sexual orientation, age, physical appearance, background, etc.

The virtual world is populated by avatars that are merely facades for real people who remain shrouded in anonymity by the net. Anonymity facilitates role playing, lies if you will, where avatars that may or may not accurately reflect the real person, display thoughts and emotions they may not really have with other avatars engaged in the same role playing make believe.

Expanding one's virtual world access point from one's personal phone or computer to the "other controlled" automobile, for example, will amend what it means to go for a drive. Human beings willing to give up their personal freedom to control their vehicle will fill the void created by the loss of their control with virtual interactions with avatars using the same real-world roads, perhaps going to the same real-world location, all directed by the unseen hands of data managers controlled by shadow men.

Your personal physician may be a virtual doctor in the not too distant future. If you haven't taken note, your real doctor has come to almost solely rely upon "the numbers" to instruct his or her diagnosis. Lab reports and clinical data were always important, but typically these data were used to confirm or rule out clinical impressions made by looking, touching, smelling and feeling the patient.

As a result of this transition from clinical to raw data, your personal digital device will monitor and measure you blood pressure, heart rate, EKG, sugar levels, hemoglobin levels, blood gasses, etc., and your virtual doctor will advise you based upon those data. At first it will be a real person on the same digital network who will advise you. Later, it will be a virtual doctor who is not real, at least in the sense that he or she is not made of flesh and blood or, if he or she is real, they are nowhere near you in the objective world.

Human beings can randomly generate their own symbolic triggers from within their virtual reality memory bank. Brains can be primed just like a water pump. Once primed human beings will continue to produce water all on their own. Post Traumatic Stress Disorder (PTSD) is a psychiatric condition that is but one example of this process gone awry.

In the instance of PTSD, a horrific physical and/or emotional experience can become embedded in the brain and resides there as a virtual library of symbolic memories of that event. Those symbols may replay when triggered by an associated stimulus (sound, image or thought) or may auto-play all on their own after being triggered by a second or thrice removed association to the traumatic event or memory. As we have demonstrated, symbols can elicit the same emotional, cognitive and behavioral responses as the actual events those symbols represent. In the case of PTSD, the patient relives cognitively, affectively and somatically whatever it was that traumatized them in the first place. Treatment for PTSD makes use of the fact that virtual reality can be modified more easily than the real world. And for PTSD patients, the problem, for the most part, resides in their CNS's data bank of symbols.

Man is, by nature, a symbol monger and trader. The vast majority of men and women *unconsciously* use symbols that convey their sexual vigor, strength and reproductive viability. The need and desire to display one's reproductive viability represents a primitive and almost universal characteristic of man. The need to display one's sexual viability continues long past man's reproductive years. I use the word "unconsciously" as it relates to the display of reproductive viability because if people are asked why they wear certain clothes, put on makeup or why they wear a moustache, beard or goatee, for example, they almost always report that "I like the way it looks" or "those things make me feel better about myself." As evidenced by these rationalizations, man, in his natural state, is divorced from what motivates much if not all of his behavior.

Facial hair on a man is an unconsciously constructed symbol displayed to other men and women that conveys: "I am a manly man." Gay men who are married to a woman may refer to their wife as "a beard," meaning, the "beard" is a cover for the closeted gay man's sexuality. Men typically display symbols that convey: "I am a force to be reckoned with." Belt buckles, large watches, pointy boots with heels, especially when paired with leather jackets, are all phallic **symbols** meant to convey "what a stud I am." Hats and cars may serve the same symbolic displays of reproductive viability and status.

My point is that we are all symbol mongers by design and nature. Not only are symbols used to control our behavior, but also, **we manipulate symbols**, as well, to control and influence other humans. This reality was not lost on those insightful social engineers who decided to use man's natural symbol mongering and trading as their point of entry in service to controlling thoughts, emotions and behaviors for their shadow men clients.

The masses have no idea that the cars they drive, the clothes they wear and all the other products they buy were sold to them using PSYOPs designed to pray upon man's need to be sexually attractive, smart, powerful and special. And while Madison Avenue honed its exploitation of man's psychological needs to sell their client's products, shadow men, by and through their human behavior expert agents, were busy exploiting similar weaknesses in man's nature to strip him of his inherent desire to be free and to control his every thought, feeling and behavior.

The Disneyland of the virtual world is social media. Social media is the generic name given to any number of "sites" where people may virtually interact with one another using symbols. Social media is a virtual world where the social physics of the real world are held in abeyance, ignored or nullified. Social physics regulate human behavior, just as the physical laws of physics control objects and people, e.g., the speed of sound, light and the law of gravity.

When a person uses Twitter, for example, he or she remains hidden between a digital curtain and objective reality. In fact, many social media users choose to use a pseudonym in lieu of their real name and in lieu of their real image they use an Avatar. Avatars may be actual photographs of the user. Often, the images chosen do not accurately reflect their objective image, e.g., some use a much younger photograph of themselves or an image so dramatically modified that their public image may as well be the photograph of another person.

Anonymity encourages lying, aggression, fantasy role-playing and the expression of urges and impulses that in the real world would be suppressed or tempered by the laws of social physics. Aggression is encouraged when the aggressor perceives that no consequences will result from their expression of aggression. Aggression in the virtual world may take the form of stalking behavior. Stalking in the virtual world is termed "cyber stalking" and has a specific legal meaning, to wit:

"The fact that cyber stalking does not involve physical contact may create the misperception that it is more benign than physical stalking. This is not necessarily true. As the Internet becomes an ever more integral part of our personal and professional lives, stalkers can take advantage of the ease of communications as well as increased access to personal

information. In addition, the ease of use and non-confrontational, impersonal, and sometimes anonymous nature of Internet communications may remove disincentives to cyber stalking. Put another way, whereas a potential stalker may be unwilling or unable to confront a victim in person or on the telephone, he or she may have little hesitation sending harassing or threatening electronic communications to a victim. Finally, as with physical stalking, online harassment and threats may be a prelude to more serious behavior, including physical violence." [3]

The reader should note that cyber stalking is a virtual world version of objective world stalking. The first stalking laws were designed to address objective world stalkers. This was because the technology that would permit cyber stalking was not widely available. Objective world stalking laws evolved into laws that addressed the use of landline phones and physical mail to carry out the stalking. Despite the differences between cyber and objective world stalking, many similarities exist, for example:

Major Similarities

Majority of cases involve stalking by former intimates, although stranger stalking occurs in the real world and in cyberspace.

Most victims are women; most stalkers are men.

Stalkers are generally motivated by the desire to control the victim.

Major differences

Offline stalking generally requires the perpetrator and the victim to be located in the same geographic area; cyberstalkers may be located across the street or across the country.

Electronic communications technologies make it much easier for a cyberstalker to encourage third parties to harass and/or threaten a victim (e.g. impersonating the victim and posting inflammatory messages to bulletin boards and in chat rooms, causing viewers of that message to send threatening messages back to the victim ("author.")

Electronic communications technologies also lower the barriers to harassment and threats; a cyberstalker does not need to physically confront the victim.

Differences Between Real World and Cyber Stalking [4]

We are now going to discuss the various forms that cyber stalking can take. This subject is important because it provides insight into the virtual world that is the playground and workplace of shadow men.

As a preface to our discussion, consider this scenario in the objective world. Imagine a door-to-door salesman who comes to your front door and rings the doorbell. You answer the door and tell the salesperson that you are not interested. The salesman walks away and that is that. Now

---

[3] Excerpted from http://www.usdoj.gov/criminal/cybercrime/cyberstalking.htm
[4] Ibid.

consider this scenario, rather than the salesman leaving your residence after you tell him that you are not interested, imagine that he continues to stand at your front door, continually ringing your doorbell. You tell him to stop, but he does not stop. Now imagine a situation where the salesman and a clan of his friends take turns incessantly ringing your doorbell. When one of these stalkers gets tired another one takes over where their colleague left off. Imagine that the stalker clan rings your doorbell, bangs on your door with their fists and bangs on your windows in unison. Of course, in the objective world most people would call the police. In the cyber stalking world there is a very similar scenario to the one I just outlined. And yes, the police should be called in the instance of cyber stalking. Police will, upon a show of proof, enforce any number of state and federal cyber staking laws, with some penalties involving jail time and others, in the civil arena, monetary damage awards.

Cyber warfare is a 21st century military strategy that can alter the balance of power and poses many real world dangers. Cyber warfare runs the gamut from simple computer and network hacking to sophisticated mind control, recruitment and other PSYOPs that exploit vulnerabilities in man's virtual reality. One military/state that has successfully used cyber warfare is ISIS/ISIL. ISIS produces high quality propaganda that is disseminated via any number of social media sites, including, but not limited to, Twitter, Instagram, Pinterest, WhatsApp, YouTube and Facebook.

In 2014 ISIS produced a recruitment video entitled, "Flames of War." ISIS also minted the hashtag #worldcup2014 and "#amessagetotheU.S. The World Cup hashtag baited unwary social media soccer-philes into accessing recruitment messages instead of information about soccer. After the United States began bombing ISIS strongholds, the message hashtag was used to directly condemn America. In 2014 ISIS captured British Broadcaster John Cantlie. Cantlie was featured on YouTube spouting ISIS propaganda with shaven head and orange T-shirt.

Proof of the effectiveness of ISIS' cyber warfare campaign was measured, in part, by the number of recruits from the western world it managed to persuade to join its army. Hundreds of western youth joined ISIS. Referring back to *The Progressive Virus*, those individuals who are awash in a meaningless sea where reality was presumed to not exist and the labels "good" and "bad" are presumed to be mere social constructs, proved to be the most vulnerable to ISIS' recruitment efforts. This is because ISIS, if nothing else, offered meaning and clarity to its new converts awash in a sea of secular humanism and relativistic values.

The reader should make note of the fact that ISIS' recruitment and brainwashing took place in the virtual world. However, at some point the transition must be made from the virtual to the objective world. Because, I suspect, recruits have conflated virtual with objective reality, once the new ISIS recruit moves into the real world, objective reality will begin the process of challenging virtual reality. Depending upon how fast that education takes place will define how long it takes for the objective world to impose its dominance upon the delusions of new recruits who have never truly experienced the real world.

CHAPTER 2: CLOAKING AND ORGANIZATION

Benjamin Disraeli, Britain's first prime minister, said this about who really controls the world:

"The world is governed by very different personages from what is imagined by those who are not behind the scenes."[5]

Pundits and political observers are fixated upon the on-stage part of shadow men's various productions. The on-stage parts of their various productions have been created to capture the attention of the masses while the deadly serious business of control and the social engineering of culture remain hidden in a backstage labyrinth of mystery and intrigue. The organizational matrix of shadow men is not unlike the matrix used by sophisticated criminal syndicates. Criminal syndicates incorporate built-in impenetrable firewalls and faux cul-de-sacs into their organizational matrix that insulate the kingpins from those charged with bringing them to justice.

One particularly fascinating characteristic of shadow men's organizational matrix structure and function is that many of their on-site agents, and proxy institutions, are comprised of people who often have no idea that their sole raison d'être is to serve the needs and wants of unseen rulers. Serving as a testament to the brilliant cloaking mechanisms found in shadow men's organizational matrix, many of their surrogates, including many of their top level agents, genuinely believe that they are NOT doing the bidding of unseen overseers. Many of shadow men's proxies sincerely deny the very notion of hidden controllers, honestly believing that assertions to the contrary have no basis in fact and are nothing more than conspiratorial nonsense.

At the lowest level of shadow men's organizational matrix we find the dupes. These people can, quite ironically, be identified by their naiveté and conformist adoption of whatever has been defined for them to be politically correct and/or trendy. Italian socialists referred to their populist supporter dupes during WWII as "useful idiots." The harshness of that descriptor strikes me as incongruous with the fact that some of these so called "useful idiots," both then and now, believe or believed in their heart that they are agents for good. In reality, these people comprise the lowest-level agents of shadow men. So called useful idiots are rather easily controlled by exploiting their need to conform to that which has been defined for them to be politically correct and/or trendy.

Shadow men's cloaking mechanisms are protected not only by their maze-like structures and their agent's blindness to their purpose, but also by their victim's failure of discernment. The failure to perceive those things hidden in plain sight is in large measure a function of the masses' psychological defenses working to protect them from a very uncomfortable reality.

Subtle factors help to protect shadow men and their minion. Ironically, one of the more interesting cloaking mechanisms is dependent upon the suspicions of those among the masses who sense something is amiss but do not possess the judgment nor the discernment acuity necessary to distinguish their rational fears and suspicions from their paranoid-laced projections.

You will learn that shadow men rely upon those suffering from paranoia and/or who lack intellectual acumen, training and education to saturate so-called alternative media with so much chaff, that it helps to cloak shadow men's elegant matrix of control. Shadow men, in large measure, remain hidden behind a curtain fabricated by paranoid projections, denial and free association-like rants. Even when one of these bloggers or broadcasters hit the mark, shadow men remain insulated within a larger sea of paranoia-fueled nonsense continually spouted from this genre of blogger/broadcaster/writer.

---

[5] Benjamin Disraeli. (1844), *Coningsby, the New Generation.* A Public Domain Book.

I am often asked: what is it about shadow men that motivate their insatiable appetite for power? The answer to that question is the proper subject matter and is the sole purview of clinical and forensic psychology. In order to answer that question, you and I will travel the geography of shadow men's minds in order to unravel their motivations and expose their strategies and tactics. Before you can effectively protect your freedom, you must come to understand the people you are up against.

Shadow men may be identified by virtue of their shared genetics, wealth and power, in short, their bio-psycho-social makeup. Many writers and commentators interested in this general subject choose to catalogue shadow men (regardless of what they call them) by labeling them by the scope of their ambitions. Two such terms are the descriptors: "Globalists" and "New World Order."

While these descriptors do accurately identify the ultimate scope of shadow men's control ambitions, these terms provide few other actionable insights, especially clinical and forensic insights. Describing anything, solely by its ultimate scope, would be like describing Ebola viruses as "pandemicists." It is much better to describe Ebola viruses by their RNA structure, replication machinery, incubation periods, what Ebola strains look like under the microscope and to what antivirals Ebola is susceptible to rather than merely by the virus' desire to go global. Still, we acknowledge and owe a debt of gratitude to those investigators who have coined the term "New World Order" because, at the very least, they have given this entity a name that can serve as a reference point.

Shadow men jealously protect their power of which they never, ever, have enough and for which they must continually control those over whom they rein. Objects of their control include other shadow men who invariably become and are their intramural competitors. Shadow men's obsessive and compulsive quest for more power and more wealth derives, in part, from the natural synergy between wealth and power. More wealth generates more power, and the more power one accumulates the more wealth one can control.

Shadow men live and work in the shadows, hence the title of this book, *Shadow Men*. Their methods of control and social engineering are, likewise, shrouded from their victims and critics, alike. The one thing that is instrumental to their continued rule and dominance is that they must exercise control without their victim's *discerned* awareness.

In fact, a key measure of success for shadow men is when their victims are not only oblivious to their control efforts, they become vocal champions for shadow men's agents, institutions, policies, aspirations and even countries, going so far as to ostracize and ridicule those who would expose shadow men and their agents.

Operationally defining that last point, this means that shadow men's victims, i.e., the general public, tend to hold dear their oppressors and their oppressor's values. Of all the major accomplishments of shadow men, that last point is their most remarkable and striking achievement.

Can shadow men's victims be catalogued by their political or ideological characteristics? Liberal, Conservative, Progressive, Labour, "Right-Wing" "Left-Wing," Libertarian, none of these political and ideological taxonomies matter to shadow men. The only real distinctions shadow men make among their victims, including on-stage political and ideological factions, has to do with fine-tuning the PSYOPs that are used to control each respective group or faction among the masses.

Shadow men who are predisposed to reject physical control measures as their first line of population management have adopted a Fabian strategy of behavioral control. The term "Fabian" derives from a dictator of Rome who lived in the 3rd century BCE by the name of Quintus Fabius Maximus Verrucosus. It is said that necessity is the mother of invention and so it was with Quintus Fabius.

This Roman dictator had been assigned the seemingly impossible task of defeating the vicious and brutal Carthaginian general named Hannibal. Hannibal had done what many considered to be the impossible when he crossed the Alps in the dead of winter and invaded southern Italy during what came to be known as the Second Punic War (218 to 202 BCE). Hannibal's brutality and win-at-all-costs approach to war resulted in horrific losses to the Roman Army despite their numerical advantage over the Carthaginians.

Faced with a seemingly invincible foe in Hannibal, Quintus Fabius devised a strategy that incorporated indirect and counterintuitive warfare strategies. He used deception, surprise attacks and tactical resistance, in addition to any number of what we call today "PSYOPs," designed to control the minds and morale of Hannibal's troops. Remarkably, Quintus Fabius's "Fabian" strategy worked and Hannibal was eventually defeated. [6]

Please appreciate the fact that while modern ruling shadow men favor Fabian style methods of population management and control, they have prepared for and have plans on the shelf that incorporate physical methods of control, many of which rely upon abject acts of dehumanization, violence and in some cases, outright genocide. Just as some members of the Roman Senate favored brute force as opposed to Quintus Fabius's approach, despite its proven success, their exists a group of shadow men who pine for the days when brute force and punitive physical means of population management were the favored approaches to achieving power and dominance over other shadow men and the masses.

Sociological and demographic based taxonomies, along with actuarial-based classifications of shadow men, have focused upon the purported genetic bloodlines disproportionately represented among them. Bloodlines correlate with race and ethnicity. A word of caution is in order here. While it may be possible to use actuarial data to categorize shadow men by their race and ethnicity, those data do not *necessarily* predict who is or is not a shadow man and are not, when used alone, reliable predictors of identity or behavior.

Racial, religious and ethnic classifications provide too few insights that will assist those who want to protect their free will and regain their lost freedoms. As with any categorization, which relies upon race, religion or genetics, the risk of committing what we researchers term a Type I Error increases exponentially.[7] In other words, just because someone belongs to a genetic/religious/racial/ethnic classification that is disproportionately represented among shadow men does not mean that person who belongs to one or another of these demographic classifications is *necessarily* a shadow man or one of their sympathizers or agents; nor does it mean that a member of one of these groups would not welcome the opportunity to thwart shadow men's mind control strategies. Taxonomies rooted in race, religion and/or ethnicity often provide a false sense of confidence for those so inclined to find comfort in such predictable, but misleading, taxonomies.

Clinically speaking, personality typologies provide more actionable data when it comes to who is likely to be one of these overseers who live in the shadows than sociological and/or demographic, genetic, racial or ethnic classifications. When I use the term "clinical," I intend to reference a subject's neuropsychological fingerprint. When I use the term "personality" I am referencing that collection of stable and predictable, across contexts, bio-psycho-social behaviors, traits and characteristics of a person. Clinical, rather than racial/religious and/or ethnic classifications are more likely to identify the most malevolent among shadow men and will shed light on how to defeat or impede these enemies of man's exercise of free will.

One genre of actuarial/demographic analysis that has proven useful is the fact of shadow men agent's disproportionate representations in those institutions and industries that are necessary for them to exercise control, e.g., banking, government, quasi-governmental institutions, data manage-

---

[6] Liddell Hart, B. H. (1967), *Strategy.* Faber & Faber, London, (2nd rev. ed.).

[7] A type I error (error of the first kind) is the incorrect rejection of a true null hypothesis. With respect to the non-null hypothesis, it represents a false positive. Usually a type I error leads one to conclude that a supposed effect or relationship exists when in fact it doesn't.

ment and the media-entertainment complex. Shadow men's relationship with these institutions and industries is one of mutual benefit in that these institutions can directly effectuate control over the masses and, in the case of banking, the material bottom line. In return, the agents manning these critical institutions can expect to reap unimaginable profits as their just reward.

The most powerful shadow men have accumulated and maintained power by profiting off the manipulation and movement of money as opposed to merely engaging in business ventures that are profit intensive or by and through inheritance. To be sure, the manipulation of money generates untold wealth that, in turn, is used to fund profit intensive businesses, which in turn generate trusts for the children of shadow men. Still, those shadow men that have control over the machinery of monetary policy, including the ability to effectuate changes in the definition of currency and the money supply, itself, are the most powerful of the powerful and are structurally very close to direct manipulation by ruling shadow men.

This author is not going to openly identify *living* shadow men by name. The reasons for this purposeful omission are three fold. First, knowing a name means nothing and serves no functional purpose, save to satisfy my reader's prurient interests and curiosity. Besides, the named person would simply deny their identity as a shadow man and that would be that. As you will learn, one of the tried and true protective mantles used by all shadow men is termed plausible deniability.

It is far better to understand personality and clinical profiles and their inherent vulnerabilities than it is to know a name, because it is shadow men and their agent's behavior that will reveal their true identity, not their name, addresses or phone numbers. Some of the names that would be properly identified as shadow men are so halo-valenced, even by so called conservatives, patriots and conspiracy theorists, that by naming these people, readers would be shocked into a state of disbelief as if they were told that the love of their life was having an affair with their best friend.

Secondly, my past relationships with shadow men are protected by an oath of confidentiality in addition to legally binding contracts that prevent me from naming names. Lastly, I am keenly aware of the risks associated with blatant, in-your-face confrontations with those more powerful than I. I am reminded of the Russian proverb in this regard: "Sometimes when you dance with the bear the bear does not let go." The bear gave me one last and very long hug before giving me its tacit approval to write this book. That last hug was punctuated, as if dotting an "i" in an essay, with one final display of brute force that had it continued I would not have been able to put pen to paper.

One final point regarding names and identities, the same bloggers and broadcasters who inadvertently run interference for shadow men have a hackneyed list of names who allegedly comprise the New World Order (NWO) that I will not repeat here, but are easily discoverable. The fact that these names are bandied about as though they are bona fide and comprise the movers and shakers of this world proves my thesis with regard to the absence of any functional utility by simply knowing names and identities. Even if you have concluded that this hackneyed listing of NWO names is complete and accurate—so what?

I was permitted to write this book because it is not a direct challenge to *all* shadow men. **This book is written on behalf of the benevolent shadow men of the prior generation who have been abandoned by their own children and are actively searching for methods and means to reestablish their once dominant rule.**

Meaningful threats made against ruling shadow men, at this point in history seldom, if ever, come to light. This is because pre-emptive strikes on the source of *genuine* threats are made *before* they appear on stage, i.e., before you would become aware of them. I shall not cite examples of pre-emptive strikes to prove my point in this regard for obvious reasons. Permit me to remind you that if someone promotes themselves in the *formal* media entertainment complex as a *formidable enemy* of the "globalists," the counter-resistance, etc., and they become popular, as noted by their multinational corporate or government sponsors, you can bank on the fact that they are **not** a bona fide threat to shadow men. In fact, some of these "counter resistance" promoters who have major corporate backing or government-subsidized operations serve only to assist shadow men by virtue of their errors in judgment and conclusions. The same goes for any number of "counter-culture" musicians, authors and directors/producers in Hollywood and New York.

A word about citizen journalists is in order here. The formal media is a branch of the media entertainment complex. That complex is under the direct control of shadow men. To be sure, the individual "stations," hosts, shows and tenor are all different, in the same way an ice cream store offers different flavors of ice cream. Be assured, however, it is all ice cream, regardless of the flavor. Citizen journalists are comprised of a mélange of some good and some not so good reporters and journalists who occasionally get things right. Navigating this sea of citizen journalists is not unlike trying the find the proverbial needle in a haystack. Some citizen journalists who started out on public access TV and who now have evolved into news-breaking investigative journalists are to be applauded for their efforts and accomplishments.

I will show you how to take back your free will and do it in a way that will provide a measure of immunity from the ruling shadow men's armamentarium of PSYOPs. It won't be easy and many of you will fail, but the few of us who demand our free will can empower old-school shadow men, who are not so ravenous and craven as are the current ruling shadow men, to challenge their children and remove them from power.

CHAPTER 3: PSYCHOANALYSIS OF SHADOW MEN

Clinically, shadow men are a motley crew of self-anointed and legacy elites whose provenance can be traced back hundreds if not thousands of years. Not all, but enough of them, display any number of psychopathological behaviors that distinguish them from those over whom they reign. Their psychopathologies are the product of their genetics and their psychosocial makeup, all of which are reinforced and exacerbated by their privileged status and their immeasurable wealth and power.

Normal, well-adjusted and good-hearted people will find it almost impossible to comprehend in a meaningful way this particular genre of human being. In some sense, this is a similar problem confronted by good-hearted people who attempt to understand the criminal mind. Good people tend to project upon others their emotional and cognitive constitutional makeup. Criminals, and certainly shadow men and their agents, exploit this tendency on the part of good-hearted people to project their own normalcy upon others. Suffice to say that in order to comprehend shadow men and their agents in a meaningful way the reader is going to have to stop projecting their cognitive and affective character traits upon them.

Keep in mind that the overarching term "shadow men" is comprised of their intramural competitors. All shadow men have more in common with one another than they do with their victims, i.e., you. But to be absolutely precise, some shadow men have, historically, been less virulent and more benevolent than others.

It is my contention, that the current crop of ruling shadow men are particularly craven and wanton when compared to their forbearers, i.e., my clients, that ruled the world post World War II through the early part of the 1960's. The children and heirs to the depression era shadow men were, like the children of the masses, stripped of many of the behavioral modifiers that kept them from unbridled indulgence of their every want, wish and desire. My work with the prior generation of shadow men took place during the last few years of their influence, i.e., the late 1980s and early 1990s.

When shadow men are left to indulge their every whim, wish and desire, there is virtually nothing that can stop their wanton, aggressive and libertine greed and desire for maniacal control. When these megalomaniacal personalities are left free to roam the earth, they will eventually destroy human and animal life in the same way that a ravenous parasite eventually kills both its host and itself.

The technological advances of the time period post 1960's, especially those digital communication technologies and devices that directly empowered the media-entertainment complex, have made it possible for the more ravenous shadow men to consume wealth and power at a pace and amount never before possible in the history of man. Man's inventions related to digital media and worldwide data management were to mind-control as the discovery of lightweight metals, flight management computers and composite materials were to aeronautical engineering.

Creative writers have *unknowingly*, over the millennia, incorporated personality typologies into their literary works that captured the clinical essence of shadow men. I refer to such literary and artist-generated insights as "they know...but they don't know" insights. I readily acknowledge, however, that a few writers appear to have an intuitive sense of the hidden world of shadow men. Shadow men-like characters and their cabals have made their appearance as central characters (villains) in almost every genre of literary work, including folklore, fairy tales, fables, children's rhymes and almost every occult ritual known to man. [8]   Others who have written or talked about the general subject matter of this book have made the error of using movies and literary works of art to document their paranoia-laced theories, as though a movie or literary work of art constitutes direct evidence or proof of their theories when such works of art don't, in fact, cannot.

When I make references to literary and other creative dramatizations of power and shadow men-like characters, I am **not** offering them as "proof" of my clinical analyses and first hand experiences. I present them solely for their ***dramatizations*** of my clinical and forensic analysis.

For example, Stanley Kubrick's last film before his untimely death, *Eyes Wide Shut*, is an exposé of shadow men's behavior, specifically their notorious sexual perversions, including their fascination with sadomasochism, pedophilia and ritualistic sacrifice. Readers who have not seen that film should consider studying it as an assignment, part of the homework component of this book. Kubrick was uncannily accurate in his depictions of shadow men in *Eyes Wide Shut*. For those of us who know the truth, we were shocked that Kubrick's highly accurate portrayal of shadow men made its way into the light of day, though most who saw the film had no idea they were provided a rare glimpse into shadow men's behind the curtain behavior. Kubrick's movie was filmed at the original home of Baron Mayer de Rothschild, located in Buckinghamshire, England, named the Mentmore Towers.

Rothschild Mansion: The Mentmore Towers, Buckinghamshire, England.
One set location for Stanley Kubrick's last film, "Eyes Wide Shut."

---

[8] I use the term "occult" intending its classic Latin meaning, i.e., "hidden, clandestine or knowledge meant for only certain people." I do NOT use the term intending to convey its colloquial meaning, i.e., referring to the paranormal.

The Mentmore Towers, Dining Area. Buckinghamshire, England.

Movie Stills from *Eyes Wide Shut*, Stanley Kubrick, 1999.

Movie Still from *Eyes Wide Shut*, Stanley Kubrick, 1999.

A rare glimpse into the world of shadow men, as depicted by Stanley Kubrick in *Eyes Wide Shut*, can be found in the photo history of a party held at Château de Ferrières in France. Marie-Hélène de Rothschild put on the party for her family and friends. I am including photographs of this party so that the reader may acquire a sense- memory of the subject matter of this book.

Château de Ferrières in France (Notice the mansion is bathed in orange lighting).

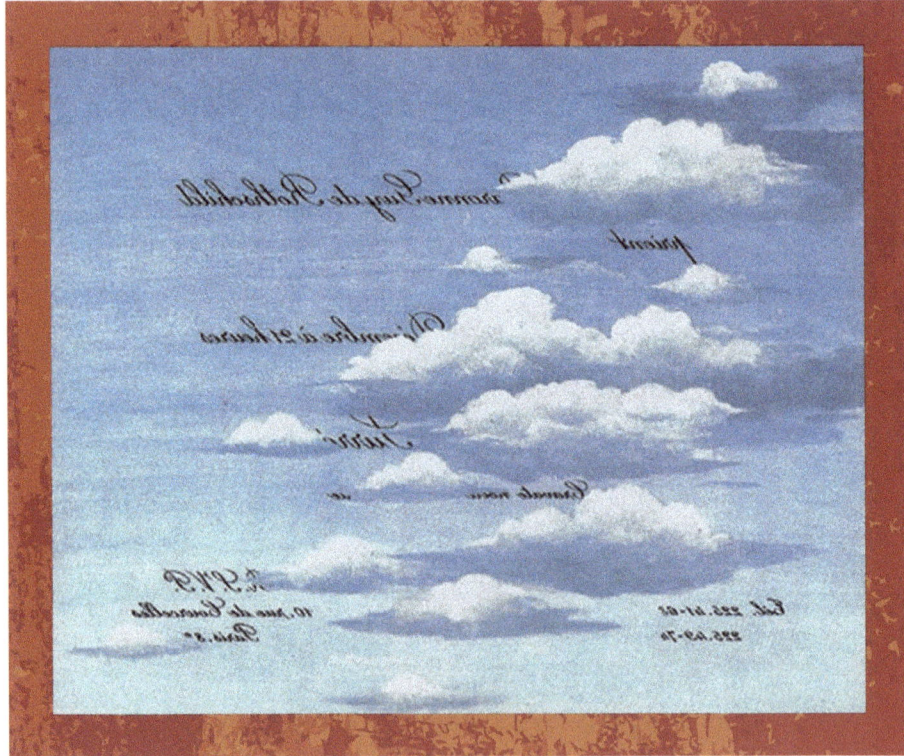

INVITATION TO THE PARTY: (Note the fact that the invitation is written in reverse).
Mirror writing is a classic occult practice. [9]

---

[9] The late Aleister Crowley, aka "the beast" and modern evangelist of Satan, has postulated several Satanic Laws, to wit: The first law, the "Law of Reversal," is the crux of Satanism. In addition to mirror writing, Crowley emphasized The Black Mass, i.e., the entire Roman Catholic liturgy of the Mass is performed backwards, or in reverse. Everything is read backwards, or in reversed speech. The Cross in the Black Mass is hung upside down (reverse) over the Satanic altar. The Anti-Christ: This signals the reverse or direct opposite of Christ. Heaven is the reversal of Hell. Heaven is up. Hell is down. God is dark. The Devil is light.

Guy de Rothschild & Marie-Hélène de Rothschild wearing a horned "giant's head" (Baphomet-like) with tears made from real diamonds.

Baroness Marie-Hélène de Rothschild and Baron Alexis de Redé.

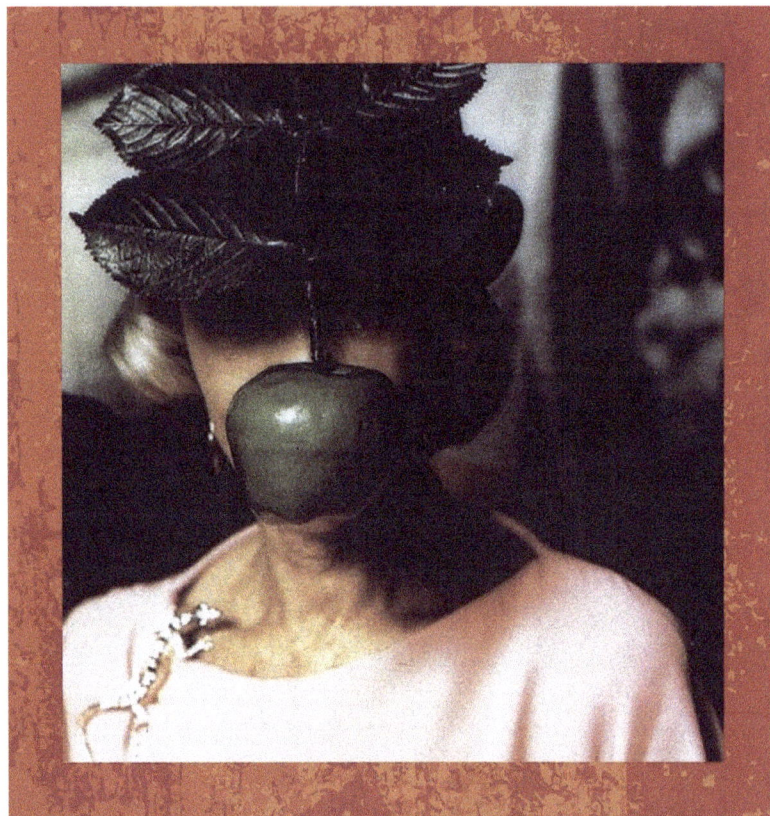

This costume made reference to the famous painting, *The Son of Man*, making a direct blasphemous Biblical reference to Eve eating Forbidden fruit from the Garden of Eden.

On the diner table are dismembered dolls and cracked skulls. The images you see here are classic occult artifacts. [10]

As one can see from this sampling of photos from an actual party that inspired Kubrick's movie *Eyes Wide Shut*, occult, Satanic and sadomasochistic images are everywhere.

Shadow men-like personalities have been cast as central characters in any number of tales of horror. This is because these men have created, throughout history, unimaginable horror. None of these literary efforts to capture the very essence of these perverse creations that live in the shadows have been more clinically accurate than the various tales and stories involving the behavior of vampires. If one were to interchange the term "shadow men" for "vampires" it would amount to a difference without a distinction from a clinical perspective. Vampires are the almost perfect *metaphor* for the worst of shadow men. [11]

---

[10] Hang the Bankers. (2013), Photos from 1972 Rothschild Party.

[11] A metaphor is a figure of speech that describes a subject by asserting that it is, on some point of comparison, the same as another otherwise **unrelated** object. Metaphor is a type of analogy and is closely related to other rhetorical figures of speech that achieve their effects via association, comparison or resemblance including allegory, hyperbole, and simile.

The worst of the shadow men are, like their literary nom de guerre, soulless creatures that live in the shadows and who must prey upon the living for their sustenance. They live off the positive life force (metaphor: blood) of the sentient beings that once bitten (do business or have sex with) by them are forever cast under their spell and for which the punishment is losing one's soul.

Once bitten by the vampire, the former living being loses his soul and will take on many of the characteristics of shadow men. Despite the similarities, one major difference exists between the vampire and his victim. The victim can never become a true member of shadow men's cabal, even though the victim will have forsaken his soul to them. Goethe's *Faust* is one of the best literary tales that chronicles the perils of striking a deal with a true shadow man. Thus, becoming the victim, unwitting or otherwise, of one of these beasts among men, is one path by which their group sustains their life but, in the process, destroys those foolish enough to enter into the bargain.

If you are a student of modern literary classics, including films based upon these archetypal tales, I suggest that you reflect upon the masterful work of Bram Stoker. Stoker's novel *Dracula* was derived, in part, from an abominable shadow man named Vlad "The Impaler" Tepus. Vlad's monstrous behavior has been chronicled in any number of historical records. [12]

Vlad "The Impaler" Tepes. (Getty Images)

One would think that being related to such a demonic figure as Vlad the Impaler would be something to keep quiet, if not ashamed of, but that is not how the elite process information. In fact, Prince Charles of England has bragged about his genetic lineage to Vlad. According to the London Telegraph, Prince Charles bragged about his bloodline relationship with Vlad the Impaler.

"The Prince himself appears in a video being used to promote the country in which he claims distant kinship with Vlad Tepes, the 15th–century Wallachian ruler on whom the Irish novelist Bram Stoker based his Dracula. "Transylvania is in my blood," he jokes in an interview first shown on satellite television last year. "The genealogy shows I am descended from Vlad the Impaler, so I do have a bit of a stake in the country."" [13]

In each of the classic Dracula dramas, filmed during the mid-20th century, there is a scene where the director focused upon the vampire's eyes as his outstretched arms rhythmically entranced his victim. The victim is not uncommonly an attractive, innocent woman who falls under the

---

[12] C.f. Florescu, Radu R.; McNally, Raymond T. (1989), Dracula, Prince of Many Faces: His Life and His Times. Little, Brown and Company.
[13] The Telegraph. *Prince Charles, heir to Dracula's blood-line.* By Victoria Ward and Andrew Hough, September 5, 2012.

vampire's spell as if by magic. If some act is not taken to frighten away the vampire, he bites his victim on the neck at which point she is forever doomed to the fate of the living dead. [14]

Bella Lugosi as Dracula.

One thing appears crystal clear, men of power congregate, and when they do their activities reflect their deepest and most ingrained personality characteristics and self-perceptions. One such group, comprised of the most powerful among the powerful, is the group known as the Bohemian Grove.

The Bohemian Grove is a 2700-acre parcel of Redwood laden land located in Northern California. The various roads leading into the Grove are guarded like Fort Knox, protected by former CIA and FBI agents. This is the sign that greets both guests and would-be trespassers:

Who comprises the members of the Bohemian Grove?

"Rumsfeld, Kissinger, two former C.I.A. directors (including Bush #41), the masters of war and the oligarchs, the Bechtels and the Basses, the board members of top military contractors—such as Halliburton, Lockheed Martin, Northrop Grumman, and the Carlyle Group—Rockefellers, Morgans, captains of industry and C.E.O.'s across the

---

[14] Please see the Movie: Dracula, 1931. Starring Bela Lugosi and Helen Chandler. Directed by Tod Browning. Written by Bram Stoker, Hamilton Deane & John Balderston.

spectrum of American capitalism. The interlocking corporate web—cemented by prep-school, college, and golf-club affiliations, blood, marriage, and mutual self-interest—that makes up the American ruling class." [15] (With Edits)

The attraction axiom of "like attracts like" normalizes the annual get together in midsummer at the Bohemian Grove. But what cannot be normalized are the activities conducted there. Keep in mind that men of wealth and power could create almost any activities list of their choosing. They could have nature walks, seminars, think sessions, recreate summer camp activities enjoyed as children, including swimming, camping, you name it. But that is not what these men of power and privilege choose to do. What these men do in midsummer is partake in a theatrical drama where they become participants/observers in an occult, satanic, macabre and sadomasochistic ritual, complete with feigned human sacrifice, known as the "Cremation of Care."

One cannot begin to understand the gravity of what goes on at Bohemian Grove until one appreciates the fact these men of power appear to have a penchant for activities and rituals that act out their sadomasochistic power over the masses. These men and women who comprise the self-anointed and legacy elite appear to enjoy dramatic reenactments of macabre human sacrifices, where members, dressed in long medieval robes, chant occult charms and missives, all the while sequestered in the middle of an otherwise beautiful Redwood forest.

I want to mention one other well-known group that originated in 1832 at Yale University named Skull and Bones. My commentary is to be distinguished from the myriad of paranoid-laced coverage of this group, which I reject because it provides unintended cover for the organization and its members. My reference to Skull and Bones is to make a *singular and unique point*, and it is this. Surreptitiously made recordings of the induction ceremony for Skull and Bones could have included almost any ritual imaginable, but it didn't. The induction ceremony for membership into Skull and Bones is accompanied by macabre images, feigned human sacrifice, blood curdling screams and role playing, if it is that, that reminds one of what actor's call "submersion." Submersion is when an actor becomes one with the character he/she is playing and, in the process, loses himself to the role. In other words, they actually come to believe they are the characters they play. Why the children of the elite would indulge behaviors that people of empathy, people of peace, find to be abhorrent is the question that captures my point.

I took images of the Bohemian Grove member's "Cremation of Care" (Just say those three words to yourself and ask why?) production and showed the surreptitiously recorded images[16] to a cross section of people. To the person, each found the images to be disturbing. Everyone who saw the images concluded that what they had seen was "some sort of Satanic or occult drama or ritual." Almost all could not believe that THIS is what men of power and wealth would actually *choose* to do in their spare time. The voice over artists who dramatize the Cremation of Care ritual at the Bohemian Grove have a vocal timber that reminds one of a supernatural evil spirit as is often portrayed in film or at Disneyland's Fantasia production where an evil spirit appears in Mickey Mouse's nightmare. The fire, smoke and Halloween-like lighting add to the emotional intensity of the production. Keep in mind that all of this goes on in the middle of the wilderness, protected from prying eyes by former FBI and CIA operatives.

---

[15] Vanity Fair Magazine. *Bohemian Tragedy*, by: Alex Shoumatoff, May, 2009.
[16] Alex Jones courageously made the surreptitiously recorded images in 1999.

Bohemian Grove "Cremation of Care" Ritual. (Photo by: Alex Jones)

What follows is the transcript of the "Cremation of Care" ritual:

The Owl is in His leafy temple
Let all within the grove be reverent before Him.
Lift up your heads oh ye trees
And be lifted up ye everlasting spires
For behold here is bohemia's shrine
And holy are the pillars of this house.
Weaving spiders come not here!
Hail, Bohemians!
With the ripple of waters
The song of birds
Such music as inspires the sinking soul
Do we invite you into Midsummer's joy?
The sky above is blue and sown with stars
The forest floor is heaped with fragrant grit
The evening's cool kiss is yours
The campfire's glow
The birth of rosy-fingered dawn.
For behold, here is Bohemia's shrine
And holy are the pillars of his house

Shake off your sorrows with the city's dust
And cast to the winds the cares of life.
But memories bring back the well-loved names of gallant friends
Who knew and loved this grove
Dear boom companions of a long ago
Aye, let them join us in this ritual!
And not a piece be empty in our midst.
All of these battles to hold
In this gray autumn of the world
Or in the springtime of your heart.
Attend our tale
Gather ye forest folks!
And cast your spells over these mortals
Touch their world-blind eyes with carry-on
Open their eyes to fancy
Follow the memories of yesterday
And seal the gates of sorrow.
It is a dream
And yet, not all a dream
Dull Care in all of his works
Harbored it
As vanished Babylon and goodly Tyre
So shall they also vanish
But the wilding rose blows on the broken battlements of Tyre
And moss rends the stones of Babylon
For beauty is eternal
And we bow to beauty everlasting
For lasting happiness we turn our eyes to one alone,
And she surrounds you now.
Great nature, refuge of the weary heart,
And only balm to breasts that have been bruised.
She hath cool hands for every fevered brow
And gentlest silence for the troubled soul.
Her councils are most wise
She healeth well
Having such ministries as calm and sleep
She is ever faithful
Other friends may fail
But seek ye her in any quiet place
Smiling, she will rise and give to you her kiss
So must ye come as children
Little children that believe do not ever doubt her beauty or her faith
Nor deem her tenderness can change or die
Bohemians and priests!
The desperate call of heavy hearts is answered.
By the power of your fellowship, Dull Care is slain

His body has been brought yonder to our funeral pyre
To the joyous singings of a funeral march;
Our funeral pyre awaits the corpse of Care
O thou, thus ferried across the shadowy tide
In all the ancient majesty of death
Dull Care, ardent enemy of beauty
Not for thee the forgiveness or the restful grave
Fire shall have its will of thee
And all the winds make merry with thy dust
Bring fire!
Fools!
Fools!
Fools!
When will ye learn?
That me ye cannot slay?
Year after year ye burn me in this grove
Lifting your puny shouts of triumph to the stars.
When again you turn your faces to the marketplace
Do you not find me waiting as of old?
Fools!
Fools!
Fools to dream you conquer care.
Say Thou mocking spirit!
It is not all a dream
We know thou waiting for us
When this out sylvan holiday has ended
We shall meet thee and fight thee as of old
And some of us prevail against thee
And some thou shall destroy
But this too we know
Year after year within this happy grove
Our fellowship bans thee for a space
Thine malevolence which would pursue us here
Has lost its power under these friendly trees.
So shall we burn thee once again this night
And, with the flames that eat thine effigy
We shall read the sign
Midsummer sets us free!
Ye shall burn me once again!
Not with these flames!
Which hither ye have brought
From regions where I reign
Ye fools and priests
I spit upon your fire!
O Owl! Prince of all mortal wisdom
Owl of Bohemia, we beseech thee

Grant us thy council
Let it be in the world
Where care is nourished
On the hates of men
And drive Him from this grove.
One flame alone must light this fire
One flame alone must light this fire
A pure eternal flame
At last, within the lamp of Fellowship
Upon the altar of Bohemia.
O Great Owl of Bohemia!
We thank thee for thy adjuration.
Begone detested care!
Begone!
Once more, we banish thee!
Begone Dull Care!
Fire should have its will of thee!
Begone Dull Care!
And all the winds make merry with thy dust
Hail, fellowship's eternal flame!
Once again Midsummer sets us free!

Photograph by Gabriel Moulin, 1915: To purge himself of worldly concerns, a member of the elite Bohemian Club participated in a 1915 Cremation of Care ceremony—complete with candles and a robed and hooded comrade to guide him. This private club of influential men still meets annually north of San Francisco and uses this symbolic ritual to kick off its summer retreat. But today the ceremony involves burning a mummy-like effigy named Care at the foot of the group's mascot: a 40-foot-tall (12-meter-tall) concrete owl.

My purpose in providing to my readers information about the Bohemian Grove rituals of the elite and organizations such as Skull and Bones is to generate in you an affective sense-memory of how the power brokers of our world recreate. I'm not declaring the members of the Bohemian Grove or any other referenced group to be comprised of shadow men, including the Rothschilds or any one particular participant or family in any of the macabre rituals that properly belong with these groups and organizations.

What I am demonstrating is that this is how one level of the self anointed and legacy elite have chosen to spend their time in the woods of Northern California and these are the kinds of fraternal organizations that have been embraced at America's so called elite universities. Of all the things these men and women could do, of all the things their wealth and power could afford them, this is what they volitionally choose to do with their "free" time? Clinically and forensically speaking, that which most human beings find to be uncomfortable at best and heinous at worst has the exact opposite effect upon these self-anointed and legacy elites. What that means is less important right now than the point I want to make. I want you to know what it feels like to be around these people and to get a feeling for who these people think they are as evinced by their recreational and fraternal activities. Whether these people are, in fact, who they think they are is a question I will hold in reserve for now.

I am going to briefly touch upon another meeting of the rich and powerful, not necessarily shadow men, named the Bilderberg Group. My information presented here will not be footnoted, as the information I am about to share with you is unknown, even among the "knowers." Bilderberg goes back to 1954. Up to about 1995 or so Bilderberg functioned as an idea laboratory where members would get together to share their latest schemes. Members would form alliances, strengthen existing alliances and plot against enemies. In that regard, Bilderberg was predominantly an intramural conglomeration of alliances seeking more power over members of their own group. Their designs on the masses were secondary.

After 1995 or so, the actual work of sharing ideas and plotting and scheming was done BEFORE the annual Bilderberg meeting. Digital and satellite communication technology was the super highway over which Bilderberg members hatched plots and came up with their newest designs on the masses. Ever since the year 2005 Bilderberg has functioned as an award's ceremony of sorts, where the movers and shakers get together to celebrate their past year's victories over the masses and their intramural competitors.

Bilderberg's location moves around, but other meeting locations exist without fanfare or notice. Few, if any, observers are aware that the island of Fiji is one location where schemes and plots are hatched. Monaco, around the time of the Grand Prix, is also a hot spot. Los Angeles, around the time of the Oscars, has served as an incubator of more than one mass PR campaign in service to mind control.

The massive and iron clad security that surrounds the Bilderberg annual meeting is not necessarily to protect its members from prying eyes in search of the business of Bilderberg; but rather, it is there to keep prying eyes from discovering the perverse and macabre recreational activities that take place there. Think of Bilderberg as shadow men's version of the Oscars, where they get together to give one another awards and celebrate being special. Far be it from me to suggest what ambitious citizen journalists should focus on when it comes to Bilderberg. But if I were to offer such advice, it would be to focus upon the agents who are brought in to service and sometimes advise the who's who of planet earth. These people are sometimes referred to as "gems." What are gems?

I want to focus upon a fascinating pattern of conduct on the part of the shadow men with regard to how they conceptualize the masses. Shadow men view the masses as an amorphous entity with indistinct borders and delineation. However, while shadow men view the masses as just so much rough material, they do expect to find uniquely talented people among the masses now and then. These special people (shadow men call them "gems") may be especially smart or they may be especially physically attractive. When it comes to the masses, intelligence and/or beauty are the two characteristics most desired by shadow men, with physical size and strength a distant third and fourth in desirability and fascination.

Shadow men do walk among the masses but you would be hard pressed to identify them. When shadow men are out and about they are on the lookout for gems among the rough. When talent is spotted, one of the shadow men's agents makes contact with the special one and, typically with the promise of fame and fortune, the unwitting gem is taken into one of the outer rings of the inner sanctum of shadow men.

As you might have already guessed, a prime hunting ground for shadow men and their agents to scout for exceptional youthful beauty is Hollywood. When it comes to intelligence, a cadre of professors at America's elite universities make it their business to be on the lookout for gems. It is interesting that Hollywood- insiders may have heard rumors about "gems" and the shadow elite but few, if any, feel comfortable talking about it.

Woe betide unto any stunningly physically attractive person who is also intelligent and curious. Some of these "special gems" have foolishly solved the puzzle of what they got themselves into but, like anyone who knowingly or unknowingly strikes a deal with the devil: "Nothing goes over the devil's back that does not come back under his belly." You'll never hear about these unfortunate souls by name, they will simply disappear as if by magic. Those who became a part of "the system" change, and often not for the better. The wear and tear on knowing or sensing celebrities can be seen in their deteriorating images and behavior. Some, who shall remain nameless, have escaped the grasp of "the system" but not without relinquishing fame and fortune. The hundreds of sweet and innocent ingénues who are purposefully transformed into drug-addled harlots are too numerous to mention. Nevertheless, not every gem falls pray to shadow men.

In 2011, James Lipton of The Actor's Studio interviewed comedian Dave Chappelle. Chappelle talked about his mysterious departure from his wildly successful comedy show and his $60 million a year contract. Dave referenced how tough people have to be to become Hollywood stars. He noted his good friend, comedian Martin Lawrence. Both Chappelle and Lawrence had "bugged out." Chappelle addressed how the public fails to understand the mysterious and unbelievable forces that can overwhelm even the strongest personalities who refuse to succumb to the forces of evil. [17] The general public simply cannot comprehend how a well-adjusted person could possible walk away from a $60 million dollar a year gig, that is, without having suffered a nervous breakdown or worse. Chappelle makes the point that such a view is dismissive. I feel confident that after reading this book, Dave's behavior will come to be admired, not dismissed or ridiculed.

On rare occasion, when shadow men's agent's fail in protecting their master's secrets, a horrific crash or suspicious accident will take place. Such incidents will soon fade into oblivion, however, as though they never occurred. This is because the PR agents working on behalf of shadow men in the media entertainment complex will simply ignore or spin the event. The "fast friends" of the victims, that is, those among the masses who espoused the moral high ground and who may have encouraged their brave friend to uncover the truth, never rise to the occasion to avenge their brave companion's untimely demise and remain as quiet as a church mouse once it becomes clear that what happened to their friend may happen to them. Again, this author refuses to cite examples for reasons already stated, but with a little bit of conscientious research on your part you will easily be able to confirm my thesis in this regard.

---

[17] James Lipton. Inside the Actor's Studio. Interview with Dave Chappelle. 2011.

CHAPTER 4: SHADOW MEN'S ACHILLES HEEL

Before I develop the allegory of vampires to shadow men, I need to warn the linear thinking reader about one particular defect the result of linear thinking. In our chapter entitled Google IQ™ we cover this very important issue in detail. For now, keep in mind that my use of this particular allegory is not to be taken literally. I will reference many allegorical images in this section to illustrate the characterological makeup of shadow men. Many of the images and references will be familiar to the reader. Again, the images and references used in this section are not to be taken literally.

Vampires, like their literary inspirations shadow men, are not without vulnerabilities. Most notably, shadow men can only work in the shadows of dusk to dawn. The sun is a metaphor for the disinfecting nature of openness and disclosure. Once the vampire is exposed to sunlight, he will perish.

Antidotes to the vampire's mind control power are not only fascinating from a literary point of view but provide clinical insight into the personalities of shadow men. You will learn later that many of the same techniques writer's created to thwart vampires, when translated from the literary metaphor into an actionable strategy in real life, constitute effective countermeasures against shadow men agent's mind control strategies, tactics and PSYOPs.

A tried and true countermeasure that impedes the mind control strategies of shadow men is the invocation of and belief in God. A belief in God saps the vampire's strength because belief in a higher power effectively dethrones both the individual shadow man and his cabal from their self-anointed demigod status. The invocation of Christian images, as has been dramatized in literary and film works of art, may take the form of displaying the crucifix, the Holy Bible or may take the form of sprinkling Holy Water upon the vampire. Anointing the vampire with Holy Water is particularly vexing to the living dead. Notwithstanding the obvious religious imagery in play here, this same religious imagery does not derive its power from the supernatural power of God or Christ, per se.

Agnostic or atheist libertarian minded people could impede the mind control power of shadow men using the strategies and tactics outlined in this chapter. However, it will be more difficult for them as a group because shadow men and their minion have less respect for agnostic or atheist resistors than they do for those who invoke the name "God." The reasons for this have to do with the personality makeup of shadow men and their provenance, not with the fact that agnostic or atheists are non-believers, per se or, as we stated earlier because of the supernatural power of God or Christ. So, if it is not the supernatural power of God or Christ, what forces explain the power that the invocation of God has over shadow men?

Both literary characters and real life shadow men believe that *they are literally Gods.* Thus, shadow men believe in the concept of God, but unlike how that belief is expressed by the masses who believe in a "higher" power or non-human God figure or figures, **shadow men believe in a very personal deity—themselves**. Shadow men's God complex manifests in their rituals where, just like an actual malevolent God, they display their power of life and death over the masses with a megalomaniacal zeal that betrays their self-perceptions. This underlying self-perception held by shadow men explains their rituals and recreational behaviors, e.g., The Bohemian Grove's Midsummer Festivities or Skull and Bones induction rituals. Thus, shadow men are deists, but with one proviso, they *are* the deity; and not just any deity, but a vengeful and malevolent deity. By invoking the concept or displaying the artifacts of a non-human God, the would-be victims of shadow men are, in effect, challenging a fundamental belief that is central to shadow men's psychological makeup. It is the invocation of "another" more powerful God that is so very vexing to shadow men, e.g., "No, you are not the almighty, there is something more powerful than you and I believe in him (it) and that God has dominion over you!"

This simple declaration in a higher power is a remarkably and counter intuitively powerful antidote to shadow men and their agent's hold on their victims. To comprehend this phenomenon one must imagine, for a moment, what it is like to believe, literally, that you are God, and to have held this belief since childhood, that your legacy pre-ordained your Godliness.

The simple declaration of a non-shadow man God strengthens the would-be victim's psychological and spiritual defenses against shadow men's control while weakening their power. The invocation of God serves as a powerful antidote to the vampire's bloodthirsty behavior (**metaphor** for the lust for power). Given this understanding, is it any wonder that removing God and the God concept from public discourse has been job number one for the agents of shadow men? Shadow men are simply knocking off their rival for control over the masses.

As previously mentioned, sunlight is lethal to the vampire. Sunlight is a **metaphor** for exposure, disclosure and revelation. Shadow men recognize that their power will all but vanish should they and their acts be bathed in the disinfecting light of the sun. In other words, if the masses came to fully understand their tactics and strategies, i.e., their methods of mind control, their effectiveness would be lessened and in some instances outright rebellion against shadow men's mind control efforts would take place. As it is now, shadow men sleep peacefully in their belief that the masses will never, ever, come to meaningfully comprehend what they are up to and how they do what they do.

The next literary antidote to the power of the vampire is particularly interesting in that it captures shadow men's perverse relationship with money. Psychoanalysts have identified the characteristics of picayune obsession with dollars and cents, greed, penuriousness and a compulsive need for control, as pathognomonic of an anal-retentive personality.

If you are someone who is unfamiliar with advanced concepts in clinical psychology or psychiatry, you will find what I am about to say unnerving if not shocking. For those who have heard the term "anal personality,' your understanding is likely deficient and more akin to a cute label you may use to disparage someone you do not like. Try to avoid transferring your repulsion or shock to the messenger (me) who is simply reporting the truth to you.

A big part of shadow men's personalities is centered-around what psychoanalysts have termed anal-sadism. Anal-sadism refers to acts of aggression and sadism that are focused upon the anus. Vlad the Impaler's behavioral proclivities are but one classic example of this perverse obsession. Vlad's victims were impaled with a long stake, bottom up, through their rectum, while still alive and left to die in the public square. Vlad loved the spectacle of this abomination and reportedly became sexually aroused at the mere thought of it. Anal sadism is where phrases like "I'm going to ream his ass," "up yours," "I'm going to kick his ass" or any number of words and phrases that all share a common perverse reservoir of psychopathology involving the confluence of the anus, with aggression and sexuality.

Aggression is not the only emotion comingled with the anus. Money and anal fixation are, likewise, connected. The statements, "he is a tight ass" or "he has a stick up his ass" refer to a person who is stingy with their money and/or stodgy and rigid. Anal-eroticism is central to shadow men's sexual proclivities, with anal-eroto-sadism a well-practiced libertine recreational activity among them. These perverse behaviors are disproportionately found among shadow men when compared to the general public, at least those who have not come to emulate their overseers.

Shadow men's culinary habits are no less perverse and cruel. Raw meat is a staple among them and takes the form of beef tartare, but is not limited to meat derived from cows. Shadow men prefer their tartare to be made from powerful and proud creatures, everything from horses that were once racing horses to endangered species. Live animals, held down with pins nailed through their writhing and terrified bodies, are eaten with ravenous zeal by shadow men who may be wearing ornate masks designed to look like medieval devils, demons and mythical beasts as they consume their living victims. Please refer to our earlier published images from the movie, *Eyes Wide Shut*. I warn the reader to not indulge your defenses and dismiss my empirically derived descriptions in order to soothe your jagged nerves. Stay engaged.

I knew of one shadow man who relished with unearthly zeal the most sickening foodstuffs one could imagine, including roasted feces derived from disemboweled animals. The more perverse and inhumanely obtained the foodstuff the more he relished it. However, if he were asked to put a pristine walnut in his mouth he would immediately gag and would not eat the walnut. And no, to the apologists out there, he was not allergic to walnuts. This particular shadow man relished feces roasted in the bowel. On the other hand, a pristine walnut taken directly from the shell and eaten caused a gagging reflex in him.

Since shadow men tend to remake society in their image, the fact that anal-eroticism has filtered down to the masses, and is now perversely popular among the libertine masses and America's youth, should come as no surprise. If you have ever wondered how is it that America's 1950's sexual mores morphed into its perverse 21st century version, well, now you know, it filtered down from the children of the prior generation of shadow men. [18] In the fall of 2014 the following headline appeared in the Huffington Post:

Texas Tech Investigating Frat For 'No Means Yes, Yes Means Anal' Sign [19]

Texas Tech was, according to the article, investigating the university's fraternity Phi Delta Theta for displaying this sign at their fraternity house:

Phi Delta Theta (2014) Fraternity House Sign.

---

[18] As the masses become more and more like their shadow men lords, their ruler's perversions will trickle down and infect the population at large. The Journal of Sexual Medicine announced in 2010 the following: 40% of women age 20-24, report having had anal sex at least once (persuaded/forced by their male partners). The number of 18-19 year-olds who've been anally penetrated rose by 20% between 1992 and 2010.

[19] Kingkade, Tyler. *Texas Tech Investigating Frat For 'No Means Yes, Yes Means Anal' Sign.* Huffington Post (Huff Post College), September 23, 2014.

Anal sadism, greed and a perverse relationship to and with money are central characteristics of shadow men's personality. Shadow men's perverse relationship with money underlay the folklore antidote of throwing grains of rice at a vampire in order to distract him and weaken his hold on his victim. The **"rice metaphor"** is based upon a brilliant observation. Once handfuls of rice are thrown at the vampire he will reflexively, according to lore, lose his focus upon his victim and begin compulsively counting the individual grains of rice. Once you begin to understand the psychoanalysis of shadow men's personality you will come to marvel at the elegant insight of throwing rice at the vampire in order to escape his control.

The precious metal silver has been reputed to have the power to weaken a vampire. The wisdom of this **metaphor** derives from shadow men's love of precious metals and how, if used against the vampire with tactical precision (silver bullet in the heart), may kill the vampire. In other words, shadow men's love of money can, under the right circumstances, bring them down. This principle also explains why simply wearing a silver bullet around one's neck, IF one's intent is to infiltrate the vampire's lair, may provide access to the vampire in order to get close enough to kill him.

A more recent, but equally fascinating **metaphor,** that explains the use of the silver bullet to kill the vampire is related to this precious metal and its relationship to silver certificates as opposed to mere reserve notes. Shadow men universally disdain returning to a precious metal-based currency, i.e., the "Gold Standard," for reasons that will become clear to you later in this book.

The methods used to kill vampires are yet another fascinating category of **metaphor** that provides insight into the vulnerabilities of these agents of evil we call shadow men. Most are familiar with the act of driving a wooden stake into the heart of the vampire in order to kill it. The wooden stake represents the wood upon which Jesus was crucified. Again, it is the invocation of God, and in this instance Christian imagery, that is lethal to the vampire.

CHAPTER 5: SECRET KNOWLEDGE

My focus in this chapter will be the etymological origins of terms, concepts and beliefs that serve as the predicate knowledge that permitted the rise of shadow men. Other authors who have dealt with this general subject matter have gone far beyond etymological data and created a labyrinth of theories, ideologies and critiques of formal religion. While I, like other modern writers on this general subject matter, owe a debt of gratitude to my predecessor's etymological research, I want to make it clear that my forensic and clinical training implores me to draw a bright line between the science of etymology on the one hand, and ideology, theory and speculation on the other. For some interesting and fascinating reasons, all of which are beyond the scope of this book, authors who have written about the etymology of power seldom limit their writings to the origination subject but extend their interests into areas that this author finds to be speculative at best and at worst delusional. Perhaps the desire to translate legitimate etymological research into a money making endeavor encourages some writers to tap into the paranormal market. Regardless, I shall stick within the goal lines demarcated by solid etymological research. So, with an acknowledged debt and respect for the etymological research of the likes of Sir Norman Lockyer, Evan Hadingham, Edwin C. Krupp, William Derham and Jordan Maxwell, we begin our review of the origins of shadow men.

The current dynasty of shadow men arose from the earliest tribal societies. An important question to ask is: How did a select few men become so powerful in the first place? One thing we know is that they did not achieve their unimaginable wealth and power from the exercise of brute force alone. Brute force may work in small groups, but even then, only for a time. Brute force won't work over the long haul because other brutish men rise-up to challenge the existent brute and, if he is not replaced by a "faster gun," then those oppressed by the brute, even though individually weaker, conspire as a group to kill him. If any man desires to rule the masses he must use methods other than brute strength alone to achieve control IF he desires to rule the masses over time.

In the very beginning a select few men possessed both uniquely higher intelligence, the desire to control others and instinctual cunning. These men discovered that if they acquired secret information, that is beyond their average tribal member's comprehension, but for which tribal members have an abiding fascination, then they could leverage their secret knowledge into the accumulation of wealth and its resultant power.

Secret knowledge related to matters that are, by their very nature, awe inspiring and fascinating to the masses, provide those who possess such secret knowledge great leverage over their fellow man. Most notably, the man with special knowledge can cultivate fear and at the same time provide a path to follow for the members of his tribe that will reduce their fear, that is, provide the fearful masses with a path to salvation from socially engineered fear. And who, pray tell, is able to offer salvation? Only God, or someone who is very close to God, can provide salvation.

With special and secret knowledge, nascent shadow men cultivated fear and awe in the tribe. To make that fear go away nascent shadow men would order up a "to-do" list for tribal members that would make their fear retreat. The "to- do" list would conveniently satisfy the nascent shadow man's wants, wishes and desires. The philosopher Hegel wrote about this principle. It has come to be known as the Hegelian Dialectic, i.e., Problem, Reaction, Solution. Note that the "reaction" part of the dialectic originates in man's nature. The problem part of the equation may be created out of thin air or may be organic. Shadow men and their agents almost always prescribe the solution to the problem regardless of its origins.

By cultivating the Hegelian Dialectic, nascent shadow men could satisfy all of their worldly needs and along the way indulge their personal perversions and peccadilloes. Being freed from the burdens of making a living provided nascent shadow men with more free time to construct an ever more elaborate story line and secret constructs that would increase their secret knowledge and thus, their control.

Nascent shadow men discovered they could make tribal members give them food, clothing, sex, land or any other earthly commodity by and through mind control. The first shadow men could make tribal members protect them by fending off his competitors and make tribal members serve his interests by attacking his enemies and taking their land and wealth for his benefit. As long as shadow men kept their special knowledge secret and cultivated the tribe's fears and ignorance, depending upon any one shadow man's degree of greed, these men could take your or your loved one's very life. So, what was that secret knowledge that provided a foothold for the very first shadow men? Let's go back to the very beginning of man in order to answer that question.

Imagine what it was like to be living 25 to 30,000 years BC. Life was a never-ending struggle for survival. Fear, misunderstanding and ignorance of almost everything in the natural world was the rule. Life was a mystery. It was divided into light and darkness. Darkness brought with it increased threat and risk. Predators came out to hunt at night and filled the air with their blood curdling howls and growls. Fire was the only thing that stood between the real and imagined terrors of the night and early man's solace. [20]

Sunrise was an event to behold each day because it brought relative safety, warmth and allowed early man the ability to see his environment. Early man did not take for granted that this fire in the sky, whatever the sun was or where it came from, would rise the next day. Like the dog that treats every return of his caretaker as a celebratory event, so it was that each sunrise was celebrated as a salvation from the evils of darkness. Likewise, every night at sunset, marked a time of heightened fear and trepidation. But it wasn't just the sun, of course, that captured man's attention and awe.

The moon was a mysterious, yet soothing light in the night sky. Early man, except for nascent shadow men/priests, did not understand the moon's movements and changing shapes in any rational sense. City dwellers that have never seen the night sky, as it appears when viewed in total darkness, are often amazed at the celestial show above them when they see it for the first time.

Man anthropomorphized the heavenly bodies, giving them personalities, histories, relationships with one another and elaborate storylines that described their existence and family dynamics. Smart people were then, as now, a statistical rarity. Those who are the smartest among the smart are even more of a statistical rarity. The men who were really smart were able to discern patterns in nature and the movement of the sun, moon and stars. They discovered that celestial bodies exhibited repeating patterns. Not only did these uniquely smart people discern patterns of movement in the celestial bodies, including identifying constellations that looked like people, places and things, e.g., The Archer (Sagittarius); The Fish (Pisces), etc., they came up with a brilliant insight when they correlated these movements with events on earth. Time, for example, was transformed from a subjective feeling to an objectively measurable phenomenon by chronicling the clock-like movement of the heavenly bodies.

Before you discount the brilliance of these insights related to the movement of the heavenly bodies, consider that in 2014 the National Science Board surveyed 2,200 people from America, the

---

[20] Note that the word "Solace" is derived from the Latin word ("Sol") for sun. It was, indeed, the sun that gave SOLace to early man.

European Union, India, Malaysia and South Korea. One simple "yes" or "no" question was asked of the test subjects: "Does the earth revolve around the sun?" Only 74% of Americans answered correctly, followed by the European Union at 66%, India 70%, Malaysia 72% and South Korea 86%. [21]

In April of 2014 a mega-church Christian pastor, John Hagee, warned of a world-changing event foretold by a celestial event known as "four blood moons."

"Megachurch pastor, televangelist and author John Hagee is warning his congregation and the rest of mankind that there's a "world-shaking event that will happen between April 2014 and October 2015. He's talking about the four 'blood moon' lunar eclipses that will make their first appearance on April 15.

Hagee, who is founder of the Cornerstone Church in San Antonio, TX, believes the "four blood moons," (four consecutive and complete lunar eclipses) also known as a lunar tetrad, is a significant event. Though NASA has also acknowledged that the 'blood moons' will be a unique sight to behold, the mega church pastor believes this event is even more significant than most understand.

The dates of each eclipse coincide with Jewish holidays but Hagee believes the event will also change world history. He discusses his research in his bestselling book Four Blood Moons: Something is About to Change, and now he's gearing people up for the event through his series of sermons and a TV special, airing on Tuesday, April 15, the first night of the tetrad....

[T]he Houston Chronicle reports that during one of his sermons last year, Hagee read from the Bible's book of Acts 2: 19-20. "And I will show wonders in Heaven above and signs in the Earth beneath, the sun shall be turned into darkness and the moon into blood before the coming of the great and awesome day of the Lord," he read.

Prophesying to his congregation, he declared, 'When you see these signs, the Bible says, lift up your head and rejoice, your redemption draweth nigh...I believe that the Heavens are God's billboard, that He has been sending signals to Planet Earth but we just have not been picking them up.'

NASA reports that the upcoming blood moon will be visible at around 2 a.m. local time from the central Atlantic westward to eastern Australia. Hagee's broadcast was aired on April 15, 2014 at 8 p.m. CT on GETV." [22]

Archaeologists have found etchings carved into animal bones and onto cave walls dating back some 27,000 years that depict the cycles of the moon and how these cycles correlated with the movement of tides and the depth of rivers. Imagine for a moment the influence, thus power, these few nascent shadow men had over their average tribal members by being able to predict the tides, river depths, seasons and the occasional eclipse!

It did not take long before the masses projected divine power upon the men who could predict the movement of the sun, the moon and the stars along with certain key events on earth. The average man presumed God made the heavens. It was God's sun, his moon and stars. To this day if you ask almost anyone where God lives they will point to the heavens above. The masses reasoned that *only* a man with a direct connection to the gods could predict the seasons, the weather and the ocean's tides. Only a God-like person could predict the best time to plant seed, harvest, plot the migration routes of food animals, avoid floods and remain peaceful during the dead of winter. These men who had discovered an early iteration of astronomy were assumed to be god-like, if not Gods, themselves.

---

[21] National Science Board "Science and Engineering Indicators, 2014. Please see:
http://www.nsf.gov/statistics/seind14/index.cfm/chapter-7/c7h.htm#page=23
[22] Christian Today, SOCIETY. *Blood Moon Lunar Eclipse April 15: Pastor John Hagee to talk 'Four Blood Moons' on GETV. April 13, 2014.*

It did not take long before these men with special knowledge began to act and FEEL like gods in response to the power given to and awe projected upon them by the masses. These nascent shadow men became what we would call today priests. They wielded great power by virtue of their predictions of earthly events that were instructed by astronomical observations, and in return, they became the beneficiaries of food, sex and protection. Then, as now, the surest proof of one's God power is the display and exercise of the ultimate power over the masses, life and death.

Over the millennia, shadow men/priests honed their strategies of control over the masses while accumulating more secret knowledge along with more wealth and power. They both attracted and sought out the most intelligent among their tribe to join their "secret society." I want to offer a word of caution here before you continue your journey.

Many writers, broadcasters and bloggers have imbued the beliefs and practices of these very first shadow men with a mysterious supernatural validity. Those intrigued by the paranormal often conflate secret societies and the elite with supernatural forces. Keep in mind that the earliest shadow men cultivated and encouraged this supernatural projection on the part of the masses. They wanted the masses to believe that they possessed supernatural powers. One of the ways shadow men/priests reinforced their power while keeping it all secret was to construct a labyrinth of secret symbols, signs and mysterious rituals that reflected their own superstitions and creativity along with their desire to promote intrigue, fear, awe and respect among the average man while keeping him in a state of ignorance. Writing, for example, was originally reserved for the exclusive use of priests in monasteries.

The Bohemian Grove's "Cremation of Care Ritual" is a dramatic reenactment of supernatural rituals that were, in shadow men's ancient past, actually carried out. In other words, in times past, ACTUAL human sacrifice was the centerpiece of shadow men's rituals. When the modern day heirs to the earliest shadow men get together, as we have documented, they retain the core psychodynamic of their ancestor's stock in trade—god-like behavior that relegates the masses into objects to be used as they see fit, including ritualistic sacrifice. The masses have always been conceptualized as canon fodder, long before there were such things as canons.

Thus, as strange as it may seem, in the very beginning it was knowledge of astronomy that soon thereafter morphed into an astrotheology that was then parlayed by the earliest shadow men into unimaginable wealth, advantage and eventual power over local and regional populations of the unwashed masses. Yes, that term "unwashed masses" derives from the fact that personal hygiene was a reserved privilege for shadow men.

The initial accumulation of great wealth was accomplished using mind control strategies fueled by fear, intrigue and awe, all made possible by the masse's tendency to project special power and supernatural abilities upon their leaders who promised salvation from cultivated fear. This desire to project great wisdom and power upon an anointed leader derives from man's almost universal and infantile need to be taken care of by an all loving and powerful surrogate mother or father.

In a perverse reinforcement of this transference on the part of the masses, shadow men would kill members of the tribe to instill fear and promote relief (if I'm "good" I won't be killed). This desire on the part of the masses continues to this day unabated, and is exploited in a myriad of ways by political and spiritual leaders in order to control the masses and, in the process, acquire untold wealth and power. The reader must ask him/herself if it is mere coincidence that each and every one of the top TV evangelists, without exception, is a multimillionaire who lives the life of a stereotypical version of the "lifestyles of the rich and famous."

The shadow men who were priests eventually spun off the theological part of their dynasty into organized astrotheologically based religions. Priests set up ever more elaborate astrotheologies that remained under the control of the shadow men in charge but appeared, to the masses, as a separate institution.

As the years passed, astrotheological-based knowledge was used by other ambitious would-be shadow men in other parts of the world outside of Phoenicia/Cana and spread to Egypt, Eastern Europe, and then Northern-Europe. The process repeated itself over and over until the earth was saturated with *competing* shadow men/priests, each with their own fiefdom, astrotheological storylines and organizational matrices.

It would be easy, if not comforting, for the reader to think of modern life as disjointed from the astrotheologically-based systems set up by these very first shadow men/priests. As evinced by Reverend John Hagee and his warnings concerning "blood moons," the tethers from the ancient to the modern world have not been broken. Most connections to the ancient world, however, remain shrouded in mystery and hidden by etymological evolution so modern man presumes there is no connection or that he has evolved past and escaped the superstitions of the past. Drawing that conclusion would be an error.

Keep in mind that while modern man believes that he is beyond the grasp of the power structure constructed by the very first shadow men, nothing could be further from the truth. What I am about to share with you may come as a shock to those readers who believe their life has remained untouched by the earliest shadow men's mind control PSYOPs. It is not my desire to undermine your deeply held beliefs, religious or otherwise, nor do I welcome the anger that some of you may direct toward the messenger for having made you aware of where some of your most deeply held beliefs originated. Simply be advised that many of you may feel uneasiness as you learn about the provenance of some of your deeply held beliefs.

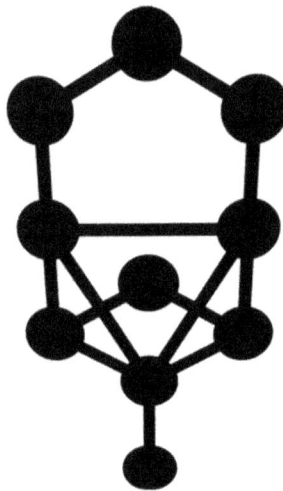

CHAPTER 6: ASTROTHEOLOGY

The very first shadow men/priests set up a matrix of power, the vestiges of which continue to this day. Even those among my readers who reject myth, the occult, and think of themselves as perfectly rational, use words and symbols whose origins can be seamlessly traced back to the earliest shadow men/priests.

Recall that the original power matrix that constituted the basis for the first mass mind control PSYOPs relied upon secret knowledge related to the movement of the sun, moon and the stars. In the beginning, shadow men/priest's secret knowledge was rooted in science but soon expanded to include anthropomorphized elaborate stories involving the heavens. The stories that came to define God for the ancient masses were routed through shadow men/priests who used fear, hope and salvation to control the behavior of their fellow tribesmen.

Earlier I stated that virtually all men and women deny the degree to which they are susceptible to mind control strategies. [23] What I am about to demonstrate is that many of the words you use, the concepts you have thought about and perhaps some of your beliefs originated with these earliest priest/shadow men. So put your cognitive and emotional seatbelt on and let's learn about our shared provenance to the very first shadow men.

Approximately 3000 BCE the Egyptians honored the sun god Horus. Horus marched across the sky each day in twelve-step intervals. His path across the sky was used to mark time. When Horus reached his highest point in the sky during the day it was then, as now, at 12:00 O'clock. This is where the term, "12 O'clock High" comes from. If you own an analog watch please note that your watch is likely to have 12 hours denoted on the dial. The English word "hour" derives from Horus, the Egyptian Sun God. English writers simply reversed the letters "u" and "o" to arrive at "HOURS" not HORUS. There also just happens to be 12 months in the calendar year, denoting Horus' seasonal trek across the heavens.

Ever notice that juries are comprised of 12 people? Ever notice that a dozen contains the number 12? Ever heard of a 12-step program? Ever contemplate why you matriculate through grades 1 through 12? What about the 12 days of Christmas? These examples of "12" can be traced to the twelve steps Horus took across the sky during the day and denotes his 12 month long heavenly trek across the calendar year. By the way, the word "light" in Latin is "Lucius" or the name "Luke" in English. Ever hear of Luke Skywalker? Luke Skywalker, the movie character from Star Wars, was derived from the Egyptian god Horus who "walked" across the sky and the seasons throughout the calendar year.

None other than Satan, himself, has a direct lineage to astrotheology. The word Lucifer can trace its origins to the planet Venus, i.e., the morning star. In the King James Version of the Bible, book of Isaiah 14:12, you find, "O Lucifer, son of the morning." Isaiah referenced a king of Babylon by addressing the image of the morning star fallen from the sky. The connection between Satan and Venus, i.e., the morning star is believed to have been borrowed from a legend in Canaanite mythology. [24] At some point in time Christian tradition began using the Latin word for morning star, i.e., Lucifer, as the formal name for Satan. Importantly, Lucifer was Satan, the angel, before he

---

[23] C.f. Fast, Nathanael J.; Gruenfeld, Deborah H; Sivanathan, Niro; Galinsky, Adam D. (2009), *Illusory Control: A Generative Force Behind Power's Far-Reaching Effects.* Psychological Science 20 (4): 502–508.

[24] Smith, Gary V. (2007), *Isaiah 1-30.* B&H Publishing Group. pp. 314–315.

embraced evil and fell from grace. Lucifer is now synonymous with Satan in the Christian Church. The term made its way into popular literature and popular culture. For example, Dante Alighieri adopted Lucifer as the proper term for Satan when he wrote Dante's Inferno. [25]

Have YOU ever commented on a beautiful sunset? "Set" was the god created by the priest/shadow men to represent darkness in ancient times. After Horus walked across the sky in 12 steps (HOURS) the 13th step resulted in darkness, or as we call it today "sunSET," named after the Egyptian god "SET". Some scholars believe that the number 13 got its bad reputation because the 13th step represented that time in a 24 hour cycle when bad things began to happen, e.g., predators and criminals prefer to hunt at night. You may have noticed that the hotels you have visited do not have a 13th floor, all thanks to "Set" and Horus' final step before he retired for the day and what was to follow.

When HORUS reaches his highest point during the year in mid-summer, modern man schooled in astronomy refers to that as the vernal equinox. When Horus is at his most high during the calendar year, Horus resides in the constellation Sirius. Have you ever said "yes sir" to someone? If you were a member of the military, you most certainly said it many times. You said yes "SIR" because the earliest shadow men required that your ancestors, who were members of the unwashed masses, submit to and pay homage to the will of Horus when he was at his most dominant (highest in the calendar year) in the constellation SIRius.

The planets that make up our solar system were imbued by the earliest shadow men/priests with supernatural power. Each planet was given its own personality, power and relative importance in the celestial heavens. Of all the planets in our solar system, the earliest shadow men and priests viewed the planet Saturn, only secondary to the Sun, as the most powerful and dominant body in the sky. Saturn was associated with darkness and chaos. It was known as "the great impeder." The people who lived on the coast of Syria, the areas we refer to today as Lebanon and Israel, were called the Phoenician/Canaanite peoples. The Phoenician's name for the planet Saturn was "El." To this day the words YOU use to describe a machine that takes you up to a higher plane or level pays homage to the god Saturn or "EL", e.g., El-evator, El-ected, El-der. Saturn was referred to as the "Lord of the Rings." Ever hear of "Lord of the Rings?" The ancients wore earrings because that was a symbol of listening, as in submission to, the Lord of the Rings, Saturn.

The hexagram (the six pointed star) belonged to Saturn and long preceded the Star of David. By the way, Saturn has its own day, "**Saturn**day" or Saturday. Interestingly, some religions use Saturn's day as their holy day during the week as opposed to **Sun's** day or Sunday.

If you travel to Israel you will notice that the word "synagogue" is NOT spelled with a "y" but with an "i", e.g., "Sinagogue." Sin was the name the Phoenicians gave to their moon god and, curiously enough, he did not come out until after sundown. Thus, some religions, including Judaism, begin their religious services only after the sun **Sets** and the moon god **Sin** rises.

In Phoenicia/Canaan, the moon would rise over a prominent mountain. In the original language of the Phoenicians, mountain was spelled "ai." Thus, in Israel, Mount **Sin ai** is that mountain where "Sin" rises over the mountain "ai." The name Israel, itself, is comprised of three parts: 1. **Is** (Isis-the moon God); 2. **Ra** (AmenRa-the successor Sun God in Egypt); 3. **El** (El-the Phoenician's name for Lord of the Rings, the planet Saturn), and later (Elohim, Hebrew for God).

---

[25] Kohler, Kaufmann, PhD. (1923, *Heaven and hell in Comparative Religion with Special Reference to Dante's Divine Comedy.* New York: The MacMillan Company.

Middle Eastern astrotheology spread like wildfire to consume most of the world. For example, the stone of Jacob is literally a stone that is placed under the British Monarch's throne.

Jacob's Stone within the British Monarch Throne.

The Union Jack Flag of Great Britain.

How does this relate to Israel, you may ask? First, the Union Jack Flag of the United Kingdom is an abbreviated version of Union **Jac**ob. According to Biblical lore, Jacob was the patriarch of all Jewish people. Jacob laid his head on a stone and dreamed of a ladder extending to heaven. (Ever hear of the song "Stairway to Heaven?") This is the same stone that has been placed within the throne of every British Monarch during their coronation ceremony.

Jacob fathered 12 Hebrew sons who invaded Canaan, the ancient land of the Philistines, and thus, became the 12 tribes of Israel. The son's names are, Manasseh, Asher, Naphtali, Zebulun, Issachar, Gad, Ephraim, Dan, Benjamin, Reuben, Simeon and Judah. Jacob's sons carved up Canaan into twelve districts and renamed the area Israel.   In 69 AD the Romans burned the city of Jerusalem to the ground and destroyed the Hebrew Temple of Solomon, except for one wall. That wall is now known as the Wailing Wall. The twelve tribes of Israel fled the land of Canaan, which was previously known as Philistine. The Romans took the land of Philistine and renamed it, using Roman lexicon, "Palestine."   The Romans gave Palestine back to the original inhabitants of what is today Israel. The same area that had been taken over by Jacob's 12 sons. As if to prove the point of how the ancient reaches into the modern world, during Prince William's marriage ceremony to Kate Middleton, a curious hymn was sang. And what was this hymn's name? *Jerusalem*. Here are the salient lyrics:

And was Jerusalem builded here
Among those dark satanic mills
Bring me my bow of burning gold
Bring me my arrows of desire
Bring me my spears o'clouds unfold
Bring me my chariot of fire
I will not cease from mental fight

Nor shall my sword sleep in my hand
Til we have built Jerusalem
In England's green and pleasant land

When the twelve tribes of Canaan fled Palestine, where did they go? The tribe of Dan became seafarers and later known by the name, Vikings. The tribe of Dan made their way to the British Isles and the rest of Europe, where they renamed many famous locations and geographical areas with the name of their patriarch "Dan." For example, the river DANube is named after Jacob's son Dan. Vowels were interchangeable in the original Hebrew, so Dan could be Din, Don or Den. The Jewish tribe of Dan has become a part of the name of cities, states and countries throughout Europe, e.g., LonDON, ScanDINavia, SweDEN, DENmark. Again, our point is to illustrate how the tethers from the ancient have made their way into the present.

The planet Saturn became synonymous with what is called a "magic square." A "magic square" is a cubic shaped figure comprised of numbers arranged in an equal number of cells that equal a square shape. If you add together all of the columns, vertically, horizontally and diagonally, you will arrive at the same number. This fascination with the "Saturnalian square" is why some scholars believe that no matter where you go on earth you are likely to find a town square, e.g., St. Peter's **Square**, Times **Square**, Tiananmen **Square**, Red **Square**, Vatican **Square**, etc. What follows are various cultural artifacts of the "magic square" of Saturn:

Numeric

2	9	4
7	5	3
6	1	8

English

B	I	D
G	E	C
F	A	H

Latin

B	I	D
G	E	C
F	A	H

Hebrew

ב	ט	ד
ז	ה	ג
ו	א	ח

Greek

β	θ	δ
ζ	ε	γ
F	α	η

Cyrillic

В	Ѳ	Д
З	Є	Г
Ѕ	А	И

Arabic

ب	ط	د
ز	ه	ج
و	ا	ح

Armenic

Բ	Թ	Դ
Է	Ո	Գ
Զ	Ա	Հ

Coptic

Ⲃ	Ⲑ	Ⲇ
Ⲍ	Ⲉ	Ⲅ
Ⲋ	Ⲁ	Ⲏ

Ancient egyptian

The ancient shadow men/priests associated each planet with a color, with Saturn being labeled as the dark planet, or one in the same with the color black. The wardrobe of the most powerful members of our society wear black, a practice that can be seamlessly traced back to the Saturnalian brotherhood who worshipped Saturn. Judges wear black robes, when you graduate from college you wear a black robe. The terms "dark side" "black hat" and a host of other negative color references linked to the color black all have their roots in the worship of the planet Saturn.

The Phoenician/Canaanite people created belief systems that eventually made their way to Northern Europe, where the populations who resided there personalized them. The Northern European shadow men and their priests were comprised of the Celtic/Druidic astrotheologies. Celtic/Druidic priests routinely spoke using a wand held in their dominant hand. This wand evolved into what we call today the "magic wand." By the way, Celtic/Druidic priests constructed their magic wands from only one species of tree. Do you know the particular species of tree? The Holly Tree. Thus, magic wands and their power over the masses have been recreated in a seamless lineage, that today we call **Holly Wood.**

When Christianity reached Northern Europe the Druids joined their worship of the Sun with that of Christ. That is why often times the Christian Cross is portrayed with a sun as part of the crucifix.

Druidic Christian Crosses

Have you ever been curious where the fish symbol comes from that we see emblazoned on the rear of some automobiles that informs other motorists and onlookers that the driver is a Christian?

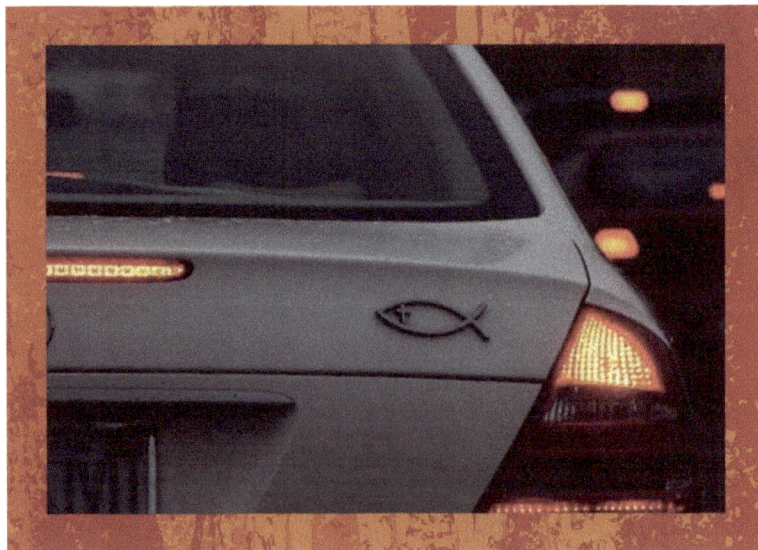

Have you ever wondered about the origin of this fish symbol with Greek letters written within it?

These symbols in the shape of a fish are all related to the fish god Dagon. Dagon was the name of the Philistine's fish-god. The Greek letters you see written within the fish symbol is the Greek word "Ichthys," referring to Dagon, the fish god. [26]

Dagon was pictured like this:

Dagon: The "Fish God"

Dagon priests in ancient Babylon wore hats that represented the open mouth of the fish. The fish's body was seen extending from that head and mouth, down the priest's back to form a robe.

The miter hat worn by the Pope is eerily similar, if not identical, to the miter hat worn by Dagon priests, the fish-god of the Philistines and Babylonians."

---

[26] Oxford English Dictionary. Definition – "Ichthyic" – "of, pertaining to, or characteristic of fishes; the fish world in all its orders."

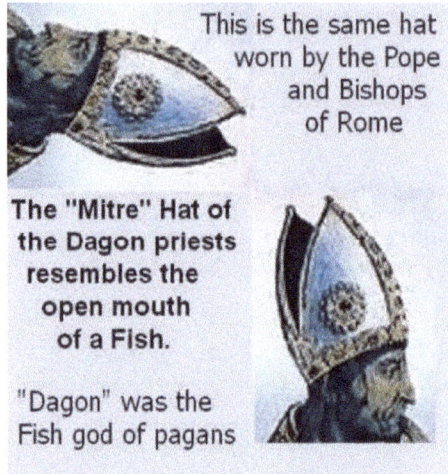

This is the same hat worn by the Pope and Bishops of Rome

The "Mitre" Hat of the Dagon priests resembles the open mouth of a Fish.

"Dagon" was the Fish god of pagans

The Pope's miter hat is a representation of a fish' head with a gaping mouth, as is the headwear worn by Catholic Cardinals on certain holy days:

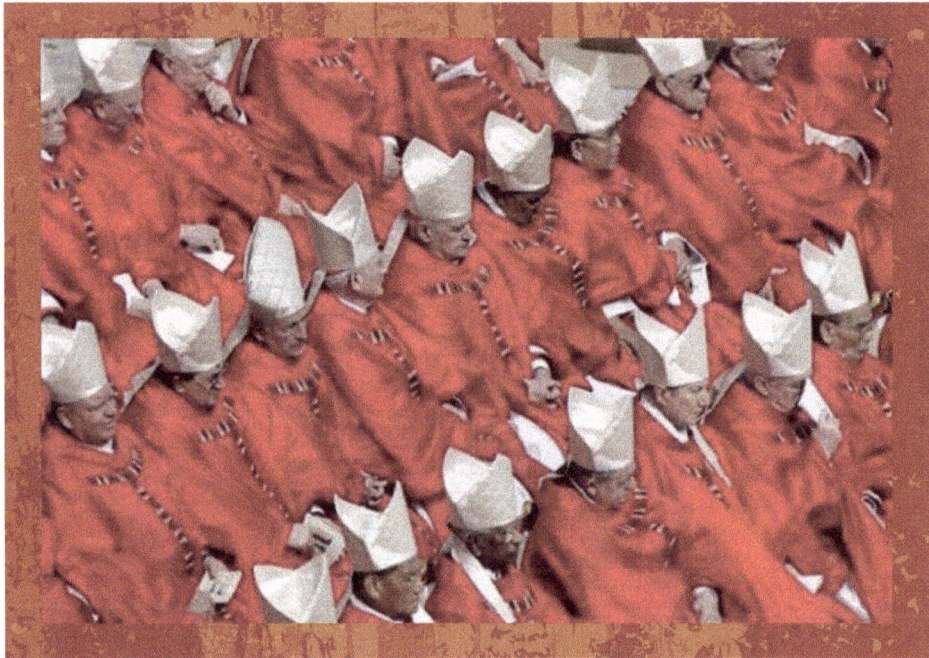

Catholic Cardinals Wearing Miter Hats Modeled after Dagon the Fish God.

Moreover, the fish symbol is emblazoned upon Papal accruements:

Pope Francis pictured with two Ichthys emblazoned on the cross.

Some Christians argue for a different provenance of the fish symbol in Christianity other than Dagon the Fish God. They say that because some of the disciples were "fisherman" or that Yahshua would make Christians "fishers of men," the fish symbol became associated with Christianity and found its way into Papal attire. But this explanation does not hold water (no pun intended, well yes).

Catholic scholars who study the origins of certain practices within their own religion corroborate the provenance of the various fish symbols in Catholicism to Dagon the fish god. Catholic scholars make the point that Catholics abstain from eating fish on all days except Fridays. This fish eating restriction is not found anywhere in Scripture. Rank and file Catholics undoubtedly have no awareness that limiting one's eating of fish to just one day a week is rooted to a reverence for Dagon the fish god.

In fact, none other than *The Catholic Encyclopedia* acknowledges this connection between limiting one's intake of fish to one day a week to an act of reverence for Dagon the fish god. Keep in mind that limiting one's intake of fish, given Christian apologists argument that many of the Disciples were fisherman and the local economy of the area was linked to fishing, makes no sense.

"As to the ritual of his worship…(referring to Dagon) we only know from ancient writers that, for religious reasons, most of the Syrian peoples abstained from eating fish, a practice that one is naturally inclined to connect with the worship of a fish-god." [27]

The earliest shadow men/priests constructed astronomical observatories that would allow them to better keep track of the heavens. Each observatory was purposefully cloaked in mystery and intrigue. A classic example is Stonehenge. Though it was built as a celestial observatory for the benefit of the shadow men of the time, the masses saw it as an edifice worthy of mystery and intrigue, a reality that continues to this very day. [28]

––––––––––––––––––––––––––––

[27] The Catholic Encyclopedia. (1913), Encyclopedia Press, Inc.

[28] Tickets are typically sold out in advance for visitors to Stonehenge. Please see: http://www.stonehenge.co.uk/Times.php

Mystery and intrigue go hand in hand. These human emotions were intentionally cultivated and served the shadow men's need to keep their secrets while, at the same time, communicating with a select few in their inner circle. As a result, the very first shadow men developed occult (hidden) symbols, words, rituals, practices and clothing that are psychologically no different than a secret handshake or an encoded message.

Before Christianity, the masses had a close relationship with the handiwork of astrotheologians who traded in the occult. The "occult" part of the equation was originally developed as a mechanism that kept the masses from becoming aware of shadow men's secret knowledge. The early church discovered that if it incorporated familiar symbols and some practices of their predecessors, the conversion of men to the Christian faith would occur faster and with relatively less resistance. Thus, whether it was the Celtic cross that incorporated worship of the sun or Papal attire that incorporated Dagon, the fish god, the purpose was the same-make the transition from astrotheology and idol worship to Christianity less threatening.

The Bible validates our thesis regarding astrotheology by specifically addressing the folly of buying into shadow men's focus upon celestial bodies, and thus, their control over man. In fact, numerous Biblical passages urge followers to turn away from the inventions of the early shadow men and their astrotheologies, to wit:

- *And when you look up to the sky and see the sun, the moon and the stars—all the heavenly array—do not be enticed into bowing down to them and worshiping things the LORD your God has apportioned to all the nations under heaven. (Deuteronomy 4:19)... and contrary to my command has worshiped other gods, bowing down to them or to the sun or the moon or the stars of the sky. (Deuteronomy 17:3)*

- *All the counsel you have received has only worn you out! Let your astrologers come forward, those stargazers who make predictions month by month, let them save you from what is coming upon you. Surely they are like stubble; the fire will burn them up. They cannot even save themselves from the power of the flame. Here are no coals to warm anyone; here is no fire to sit by. That is all they can do for you—these you have labored with and trafficked with since childhood. Each of them goes on in his error; there is not one that can save you. (Isaiah 47:13-15)*

- *Hear what the LORD says to you, O house of Israel. This is what the LORD says: "Do not learn the ways of the nations or be terrified by signs in the sky, though the nations are terrified by them." (Jeremiah 10:1-2)*

- *In every matter of wisdom and understanding about which the king questioned them, he found them ten times better than all the magicians and enchanters in his whole kingdom. (Daniel 1:20)*

The mystery and intrigue intentionally created by those who wished to monopolize power had its desired effect. Today, people who are intrigued by the "dark side" revel in the symbols, rituals and beliefs of the original shadow men. A myriad of secondary, tertiary and other secret societies were built upon the original matrix created by the earliest priest/shadow men. For our purposes, just know the general origin of these practices and the mind control value these occult practices served then and now. Nothing is new under the sun, including the "dark side."

CHAPTER 7: THE TRANSFORMATION

Once shadow men accumulated massive amounts of wealth and power they spun off various parts of their enterprise. This organizational transformation took various forms similar to what we would call today shell corporations, subsidiaries and vertically integrated units of the same parent corporation. These transformations occurred because shadow men's empires became too large and had too many moving parts to manage as a single entity. For our purposes, we are interested in how certain institutions became the proxy agents of the shadow men. More importantly, we want to know how some of these secondary institutions garnered so much wealth that they evolved into semi-independent bases of power.

As previously mentioned, the first part of the shadow man's dynasty spun off as a separate institution that comprised the theological component of their empire. Although the religious part was spun off it remained as one with the rulers who retained control. Only the masses erroneously believed that the religious component was separate from the shadow men in charge. A classic modern day example of this synergistic union between shadow men and their religious subsidiary is The Church of England.

The next organizational rearrangement involved the military. Shadow men's fighting forces functioned best when their commanders were chosen from within their own ranks. Nevertheless, the military remained under their shadow man's ultimate control. This formed the model used today, in much of the western world, where a non-military civilian leader commands the military. What the shadow men spun off next proved to be a turning point in the history of mankind. Like Dr. Frankenstein, shadow men unwittingly spun off a part of their enterprise that ultimately rose to rival their power.

The original shadow men were unable to effectively manage their massive amounts of wealth because they had so much of it and because their perversions and libertine lifestyle made them incapable of managing their money. Their innate penuriousness encouraged them to look elsewhere to finance their adventures. Greed fueled the desire to use other people's money to finance castles, wars and other massive expenditures related to the imperialistic desires of ruling shadow men.

Long before shadow men came to the realization that they needed to have experts manage their money, and long before there were actual lenders, a group of people existed who had learned to make money from managing money. It was this group of people who would eventually evolve into becoming shadow men's money managers and financiers. Some researchers cite to those men who fronted funds for grain purchases as far back as 2000 BCE as the first nascent bankers; but we view those operations as merely a cooperative enterprise and not, like a bank, *predominantly* in business to make money from money.

The first money managers in ancient times were called moneychangers. This is an apt name given that this is exactly what they did for a living, i.e., they converted currencies.

Ancient Moneychanger at Work.

E.P. Sanders and Burt D. Ehrman have written extensively on this subject. Their combined works, quoted here in part, serve as an excellent primer on the history of money changing:

"In ancient times in Jerusalem, pilgrims visiting the Jewish Temple on Holy Days would change some of their money from the standard Greek and Roman currency for Jewish and Tyrian money, the latter two being the only currencies accepted as payments inside the Temple. With this Temple money in hand the pilgrim would purchase a sacrificial animal, usually a pigeon or a lamb, in preparation for the following day's events.

During medieval times in Europe, many cities and towns issued their own coins, often carrying the face of a ruler, such as the regional baron or bishop. When outsiders, especially traveling merchants, visited towns for a market fair, it became necessary to exchange his foreign coins to local ones at local moneychanger establishments. Moneychangers would evaluate a foreign coin for its type, wear and tear, and possible counterfeit, then accept it as deposit, recording its value in local currency. The merchant could then withdraw the money in local currency to conduct trade or, more likely, keep it deposited and use its clearing facility to conduct trade. In the market, most large transactions were done not by cash/coins, but by transfer order of funds on the books kept at the local moneychangers, for a fee, of course. After a market/fair ended, merchants gathered at the local moneychangers and withdrew their deposit in their own different currencies. The rate of exchange between different foreign currencies and the local one were fixed between the opening and the closing days of the market.[29]

What began as a simple currency exchange operation related to religious sacrifice took on a life of its own as moneychangers continued to add financial services to their repertoire.

---

[29] Sanders, E. P. (1993), *The Historical Figure of Jesus.* Penguin Books.
Ehrman, Bart D. (2009), *Jesus, Interrupted*, HarperCollins Publishing.

It is fascinating that in Matthew 21:12 we are told that Jesus had a run-in with one of these money changing operations. Jesus' displeasure with the practices of moneychangers, including the sale of sacrificial animals, was expressed in an atypical expression of physical violence on his part. Here are three separate translations of Matthew 21:12 that describe this physical confrontation between Jesus and temple moneychangers:

New International Version
Jesus entered the temple courts and drove out all who were buying and selling there. He overturned the tables of the moneychangers and the benches of those selling doves.

New Living Translation
Jesus entered the Temple and began to drive out all the people buying and selling animals for sacrifice. He knocked over the tables of the moneychangers and the chairs of those selling doves.

English Standard Version
And Jesus entered the temple and drove out all who sold and bought in the temple, and he overturned the tables of the moneychangers and the seats of those who sold pigeons.

Biblical scholars time this confrontation between Jesus and these particular moneychangers as taking place a week or so before Jesus was crucified. Scholars have speculated that either the Temple guards arrested Jesus on the spot or Temple guards called in the Romans to arrest Jesus.

Over the years, moneychangers developed ever-more creative ways of making money from money. As previously mentioned, the first source of the "changers" burgeoning wealth came from converting currencies. Sometime later, the moneychanger's operation evolved into the creation of financial institutions that both held and lent money to whomever could afford their services, including their libertine clients living in the shadows. In other words, money changing evolved into what we would recognize today as an early form of banking.

As we stated earlier, classifications that rely exclusively upon race, ethnicity or religion are fraught with any number of problems. And so it is here for those who would conclude that money changing, and all that evolved from it, is a uniquely Jewish practice, rooted to the precepts of the religion, itself. Such is not the case. In fact, charging interest is described in the Book of Ezekiel as being among the worst sins,[30] and is forbidden according to Jewish law. The Talmud dwells on Ezekiel's condemnation of charging borrowers interest,[31] where Ezekiel denounces it as an abomination, and metaphorically portrays usurers as people who have shed blood.

As these nascent bankers added more and more money services, their power grew and grew until they became the financiers to shadow men. For example, those shadow men who wanted to expand their reign of influence or build a new castle or finance a new "this or that" came to these nascent bankers for money. Money changing took on a life of its own, and it didn't take long before these nascent bankers routinely financed the military escapades of their shadow men/clients.

Eventually, both shadow men and the wealthier among the masses became dependent upon banking institutions because of the allure of using other people's money for what would eventually become credit. It would take yet another transformation before these early money-changing operations would morph into international banks, with a much broader and more powerful sphere of influence.

---

[30] Ezekiel 18:13, 18:17.
[31] Baba Metzia 61b.

Scholars often cite to The Knights Templar as the beginning of international banking. [32] Some writers have suggested that The Knights Templar was started by one of a few select secret societies sometime in the 1100's A.D. We cannot confirm what group or groups began The Knights Templar, though we are aware of the names of the candidates often cited in the literature. As a result of this lack of empirical proof, we shall limit our analysis to what we believe to be true and not engage in speculation.

The Knights Templar was comprised of warriors closely associated with the Catholic Church. The Knights were originally tasked with protecting Christian pilgrims who traversed the roadways to and from the Holy lands between various parts of Europe. When you think of The Knights Templar, think of the Roman Catholic version of Wells Fargo during its stagecoach era, only much, much earlier.

Aspiring knights took an oath of poverty and loyalty to the Roman Catholic Church before they could become full-fledged Knights Templar members. The Knights were an elite group of fighting men who were fiercely loyal to the Pope. They were an early version of America's Navy SEALS, only these soldiers/warriors limited their work to land operations.

The Knights protected the treasures of wealthy European clients as they traveled to and fro the Holy Land in the Middle East. The Knight's services evolved to include what we might call today "safety deposit boxes," wherein wealthy clients left their treasures in the care of the Knights Templar while away or when threatened by a competing shadow man or roving gangs. As with any repository service that insured its wealthy client's money, the Knights garnered the trust of Europe's elite as their trust in the Knights was affirmed time and time again.

The Knights eventually came to provide what we would recognize today as an early form of "check writing." For example, a wealthy London royal might place some of his assets with the Knights for safe keeping while he traveled to Jerusalem. While in Jerusalem this wealthy traveler could write a check to a local merchant. The check was underwritten by funds held by the Knights Templar in Rome. Both the merchant and the check writer could trust that the Knights would facilitate the transaction and the timely transfer of the funds, for a fee, of course.

Then, as now, carrying proxy money in the form of a check or I.O.U. was an attractive option for the elite who valued the safety and convenience provided by the Knights Templar. Wealthy clients from all over Europe and the Middle East retained the services of the Knights; thus, they became the first semi-international bankers. For the next 300 years the Knights both earned and managed huge sums of money with virtually all of the profits going to the Catholic Church.

What happened next illustrates two principles that are the ever-present companions of large sums of money. I refer to these principles as the Napoleon Money Axiom. The first principle in this axiom is that *large sums of money attract would-be thieves*. The second principle has to do with the fact that *there will always be manipulation when large sums of money is involved*. In fact, Napoleon's Money Axiom states that the relationship between thievery and manipulation is directly proportional to the amount of money involved. Thus, the larger the amount of money the greater the amount and sophistication of manipulation and greater is the threat of thievery. Napoleon's Money Axiom not only applies to money, itself, but also to people who have the ability to make large sums of money. Thus, Napoleon's Money Axiom states that if you are someone who can create large amounts of

---

[32] Martin, Sean (2005), *The Knights Templar: The History & Myths of the Legendary Military Order*. New York: Thunder's Mouth Press. ISBN 1-56025-645-1.

wealth, you will attract thieves and be subjected to manipulation. Without going into detail, I encourage the reader to apply Napoleon's Money Axiom to any number of music stars or prize fighters who, despite having made billions for record companies and promoters, ended their life as destitute paupers.

In 1307 A.D., on Friday the 13th in October, Pope Clement V issued an official edict accusing the Knights Templar of heresy. Papal edicts of this magnitude are termed "Papal Bulls." One might reason in support of the validity of this accusation of heresy that with access to such huge sums of money, the Knights may have set up an embezzlement ring. But that is not what happened. It appears that the men who had sworn an oath of poverty in order to join the Knights Templar had remained true to their oath. So what happened?

Phillip the IV of France, true to his shadow man's perverse obsession with greed, stinginess and anal retentiveness, went to war with England but chose to finance the war with other people's money. True to the shadow man's penchant for penuriousness, Phillip borrowed money from the Knight's treasury (The Catholic Church) to finance his war, rather than pay out of pocket with France's (Phillip's) gold. This meant, of course, that Phillip owed a tremendous debt to the Knight's Templar Bank. In yet another act of ultimate stinginess and duplicity, Phillip understood the power behind the Knight's power and approached the Pope to forgive his debt. Some believe that Phillip pitched to Pope Clement the idea of blaming the Knights for raiding the Papacy's bank, so that Phillip could avoid the stigma of being known as the French King who reneged on his Papal loan.

Pope Clement the V rejected, out of hand, the proposal made by King Phillip. Pope Clement had a vested interest in recouping the principal plus interest owed by King Phillip, not to mention the fact that the Pope trusted the Knights Templar implicitly. After all, The Knights Templar had garnered the trust of elites throughout Europe, Scandinavia and the Middle East. The Knights Templar had helped to make Rome's Papacy rich beyond the Pope's wildest imagination. But this didn't stop King Phillip's greed frenzied insistence that the Pope forgive his debt. What happened next between Pope Clement V and King Phillip IV is a perfect illustration of Napoleon's Money Axiom at work.

King Phillip not only demanded that his debt be forgiven, but also, he schemed that if he could get the Knights Templar outlawed or disbanded, he would have effectively stripped the Roman Papacy of its mantle of protection. King Phillip reasoned that should he be able to convince the Pope to outlaw the Knights, HE could then commandeer the wealth held by the Vatican's banking operation with a military invasion that would be virtually unopposed. Without the Knights Templar, who or what would effectively protect the Papacy?

To reinforce this point about the inherent ruthlessness of shadow men, King Phillip IV kidnapped relatives of Pope Clement V and held them hostage under threat of death if the Pope did not give into the King's demands. Pope Clement V reluctantly gave in and, the Papal Bull was issued against the Knights.

This drama between Pope Clement V, King Phillip IV and the Knights Templar led to a ruinous divorce between the Catholic Church and Knights Templar members and their supporters. Former members of the Knights Templar helped to finance the so-called "protesters" of Catholicism, eventually garnering the name "Protestants." These were the same men who once protected the Papacy but were betrayed by the Pope. Although the rest of the story is beyond the scope of this book, just appreciate that this battle between the earliest banks, religious enterprises and shadow men continues to this day in one form or another and influences YOUR life in ways that most readers would never imagine.

CHAPTER 8: THE PSYCHOLOGY OF BANKING

Shadow men split off two major parts of their empire as a first step to diversification, religion and banking. The first "new" subsidiary of shadow men, religion, utilized astrotheology as a means to control the masses and enshrine shadow men's power. This venture resulted in great wealth for shadow men. Efforts to manage and protect that wealth generated the second venture we know today as banking.

We chronicled the next quantum leap in the development of banking by discussing the moneychangers and The Knights Templar. The Knight's relationship with the Roman Catholic Church ended badly but not before unimaginable wealth had been generated for the Papacy. Since international banking as a subject would result in a book that would rival the length of Tolstoy's War and Peace, we will limit our focus in this chapter to a general discussion of banking in the United States. The archetypal principles we will cover here apply, however, to banking operations all over the world.

What follows is a timeline of American banking prepared by Daniel Freeman. His timeline chronicles major events in the history of American banking beginning in 1690. I'm providing this outline in order to give you a sense of how this one institution has embedded itself within American culture.

Timeline of Banking

Daniel Freeman

	Event Date:	Event Title:	Event Description:
	1st Jan, 1690	Colonial Notes	Before the American revolution, Americans used the French, English and Spanish currencies. The Massachusetts Bay Colony issued the first paper money in the colonies that would later form the United States.
	1st Feb, 1775	Continental Currency	American colonists issued paper currency for the Continental Congress to finance the Revolutionary War. The notes were backed by the "anticipation" of tax revenues. Without solid backing and because they were easily counterfeited, the notes quickly became devalued.
	28th Sep, 1781	The Nation's First Bank	The Continental Congress chartered the Bank of North America in Philadelphia as the nation's first "real" bank to give further financial support to the Revolutionary War.
	10th Oct, 1785	The Dollar	The Continental Congress adopted the dollar as the unit for national currency. At that time, private bank-note companies printed a variety of notes.
	9th Sep, 1789	First Bank of the USA	After adoption of the Constitution in 1789, Congress chartered the First Bank of the United States and authorized it to issue paper bank notes to eliminate confusion and simplify trade. The bank served as the U.S. Treasury's fiscal agent, thus performing the first central bank functions.
	31st Dec, 1792	US Mint	The Federal Monetary System was established with the creation of the U.S. Mint in Philadelphia. The first American coins were struck in 1793.

	12th Sep, 1809	**First Bank Failure**	The Farmer's Exchange Bank in Glouchester, Rhode Island, fails—the first U.S. bank failure.
	8th Feb, 1816	**Second US Bank**	The Second Bank of the U.S. was granted a 20-year charter.
	10th Sep, 1820	**More Banks Open**	Approximately 300 banks operate in the U.S.
	13th Jan, 1849	**Gold Rush**	The Gold Rush begins.
	30th Nov, 1863	**National Currency Act of 1863**	Established a national currency: the dollar Established national banks, which creates the dual banking system with national and state chartered banks—the only such system in the world.
	12th Oct, 1877	**Chase**	The Chase National Bank is chartered.
	10th Sep, 1900	**Checking**	Checks become a more popular mean of payment
	11th Sep, 1900	**The Standard Gold Act**	This act stabilizes the economy, establishes gold as the only standard for redeeming paper money, and prohibits the exchange of silver for gold.
	11th Sep, 1913	**The Federal Reserve Act of 1913**	-Establishes the Federal Reserve System, commonly known as the Fed, as the central bank—the nation's third central bank. -Gives the Fed authority to regulate and supervise state-member banks -Allows national banks to open branches overseas -Moderately expands national banking powers by permitting real estate loans, time and savings deposits, trust services, and foreign branches.
	11th Sep, 1925	**The Roaring 20's**	The stock market undergoes an extraordinary, unprecedented expansion and is caught in a speculative euphoria between 1925 and 1929.
	11th Sep, 1929	**The Great Depression**	The Great Depression, a worldwide economic downturn, hits the U.S. in 1929 and lasts until about 1939. It is the longest and most severe depression experienced by the U.S. Its social and cultural effects are staggering. Many banks fail, many because they have made loans to stock market speculators that are never repaid.
	14th Jan, 1996	**Currency Redesign**	US currency was redesigned to incorporate a series of new counterfeit deterrents
	13th Aug, 2004	**Three banks**	Three US banks exceed a trillion dollars in assets. The number of branches increases. Interest rates are low. A housing boom occurs.

Most Americans have little appreciation for the impact that banking has had on their lives. The mind control mechanisms exploited by the banking industry are very old in that they often result in an ancient control mechanism called indentured servitude. Although primitive in origin, modern day indentured servitude relies upon very sophisticated 21st century PSYOPs. This is because, like so many other power brokers, bankers have chosen to use Fabian strategies and tactics to achieve their goals. Fabian methods of influence have replaced brutish methods used by the feudal lords who popularized the original versions of indentured servitude.

Lending money to citizens who do not have the funds to purchase what they want represents the Achilles Heel point of contact between bankers and their indentured servants. Thus, mind control strategies that encourage hedonistic material indulgence, regardless of actual financial wherewithal, work hand and glove with those lending institutions that are more than willing to indebt citizens so that they may live in a virtual reality that looks and feels real but is not. Striking a balance between indebtedness and economic freedom is not easy.

Keep in mind that something as simple as having bankers and borrowers exercise personal responsibility would provide significant immunity to many of the pitfalls of indentured servitude for both the borrower and the bank. Exercising personal responsibility would also go a long way toward preventing the economic debacles that routinely occur in capitalist economies, including the 2008 catastrophe that began in the United States and spread to infect most of planet earth shortly thereafter. Despite this rather simple solution involving personal responsibility, the mind control artists have been wildly successful, not only by encouraging, but also by normalizing, financial indentured servitude and insolvency-threatening banking practices.

I offer the following examples of cognitive distortions and delusions, related to money changing, in order to remind you how mankind has been manipulated by a cottage industry of mind controllers whose stock in trade is making money from money. These social engineers persuade otherwise intelligent citizens to become serfs on the lender's plantation. Almost everyone has made these or similar cognitive errors in judgment. I want to make it clear, that I am not chastising you if you are one of the vast majority who has made the errors I am about to discuss. I am only setting the stage so that you can begin to appreciate the fact that all of us have been victims of mind control artists who are dedicated promoters of indentured servitude.

Consumers (all of us) are universally delusional as evidenced by how most of us use words that describe our relationship with material possessions purchased on credit. Citizens who are indebted to the bank or lending institution for "X" number of years (home mortgage, for example) actually believe that they are home "owners." This is delusional. [33]

Fail to pay the lending institution its monthly fees and it will become readily apparent who actually owns the home (with a mortgage) you live in or rent to others. By the way, if you study the etymological provenance of the word "mortgage," you will find that it is comprised of two root words, "dead" and "pledge." The word "mortgage" truly is the best word to describe this form of indentured servitude because the shadow men who originally designed the "dead-pledge" understood all too well what they were doing to the person who entered into a contract with them. By logical extension, one would conclude that anywhere where property taxes are assessed means that the state is a co-owner of "your" property even when there is no mortgage to pay. How can I

---

[33] **Delusion**: noun. An idiosyncratic belief or impression that is firmly maintained despite being contradicted by what is generally accepted as reality or rational argument.

prove this? Easy, simply fail to pay your property taxes and the state will lay claim to "your" home and then auction "your" (their) home to the highest bidder in short order.

A typical 30-year mortgage has terms that will, more or less, double the purchase price of the home. The indentured term is approximately 40% of the lifespan of the dead pledger. The litany of false beliefs regarding mortgages does not stop there. The dead pledger, if asked what was the cost of their mortgaged home, will report the sale's price NOT the actual out of pocket cost of the home (interest plus principal plus mortgage insurance, etc.). If a consumer actually pays, out of pocket, $500,000 for a home BEFORE the title is officially recorded solely in his or her name, it is delusional to report that the home you are living in cost $250,000 dollars.

The term "dead pledge" is not the only moribund term used in the credit industry. When a "pledger" has made the last payment to the lender the home's title is not "transferred" to the consumer, the official term that is used is "redemption." The term derives from the Latin meaning to "buy back" (from the lender, of course), which proves, once again, who really owned the home all along.

While consumers live in a delusional world, where virtual and objective realities are conflated with one another, lending institutions do not suffer from those same delusions. When a consumer enters into an indebtedness relationship with a lender, the interest costs are paid upfront. Thus, this same delusional consumer looks at his $2,000 per month mortgage payment, for example, and it feels like he is reducing his principal amount in a commensurate amount. But that is delusional. In a typical 30-year mortgage, the monthly payment that exceeds the interest payment does not occur until the 18th year of the loan! [34]

One measure of the degree to which 21st century Americans and, to a large extent, the rest of the Western world have become indentured servants to banking lords is related to net worth. The median American household in 2010 had a net worth (assets minus liabilities) amounting to $10,890 dollars according to calculations by Edward N. Wolff, an economics professor at New York University. [35] We also know that over 50% of retirees depend wholly upon their social security checks for their sustenance. And surprising to many, the story isn't all that rosy for those who retire in the top 10% of household incomes either, those with one million dollars of net worth. How can this be?

Back in the day, if a person was a "millionaire," that was considered rich. American movies reflected this long faded reality with titles like "How to Marry a Millionaire," a 1953 movie starring Marilyn Monroe, "The Happiest Millionaire," a 1967 movie starring Fred MacMurray, and a long list of other "millionaire" movies. According to Jeff Sommer, writing for the New York Times in 2013, the picture for "millionaire" retirees is not what it used to be:

*"A typical 65-year-old couple with $1 million in tax-free municipal bonds want to retire. They plan to withdraw 4 percent of their savings a year — a common, rule-of-thumb drawdown. But under current conditions, if they spend that $40,000 a year, adjusted for inflation, there is a 72 percent probability that they will run through their bond portfolio before they die." [36]

---

[34] Here is a link to an on-line credit calculator that will permit you to see how mortgage payments actually work. http://www.practicalmoneyskills.com/wizards/credit/index.php
[35] Recent Trends in Living Standard in the United States, in Edward N. Wolff editor, *What Has Happened to the Quality of Life in the Advanced Industrialized Nations*? Edward Elgar Publishing Ltd., 2004, pp. 3-26., April, 2002.
[36] New York Times. *For Retirees a Million-Dollar Illusion.* By Jeff Sommer, June 8, 2013.

If the picture is less than rosy for the median American household, and troublesome for the top 10%, then something appears to be amiss. We caution those who have been conditioned to displace responsibility upon others, including lenders or the "rich," to realize that the problem we are addressing here transcends the banking industry and those who are relatively well off. The underlying problem is one of loss of personal control and the cognitive distortions promulgated by mind control agents. Add a collectivist component, overseen and enforced by a federal government controlled by financial interests, and you can see that even responsible people can be caught up in the delusions of the indentured servants and their banking masters.

There exists an entire catalogue of PSYOPs that are designed to do one thing and one thing alone: Encourage the consumer to indebt himself to lending institutions, in pursuit of material goods and services he really can't afford and does not need. Thus, the mind control agents who are selling you things you really can't afford and don't need are merely agents of shadow men, or more specifically, their diversified wealth management arm called banks and related financial management organizations, including shadow men's PR arm, the media entertainment complex.

When we reach that point in our book where we discuss the elegant manipulative PSYOPs used to promote this disastrous state of affairs, you'll begin to understand that Fabian strategies of mind control can and do enslave man better than any slave master or feudal lord could have ever dreamed of mastering using brutish methods. Before we get into the details of the psychological operations involved with promoting indentured servitude, take a look at the data that empirically demonstrate how wildly successful indentured servitude promoting PSYOPs have been over the past 60 or so years (2014 reference point). In order to get some idea of how successful, look at these data:

In the 1950's people from all walks of life made less money, per capita, when compared to today, but workers back then had more disposable income. Not only did people back then not have super easy access to credit, they believed in the virtues of frugality and saving for posterity. People actually owned material items. Cars were owned back in the 1950's, not "bought on time" and certainly not leased.

When the title of anything is solely in your name, that fact encourages pride of ownership (an old term slated for extinction as we move further into the 21st Century). People in the 1950s and 60s did not drive their cars as though there was no tomorrow. This meant that they respected other people's cars, as well, because of the shared virtue of pride of ownership.

One of the best examples of pride of ownership is the Zippo™ lighter. Notwithstanding the reduction in smoking behavior, in the 1950's, 60's and the first part of the 70's, Zippo lighters were bought and cared for and passed down to one's heirs. Before people reduced their smoking behavior the introduction of the disposable lighter began to replace the venerable Zippo lighter. Disposable lighters are abused and then thrown away, a metaphor for today's live for today mindset. Take a look at the origins of the word "credit." It is derived from the words "belief" and "trust." Lending institutions don't have to "trust" or "believe" they will be paid the money they lend plus interest because they can enforce their loan contracts using any number of laws, regulations and enforcement agencies that insure that they either get back their money or their property, sometimes both. Even when a financial tsunami hits, like in 2008, where creditors defaulted on their loans and their property value dropped to only a fraction of its prior value, the taxpayer ended up bailing out the banks. Win, lose or draw, bankers and their political agents have devised a system where bankers almost always win.

Banker's gaming of the system, so that "heads they win, tails they win," has created a cottage industry that takes back lender's property when the consumer stops paying his monthly fees. Repossession businesses are a multi-billion dollar a year business and growing. On the top end, lawyers familiar with the repossession business tell me that banking and insurers trade in billions of dollars when it comes to repossession of real property. One big bank, for example, settled one of its cases involving repossession of real property post the 2008 financial collapse for 25 billion. Repossession agents who take back automobiles for their financial service's clients will tell you that the most common response they get from consumers, when they come to repossess the lender's car, is words to the effect, "You can't take my car," to which the agent invariably replies, "it isn't your car, it's the bank's car."

A fascinating political movement came to power in 2008 with the election of Barach Hussein Obama. Mr. Obama's administration moved closer than any executive, since FDR, to adding fuel to entitlement minded citizens who had indentured themselves to bankers in service to living beyond their means. Loan forgiveness and pressure upon banks to modify loan terms did little to impact bank's bottom line but did encourage further indentured servitude on the part of greed frenzied and entitlement minded citizens.

"In 2007 auto repossessions in the U.S. rose to a 10-year high of about 1.5 million. In 2008 the total jumped to 1.67 million. By 2009 it had reached almost 2 million, the worst in a generation. The number dropped to 1.3 million in 2011, in part because repossessions depend on people buying cars in the first place." [37]

Take a look at the debt to Gross Domestic Product ratio that compares 1950 to 2013.

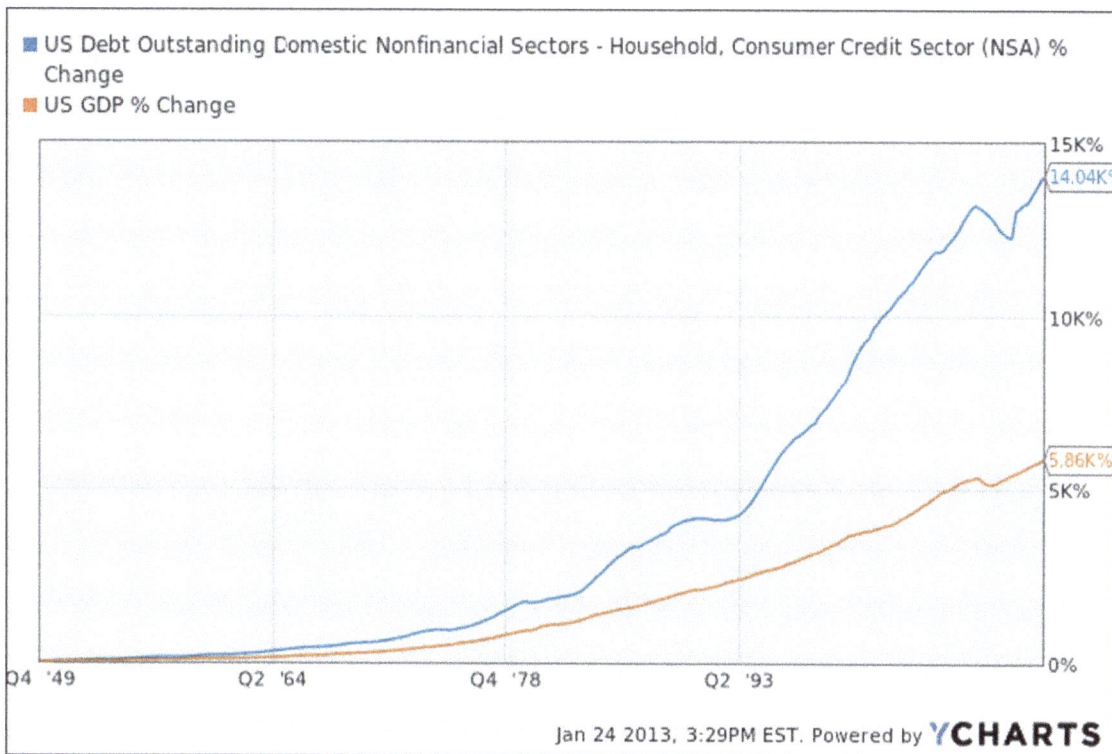

Consumer debt has risen 14,040% since 1950 while GDP has only grown by 5,860%.
Next, study the personal savings rate during that same time period:

---

[37] Bloomberg Business Week. (2012), *Luxury Repo Men.* Matthew Teague, October 25.

US Personal Savings Rate

Jan 24 2013, 3:34PM EST. Powered by Y**CHARTS**

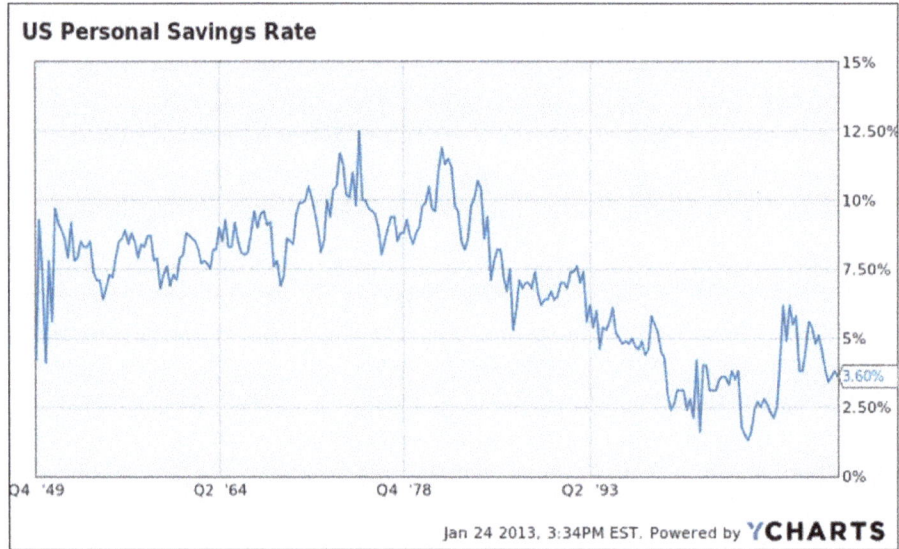

The percent of savings rate has been on a steady decline since the early 1970s. [38]

As the media entertainment complex provided ever more creative and entertaining ways to enter our consciousness, especially since the digital revolution ushered in the smart phone, consumer debt has skyrocketed while personal savings has plummeted.

Take a look at what things cost back in 1950 compared to 2012 when these data were compiled:

The average house cost $15,796

Equivalent 2012: $143,530

The average car cost $1,480

Equivalent 2012: $13,448

The average wage was $2,686

Equivalent 2012: $24,406

In 1950, a gallon of gasoline cost about 27 cents.

In 2012, a gallon of gasoline costs $3.69.

In 1950, you could buy a first-class stamp for just 3 cents.

In 2012, a first-class stamp will cost you 45 cents.

In 1950, more than 80 percent of all men were employed.

In 2012, less than 65 percent of all men are employed.

In 1950, the average duration of unemployment was about 12 weeks.

In 2012, the average duration of unemployment is about 40 weeks.

In 1950, the average family spent about 22% of its income on housing.

In 2012, the average family spends about 43% of its income on housing.

In 1950, the United States was #1 in GDP per capita.

In 2012, the United States is #13 in GDP per capita.

In 1950, about 13 million Americans had manufacturing jobs.

---

[38] Paul Grabil. (2012), *Capitalist Manifesto, CONSUMER DEBT VS GDP GROWTH SINCE 1950. A REASON FOR CONCERN?* January 13.

In 2012, less than 12 million Americans have manufacturing jobs even though our population has more than doubled since 1950.

In 1950, there were about 2 million people living in Detroit and it was one of the greatest cities on earth.

In 2012, there are about 700,000 people living in Detroit and it has become a bastion of urban blight.

In 1950, corporate taxes accounted for about 30 percent of all federal revenue.

In 2012, corporate taxes will account for less than 7 percent of all federal revenue.

In 1950, the median age at first marriage was about 22 for men and about 20 for women.

In 2012, the median age at first marriage is about 28 for men and about 26 for women.

In 1950, each retiree's Social Security benefit was paid for by 16 workers.

In 2012, each retiree's Social Security benefit is paid for by approximately 3.3 workers.

In 1950, the United States loaned more money to the rest of the world than anybody else.

In 2012, the United States owes more money to the rest of the world than anybody else.

In 1950, the U.S. national debt was about 257 billion dollars.

In 2012, the U.S. national debt is 59 times larger. It is currently sitting at a grand total of $15,435,694,556,033.29. (As of 2014, $19 trillion plus and counting).

(Emphasis Added) [39]

Anyone who dares to make socio-economic comparisons between the 1950's and 21st century America is reflexively attacked by those mind control agents whose stock in trade is to cultivate perma-victimhood, especially those agents whose job it is to pit African Americans and women against Anglo-European Americans and men. Notwithstanding each and every social inequity and racial bias heaped upon African Americans in the 1950's, consider the economic reality for African Americans using the same time frame comparison:

"The economic milieu in which the War on Poverty arose is noteworthy. As of 1965, the number of Americans living below the official poverty line **had been declining continuously** *since the beginning of the decade and was only about half of what it had been fifteen years earlier. Between 1950 and 1965, the proportion of people whose earnings put them below the poverty level, had decreased by more than 30%.* **The black poverty rate had been cut nearly in half between 1940 and 1960.** *In various skilled trades during the period of 1936-59, the incomes of blacks relative to whites had more than doubled.* **Further, the representation of blacks in professional and other high-level occupations grew more quickly during the five years preceding the launch of the War on Poverty than during the five years thereafter.**

Despite these trends, the welfare state expanded dramatically after the passage of LBJ's "war on poverty." Between the mid-Sixties and the mid-Seventies, the dollar value of public housing quintupled and the amount spent on food stamps rose more than tenfold. From 1965 to 1969, government-provided benefits increased by a factor of 8; by 1974 such benefits were an astounding 20 times higher than they had been in 1965. Also, as of 1974, federal spending on social-welfare programs amounted to 16% of America's Gross National Product, a far cry from the 8% figure of 1960. By 1977 the number of people receiving public assistance had more than doubled since 1960. [40]

According to Robert Kessler, author of "Inside the White House," he quotes LBJ as uttering these words on Air Force One to a small group of confidants in 1964. LBJ was referencing his landmark Civil Rights Legislation and the now famous "War on Poverty.":

"We'll have those Niggers voting for us for the next 100 years." [41]

---

[39] Michael Snyder, (2012), *America 1950 vs. America 2012.* February 26th.

[40] David Horowitz and John Perazzo, (2012), *How the Welfare State Has Devastated African Americans.* In, DISCOVERTHENETWORKS.ORG.

[41] Kessler, Ronald. (2008), *Inside the White House.* Blackstone Audio Books.

Applying Napoleon's Monetary Axiom to the huge sums of money literally thrown at one social welfare program after another, no one should be all that surprised that people are financially worse off today, especially Black people, and that America's coffers are running a huge deficit. The only part of the program that helped anyone, it would appear, is the socially engineered changes in voting patterns on the part of Black Americans for Democrat candidates and the bureaucrats whose living depends upon allocating taxpayer funded subsidies and benefits to a dependent and permanent under class.

Two things occurred between 1950 and the new millennium that changed everything. The first was a collectivist cultural revolution that reached critical mass in the 1960's and has been growing ever since. The second involved the delivery systems of the mind control PSYOPs that made it possible, for the first time in human history, to brainwash almost everyone on earth so that they would think and feel the way mind controllers desired. And one of the central mindsets cultivated over the past half-century involved the dissolution of pride of ownership, replaced by wanton consumption using other people's money.

Banking is not a monolithic enterprise. The banking industry and its related businesses are comprised of competing seats of power, each with a ravenous appetite to consume their competitor's money. Keep in mind our two guiding principles (Napoleon's Monetary Axiom) when evaluating banking and its related industries. Large sums of money attract thieves and manipulation.

Consider the following as a reminder of our three ancient bedfellows: banking, religion and government:

"A true world political authority" was called for by Pope Benedict XVI during his Dec. 3, 2012 remarks to the Pontifical Council for Justice and Peace, citing his 2009 encyclical Caritas in Veritate. The same council had "called for the establishment of a **'central world bank'** *to regulate the global financial industry and the international money supply as a step toward the world authority envisioned by Pope Benedict." The council's president is Cardinal Peter Turkson of Ghana.* [42]

Two weeks later the following took place,

The European Central Bank, headed by Mario Draghi, former Goldman Sachs International vice chairman and managing director, was given the authority to directly police at least 150 of the euro zones' biggest banks. The deal foresees banks with assets of 30 billion Euros, or larger than one-fifth of their country's economic output, being supervised by the ECB rather than national supervisors....[C]ritically, it also gives the ECB authority to widen its authority to smaller banks if problems arise.

Draghi is now 'Europe's most powerful person" and "chief banker of the world's largest currency area. **Some of Goldman Sachs' financiers who brought austerity and submissive national economies to Europe are also** <u>**advisers to the Vatican.**</u>

Perhaps the most prominent ex-politician inside the European Central Bank is Peter Sutherland. **He is now non-executive chairman of Goldman's UK-based broker-dealer arm, Goldman Sachs International. Sutherland also carries the title Consultor of the Extraordinary Section of the Administration of the Patrimony of the Apostolic See, the Vatican department, which controls their vast real estate and investment portfolios.**

Mario Monti has maintained an excellent relationship with the Vatican. Monti is an international adviser to Goldman Sachs whose appointment as Italian prime minister in November 2011 was highly praised by Italian churchmen, his photo appearing on the front page of the Vatican's newspaper, L'Osservatore Romano, six times in his

---

[42] Daily Kos. Vatican and Goldman Sachs, *A "One-World Government" Aimed at Africa.* Betty Clermont, January 10, 2013.

first two months in office. Monti, a frequent visitor to the Vatican, has already been endorsed by the Church should he decide to seek a second term as head of a new coalition.

Early in 2010, Mario Draghi went to the Vatican to discuss the Greek financial crisis with Hans Tietmeyer, former president of the Deutsche Bundesbank **and first choice of Popes John Paul and Benedict for president of the IOR (Vatican Bank);** *the then IOR president, Opus Dei member and former president of Santander Consumer Bank SpA, Ettore Gotti Tedeschi; and then president of the Bank of Greece, the technocrat later installed as unelected prime minister, Lukas D. Papademos. Draghi said in an interview at the time that Greece needed to "slash the minimum wage, pensions and benefits – including deep cuts in the health service."* [43] (Emphasis Added)

It may be soothing to some readers that Goldman Sachs and the Vatican are consulting with one another on matters that do not directly involve the United States. If you have concluded that, you would be wrong. In June of 2015 Jeffrey Sachs, a high level advisor to Pope Francis and the Catholic Church, had this to say about America. What follows was taken from an article published by Western Journalism and corroborated by multiple sources:

"Top Vatican adviser Jeffrey Sachs says that when Pope Francis visits the United States in September, he will directly challenge the "American idea" of God-given rights embodied in the Declaration of Independence.

Sachs, a special advisor to the United Nations and director of the Earth Institute at Columbia University, is a media superstar who can always be counted on to pontificate endlessly on such topics as income inequality and global health. This time, writing in a Catholic publication, he may have gone off his rocker, revealing the real global game plan." [44]

Jeffrey Sachs

AKA Jeffrey David Sachs

Born: 5-Nov-1954
Birthplace: Detroit, MI

Gender: Male
Religion: Jewish
Race or Ethnicity: White
Sexual orientation: Straight
Occupation: Economist

Nationality: United States
Executive summary: *The End of Poverty*

Father: Theodore Sachs
Mother: Joan
Wife: Sonia Ehrlich (two daughters, one son)
Daughter: Lisa
Son: Adam
Daughter: Hannah

Jeffrey Sachs, Top Advisor to the Vatican.

What you see illustrated here is that banking power centers both compete and cooperate with one another. When they cooperate they frequently plot and plan to unite the entire world into one big customer base using a single currency controlled by a cabal made up of the most powerful men on earth. Enter the International Monetary Fund.

---

[43] Ibid.
[44] Western Journalism. *Vatican Adviser Says America's Founding Document Is Outmoded, Reveals Global Game Plan.* Reported by: Cliff Kincaid, May 19, 2015.

The International Monetary Fund has made the following glowing comments about itself:

"The International Monetary Fund (IMF) is an organization of 188 countries, working to foster global monetary cooperation, secure financial stability, facilitate international trade, promote high employment and sustainable economic growth, and reduce poverty around the world." [45]

Shortly after the financial debacle in 2008, an investigative reporter writing for *The Atlantic* gained access to a high-ranking official at the International Monetary Fund (IMF). How high ranking? How about the Chief Economist for the IMF. Investigative reporter Simon Johnson wrote the following:

"The crash has laid bare many unpleasant truths about the United States. One of the most alarming, says a former chief economist of the International Monetary Fund, is that the finance industry has **effectively captured our government**—*a state of affairs that more typically describes emerging markets, and is at the center of many emerging-market crises. If the IMF's staff could speak freely about the U.S., it would tell us what it tells all countries in this situation: recovery will fail* **unless we break the financial oligarchy** *that is blocking essential reform. And if we are to prevent a true depression, we're running out of time."* (Emphasis Added) [46]

Applying the knowledge we have learned thus far concerning the origins of shadow men and their financial empires, we should find this would-be whistle blower's revelations refreshingly candid, but certainly not a surprise. We should be able to, at this point in our studies, find revelations concerning the relationship between The Vatican, Goldman Sachs and their political arms *to be expected, not shocking*. If the reader is shocked at this revelation, be aware that shock in response to facts is simply your defenses, and the false beliefs they protected, dissolving right before your very eyes.

And lest you conclude that my comments are solely focused upon the Catholic Church, they are not. The Catholic Church has accumulated huge sums of money and manages its own bank. Applying Napoleon's Axiom to this situation would predict that The Roman Catholic Church is now and will continue to be besieged with thievery and manipulation as long as it maintains control over its large sums of money. Again, if you understand the origins of power and its evolution over time, what should be surprising is the fact that it is not common knowledge that these three bedfellows (Government/Religion/Banking) have been together since the very beginning and are controlled by those living and working in the shadows.

The former chief economist for the IMF, in a moment of stark candor fueled by the realization that we were facing the worst financial debacle since the great depression of the 1930's, gave voice to this book's précis:

*"Typically, these countries are in a desperate economic situation for one simple reason—***the powerful elites within them overreached in good times and took too many risks.** *Emerging-market governments and their private-sector allies commonly form a tight-knit— and, most of the time,* **genteel—oligarchy**, *running the country rather like a profit-seeking company in which they are the controlling shareholders. When a country like Indonesia or South Korea or Russia grows, so do the ambitions of its captains of industry. As masters of their mini-universe, these people make some investments that clearly benefit the broader economy, but they also start making bigger and riskier bets.* **They reckon—correctly, in most cases—that**

---

[45] International Monetary Fund Homepage (2014), https://www.imf.org/external/about.htm
[46] The Atlantic. *The Quiet Coup.* Simon Johnson, May 1, 2009.

their political connections will allow them to push onto the government any substantial problems that arise." [47]

And while we are examining the relationships between bankers, religion and politics, consider the World Bank. The World Bank published these glowing descriptions of itself on its website:

"The World Bank is a United Nations international financial institution that provides loans to developing countries for capital programs. The World Bank is a component of the World Bank Group, and a member of the United Nations Development Group.

The World Bank's official goal is the reduction of poverty. According to its Articles of Agreement, all its decisions must be guided by a commitment to the promotion of foreign investment and international trade and to the facilitation of capital investment." [48]

Permit me to share with you a comment by Richard Clarke, one of the, if not the, most informed intelligence officers both before and after 9/11 and the invasion of Iraq under President George W. Bush. For those of you who don't know, here is a brief dossier on Clarke:

"Richard Alan Clarke is the former National Coordinator for Security, Infrastructure Protection, and Counter-terrorism for the United States.

Clarke worked for the State Department during the presidency of Ronald Reagan. In 1992, President George H.W. Bush appointed him to chair the Counter-terrorism Security Group and to a seat on the United States National Security Council. President Bill Clinton retained Clarke and in 1998 promoted him to be the National Coordinator for Security, Infrastructure Protection, and Counter-terrorism, the chief counter-terrorism adviser on the National Security Council. Under President George W. Bush, Clarke initially continued in the same position, but the position was no longer given cabinet-level access. He later became the Special Advisor to the President on cyber security. Clarke left the Bush administration in 2003."

Clarke attended a meeting with soon to be head of the World Bank, Paul Wolfowitz, along with Richard Perle and President G.H.W. Bush. Clarke assumed, like everyone else in the know, Osama bin Laden was the perpetrator of 9/11. Much to Clarke's chagrin, however, he walked into a chorus of drumbeats for war blaming, of all people, Saddam Hussein.

President George W. Bush welcomes Deputy Secretary of Defense Paul Wolfowitz to the Oval Office Wednesday, March 16, 2005. President Bush is recommending Secretary Wolfowitz to be elected as the next President of the World Bank. White House photo by Paul Morse.

---

[47] Ibid.
[48] World Bank. (2011), *About Us.*

Richard Clarke wrote about this meeting attended by Wolfowitz in his book *Against All Enemies*:

> *"Wolfowitz fidgeted and scowled, "I just don't understand why we are beginning by talking about this one man bin Laden." "We are talking about a network of terrorist organizations called al Qaeda, that happens to be led by bin Laden, and we are talking about that network because it and it alone poses an immediate and serious threat to the US," I answered.*
>
> *Wolfowitz turned to me. "You give bin Laden too much credit. He could not do all these things like the 1993 attack on New York, not without a state sponsor. Just because FBI and CIA have failed to find the linkages does not mean they don't exist."*
>
> *I could hardly believe it, but* **Wolfowitz was actually spouting the totally discredited theory that Iraq was behind the 1993 truck bomb at the World Trade Center**, *a theory that had been investigated for years & found to be totally untrue. I had a flashback to Wolfowitz saying the very same thing in April. The focus on al Qaeda was wrong, he had said, we must go after Iraqi-sponsored terrorism."* [49]

Richard Perle, aka, "The Dark Prince" was another self-proclaimed neo-conservative, along with Paul Wolfowitz and others, who lobbied vociferously for an invasion of Iraq based upon a 9/11 and Saddam Hussein connection, a connection that was utterly and totally without merit, specious and not reasonably plausible. In other words, NO ONE with both knowledge AND intelligence experience believed there to be even a distant connection. Hussein was a tyrant, but he was a secular tyrant who understood Islam's threat to his secular government better than anyone in the American administration.

> *"Like many in the neoconservative movement, Perle had long been an advocate of regime change in Iraq. In 1998 Perle led an effort known as the Project for the New American Century with close neoconservative allies Wolfowitz, Woolsey, Elliott Abrams, and John Bolton. The Project culminated in a letter sent to US President Bill Clinton calling for the military overthrow of Saddam Hussein's regime.[2]"* [50]

Richard Perle, aka "The Dark Prince."

Viewing this situation using a forensic scientist's prism, it is perfectly logical that the World Bank's President, before he became president of the bank, would be instrumental in lobbying for an invasion of Iraq. Wolfowitz opened an office in Baghdad, once American, British and other members of the coalition had done the dirty work. Why the office in Baghdad?

---

[49] Clarke, Richard A. (2004), *Against All Enemies: Inside America's War on Terror.* Free Press, New York, New York.

[50] Shadow Elite, Janine R. Wedel, (2009), pgs.147-191.

Wolfowitz began the process of indebting Iraq to the World Bank by making loans to this oil rich country to rebuild infrastructure destroyed the result of his war lobbying while Assistant Secretary of Defense. Global Policy Forum (GPF) said this about the World Bank and Iraq: [51]

"Reports that a World Bank staffer was shot at an Iraqi checkpoint surfaced in late February. The Bank apparently suppressed the news for several days, presumably in an effort to quell concerns about Bank President Paul Wolfowitz's recent push to re-open a World Bank office in Baghdad. What should the Bank be doing in Iraq? Following is an overview of current Bank involvement in the country, and some reasons why you should be concerned.

The World Bank's stated mission for Iraq is to "help Iraq build efficient, inclusive, transparent, and accountable institutions for stability, good governance, and sustainable economic prosperity." Activities are guided by a 2006-7 Interim Strategy Note (ISN) and based on four pillars: restoring basic service delivery, enabling private sector development, strengthening social safety nets, and improving public sector governance. The Bank is currently providing both lending and technical advice to the country. It also administers one part of the International Reconstruction Fund Facility for Iraq: the World Bank Iraq Trust Fund (the UN's Development Group Trust Fund is the other part).

* Lending: The ISN provides a framework for up to $500 million in IDA resources. Another $500 million in IBRD resources may also be available, contingent upon improvements in creditworthiness. The Bank's website lists three active IDA projects with commitments totaling almost $300 million. The IFC, the Bank's private-sector arm, is supporting four private investments in the country totaling $297 million, including a SME-based project involving a Jordanian bank and a Commercial Bank project involving the National Bank of Kuwait (which is also, incidentally, part of a consortium managing the Iraq Trade Bank).

* Analytical & Advisory Services: The Bank is also providing policy reform papers on key issues and sectors, and organizing policy dialogues. Examples of Iraq reform paper topics include: economic reform, investment climate, and state-owned enterprises. One WB policy reform paper (United Nations and World Bank Joint Needs Assessment: Investment Climate (October 2003)) urges Iraq to quickly develop institutions and laws in favor of private and foreign investment. The Bank is also the lead adviser to the IMF's Iraq program on sectoral strategies including, inter alia, the oil sector.

* Iraq Trust Fund: Through the World Bank Iraq Trust Fund, the Bank finances at least 15 active and completed projects totaling over $400 million, primarily in the Water/Sanitation, Transportation, and Education sectors.

* Office: Bank activities in Iraq have been directed through an office in Amman, Jordan since shortly after the fall of Saddam Hussein. Country Director Joseph Saba is based in Washington, DC. However, Paul Wolfowitz has recently made moves to beef up the Bank's presence in the country, negotiating a contract with a new resident country director to be based in Baghdad's 'Green Zone'." [52]

I reiterate that the vast majority of politicians are merely the onstage handmaidens working on behalf of shadow men and their financial arms in banking and related institutions. Can you now

---

[51] Global Policy Forum is an independent policy watchdog that monitors the work of the United Nations and scrutinizes global policymaking. We promote accountability and citizen participation in decisions on peace and security, social justice and international law.
[52] Global Policy Forum (2007), *Why you should care about the World Bank and Iraq.*

begin to see how foolish it is to focus upon the on-stage productions we refer to as politics, as though those men and women are the true decision makers? And if you are beginning to realize that this on-stage production is little more than a high-school play designed to entertain and motivate the student body to do shadow men's dirty work, then imagine how asinine it is to take seriously the so-called political pundits whose stock in trade it is to wax-on about this high school production while the true power centers and their blatant manipulation go unnoticed, misunderstood and ultimately unchallenged.

My implied criticisms of where average citizen's focus their attention are not so much that people may choose to watch and listen to those who debate political ideas and current events broadcast by your favorite cable provider, but that the masses fail to appreciate that what is presented to them is comprised of illusions with a purpose. The men and women who discuss politics are, with few exceptions, the public relations arm of the shadow men in charge and their branch power centers. Keep in mind that only a very few, if any, of media pundits (left, middle or right) know what they are up to while the rest of them have no idea, none whatsoever, that they are poorly sharpened tools in service to the people who control the entire production from start to finish. Simply put, "they sing the song of whose bread they eat."

CHAPTER 9: THE FEDERAL RESERVE

If you ask the average American to describe The Federal Reserve, you are likely to get a blank stare in response to that question. If you ask informed Americans to describe The Federal Reserve, they will likely tell you in error that "The Fed" is a government institution having something to do with banking.

Ignorance of The Federal Reserve is the rule and, unlike other vacuums of insight or knowledge, this ignorance can result in any number of profoundly negative consequences. Consider what President John Adams had to say in this regard:

> *"All the perplexities, confusion and distresses in America arise not from defects in the constitution or confederation, nor from want of honor or virtue, as much from downright ignorance of the nature of coin, credit, and circulation."* [53]

Reflect upon our analysis of how formalized banking began in the religious temples of the Middle East as you read President James Madison's words:

> *"History records that the money changers have used every form of abuse, intrigue, deceit, and violent means possible to maintain their control over governments by controlling money and its issuance."* [54]

In a Presidential speech on the topic of international bankers, President Andrew Jackson said this:

> *"You are a den of vipers! I intend to rout you out, and by the Eternal God I will rout you out. If the people only understood the rank injustice of our money and banking system, there would be a revolution before morning."* . . . *"If congress has the right under the Constitution to issue paper money, it was given them to use themselves, not to be delegated to individuals or corporations."* [55]

The Federal Reserve is ***not*** a government institution. It is an association of PRIVATE banks. In fact, in 1982 a Federal Court declared the private legal status of The Fed:

> *"Examining the organization and function of the Federal Reserve Banks, and applying the relevant factors, we conclude that **the Reserve Banks are not federal instrumentalities for purposes of the FTCA, but are independent, privately-owned and locally controlled corporations.***"* (Emphasis added) [56]

One can tell a great deal about almost anything by the circumstances surrounding its inception and how it operates. Are the principals and owners easily identified? Are the dealings of the subject institution conducted in open or shrouded in secrecy? Is the subject institution characterized by an organizational maze that makes it almost impossible to know who and what is in control? Was the subject institution created under the scrutiny afforded by the light of the day or was it conceived and brought into existence in the dead of night? These questions, if asked in regard to The Federal Reserve, result in answers that when understood are enough to take a considered man's breath away.

---

[53] John Adams, 1735-1826, letter to Thomas Jefferson.
[54] James Madison, arguing against Alexander Hamilton's plan to establish a central banking corporation in 1791.
[55] President Andrew Jackson, 1829-1837.
[56] Lewis vs. U.S., 680 F. 2d 1239, 1241.

In 1913, shortly after the creation of The Federal Reserve Act, American hero and Congressman, Charles Lindberg Sr., said this:

> *"This Act (Referring to the establishment of The Federal Reserve) establishes the most gigantic trust on earth. [W]hen the President signs this Act,* **the invisible government by the money power, proven to exist by the Money Trust Investigation, will be legalized.** *[T]he new law will create inflation whenever the trust wants inflation. [F]rom now on depression will be scientifically created."* (Emphasis Added) [57]

A word of caution is in order at this point in our review of The Federal Reserve. We are painfully aware that The Federal Reserve, mostly because of its secrecy, complexities and obvious power, has attracted the attention of any number of bloggers, commentators and observers who are plagued by paranoia and/or who lack the intellectual rigor necessary to separate truth from fiction.

To be sure, The Federal Reserve's organizational matrix incorporates any number of "blinds" that encourage this genre of paranoia-laced speculation. It is this author's contention that the power brokers within The Federal Reserve and others in similar endeavors welcome this hailstorm of speculation and conspiratorial fantasy because it serves the function of cover.

It is a point worth repeating: true power is protected by a matrix of impenetrable firewalls and blind cul-de-sacs. True power is also protected by the paranoia-laced commentary of citizen journalists who virtually insure that when attempts are made to uncover the truth about The Fed, such efforts are frequently lost in a sea of their well intentioned, but nonetheless, paranoia-laced nonsense.

Our analysis herein is made using forensic techniques honed over the past 25 years (forensic and clinical psychology). My professional practice has relied upon a skill set that makes possible the construction of a provable or defensible case (prosecution or defense) in a court of law from an incomplete fact portrait. After all, human beings engaged in clandestine, immoral or illegal behavior make every effort to hide their tracks. If those involved in illegal or immoral activity did not make every effort to hide their tracks, they would not be so easily tracked down and brought to justice. On the other hand, and this is the crook's dilemma, if they don't hide their tracks their devious acts are often detected and they are brought to justice.

I am fully cognizant of the fact that sometimes innocent people and organizations simply prefer to keep things secret for security reasons or because they believe that should the public get wind of what they are up to, the public may withdraw its support from their venture. As Freud taught us, "Sometimes a cigar is just a cigar." Forensic psychology uses known patterns of human behavior and applies both inductive and deductive reasoning to any given situation in order to construct a portrait of what really happened and/or what is really going on. I am going to cover the genesis of The Fed by examining a meeting that took place on Jekyll Island in 1910. This meeting has garnered the attention of any number of bloggers and paranoia-prone citizen journalists and professional historians, alike.

The critics of those who focus upon Jekyll Island have been consistently snide and condescending in their remarks. The thrust of their criticisms is that the Jekyll Island meeting is just so much conspiratorial nonsense. I purposefully took the position that these critics were more correct than not before beginning my analysis. My null hypothesis going into my research was that when it came to Jekyll Island and The Fed, there was no "there, there." Since none of us were there,

---

[57] Congressman Charles Lindberg, Sr. Congressional Record, Vol. 51, p. 1446. December 22, 1913.

I relied upon independent scholars with impeccable credentials to form the factual basis for my opinions.

For example, James Neal Primm (1918 - 2009) chronicled the provenance of The Federal Reserve, including Jekyll Island. Mr. Primm was the Curators' Professor of History Emeritus at the University of Missouri-St. Louis. A noted scholar and historian, Professor Primm was the author of a number of works on American and St. Louis history, including *Lion of the Valley: St. Louis; Economic Policy in the Development of a Western State; and The American Experience*. We rely upon Primm, in addition to other scholarly authors and writers cited herein, because in our judgment Primm, like the others, were objective historians and not prone to speculation or paranoia-laced theories when it came to Jekyll Island.

In Chapter Two of Primm's, *A Foregone Conclusion*, entitled "Banking Reform," we learn of a central figure in The Fed's development. Please notice that I will highlight, in bold type, the key parts of Mr. Primm's narratives that have, in my opinion, forensic significance:

> *"Senator Nelson W. Aldrich of Rhode Island was named chairman of the commission which guaranteed the hostility of Democrats and insurgent Republicans such as Robert W. La Follette of Wisconsin to anything it might recommend. Aldrich, a former banker, was allied with the House of Morgan**; he had written the Gold Standard Act of 1900**, and **he was the Senate's leading protectionist.** He was as obnoxious to Democrats and insurgents as Bryan was to conservatives.*
>
> ***After touring Europe*** *to study its banking systems and techniques, Aldrich and the other commissioners **returned convinced** that the United States **should have a central bank controlled by bankers** and issuing notes based on commercial paper. **This was a surprising reversal for Aldrich,** who previously **had opposed** __any__ significant changes in the existing system, believing that only bond-related notes should be issued. The commission made no immediate proposal for legislation, knowing that an extensive campaign would be required to educate bankers and the public, especially after the Democrats gained control of the House of Representatives in 1910."* [58]

**Nelson Aldrich, Senator from
Rhode Island.**

---

[58] Primm, James Neal. (1989), *A Foregone Conclusion. The Founding of The Federal Reserve Bank of Saint Louis.* Federal Reserve Bank of St. Louis.

As a forensic psychologist, I find Senator Aldrich's "surprising" conversion as an entry point for my analysis. I can't overstate the importance of Aldrich's conversion after his European trip. Aldrich's conversion represented a 180-degree turnaround on the issue of creating a Federal Reserve-type banking entity. It would be like Karl Marx adopting the opinions of Adam Smith or Thomas Jefferson joining forces with the English Crown.

Surprising reversals, especially for notoriously stubborn personality types like Senator Aldrich (numerous biographies of Aldrich have made note of his stubborn personality), imply a cataclysmic act or acts of persuasion on the part of someone(s). Furthermore, consistent with my forensic and clinical training, the people doing the persuading must have been very powerful, indeed. Social scientists know, for example, that it takes **greater power to persuade great power.**

Keep in mind that Aldrich was a sitting Senator of the United States. Not only was he notoriously stubborn, a powerful man in his own right, but also **he had authored** the Gold Standard Act of 1900 and was a staunch protectionist against foreign involvement in America's banking system.

Senator Aldrich was also the Chairman of Congress' National Monetary Policy Committee whose charge was to review America's banking policies. Aldrich occupied that position that controlled America's monetary policy. Then, as now, international power centers had their eye on America's monetary policy as a means to access America's wealth (Please refer to Napoleon's Monetary Axiom). Clinical psychology informs us that human nature insures that we are jealously protective over that which we authored. Aldrich was not merely a supporter of the Gold Standard; he authored it!

The piece de resistance prize for any ambitious shadow man would be to commandeer a powerful nation's money supply and the machinery thereof. Commandeering America's monetary system would be tantamount to winning every gold medal in every Olympic event. Bankers, since time immemorial, have had as their number one goal the control of powerful nation's money supply machinery. Although this should strike the reader as common sense, it may be worth reiterating, that shadow men can never, ever, have enough power, that is, wealth. They understand wealth creation and are habitually looking to find new ways to make more.

The most authoritative opinion on the ultimate means of wealth creation was voiced by none other than Baron Amschel Bauer Rothschild (February 23, 1744 –September 19, 1812), a banking baron whose familial provenance in banking goes back further than any other blood line or family enterprise. Here is what this particular Rothschild had to say:

> *"The few who understand the system, will either be so interested from its profits or so dependent on its favors, that there will be no opposition from that class."* . . . *"Let me issue and control a nation's money and I care not who writes the laws."*

As previously mentioned, forensic scientists can tell a great deal about anything by how it came into existence. So let's now explore Jekyll Island.

Jekyll Island is located off the coast of Georgia. In 1910 Aldrich organized a clandestine meeting of the who's who of banking under the guise of a "duck hunt." It is important to pay special attention to the built-in secrecy of the meeting (duck hunting ruse) along with a "first name only" protocol (attendees only used one another's first names) before, during **and long after** the clandestine meeting was over.

Forensically, we could explain the duck-hunting ruse as merely an attempt to keep the press from learning about an important meeting and/or an effort to keep detractors in the dark so that opponents to their plan could not sabotage it before it came to fruition. But when those in attendance, those who already knew one another, used only their first names, and continued this cover-gambit long after the meeting was over and their work was done, we conclude that the attendees knew that what they had done would be investigated. Good acts are usually broadcast to the general public or, at the very least, those responsible for good acts do not attempt to make the discovery of those good acts almost impossible. In essence, the attendees on Jekyll Island, by and through their various attempts to prevent investigators from knowing who, when, why and how they did what they did, demonstrated a consciousness of guilt; but guilt over what? [59]

According to Nathaniel Wright Stephenson's biography of Aldrich, [60] the secret meeting was attended by Dr. A. Piatt Andrew, a Harvard Economics professor, Henry P. Davison, a J.P. Morgan & Co. partner, Frank A. Vanderlip, National City Bank president (Now known as CitiBank), along with Kuhn, Loeb, and Company partner, Paul M. Warburg. Each of these men had a direct linkage to European banking interests and families. Stephenson had to move heaven and earth, by the way, to learn of the names in attendance on Jekyll Island, risking his personal safety in the process.

Neil Irwin, author and writer for The Washington Post, corroborated Stephenson's 1930 accounting of the secret meeting and those in attendance on Jekyll Island. Irwin is one of many writers who corroborate the "first name only" before, during and **after** component of the Jekyll Island meeting. [61]

We want to remind the reader of Aldrich's "miraculous conversion" following his trip to Europe where he met with European shadow men impresarios. We do not know whom he met with on the continent. Aldrich made sure that his meetings were cloaked in secrecy. Back in 1910, cameras and reporters were not everywhere like today. But one thing is for certain: though I cannot provide to you the exact names, I do know that he met with Europe's most powerful banking dynasties. How do we know this?

We rely upon our forensic expertise regarding how power works and Aristotelian logic. Recall that Aldrich was in the proverbial "catbird's seat" when it came to having the capacity to change America's monetary system, a fact known to every banking impresario in Europe and America. Keep in mind that America's monetary system was the prize of all prizes because up until 1913, America had resisted the inherent vulnerabilities associated with a central banking establishment in control of the nation's monetary system. In fact, as you will learn later in this book, one of the key factors that set America apart from all other nations on earth was that it retained control of its own monetary system. This was true despite the fact that European investment banker types had financed the colonization of the "new" world. I will also remind you of the gravity of the issue of who controls a nation's money supply, to quote Thomas Jefferson's prescient warning on the subject:

> *"If the American people ever allow private banks to control the issue of their currency, first by inflation, then by deflation, the banks…will deprive the people of all property until their children wake-up homeless on the continent their fathers conquered…. The issuing power should be taken from the banks and restored to the people, to whom it properly belongs."* . . . *"Paper is poverty. It is the ghost of money and not money itself."*

---

[59] Criminals frequently use nicknames, first names only or made up names, such as colors (Mr. Red or Mr. Blue), when identifying one another in order to protect them from prosecution should they be caught.
[60] Stephenson, Nathaniel Wright. (1930), *Nelson W. Aldrich, A Leader in American Politics.* C. Scribner's Sons.
[61] Irwin, Neil. (2013), *The Alchemists: Three Central Bankers and a World on Fire.* Penguin Publishing,

So who did Senator Aldrich meet in Europe? We suggest the likely candidates are to be found from this group of banking impresarios or their designated representatives:

Family ⬥	Companies ⬥	Place of origin ⬥	Principal countries of residence ⬥
Bardi family	Compagnia dei Bardi		🇮🇹 Italy
Baring family	Barings Bank	Bremen	🇩🇪 Germany 🇬🇧 UK
Berenberg-Gossler-Seyler banking dynasty	Berenberg Bank	Antwerp	🇧🇪 Belgium, 🇩🇪 Germany
Cerchi		Florence	🇮🇹 Italy
Clifford family (bankers)		Clifford, Herefordshire	🇬🇧 UK, 🇳🇱 The Netherlands
Fugger		Augsburg	🇩🇪 Germany
Gondi family		Florence	🇮🇹 Italy
Hoare Family	C. Hoare & Co	London	🇬🇧 UK
Hope family	Hope & Co.	Amsterdam	🇳🇱 Netherlands
Hochstetter		Höchstadt	🇩🇪 Germany
Oppenheim family			🇩🇪 Germany
Rockefeller family	Rockefeller Financial Services (Rockefeller & Co), J.P. Morgan Chase	Cleveland, OH, New York, NY	🇺🇸 USA
Rothschild family	RIT Capital Partners, N M Rothschild & Sons	Frankfurt	🇩🇪 Germany, 🇦🇹 Austria, 🇫🇷 France, 🇬🇧 UK
House of Medici		Florence	🇮🇹 Italy
Mellon family	Bank of New York Mellon	Pittsburgh, PA	🇺🇸 USA
Metzler	Metzler Bank	Frankfurt	🇩🇪 Germany
Morgan family	Morgan Stanley, J.P. Morgan Chase	New York, NY	🇺🇸 USA
Peruzzi		Florence	🇮🇹 Italy
Solaro (family)		Asti	🇮🇹 Italy
Wallenberg family			🇸🇪 Sweden
Warburg family	Warburg Pincus, UBS		🇩🇪 Germany
Welser		Augsburg	🇩🇪 Germany

Credit: **WikiCharts**

How is "up" converted into "down" or "good" into "bad?" Aldrich and his cohorts were either bought off and/or muscled into helping to turn over America's money supply to one or more of the powerful banking interests identified above. One scenario goes like this, banking impresario's agents, residing in the United States, would serve as on-site agents, powerful in their own right but subservient to the European shadow men who had pulled off a coup that rivaled the one used against Pope Clement V involving the Knights Templar.

Aldrich's miraculous conversion left footprints. Aldrich's daughter, Abigail Greene "Abby" Aldrich, married philanthropist John Davison Rockefeller, Jr. Their second son, Nelson Aldrich Rockefeller, was a four-term Governor of New York who campaigned for the Republican presidential nomination in 1960, 1964, and 1968, and was named Vice President of the United States under President Gerald Ford by the Congress in 1974. Aldrich's son, Richard S. Aldrich, served in Congress from 1923 to 1933. Nelson Aldrich's grandson, Winthrop Williams Aldrich, served as chairman of Chase National Bank. As far as Nelson Aldrich, he became wealthy after making some insider investments in railroads, sugar, and rubber, among other investments.

We began this chapter by applying our forensic science expertise to the genesis of the Federal Reserve. When institutions are created in the dead of night, when monumental changes are made in a rush or when no one is looking, you can count on the fact that something important and, perhaps, nefarious is afoot. Consider this:

The Federal Reserve was chartered by an act of Congress when most members
had gone home for Christmas holiday on December 23rd, 1913. The Federal Reserve

Act of 1913 had made its way out of the Congress but it was having difficulty finding enough Senators to pass it.

Only three senators passed the act with a unanimous voice vote despite the fact that no recess had been called and virtually all the other senators had left Washington, D.C. for Christmas break. There were no objections.

I certainly recognize that just because an institution was born in secrecy and passed into law by a small, non-representative sample of legislators when the opposition had left town for the holidays, does not *necessarily* mean that the institution is involved in something nefarious. On the other hand, I stand by Napoleon's Monetary Axiom: *Large sums of money invariably attract the attention of thieves and encourages manipulation.*

The caretaking and management of large sums of money is one thing, but imagine if we were talking about actually making and defining the value of money, what kind of personalities would be interested in manipulating and exploiting that system? How far would these people go and what wouldn't they do in order to commandeer the money supply of the United States of America?

The inner workings of The Fed ONLY come to light when a flaw occurs in one or more of its cloaking mechanisms. And even then we only get a fleeting glimpse into its inner workings. In 2012 one of these lapses in The Fed's cloaking mechanisms provided a glimpse into how the Fed deals with transgressions of one of its member banks.

Jake Bernstein, an investigative reporter for the Washington Post (a dying breed of journalist), wrote a story about a New York Fed examiner by the name of Carmen Segarra. Here is an excerpt from Mr. Bernstein's story:

"In the spring of 2012, a senior examiner with the Federal Reserve Bank of New York determined that Goldman Sachs had a problem.

Under a Fed mandate, the investment banking behemoth was expected to have a company-wide policy to address conflicts of interest in how its phalanxes of dealmakers handled clients. Although Goldman had a patchwork of policies, the examiner concluded that they fell short of the Fed's requirements.

That finding by the examiner, Carmen Segarra, potentially had serious implications for Goldman, which was already under fire for advising clients on both sides of several multibillion-dollar deals and allegedly putting the bank's own interests above those of its customers. It could have led to closer scrutiny of Goldman by regulators or changes to its business practices.

Before she could formalize her findings, Segarra said, **the senior New York Fed official who oversees Goldman Sachs pressured her to change them. When she refused, Segarra said she was called to a meeting where her bosses told her they no longer trusted her judgment. Her phone was confiscated, and security officers marched her out of the Fed's fortress-like building in lower Manhattan, just 7 months after being hired.**

"They wanted me to falsify my findings," Segarra said in a recent interview, "and when I wouldn't, they fired me. (Emphasis Added)"*" [62]

The New York Fed is considered, by scholars to be the most powerful among all of the other banks that comprise The Federal Reserve System. To that point, Elliot Spitzer, former Governor and Attorney General of New York, wrote the following in Slate Magazine, May of 2009:

---

[62] Washington Post & ProPublica Joint Publication. *New York Fed Fired Examiner Who Took on Goldman.* October 10, 2013.

> *"A quasi-independent, public-private body, the New York Fed is the first among equals of the 12 regional Fed branches. Unlike the Washington Federal Reserve Board of Governors, or the other regional fed branches, the N.Y. Fed is active in the markets virtually every day, changing the critical interest rates that determine the liquidity of the markets and the profitability of banks. And, like the other regional branches, it has boundless power to examine, at will, the books of virtually any banking institution and require that wide-ranging actions be taken—from raising capital to stopping lending—to ensure the stability and soundness of the bank. Over the past year, the New York Fed has been responsible for committing trillions of dollars of taxpayer money to resuscitate the coffers of the banks it oversees."* [63]

The former New York Governor and Attorney General mentioned that The New York Fed has "boundless power to examine ANY financial institution." I suppose that is true, but Ms. Segarra's dismissal and the confiscation of her records suggests that perhaps a better way to describe The New York Fed is that it has "boundless power to examine, then squelch or expunge the findings of any examination it makes of any financial institution."

Professor Fekete is a mathematician by training and scholar of The New School of Austrian Economics. He has commented that the Federal Reserve Act of 1913 was less virulent than many contend. Professor Fekete believes that the transformation of the Fed in 1922 was the mutation that made The Fed into a virulent entity. What happened in 1922? After WWI ended the American bond market collapsed in 1921. The year after the bond collapse, The Fed intervened in the bond market. In violation of all relevant laws at the time, The Fed began buying T-Bills from the Treasury in order to re-inflate the collapsed bond market. It was not until 1935 that Congress passed a law that legalized what The Fed had done some 13 years earlier. Yes, The Fed's bond buying spree was made *retroactively* legal. In 2014 central bankers are, as professor Fekete termed it, "sowing inflation with quantitative easing, but are reaping, instead, devaluation." [64]

I am always amazed at how institutions that "run money" (a term bankers prefer) can get away with the most duplicitous and scandalous behavior imaginable. Even when The Fed blatantly violated the law in 1922, when it began its bond- buying spree, never fear, Congress was there to cleanse The Fed of its sins by rewriting the law and making it retroactive.

Referring back to Mr. Bernstein's article on Goldman Sachs, that investment- banking institution took both sides of multi-million dollar trades. That means that while Goldman was busy promoting and selling "buy calls" (a bet that the price will go up on a security within a certain time frame) on various securities it was using its own cash hoard to "buy puts" that the price of the security would go down. Of course it turned out that Goldman's money was on the "right side" of the bet. They are, after all, "investment bankers."

But never mind that, when The Vatican ran into its own trouble with some of its investments, it was Goldman Sachs that imposed itself on the Vatican as a consultant. (Napoleon's Monetary Axiom at work) And when politicians pressured the New York Fed to examine Goldman Sachs for any number of questionable practices, the New York Fed, in a moment of clarity for the rest of us, demonstrated who was truly in charge, was it The Fed or the politicians in Washington? Just ask Carmen Segarra who's the boss, she'll tell you. Occasionally, one finds people like Ms. Segarra who "didn't get the memo" on how to whitewash questionable behavior.

---

[63] Slate Magazine. (2009), *Fed Dread*, by Elliot Spitzer. May 6.
[64] Keiser, Max. The Keiser Report. *An Interview with Antal Fekete.* RT Television, October 18, 2014.

Jeffrey Sachs is an economist who shares my perspective on the gravity of what we are dealing with here. Mr. Sachs was ranked as one of Time Magazine's Top 100 most influential people in the world. James Legge, writing for The Independent, reported on Sach's view of Wall Street and the politicians who would like for you to believe that they control big money and not the other way around, to wit:

> *"In a cutting attack on America's financial hub, one of the world's most respected economists has said Wall St. is full of "crooks" and hasn't reformed its "pathological" culture since the financial crash.*
>
> *Professor Jeffrey Sachs told a high-powered audience at the Philadelphia Federal Reserve earlier this month that the lack of reform was down to "a docile president, a docile White House and a docile regulatory system that absolutely can't find its voice."*
>
> *Sachs, from Colombia University, has twice been named one of Time magazine's 100 Most Influential People in the World, and is an adviser to the World Bank and IMF. "What has been revealed, in my view,* **is prima facie criminal behavior,***" he said. "It's financial fraud on a very large extent. There's also a tremendous amount of insider trading - you can even* **watch when you are living in New York** *how that works."*
>
> *In his live remarks, via videophone from New York, an emotionally charged Sachs also ripped into practices at Goldman Sachs and into the* **political classes on both the left and right,** *according to the New York Post.*
>
> *"We have a corrupt politics to the core, I am afraid to say, and . . . both parties are up to their neck in this.* **This has nothing to do with Democrats or Republicans."**[65]

Let's take a look at The Federal Reserve's organizational matrix. The Federal Reserve consists of twelve central banks, one for each of the 12 geographical areas of the Continental United States.

---

[65] The Independent. *Top economist Jeffrey Sachs says Wall Street is full of 'crooks' and hasn't changed since the financial crash.* By James Legge, April 29, 2013.

Geographic Boundaries
of the Federal Reserve Districts

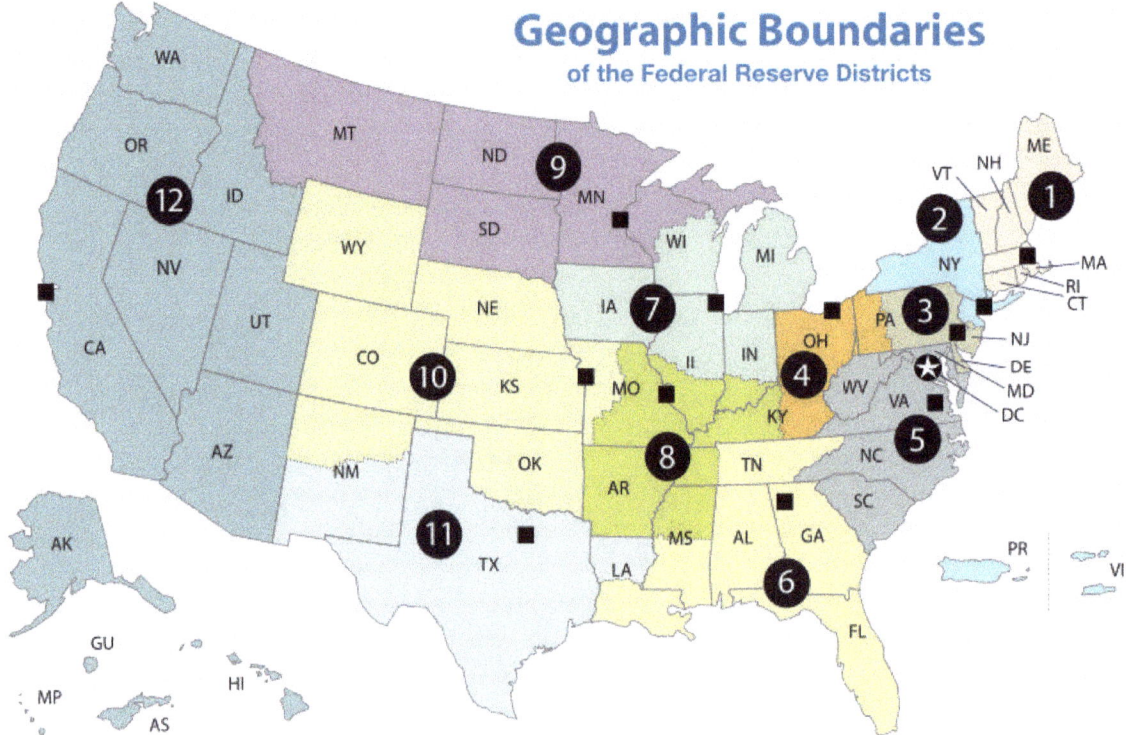

1. Boston	7. Chicago
2. NewYork City	8. St. Louis
3. Philadelphia	9. Minneapolis
4. Cleveland	10. Kansas City
5. Richmond	11. Dallas
6 Atlanta	12. San Francisco

There are four levels at The Federal Reserve.

1. The Board of Governors,
2. The Federal Open Market Committee (FOMC),
3. 12 regional banks and,
4. 25 smaller member banks.

The President of The United States appoints the 12 members of The Fed's Board of Governors. Their appointment lasts 14 years. Seven of the 12 members make up the FOMC. The remaining Five come from The 12 Reserve Banks that comprise the member banks. Four of these members rotate in and out every three years (not fixed) but the President of the New York Bank has a special place in the scheme of things because **The New York Bank Chairman is a permanent member.** Keep this in mind as you study the workings of The Fed because this is just one example of how New York is the hub of the machinery of money in the United States. Even though New York is the hub, during the cocaine cowboy days of South Florida in the 1980s, region 6 of The

Federal Reserve banks had more money in its coffers than all the other 11 Fed Banks combined. What does that factoid tell you?

What follows is a complete listing of The Federal Reserve's Chairmen, presented in their order of appointment:

The first chairman of the American Federal Reserve was Charles Sumner Hamlin.

Second, William Proctor Gould Harding.

Third, Daniel Richard Crissinger.

Fourth, Roy Archibald Young.

Fifth, Eugene Isaac Meyer. (Also, first president of the World Bank).

Sixth, Eugene Robert Black.

Tenth, Arthur Frank Burns. .

Twelfth, Paul Adolph Volcker.

Thirteenth, Alan Greenspan.

Fourteenth, Chairman is Ben Bernanke.

Fifteenth, Chairperson Janet Yellen.

The Federal Reserve regulates something called "fractional banking." Fractional banking is a system where a bank retains a mere fraction of the actual deposits its customers have left in its care. The average American is often shocked to learn that any given bank's investable money is a multiple of its actual deposits, i.e., cash left in its care by its customers.

"You mean the money I've deposited with my bank may not be there?" Not only is your money NOT likely to be in your bank's vault, your bank invests your and your fellow depositor's money, along with borrowed money, in things like mortgages, commercial ventures and the purchase of commodities as well as other investments. And what happens if my bank's investments go belly up? Well, The Federal Government's FDIC (Federal Depository Insurance Company) insures your money up to $250,000 dollars. After that, you're on your own.

On paper, fractional banking was developed by the financial barons to expand the economy by *freeing up* capital that can be loaned out to other parties. Nothing needed to be "freed up." Fractional banking is one of those money machinery prestidigitations that simply refers to a made-up machination whereby financial barons declared that they only needed to keep a fraction of the money given to them for safe keeping by their customers so that they could leverage their risks beyond their own resources. Think of fractional banking as the banker's version of trading on margin (borrowed money). Fractional banking only works, by the way, if EVERYONE is living in the same delusional world; that is, living in a virtual world where other people's money is treated as your own and people can "use" borrowed money to speculate. So what happens if so many depositors want their money back from the bank that the bank runs out of money? (They call this a "run on the bank") Never fear, The Fed is there to help.

The Federal Reserve was originally designed to be the lender of "last resort." It operates under what it calls its "dual mandate," to wit,

> *"The Board of Governors of the Federal Reserve System and the Federal Open Market Committee shall maintain long run growth of the monetary and credit aggregates commensurate with the economy's long run potential to increase production, so as to promote effectively the goals of maximum employment, stable prices and moderate long-term interest rates."* [66]

---

[66] The Federal Bank of Chicago. (2014), *The Federal Reserve's Dual Mandate.* The Federal Reserve of Chicago's Publications.

So if banks run out of enough money to pay their depositors, and they can't borrow it from another banker because that other banker doesn't trust them, they can come to The Fed (The Fed's Window). So who determines the interest rate at which banks can make short-term loans to other banks?

First of all, this rate is very important as one might imagine. After all, if a bank needs to borrow money from another bank the interest rate will determine the degree to which that bank can afford to pay back such a loan and the amount it will be able to borrow. By the way, banks are moving money back on forth each and everyday across the globe. The rate at which *overnight rates* are set is determined in London. London you say? Yes.

Many otherwise intelligent people scoff at the notion that international bankers are intimately involved in America's financial system, with special reference to The Fed. These same critics derive great pleasure by snidely ridiculing anyone who would dare mention the term "international bankers" in the same sentence with The Federal Reserve. By the way, if you do mention these two terms in the same sentence then these snide and overly confident critics liken you to people who report seeing Elvis from time to time. For these people I issue this warning, you might want to cover your eyes or plug your ears, as the case may be, when it comes to what I am about to tell you.

The short-term interest rate that America's banks use when they borrow from other banks is called the LIBOR rate. That is, THE LONDON INTERBANK OFFERED RATE. And yes, as the name implies, the LIBOR rate is set in London, England by The British Banking Association (BBA). And what, pray tell, is the BBA? It consists of 16 *international* member banks. Every day at 11:45 a.m. GMT the BBA publishes that day's rates. And how much of the world's economy is influenced by the LIBOR rate? By some estimates, LIBOR sets the rate for a whopping **$360 trillion dollars of financial products across the globe**. What countries, you may ask, rely upon LIBOR? United States, Canada, Switzerland and the United Kingdom.

America has four banking empires that are the behemoths in the banking industry and are subsumed under The Fed's regulatory control. They include: Bank of America, CitiGroup, J.P. Morgan Chase and Wells Fargo. These four banks are major stockholders, by the way, in the vast majority of Fortune 500 companies. Thank God for fractional banking, right? [67]

Bank of America owns something called The US Trust Corporation. This organization was founded in 1853. A recent US Trust Corporate Director and Honorary Trustee was Walter Rothschild, a European financial baron whose family and banking provenance extends as far back as the 17th Century. The directors of the trust include a who's who in banking, e.g., Daniel Davison of JP Morgan Chase, Richard Tucker of Exxon Mobil, Daniel Roberts of Citigroup and Marshall Schwartz of Morgan Stanley. All of these corporations are multi-national by charter. [68]

With reference to Exxon Mobil, it is fascinating that the four largest banking empires are major owners of the world's major oil companies, e.g., Exxon Mobil, Royal Dutch/Shell, British Petroleum (BP) and Chevron Texaco. Other major shareholders include Europe's who's who in banking, e.g., Deutsche Bank, BNP, Barclays, among others. [69] Deutsche Bank's derivatives portfolio has been estimated to be worth 72 Trillion (yes, with a "T") dollars. Imagine if that derivative's portfolio went belly up.

---

[67] 10K Filings of Fortune 500 Corporations to SEC. 3-91.
[68] 10K Filing of US Trust Corporation to SEC. 6-28-95.
[69] Ibid.

On The New York Fed's official website the following international banking relations are listed as part of The Fed's wheelhouse:

1. Federal Reserve monetary policy is one influence on the foreign exchange (FX) value of the dollar.

2. In conjunction with the U.S. Treasury, the Fed sometimes intervenes in the FX market, though in recent years intervention has become much less frequent.

3. The Fed provides a variety of services to more than 200 foreign central banks, foreign governments and international official institutions.

4. As part of its bank supervision responsibility, the Fed conducts annual examinations of most foreign bank branches and agencies operating in the United States. [70]

From our review, America's Federal Reserve sits atop the international banking heap. Applying Napoleon's Monetary Axiom that large sums of money attract thieves and manipulation, can we cite to any such problems involving LIBOR? During the 2007-2009 period Barclays, and allegedly other banks, manipulated the LIBOR rate. Barclay's submitted artificially low LIBOR rates to the BBA so as to project an appearance of strength and to boost trader's profits.

Mark Ross, writing for Investopedia, chronicled the scandal:

"Allegations that the major banks colluded in suppressing their funding costs to appear healthier than they actually were during the financial crisis of four years ago, and the manipulation of rates through an opaque setting process, have come to a head with the resignation of Barclays CEO Bob Diamond. Diamond admitted to manipulating the rates at his firm, which incurred a $450 million (290 million pound) fine. COO Jerry Del Missier and Chairman Marcus Agius stepped down as well, which was also followed by 20 banks undergoing investigation, including Citigroup, UBS, RBS, BOA, JP Morgan, HSBC, Deutsche Bank and Credit Suisse.

Greg Smith resigning from Goldman Sachs in disgust at a culture gone awry, JP Morgan admitting to a botched hedging strategy in its Chief Investment Office, MF Global collapsing beneath the weight of bad trading and a failure to protect its clients, Fabrice Tourre, Jérome Kerviel and Kweku Adobole caught out in bad trades and now this. Has scandal become sufficiently commonplace in the banking community that, like a road show, we can pick it up anywhere? Has the culture of serving clients been turned on its head? There would most definitely appear to be something wrong somewhere." [71]

So getting back to this notion of The Fed being the lender of last resort, what happens if The Fed runs out of money? The Chairman or one of his/her representatives gets on the phone to The Bureau of Engraving and Printing and puts in an order for some more money to be printed. I know, it doesn't seem real, but it is. How much does The Fed pay for the bills it has printed? Four (4) cents for each bill. As of July 2013 there was approximately 1.2 trillion dollars worth of currency in circulation. But never fear, it is not quite as bad as its sounds, or is it?

Every time The Fed has more money printed the buying power of the money in circulation is reduced (devaluation). However, whenever The Fed has more money printed it collateralizes the freshly printed money by providing Treasury securities to The Treasury of the United States. But who or what underwrites and pays the interest on the Treasury securities? The Fed does. The lynch pin to this otherwise Ponzi-like program relies upon people and countries buying America's Treasury Notes.

---

[70] www.newyorkfed.org. *Federal Reserve in the International Arena.*
[71] Investopedia. *THE LIBOR SCANDAL.* By Mark Ross, July 18, 2012.

Who owns America's debt, that is, who or what is buying our Treasury notes? It is NOT primarily China as you may have learned from your friends in the media-entertainment complex, though China is an important purchaser and holder of America's debt. Are you sitting down?

By a long shot it is The Social Security Trust. How does that work you might ask, I thought that there was a problem with the solvency of our Social Security System? Well no, actually, the Social Security Trust takes in MORE (a lot more) money than it pays out. If that is true, where is the problem with the trust's solvency? The Trust takes that extra money taxpayers put into it, money that is supposed to be earmarked for THEIR RETIREMENT YEARS, and your politicians (the political arm of shadow men) move those extra funds into THE GENERAL FUND. What is the general fund? Think of The General Fund of The United States as your politician's petty cash hoard that can be used for paying for Las Vegas junkets for "team training" (dance classes) for I.R.S. Employees, paying for statues of glass camel's in Pakistan or for helping to finance the building or refurbishment of Islamic mosques in Muslim countries.

FactCheck.org published these data with regard to who owns America's debt:

> *"Our primary source is Table OFS-2 in the September issue of the Treasury Bulletin, which can be found under the heading "Ownership of Federal Securities." For additional details, we've also drawn on reports of the Federal Reserve System and other U.S. Treasury documents.*

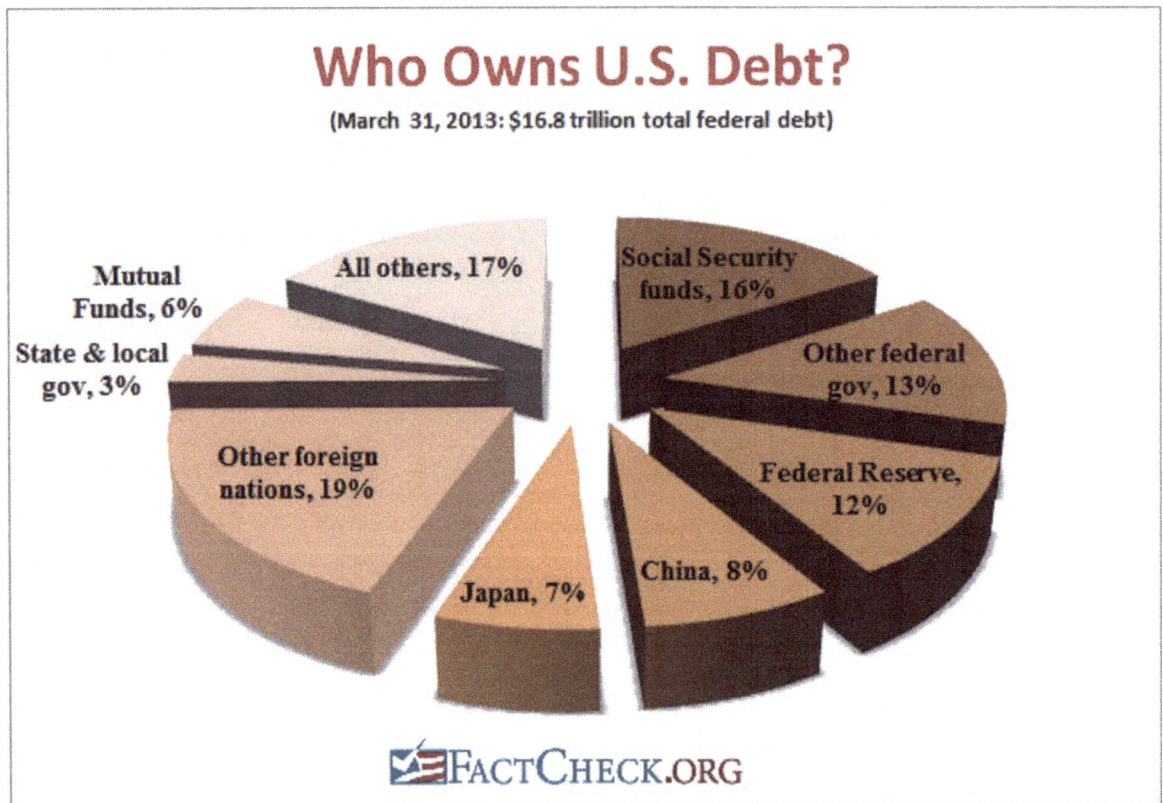

Who Owns U.S. Debt?
(March 31, 2013: $16.8 trillion total federal debt)

> *As of the end of March 2013 — the most recent period for which the Bulletin provides a breakdown — total federal debt stood at $16.8 trillion. It has since grown to nearly $17.2 trillion, but the share of debt held by various lenders cannot have shifted by much.*
>
> *The largest portion of the total debt — about 40 percent — was held by federal government accounts plus the Federal Reserve banks. Since 2009, the Federal Reserve banks have been sharply increasing their holdings of Treasury securities to stimulate the economy, and as of March 31, they held just under $2 trillion*

of the national debt, or about 12 percent. The federal government accounts include the two Social Security trust funds, which together hold 16 percent of the total federal debt. Other federal government accounts include the federal civil service retirement and disability fund (5 percent of total debt), the military retirement fund (3 percent), the Medicare hospital insurance fund (1 percent), and several other smaller funds.

Another 34 percent of total federal debt is owed to foreigners, including China (which owned nearly $1.3 trillion of the total debt, or about 8 percent), closely followed by Japan, which owned $1.1 trillion, or 7 percent. Previously, Japan had been the top foreign owner of U.S. debt, but China surpassed Japan in September 2008. Other major foreign lenders are various Caribbean banking centers, including the Cayman Islands (2 percent altogether), various oil-exporting nations including Saudi Arabia (2 percent altogether) and Brazil (2 percent).

The remainder of the total federal debt is spread among mostly private, domestic investors, including 6 percent owned through mutual funds, such as money-market funds. Another 3 percent is owned by state and local governments. The remaining 17 percent is spread among banks and other depository institutions (2 percent), owners of U.S. savings bonds (1 percent), private pension funds (3 percent), state and local pension funds (1 percent), and insurance companies (2 percent), with the remaining 9 percent held by various "individuals, Government-sponsored enterprises, brokers and dealers, bank personal trusts and estates, corporate and non-corporate businesses, and other investors," according to the Treasury.[72]

The Fed's monetary policy has had the intended effect of devaluing the dollar. Why is this important to the average citizen? Charles Kadlec, writing for Forbes Magazine in 2012, said this about the devaluation of the dollar:

"The Federal Reserve Open Market Committee (FOMC) has made it official: After its latest two day meeting, it announced its goal to devalue the dollar by 33% over the next 20 years. The debauch of the dollar will be even greater if the Fed exceeds its goal of a 2 percent per year increase in the price level.

An increase in the price level of 2% in any one year is barely noticeable. Under a gold standard, such an increase was uncommon, but not unknown. The difference is that when the dollar was as good as gold, the years of modest inflation would be followed, in time, by declining prices. As a consequence, over longer periods of time, the price level was unchanged. A dollar 20 years hence was still worth a dollar.

But, an increase of 2% a year over a period of 20 years will lead to a 50% increase in the price level. It will take 150 (2032) dollars to purchase the same basket of goods 100 (2012) dollars can buy today. **What will be called the "dollar" in 2032 will be worth one-third less (100/150) than what we call a dollar today.**

The Fed's zero interest rate policy accentuates the negative consequences of this steady erosion in the dollar's buying power by imposing a negative return on short-term bonds and bank deposits. In effect, the Fed has announced a course of action that will steal — there is no better word for it — nearly 10 percent of the value of American's hard earned savings over the next 4 years."[73]

Just so the reader understands what The Fed is doing, its monetary policy explicitly is designed to reduce the value of YOUR money (buying power) by AT LEAST 33% in the next 20 years, according to Mr. Kadlec and many other experts on The Fed. The Fed is introducing "liquidity" into the market in order to encourage easy "dead-pledging" for businesses and consumers. Oh, by

---

[72] FactCheck.org. *Who Owns The U.S. Debt?* By: Brooks Jackson, November 19. 2013.
[73] Forbes Magazine. *The Federal Reserve's Explicit Goal: Devalue The Dollar 33%.* By: Charles Kadlec. February 6, 2012.

the way, since the creation of The Fed in 1913, your dollar has lost 96% of its value when compared to today (2015). How does The Fed do this? Here are the three ways The Fed introduces liquidity into the market:

1. The Fed can influence the money supply by modifying reserve requirements, which is the amount of funds banks must hold against deposits in bank accounts. By lowering the reserve requirements, banks are able loan more money, which increases the overall supply of money in the economy. Conversely, by raising the banks' reserve requirements, the Fed is able to decrease the size of the money supply.

2. The Fed can also alter the money supply by changing short-term interest rates. By lowering (or raising) the discount rate that banks pay on short-term loans from the Federal Reserve Bank, the Fed is able to effectively increase (or decrease) the liquidity of money. Lower rates increase the money supply and boost economic activity; however, decreases in interest rates fuel inflation, so the Fed must be careful not to lower interest rates too much for too long.

3. Finally, the Fed can affect the money supply by conducting open market operations, which affects the federal funds rate. In open operations, the Fed buys and sells government securities in the open market. If the Fed wants to increase the money supply, it buys government bonds. This supplies the securities dealers who sell the bonds with cash, increasing the overall money supply. Conversely, if the Fed wants to decrease the money supply, it sells bonds from its account, thus taking in cash and removing money from the economic system.

I'm now going to use the financial meltdown of 2008 in order to illustrate the perils and pitfalls of credit and a nation's money supply. Sometimes it helps to jump to the end of the story before we delve into how it all happened because the financial debacle of 2008 was in the making for a number of years.

The end of the story finds The Fed's Fund Rate at 0%.[74] The Fed purchased troubled (foreclosed or near foreclosure) mortgage backed securities from banks (financial instruments, commonly named "collateralized debt obligations" (CDO's), and The Fed purchased U.S. Bonds. All of these money-changing operations were financed, by the taxpayer, through a process of devaluation of the dollar.

The profiteers who benefited from the 2008 economic meltdown were nowhere to be found when the dust finally settled. Perhaps more importantly, even if ALL of the investment banks and

---

[74] The interest rate at which a depository institution lends funds maintained at the Federal Reserve to another depository institution overnight. The federal funds rate is generally only applicable to the most credit worthy institutions when they borrow and lend overnight funds to each other. The federal funds rate is one of the most influential interest rates in the U.S. economy, since it affects monetary and financial conditions, which in turn have a bearing on key aspects of the broad economy including employment, growth and inflation. The Federal Open Market Committee (FOMC), which is the Federal Reserve's primary monetary policymaking body, telegraphs its desired target for the federal funds rate through open market operations. Also known as the "fed funds rate".

banker's money had been confiscated after the crash of 2008, the hole they helped to dig was so deep that their wealth would not have been enough to fully compensate for the losses suffered by millions upon millions of people and corporations, public entities, etc. Hence, the American dollar with its broad base was the only source large enough to help fill the deficits created by the 2008 crash.

The investment bankers who made out like bandits selling CDO's and bankers and mortgage operations that handed out mortgages like candy to any greed frenzied borrower/speculator who asked, the same people who were in bed with the insurers who underwrote the solvency of these mortgages and CDO's, e.g., A.I.G., the rating agencies like Standard and Poors and Moody's who were also in bed with the bankers and reassured consumers that "these investments instruments were AAA rated," held the American taxpayer hostage.

Hank Paulson, former Secretary of the Treasury, who was appointed by G.W. Bush to that position, painted a frightening portrait of impending disaster to politicians in 2008, the likes of which had not been seen since the great depression of the 1930's. [75] According to U.S. News and World Report, Paulson got on his knees to then Speaker of the House, Nancy Pelosi, begging for her support of the bailout called TARP (Troubled Asset Relief Program). [76]

Mr. Paulson was the former Chairman and Chief Executive Officer of Goldman Sachs. Paulson's colleagues referred to him as "God" during his tenure at Goldman Sachs. [77] And bail the bankers out they did using The Fed's money machinery funded by The Bureau of Engraving and Printing at the expense of the American taxpayer. In times of crisis, the political arm of shadow men walk the point. Ms. Pelosi had been voted into office by the residents of the notorious libertine Castro District in San Francisco, California, a constituency comprised of a demographic that knows or cares little about The Fed or monetary policy. But here she was, The Castro District's finest, with her hand on the trap door of a looming depression.

When The Bureau of Engraving and Printing provides The Fed with money hot off the printing presses, The Fed sends an I.O.U. to the U.S. Government for the tab. Now that is the end of the story, here is a brief summary of the beginning of the financial debacle of 2008. Recall that I stated earlier that bankers have employed various Fabian strategies to encourage citizens to live in a virtual reality where they are permitted to acquire the use (not own) of material goods that they otherwise could not afford (homes, cars, gadgets, you name it).

These mind control PSYOPs relied upon tuned-in, plugged-in, media-addicted citizens that became nothing more than experimental subjects who were fed an endless stream of PSYOP laden messaging that persuaded consumers to become indentured servants to lenders. By and through the creation of psychological attitudes like entitlement, envy and class warfare, the average citizen came to believe that he or she was ENTITLED to have any material item even if they could not afford that item. But it wasn't just the banks, by and through their PR arm, the media-entertainment complex that had modified the public's cognitions and values regarding credit-based consumption.

Politicians added fuel to the credit and entitlement culture fire in America. Progressive politicians favor equal outcomes over equal opportunity and conservatives are often motivated to assist their banking patrons. When it came to "owning" a home, i.e., entering into a "dead-pledge"

---

[75] Reporter Charles Gasparino, a correspondent for CNBC at the time, reported that Hank Paulson was nicknamed the "snake" by his co-workers in the financial industry because he could not be trusted under any circumstances.

[76] U.S. News and World Report. *Hank Paulson: Kneeling Before Pelosi.* By Liz Wolemuth. September 26, 2008.

[77] Ibid.

with a lender, the U.S. Government under **both** major political parties, pressured lenders to enter into a dead-pledges with citizens who could not financially qualify for a mortgage using time tested qualification standards such as 20% down and a 28% debt to asset ratio. The 20% down standard had served everyone's best interest because it meant that the dead-pledger had skin in the game. The 28% debt to asset ratio served as a braking mechanism against those consumers who either gambled on appreciating home prices to make a quick buck or those consumers whose eyes were bigger than their stomach or who simply felt entitled. Both political parties along with bankers encouraged the average man to make a mess of his life by indulging his greed and grandiose delusions.

To understand why equal outcomes was promoted in order to supplant equal opportunity one must understand the collectivist's promotion of the psychological mindset of "entitlement." Entitlement is a cognition (a thought and/or belief) that asserts: "I am entitled (I have a right) to have what any other person has regardless of my intelligence, education, work ethic, inheritance or financial wherewithal. The only thing that is necessary to have almost anything, in an entitlement society, is envious desire, and that is easy to promote using any number of PSYOPs and soon becomes the cultural norm. This is because mankind, absent a moral imperative against it, become envious and jealous of other people more successful than are they. The only other ingredient is "easy" money, and there was plenty of that in the years before the crash of 2008.

Entitlement just happens to be a bulwark precept of all Marxist and Marxist-inspired ideologies. This is because entitlement justifies government's redistribution of wealth (from the haves to the have-nots). Without government's having at their disposal the redistribution of wealth machinery and a citizenry that supports their redistribution schemes, ALL collectivist ideologies will eventually fail.

I would be remiss were I not to declare that community banks who know their clients have, over the years, helped people realize their business dreams by placing a bet on people they trust by lending money to those who would otherwise no be able to finance their realistic dreams. In this respect, banking can and has helped many, many people. Banking is not, necessarily bad, as long as both the lender and borrower exercise personal responsibility. When all is said and done, no one twists a creditor's arm to borrow money to buy things he can't afford or to finance narcissistic and self-aggrandizing dreams.

Now let's go to the beginning of the story in order to put all of the pieces together. What follows is an excerpt from a chapter in a book entitled, *The Progressive Virus*. The Chapter we'll focus upon is entitled, *The Financial Meltdown of 2008*. This chapter excerpt explores the beginning of the story of the financial debacle of 2008:

"In1994 President Clinton directed HUD Secretary Henry Cisneros to come up with a plan to increase home ownership. Cisneros convened what HUD called a "historic meeting" of private and public housing-industry organizations in August of 1994. The group eventually produced a plan that incorporated creative measures to promote home ownership. The underlying motivation to increase home ownership was rooted in classic progressive dogma. That dogma asserts that all people, regardless of financial wherewithal, are entitled to own a home. The fact that people may no be able to afford to buy a home is, according to the cognitive distortions created by the progressive virus, nothing but one more example of social injustice.

Another die-hard progressive by the name of Congressman Barney Frank pressured Fannie Mae to make loans to people who would otherwise not qualify to buy a home, people who were likely to default on their loans. Frank pressured then Federal Reserve Chairman, Alan Greenspan, to lower interest rates to make it easier for the have-nots to qualify for a loan. Banks, under pressure from both the Clinton and Bush Administrations, were coerced into weakening home loan qualification criteria. Unfortunately, all of this progressive social engineering took place as the housing market bubble was reaching its "pop" point.

In the mid-2000's, the looming housing bubble was denied to exist. During a House Financial Services Committee Hearing held on September 10, 2003, Congressman Frank, along with his fellow progressives on the committee, arrogantly dismissed the idea of a housing bubble and insolvency at Fannie Mae and Freddie Mac.

Rep. Barney Frank (D., Mass.): "I worry, frankly, that there's a tension here. The more people, in my judgment, exaggerate a threat of safety and soundness, the more people conjure up the possibility of serious financial losses to the Treasury, which I do not see. I think we see entities that are fundamentally sound financially and withstand some of the disaster scenarios. " [78] *When the committee reconvened on September 25, 2003, Frank had this to say: Rep. Frank: "I do think I do not want the same kind of focus on safety and soundness that we have in OCC [Office of the Comptroller of the Currency] and OTS [Office of Thrift Supervision].* **I want to roll the dice a little bit more in this situation towards subsidized housing.** *"* [79] *(Emphasis added) With reference to Congressman Frank's gambling analogy, the only problem with "rolling the dice" is that Mr. Frank was betting the taxpayer's money, not his own. One committee member not infected with the progressive virus predicted the disaster that was about to happen. It should go without saying that this committee member's prescient concerns were catalogued by the progressives on the committee as nothing more than an expression of social injustice....*

[W]all Street bankers, who are never at a loss to exploit a bad situation and feather their own nest, took these subsidized and fragile loans and packaged them into what investment bankers called "Collateralized Debt Obligations." (CDO's) Not only did the bankers package loans into a portfolio whose contents were a mystery to everyone, including the bankers who created them, they insured them through the likes of A.I.G. And just to make sure that unsuspecting "investors" had no fear about buying these CDO's, the bankers had their friends at the rating agencies, e.g., Standard and Poors, gave these house of cards investments their highest rating.

The general population who had been thoroughly infected with the progressive virus lapped up the little or no money down loans with a sense of entitlement. Some mortgage companies were giving loans equal to 125% or even more of the home's inflated appraisal price. Americans infected with the progressive virus asked: Why should I not be able to buy a home just because I can't afford to buy it? It is said that a fool and his money soon part.

These nouveau pseudo rich included house "flippers" who would buy homes on credit with no down payment, slap a coat of cheap paint on and in it, then "flip" it within a couple of weeks for a net profit to another greed frenzied person, often like himself. Real Estate Agents were rolling in the dough. House salesmen leased Mercedes, BMW's and Lexus automobiles to drive their greed-frenzied clients to the next open house. Dilapidated shacks near the California coast with less than 900 square feet on average size lots were going for over a million dollars, sometimes more.

An entire generation of entitled Americans thought of their home as their personal piggy bank. They sucked the money out of their over-inflated homes and used it to buy fancy cars, take grand vacations, buy luxury goods and live the lifestyle the progressive virus had convinced them they were

---

[78] House Financial Services Committee Hearing, Sept. 10, 2003.
[79] House Financial Services Committee Hearing, Sept. 25, 2003.

entitled to have. This was all done on credit and none of the progressives in the government seemed concerned, that is, until the bubble burst in 2008.

Those who took out their easy loans defaulted on them with an equivalent easiness. Banks had so much red on their books that even they got scared. Their insurers were asked to underwrite so many bad loans that they, too, went bust. The collapse scared everyone and when all was said and done, it was the taxpayer who was coerced into bailing out those who, because of their progressive infection, raped and pillaged the American economy." [80]

No one has gone to jail for having been instrumental in causing the financial meltdown of 2008. Former Speaker of the House, Newt Gingrich, has argued for the arrest of former Representative Barney Frank (D-MASS) and Christopher Dodd, former Senator (D-CONN) for their participation in helping to cause the financial collapse. People like Angelo Mozilo, the former head of subprime mortgage giant Countrywide Financial, who was one of the poster-boys for why things turned out the way they did is, according reports, very happy, content and "sleeps like a baby." Mark Gongloff, writing for the Huffington Post, said this about Angelo Mozilo:

"Meanwhile, in just the five years it took Mozilo to turn Countrywide into a giant subprime-mortgage machine, he took home $471 million. He netted more than $139 million in insider stock sales alone between November 2006 and August 2007, according to a Securities and Exchange Commission lawsuit. According to that lawsuit, while Mozilo was selling his stock, he and other Countrywide officers were increasingly worried about the quality of the loans they were churning out. At the top of the bubble, in 2006, Countrywide originated $461 billion in mortgages, including $41 billion in subprime. Despite his concerns about those loans, Mozilo told Countrywide investors that everything was fine, according to the SEC lawsuit.

Mozilo settled that lawsuit in 2010 for $67.5 million. He didn't have to admit or deny any wrongdoing, and he has avoided criminal prosecution. He regularly appears on lists like Time's "25 People to Blame For the Financial Crisis" or Portfolio's "Worst American CEOs Of All Time," but nobody reads those things anyway, and it's not exactly the same as going to jail.

Meanwhile, aside from having to appear for the occasional deposition, where rude lawyers ask him "nonsensical and insulting" questions, he has not had to bear the damage still being done to the bank that bought Countrywide, Bank of America.

The lawsuit in which Mozilo testified was one brought by a bond-insurance company, MBIA, accusing Countrywide of fraud. BofA shareholders could have to pay more than $1 billion if MBIA wins. Separately, the U.S. government has sued BofA for more than $1 billion over a Countrywide lending scheme dubbed "the hustle."

---

[80] Napoleon, Anthony. (2012), *The Progressive Virus*. VBW Publishing, College Station, Texas.

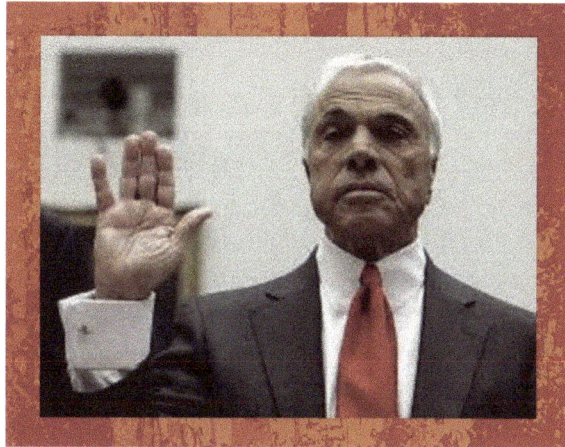

Angelo Mozilo.

BofA shareholders have already shelled out $40 billion to cover losses from the toxic garbage Mozilo handed to them in the Countrywide sale, Bloomberg points out. Just months after it bought Countrywide, BofA paid $8.7 billion to settle predatory-lending charges. The bank has also paid hundreds of millions of dollars to settle shareholder lawsuits, charges of discriminatory lending and accusations that Countrywide overcharged customers.

Meanwhile, Mozilo has nothing but free time to golf, work on his tan and spread blame for what happened to the economy to everybody else in the world -- to the Federal Reserve and other regulators, greedy homebuyers, Fannie Mae and Freddie Mac -- to anybody but him and Countrywide. So, yeah, why wouldn't Angelo Mozilo feel just fine?" [81]

The Chairman of The Federal Reserve during the lead up to the financial debacle of 2008 was Alan Greenspan. Mr. Greenspan denies having had an awareness of the impending debacle, though he described the housing market in 2005 as "frothy." [82]

In an interview with Lauren Victoria Burke of CNBC, Mr. Greenspan made these key points about the 2008 meltdown:

1. "The core of the subprime problem lies with the misjudgments of the investment community."
2. "Subprime-mortgage securitization exploded because it appeared mis-priced and there were few delinquencies and defaults, creating the illusion of great profit opportunities."
3. "Lenders were then pressed by securitisers for mortgage paper "with little concern about its quality." Greenspan also said he doubts tightening of regulation would have solved the problem.
4. "The problem is not the lack of regulation but unrealistic expectations about what regulators are able to prevent." [83]

I ask the reader to consider the provenance of these modern day moneychangers to those men who preceded them in the ancient world. They are kindred spirits and then, as now, their ultimate

---

[81] The Huffington Post. *Angelo Mozilo Has 'No Regrets,' Former Countrywide CEO Sleeps Like Big Leathery Baby.* By Mark Gongloff, December 13, 2012.
[82] New York Times. *In a Word; Frothy.* By Leon Lionhardt. December 25, 2005.
[83] CNBC with Reuters News Service. (2008), *Greenspan Says Fed Didn't Cause Housing Bubble.* April 8.

goal was to commandeer the machinery of money. In 1913, the machinery of money became the exclusive purview of 12 Regional, privately owned banks collectively known as The Federal Reserve.

We have documented interconnectedness between The Fed and the investment banks, e.g., Goldman Sachs, et al. We have documented the interconnectedness between The BBA and The Fed. We have documented The Vatican's explicit plans to create a world banking operation. The interconnectedness between banking, religion and government has been empirically demonstrated.

Author Nomi Prins has researched the relationships between bankers and American presidents over the past 100 years. What she found is that every executive administration, from the president on down, has had close business, political and often times familial (genetic/marriage) ties to banking.

Paul Craig Roberts, former editor of The Wall Street Journal and Assistant Secretary of the U.S. Treasury, said this about Prin's research:

> *"Nomi Prins reveals how U.S. policy has been largely dominated by a circle of the same banking and political dynasties. For more than a century presidents often acquiesced or participated as bankers subverted democracy, neglected the public interest and stole power from the American people."* [84]

I noted with some interest that Miss Prins, like Stephenson, Griffin, Primm and my analysis herein, highlighted the 1910 meeting on Jekyll Island as a watershed event in American financial history.

My contribution to understanding the significance of the Jekyll Island meeting derives from my expertise in forensic science. This expertise permitted me to test known standards of human behavior to the historical record chronicled by any number of scholars, including Miss Prins. Miss Prins identifies, by name, the who's who of the banking dynasties that have had a disproportionate influence on American politics and world events for at least the last 100 years. The names are all familiar. What is fascinating and consistent with our clinical and forensic analysis is that these men have a shared provenance with families who originated in and from the shadow men dynasties of old Europe.

Far from being a mysterious cabal, the fact that old wealth and power go hand in hand is both logical and to be expected. The fact is that when it comes to power "blood is always thicker than water." Power once achieved is jealously protected and it transfers from one generation to another in the same way that genetics transfers from mother and father to their progeny.

The history of bankers and banking is a provenance of dynasty funded by wealth and motivated by power. The application of Napoleon's Monetary Axiom accounts for both the intrigue and mystery surrounding money, banks, economies and The Fed. The only thing mysterious about banking dynasties is the public's relative ignorance of them.

---

[84] Prins, Nomi. (2014), *All the President's Bankers: THE HIDDEN ALLIANCES THAT DRIVE AMERICAN POWER.* Nation Books, New York.

CHAPTER 10: EARLY AMERICA AND ITS FOUNDERS – ESCAPE FROM SHADOW MEN

America's founding documents represent an explicit effort to permanently block the insatiable appetite of shadow men to consume freedom and free will. The founding documents are reflections of the personalities and motivations of the men who wrote them.

I respectfully suggest that true American patriotism should naturally flow from an appreciation of the fact that America's founders constructed barriers and firewalls designed to permanently block shadow men and their progeny from consuming other men's free will. Thwarting evil, especially organized evil, is THE issue that sooner or later engulfs every thinking person's life.

Of course other people, from other times and countries, have resisted tyranny since time immemorial, but these efforts, noble though they were, were reactions to specific acts of oppression within a given time frame at a given place. They were cures for a specific problem in a specific time. America's founders, on the other hand, understood that the wellspring from which oppressive rulers are born is an ever-present and self-regenerating evil. Our founders took the measure of not only the specific shadow men who ruled over them, but also, more importantly, the archetypal characters they represented. They took their brilliant insights and explicitly set about to gift to all future generations a means by which free men can remain free though surrounded by the successors and kindred spirits of their particular oppressors.

To accomplish our task of understanding the unique nature of America's founding father's intent, we are going to go back in time a few hundred years. We are also going to explore other parts of the world in order to document the zeitgeist of America's founders. Keep in mind that America's founders were extremely well read and understood world history. It is my contention that their understanding of world history motivated their drive to set ALL men free, not just their fellow Colonists.

Government, no matter how lofty its intentions or rational its members may be or its racial, religious or national creed will, through a process of entropy, devolve into a means by which evil men and women will seek to satisfy their insatiable appetite for power. The founders understood that evil men, because of their nature, would attempt to take control of any government and use that government to impose its will upon mankind. America's founders understood that governments are the devil's playground in the same way a warm agar plate is a breeding ground for bacteria.

My purpose in this chapter is to capture the personality and motivational fingerprints of all the players before, during and after the American Revolution. My clinical and forensic insights, applied to facts compiled and presented here from a broad cross section of historians, will make my review distinct from all of the other reviews of America's early history.

Doctoral level understanding of personality and motivation has been instructed by any number of scientific studies on how these human behavior-dynamos operate. I have conducted hundreds of personality and other psychological assessments using the most sophisticated psychometric tools available. I have conducted these analyses in hospitals, clinics, government institutions and courtrooms. I've tested all nationalities, races, creeds and genders. My professional life could be accurately described as a developer of mind control antidotes and working as a scientist whose livelihood depended upon my ability to shepherd my clients through the rough waters of complex legal and national and international conflicts. My work here represents a historical psychoanalysis of people, their ideas and their governments.

Personality, as a construct, is comprised of those enduring and consistent across contexts, core characteristics that are the product of one's unique biological, psychological, cultural and spiritual fabric. Clinical psychologists and psychiatrists chronicle personality on Axis II of the five psychiatric diagnostic Axes.

Historians have gifted to us a compendium of documented facts that accurately reflect early America. When these facts are assembled into a clinical and forensic framework, these facts morph from mere factoids into a digestible storyline that transcends the usual and customary historical recantation that best describes other treatments of early American history.

My analysis herein will be purposefully politically agnostic. I am going to reconstruct early America and its first European settlers and their world environment using the same clinical and forensic insights I would use had I been tasked with uncovering motive and identifying the key players in a criminal matter. So without further ado, let's begin.

56 men comprised the first Continental Congress. Of those 56, five men were assigned the task of writing the Declaration of Independence: John Adams, from Massachusetts, Thomas Jefferson from Virginia, Benjamin Franklin from Pennsylvania, Roger Sherman from Connecticut and Roger Livingston from New York.

Jefferson began work on the Declaration of Independence on June 11, 1776 and finished the document on June 28, 1776. The weather in Philadelphia during the latter part of June and into July was uncharacteristically cool. How do we know what the weather was like? Thomas Jefferson, true to his rather obsessive personality, kept a weather journal. Here is a page from Jefferson's weather journal that chronicles the weather for Philadelphia during the first part of July 1776:

Thomas Jefferson's weather journal for July 1776.

I draw the reader's attention to Jefferson's precise cursive handwriting. Forensic hand writing analysts who studied Jefferson's handwriting informed me that Jefferson was a careful and patient man who cared about detail and precision.

Jefferson gave his draft version of the Declaration of Independence to Adams and Franklin who proof read it. They, along with other members of the Continental Congress, made edits. The completed document was presented to delegates in the Pennsylvania State House on July 1, 1776. Delegates reviewed it on July 2nd and, on July 4, 1776, they formally voted in favor of its approval.

Jefferson acknowledged that he wrote the Declaration of Independence so that the common man would readily comprehend and be motivated by its content. In New York City, the Declaration of Independence was read aloud to a gathering of colonists near a statue of King George III. The reading of the new Declaration of Independence so motivated the gathering of soon to be Americans that they spontaneously pulled down a statue of the English King. The following drawing created by Habermann depicts this event:

Franz Haberman: Independentists Pulling Down Statue of King George III in New York, July 9, 1776.

Declaration of Independence (Rough Draft).

What follows is the typewritten text of the rough draft version of the Declaration of Independence. Notice Jefferson's edits as he wrote and rewrote this document. His edits suggest the mindset of a man striving to connect with the common man:

one
```
    When in the course of human events it becomes necessary for a^
```

dissolve the political bands which have connected them with another,
```
  people to ^advance from that subordination in which they have
hitherto
```

and to
separate and equal
```
  ^remained, & to assume among the powers of the earth the
  ^equal and independent station to which the laws of nature and of
nature's god
```
```
  entitle them, a decent respect to the opinions of mankind requires
```

the separation
```
  that they should declare the causes which impel them to ^change.
```

self-evident,
```
  We hold these truths to be ^sacred & undeniable; that all Men
```

they are endowed by their creator with
```
  are created equal & independent; that ^from that equal creation
they
```

equal rights, some of which are   rights; that   these
```
  derive in rights inherent & inalienable ^ among ^which are the
```
```
  preservation of life, & liberty, & the pursuit of happiness;
```

rights
```
  that to secure these ^ends, governments are instituted among men,
```
```
  deriving their just powers from the consent of the governed; that
```
```
  whenever any form of government shall becomes destructive of these
```
```
  ends, it is the right of the people to alter or abolish it, & to
```
```
  institute new government, laying it's foundation on such
principles,
```
```
  & organizing it's powers in such form, as to them shall seem most
```
```
  likely to effect their safety & happiness.  prudence indeed will
```
```
  dictate that governments long established should not be changed for
```

light & transient causes; and accordingly all experience hath shown

that mankind are more disposed to suffer, while evils are sufferable,

than to right themselves by abolishing the forms to which they are

accustomed. but when a long train of abuses & usurpations pursuing

invariably the same object, evinces a design to ~~subject~~ reduce them

under absolute Despotism [FRANKLIN]
^~~to arbitrary power~~, it is their right, it is their duty to throw off

such government, & to provide new guards for their future security

such has been the patient sufferance of these colonies; & such is now

the necessity which constrains them to alter their former systems of

the   *king of Great Britain*
[ADAMS]
government. the History of ^~~his~~ the present ^~~majesty~~ is a history of

appears no solitary fact
repeated injuries & usurpations, among which ^~~no one fact stands single~~

but all
~~and solitary~~ to contradict the uniform tenor of the rest, ^~~all of which~~

have in direct object the establishment of an absolute tyranny over

these states. to prove this, let facts be submitted to a candid world,

for the truth of which we pledge a faith yet unsullied by falsehood.

he has refused his assent to laws, the most wholesome & necessary for

the public good:

he has forbidden his governors to pass laws of immediate &

pressing importance, unless suspended in their operation

till his Assent should be obtained; and when so suspended,

he has neglected utterly to attend to them.

he has refused to pass other laws for the accommodation of large

   districts of people, unless those people would relinquish the right
of

                       in the Legislature
   representation ^, a right inestimable to them, & formidable to
tyrants

   only:

he has called together legislative bodies in places unusual,

   uncomfortable & distant from the depository of their public records

   for the sole purpose of fatiguing them into compliance with his

   measures:

he has dissolved Representative houses repeatedly & continually, for

   opposing with manly firmness his invasions on the Rights of the
People.

                                          time after such
dissolutions
~~he has dissolved,~~ he has refused for a long ^ ~~space of time~~, after

   such dissolutions, to cause others to be elected, whereby the

   legislative Powers, incapable of annihilation, have returned to the

   people at large for their exercise; the state remaining in the

   meantime exposed to all the dangers of invasion from without, &

   convulsions within:

he has endeavored to prevent the population of these states; for

   that purpose obstructing the laws for naturalization of foreigners;

   refusing to pass others to encourage their migrations hither;

   & raising the conditions of new appropriations of lands:

he has suffered the administration of justice totally to cease
in

                    states
   some of these ^ ~~colonies~~, refusing his assent to laws for

establishing judiciary powers:

he has made our judges dependent on his will alone, for the tenure

of their offices, and ^ the amount ^ and payment [FRANKLIN] of their Salaries:

he has erected a multitude of new offices by a self-assumed power,

& sent hither swarms of new officers to harass our people and eat

out their substance.

he has kept among us in times of peace ^ without our consent standing armies,

& ships of war^: without ^the our consent. of our legislatures

he has affected to render the military independent of, & superior

to the civil power:

he has combined with others to subject us to a jurisdiction foreign

to our constitutions, and unacknowledged by our laws; giving his

assent to their ^ acts of pretended acts of legislation,

for quartering large bodies of Armed Troops among us;

for protecting them, by a mock-trial from punishment for any

murders ^ which they should commit on the inhabitants of these states;

for cutting off our trade with all parts of the world;

for imposing taxes on us without our consent;

for depriving us of the benefits of trial by jury;

for transporting us beyond seas to be tried for pretended offences;

for abolishing the free system of English laws in a neighboring province,

   establishing therein an arbitrary government, and enlarging it's

   boundaries so as to render it at once an example & fit instrument

   for introducing the same absolute rule into these ~~colonies~~ states;

                                                   valuable
                              abolishing our most ^~~important~~
laws [FRANKLIN]
   for taking away our charters, ^ & altering fundimentally the forms of

      our governments;

   for suspending our own legislatures & declaring themselves

      invested with power to legislate for us in all cases

      whatsoever:

he has abdicated government here, withdrawing his governors,

   & declaring us out of his allegiance & protection:

he has plundered our seas, ravaged our coasts, burnt our towns,

   & destroyed the lives of our people:

he is at this time transporting large armies of foreign mercenaries

   to compleat the works of death, desolation & tyranny, already begun

   with circumstances of cruelty and perfidy unworthy the head of a

   civilized nation:

he has endeavored to bring on the inhabitants of our frontiers the

   merciless Indian savages, whose known rule of warfare in an

   undistinguished destruction of all ages, sexes, & conditions of

   existence:

he has incited treasonable insurrections of our fellow-citizens,

   with the allurements of forfeiture & confiscation of our
property:

                              taken captives
he has constrained others, ^~~falling into his hands,~~ on the high

   seas to bear arms against their country, ~~& to destroy & be~~

   ~~destroyed by their breteren whom they love,~~ to become the

   executioners of their friends & brethren, or to fall
themselves

   by their hands.

he has waged cruel war against human nature itself, violating

   it's most sacred rights of life & liberty in the persons of

   a distant people who never offended him, captivating &
carrying

   them to slavery in another hemisphere, or to incur miserable

   death in their transportations thither. this piratical
warfare,

   the opprobrium of infidel powers, is the warfare of the
Christian

   king of Great Britain. determined to keep open a market where
MEN

   should be bought & sold, **he has prostituted his negative for**

   suppressing every legislative attempt to prohibit or to
restrain

~~determining to keep open a market where MEN should be bought &~~
~~sold~~
   this excrable commerce ^ and that this assemblage of horrors
might

   want no fact of distiguished die, he is now exciting those
very

   people to rise in arms against us, and to purchase that
liberty

   of which he has deprived them, by murdering the people upon
whom

he also obtruded them; thus paying off former crimes which he

urges them to commit against the lives of another.

in every stage of these oppressions we have petitioned for

redress in the most humble terms: our repeated petitions have

<pre>   only [FRANKLIN]</pre>
been answered ^ by repeated Injury. a Prince whose character

is thus marked by every act which may define a tyrant, is

unfit to be the ruler of a people who mean to be free. future

ages will scarce belive that the hardiness of one man,
adventured

<pre>   build</pre>
to ^lay a foundation so broad & undistiguished for
tyranny
within the short compass of twelve years only, ^on so many
acts

of tyrany without a mask, over a people fostered & fixed in

<pre>   freedom</pre>
principles of ^liberty.

Nor have we been wanting in attentions to our British Brethren.
we

have warned them from time to time of attempts by their

legislature to extend a jurisdiction over these our states. we

have reminded them of the circumstances of our emigration &

settlement here, no one of which could warrent so strange a

pretention: that these were effected at the expence of our own

blood & treasure, unassisted by the wealth or the strength of

Great Britain: that in constituting indeed our several forms

of government, we had adopted one common king, thereby laying
a

foundation for perpetual league & amity with them: but that

submission to their parliament was no part of our
constitution,

nor ever in idea if history may be credited: and we appealed to

their native justice and magnanimity as well as the ties of our

common kindred to disavow these usurpations which were likely to

connection &
interrupt our ^ correspondence. they too have been deaf to the

voice of justice & of consanguinity & when occations have been

given them, by the regular course of their laws, of removing from

their councils the disturbers of our harmony, they have by their

free election re-established them in power. at this very time too

they are permitting their chief magistrate to send over not only

soldiers of our common blood, but Scotch & foriegn mercinaries to

destroy us [FRANKLIN]
invade & ^~~deluge us in blood.~~ these facts have given the last stab

to agonizing affection, and manly spirit bids us to renounce

forever these unfeeling bretheren. we must endeavor to forget our

former love for them, and to hold them, as we hold the rest of

mankind, enemies in war, in peace, friends. we might have been a

free & a great people together; but a communication of gradeur &

of freedom it seems is below their dignity, be it so, since they

& to glory
will have it: the road to ~~glory &~~ happiness ^ is open to us too;

```
                        apart from them
we will climb it ^ in a separatly state, and acquiesce in the

                        de              eternal separation!
necessity which pro^nounces our ^everlasting adieu!

We therefore the representatives of the United States of

   America in General Congress assembled, do, in the name & by
the

   authority of the good people of these states, reject and

   renounce all allegiance & subjection to the kings of Great
Britain

   & all others who may hereafter claim, by through or under
them;

   we utterly dissolve & break off all political connection which

                        have
   may have heretofore ^ sibsisted between us & the people or
parliament

   of Great Britain; and do finally we do assert and declare
these

   colonies to be free and independent states, and that as free &

                                            full
   independent states they shall hereafter have ^ power to levy war,

   conclude peace, contract alliances, establish commerce, & do all

   other acts and things which independent states may of right do.

And for the support of this declaration we mutually pledge to each

other our lives, our fortunes, & our sacred honor. 85
```

I want to give you a glimpse into the personalities of the men who were at the center of this new venture that intended to permanently hobble oppressors, both in and out of the government, for not only their personal piece of mind but their progeny and future Americans and world citizens, as well. If you study Jefferson's rough draft of The Declaration of Independence you can readily see that oppression and mind control were on his mind and that he intended, along with his fellow "worthies," to grant to future generations the gift of protection from the archetypal enemies of free will.

---

85 Independence Hall Association. (1995), Philadelphia, Pennsylvania, founded in 1942.

All of America's founders retained a British accent, though a hint of what today we would describe as, a gentlemen's Eastern/Southern accent, would be noticeable to the trained ear. Keep in mind that America's founder's parents were all born in the "old" country, part of the British Empire. America's founders grew up in households where the first vocal inflections and accents they heard were the King's English. People living in the port cities of Boston, New York and Savannah, for example, retained their status-giving English accents well into the 20th century. However, as port cities gave way to industrial centers like Pittsburg, Cleveland, Chicago and Detroit, the English accent lost favor and what are now recognized as regional American accents supplanted the King's English. Linguists have noted that regional accents as spoken in The Hamptons or Hyannis Port, for example, are remnants of the linguistic artifacts of America's first English settlers.

Jefferson was only 33 years old when he wrote the Declaration of Independence. He stood 6' 2 1/2" tall and was a lanky 181 pounds. He had bright red hair and was not physically attractive. Red hair is typically comprised of a "flatter" as opposed to "rounder" hair shaft; therefore, his hair was curly and wavy.

Jefferson was an extremely reserved person. He was the kind of person who sat quietly in the back of the room taking precise notes, handwritten in carefully penned cursive. He made up for his taciturn nature, in part, by becoming an elegant writer. Jefferson was so reluctant to speak in public that he didn't even give a State of the Union Speech as President, choosing instead to send a letter to Congress.

Near the end of his life, Jefferson explained his goal in writing the Declaration of Independence. In a letter to Henry Lee, May 8, 1825 he stated:

> *"This was the object of the Declaration of Independence. Not to find out new principles, or new arguments never before thought of, not merely to say things which had never been said before;* **but to place before mankind the common sense of the subject, in terms so plain and firm as to command their assent, and to justify ourselves in the independent stand we are compelled to take.** *Neither aiming at originality of principle or sentiment, nor yet copied from any particular or previous writing,* **it was intended to be an expression of the American mind,** *and to give to that expression the proper tone and spirit called for by the occasion. All of its authority rests then on the harmonizing sentiments of the day . . ."*

The last letter Jefferson ever wrote provides confirmation of our central thesis that Jefferson understood that he and his fellow founders were engaged in an **archetypal battle for all of mankind,** not merely the few in the colonies who insisted upon their freedom from the English Crown.

On June 24, 1826, Jefferson wrote to Roger C. Weightman, declining to attend the celebration of the fiftieth anniversary of the Declaration of Independence in the District of Columbia.

> *'Monticello, June 24, 1826*
> *Respected Sir-*
>
> *The kind invitation I receive from you, on the part of the citizens of the city of Washington, to be present with them at their celebration of the fiftieth anniversary of American Independence, as one of the surviving signers of an instrument pregnant with our own, and the fate of the world, is most flattering to myself, and heightened by the honorable accompaniment proposed for the comfort of such a journey. It adds sensibly to the sufferings of sickness, to be deprived by it of a personal participation in the rejoicings of that day. But acquiescence is a duty, under circumstances not placed among those we are permitted to control. I should, indeed, with peculiar delight, have met and exchanged there congratulations personally with the small band, the remnant of that host of worthies,*

who joined with us on that day, in the **bold and doubtful** *election we were to make for our country, between submission or the sword; and to have enjoyed with them the consolatory fact, that our fellow citizens, after half a century of experience and prosperity, continue to approve the choice we made.* **May it be to the <u>world</u>, what I believe it will be, (to some parts sooner, to others later, but finally to all,) the signal of arousing men to burst the chains under which monkish ignorance and superstition had persuaded them to bind themselves, and to assume the blessings and security of self-government. That form, which we have substituted, restores the free right to the unbounded exercise of reason and freedom of opinion. All eyes are opened, or opening, to the rights of man.** *The general spread of the light of science has already laid open to every view the palpable truth, that the mass of mankind has not been born with saddles on their backs, nor a favored few booted and spurred, ready to ride them legitimately, by the grace of God. These are grounds of hope for others. For ourselves, let the annual return of this day forever refresh our recollections of these rights, and an undiminished devotion to them.*

I will ask permission here to express the pleasure with which I should have met my ancient neighbors of the city of Washington and its vicinities, with whom I passed so many years of a pleasing social intercourse; an intercourse which so much relieved the anxieties of the public cares, and left impressions so deeply engraved in my affections, as never to be forgotten. With my regret that ill health forbids me the gratification of an acceptance, be pleased to receive for yourself, and those for whom you write, the assurance of my highest respect and friendly attachments.

Th. Jefferson"

Whether you are friend or foe of America, after reading Jefferson's thoughts on the subject of his efforts under threat of torture or death, those politicians and subversives who would undo the work of Jefferson and his fellow worthies should have reserved for them a special place in hell or, at the very least, a dedicated biography chronicling the most arrogant and brazen narcissists who have ever lived on earth.

After studying every major treatise in print on American history, it is my opinion that students of American history have been subjected to too many unconsciously tainted recantations of history. I say "unconsciously tainted" because I believe that the vast majority of historians try to be objective, but absent that peculiar ability that needs to be tempered with a rigorous education joined with an almost obsessive passion for objectivity, all men pray before their unconscious prejudices. Historians who bowed before the delusion of "everything written is a subjective expression" mantra have proven themselves to be incapable of chronicling the American idea without their own unique personalities and biases entering into their work.

In the 1940's and 50's students were typically presented with a two-dimensional history of America that was heavy on dates and names but absent contextual motivation of the actors. In 1980 and later, students were literally pummeled with Communist inspired recantations of American history, e.g., Howard Zinn's: "*A Peoples History of the United States.*" Communist inspired books on American history were thinly veiled PSYOPs designed to accomplish what many of them did, indeed, accomplish, to deny Americans a justifiable pride in their country's founders and mold readers into anti-American martinets.

The 21st Century handmaidens of shadow men, masquerading as Congressman, Senators and Presidents, have set about to undo what Jefferson and his valiant "worthies" [86] accomplished that came to be known as the American idea. The agents of shadow men who have literally put the American idea in their crosshairs use manipulative slight of hand trickery more appropriate for the hypnotist's stage as a means of accomplishing their subversion of America and its citizens. Subversion encourages arrogant politicians and some academics to deconstruct the American idea as manifest in its founding documents. What follows are a couple examples of this most destructive pattern:

James Madison wrote the First Amendment to the Constitution. Madison had witnessed, first hand, the Crown's attack upon those men and women who spoke the truth and dared to expose the graft, fraud and embezzlement of men like William Cosby, a British Governor appointed by the King. Madison recognized that men are gifted (entitled to), from God or nature, the freedom to express words, thoughts and speech. When this God given right is recognized (not granted) by governments as a **transcendent right**, then oppressors of men will have a much more difficult time enforcing their will. The brilliance of Madison's gift to all Americans is under attack by a 21st century New York Senator named Charles Schumer (D-NY) in 2001.

Schumer is a progressive activist whose intellectual prowess is inversely proportional to his presumptuous arrogance and blatant pomposity. For the likes of Schumer to assume that he is the intellectual and moral equal of Madison, so much so that Schumer would declare, on the Senate floor of the United States of America, that he desired to *rewrite* Madison's gift to America, then it is clear that Chutzpah and malignant narcissism have no bounds. Permit me to use an analogy: Schumer's desire to rewrite Madison's First Amendment to the Constitution is like the high school literature teacher who declares his intention to rewrite Hamlet.

To understand what Madison experienced that inspired him to give to all of us this novel notion of "freedom of speech," the same notion that the likes of Schumer would rewrite if he were unbridled, consider this exemplar history of how oppressors behave if given the opportunity.

'John Peter Zenger was a German immigrant and publisher of The New York Daily Journal. Zenger's newspaper was considered, at the time, (1730's) to be pro-colonist and anti-Royal. It was financially supported by the Morrisites, a political party that stood in opposition to many of the Tory-like policies of its political rival, the Court party. Some of Zenger's more threatening editorials included exposés on a British Governor by the name of William Cosby. In particular, Cosby's rigging of the 1734 elections; Cosby's personal use of tax monies and Cosby's illegal appropriation of Indian lands, among other transgressions.

In November 1734, Governor Cosby ordered his men to burn four editions of the New York Daily Journal. These editions contained the allegedly seditious, truth-telling material that so bothered Governor Cosby. On November 17, 1734, Zenger was arrested for "seditious libel" for having published the truth about Cosby. This arrest took place despite the fact that a New York grand jury, consisting of American colonists, refused to indict Zenger. During Zenger's incarceration awaiting trial, his wife Anna, in a display of bravery and patriotism, continued printing the newspaper.

---

[86] "Worthies" is the term Mr. Jefferson used when referring to his fellow Colonists who put their life on the line for this new venture called The American Idea.

The Zenger trial provides us with a classic example of how far vested interests (shadow men's agents) can and will go to attack the speaking of truth in the absence of a Constitutional guarantee to speak the truth.

Governor Cosby disbarred the local defense counsel for Zenger using his executive authority. In response, the Morrisites hired Andrew Hamilton, a talented trial lawyer from Philadelphia, to defend Zenger. Even Cosby realized that he could not attack Hamilton's credibility. Therefore, Cosby concluded that the only way he could sway the jury was to hire a lawyer with very powerful connections, a sinecure of the King himself. Zenger's lawyer, Alexander Hamilton, argued that the newspaper couldn't be punished unless what it had printed was falsely seditious. Hamilton's defense of Zenger created in that trial a concept we all have come to accept as a given: The truth can never be libelous.

It was the Zenger trial and similar assaults upon truth telling by the British Monarchy and their agents in the colonies that motivated James Madison to draft the First Amendment to the Constitution.

'Madison's version of the speech and press clauses, introduced in the House of Representatives on June 8, 1789, provided:

"The people shall not be deprived or abridged of their right to speak, to write, or to publish their sentiments; and the freedom of the press, as one of the great bulwarks of liberty, shall be inviolable." [87]

I want to take this opportunity to remind you that Zenger had incurred the wrath of Cosby, in part, because he had expressed a criticism of Governor Cosby's appropriation of Indian land. That may surprise some of you, that an American Colonist would take the side of the indigenous population. Despite what you may have learned if you studied American history post 1960, Colonists had a symbiotic relationship with many Native American tribes. You'll learn about this symbiotic relationship later in this book when I share with you information purposefully kept from you and replaced with a nightmarish scenario designed to portray European Christian settlers as rapists and pillagers of the indigenous peoples in North America. For now, realize that Zenger's newspaper printed editorials that decried the exploitation of Native Americans by the British and non-Christian colonists.

Attacks upon the First Amendment often make their way into the public's awareness because the media entertainment complex tend to emphasize their freedoms as enshrined in the First Amendment. One of the most recent examples is to label some speech as "hate" speech. No doubt, William Cosby would have labeled Zenger's critical editorials of his graft as "hate" speech just as today's politicians would love to be able to label those who would uncover their foul deeds as guilty of "hate speech." Madison would have never carved out an exception for "hate" speech because men in power tend to label all speech that is critical of them or their pet causes as "hateful" speech.

Other blatant Constitutional violations are more insidious because that same media entertainment complex couldn't care less or, more insidiously, actually support such violations. One such erosion of America's founding document involves the 10th Amendment,

---

[87] Napoleon, Anthony. (2012), *The Progressive Virus: Why you can't permit it to go forward.* VBW Publishing, College Station, Texas.

> "The powers not delegated to the United States by the Constitution, nor prohibited by it to the States, are reserved to the States respectively, or to the people."

The 10th Amendment was intended to be the bulwark amendment that insured that at some time in the future the American idea would not devolve into another all powerful and central planning monstrosity run by shadow men. The 10th Amendment had its origins in a provision written into the Articles of Confederation, to wit,

> "Each state retains its sovereignty, freedom, and independence, and every power, jurisdiction, and right, which is not by this Confederation expressly delegated to the United States, in Congress assembled."

The Tenth Amendment did not itemize those powers not specifically given to the Federal Government nor, in the alternative, itemize those rights reserved for the states. As in virtually all conflicts arising from Constitutional challenges, the U.S. Supreme Court has become the arbiter of what any particular amendment to the Constitution means. The U.S. Supreme Court has traditionally ruled that laws affecting such matters as marriage, divorce and adoption are reserved for the states. This tradition, involving states' regulation of marriage, was broken in June of 2015 when the U.S. Supreme Court overruled some states' prohibition of gay marriage as unconstitutional. Commerce or trade limited to the confines of a state's own borders are reserved for state control. Local law enforcement activities fall within the confines of the 10th Amendment.

Notwithstanding the clear intent of the 10th Amendment, the 20th Century ushered in a rapacious expansion of the Federal Government's powers. Keep in mind that America's founders were adamant in their opposition to shadow men and knew all too well that shadow men's lifeblood was centralized authoritarian power. Despite built in protections in America's Constitution, shadow men and their agents have successfully circumvented the original intent of the 10th Amendment. They have done so, in part, by deviously artful uses of the Commerce Clause:

> Article 1, Section 8, Clause 3 of the U.S. Constitution gives Congress the power "to regulate commerce with foreign nations, and among the several states, and with the Indian tribes."

Modern technology means that business and commerce in the 21st Century is seldom confined to the borders of any one particular state; thus, those with a vested interest in expanding the powers of the federal government argue that the Commerce Clause should apply; essentially nullifying the 10th Amendment's clear intent. The means by which shadow men's agents, both in and out of the government, have schemed to circumvent the 10th Amendment could only be done justice by writing an entire book on the subject.

One particularly devious strategy to circumvent the Constitution involves the Federal Government's use of the strategy of double binding states when it comes to the issue of border security. The Federal Government has the exclusive power to control America's borders, including implementing border security and regulating immigration. Border states, on the other hand, are on the front lines of border security issues because of their proximity to Mexico and Canada.

So what happens when the Federal Government chooses to stand down, turn a blind eye to or simply refuse to enforce immigration laws? Putting aside the underling motivation of agents within the federal government to obviate the solvency of the border, imagine if a federal government was taken over or simply became ineffective for any number of reasons. Are states helpless in any of those circumstances where the federal government fails in protecting America's border? Notwithstanding their sovereignty, border states find themselves in the unenviable position of "damned if we do and damned if we don't." In 2012 the Supreme Court heard the case of Arizona v. The United States. Justice Kennedy wrote the following introduction to the court's ruling:

> "To address pressing issues related to the large number of aliens within its borders who do not have a lawful right to be in this country, the State of Arizona in 2010 enacted a statute called the Support Our Law Enforcement and Safe Neighborhoods Act. The law is often referred to as S.B. 1070, the version introduced in the state senate. See also H. 2162 (2010) (amending S. 1070). Its stated purpose is to "discourage and deter the unlawful entry and presence of aliens and economic activity by persons unlawfully present in the United States." Note following Ariz. Rev.Stat. Ann. § 11-1051 (West 2012). The law's provisions establish an official state policy of "attrition through enforcement." Ibid. The question before the Court is whether federal law preempts and renders invalid four separate provisions of the state law." [88]

When all was said and done, the Supreme Court nullified three of the four provisions of Arizona's SB 1070, to wit:

> "In the end, by a vote of 5-3, the Court nullified three of the four provisions because they either operated in areas solely controlled by federal policy, or they interfered with federal enforcement efforts. Nullified were sections making it a crime to be in Arizona without legal papers, making it a crime to apply for or get a job in the state, or allowing police to arrest individuals who had committed crimes that could lead to their deportation. The Court left intact — but subject to later challenges in lower courts — a provision requiring police to arrest and hold anyone they believe has committed a crime and whom they think is in the country illegally, and holding them until their immigration status could be checked with federal officials." [89]

Suffice to say that where there is a will to circumvent the Constitution of the United States, shadow men will always find a way. What is missing in modern America is the counter-point to revolutionaries who would subvert the Constitution. Counter revolutionaries would reify the solvency of the Constitution in general and the 10th Amendment in particular. In other words, much to the chagrin of America's founders, I am sure, modern Americans, including state governors, have had their natural love of freedom and constitutional mettle removed from their psyche by the subjects of this book. Recovering one's love of freedom and passion is as simple as rediscovering the fire of freedom that resides in man's soul, then having the courage to force the issue on tyrants, *no matter what it takes*. Let's now return to those men who possessed the intestinal fortitude and passion to do just that.

A cover letter accompanied the Declaration of Independence. This is what the British shadow men read that put them on notice:

> *"Gentlemen, Altho it is not possible to forsee the consequences of human actions, yet it is nevertheless a duty we owe ourselves and posterity in all our public councils to decide in the best manner we are able and to trust the event to That Being who governs both causes and events, so as to bring about his own determinations.*

---

[88] Arizona v. US132 S. Ct. 2492, 567 US __, 183 L. Ed. 2d 351
[89] Supreme Court Blog (2012), ARIZONA V. UNITED STATES.

Impressed with this sentiment, and at the same time fully convinced that our affairs will take a more favorable turn, The Congress have judged it necessary to dissolve all connection between Great Britain and the American Colonies, and to declare them free and independent States as you will perceive by the enclosed Declaration, which I am directed to transmit to you."

John Adams was a little older than Jefferson at the time of the drafting of the Declaration of Independence (40 years-old), stood 5' 7" tall and had a muscular build. He had light brown to dishwater blond hair that fell over his ears. Without his powdered wig on you would have seen a receding hairline and a high forehead. He was as boisterous and talkative, if not obnoxious, as Jefferson was quiet and polite. For example, John Adams holds the record for the longest continuous sentence ever spoken before Congress at 755 words. An interesting factoid is that Adams and Jefferson would both pass away on July 4th within hours of one another in 1826.

John Adams had to do a little arm-twisting to get Jefferson to write the Declaration of Independence. In fact, Jefferson argued that Adams should be the one to write the document. In one of Adam's letters on the subject, Adams recounted the back and forth regarding who would write the Declaration of Independence:

"[J]efferson proposed to me to make the draft. I said, 'I will not,' 'You should do it.' 'Oh! no.' 'Why will you not? You ought to do it.' 'I will not.' 'Why?' 'Reasons enough.' 'What can be your reasons?' 'Reason first, you are a Virginian, and a Virginian ought to appear at the head of this business. Reason second, I am obnoxious, suspected, and unpopular. You are very much otherwise. Reason third, you can write ten times better than I can.' 'Well,' said Jefferson, 'if you are decided, I will do as well as I can.' 'Very well. When you have drawn it up, we will have a meeting. [90]

Ben Franklin stood 5'9" tall and was a slightly heavy man with blond to light brown hair. He was 70 years old in 1776. He wore spectacles on the end his nose when he read and had a personality rather like a mad scientist who was always tinkering with something to figure out how it worked. He was an iconoclast who liked the ladies, reputedly, much younger women. He was a charmer because of his warmth and good nature. He would have made the perfect Santa Claus because of his personality and physical dimensions. At the risk of focusing too much on Benjamin Franklin at the expense of his fellow worthies, Franklin's accomplishments deserve enumeration, if for no other reason than to give the reader a sense of the quality of the men who founded America:

1. To his life's end, Ben Franklin remained a printer and took pride in it. Wherever he lived in Europe or America, he managed to have a printing press at his disposal. It is no accident that his last will and testament, written at age eighty-three (the year before he died) begins "I, Benjamin Franklin of Philadelphia, printer…".

2. Ben Franklin first saw himself in print at age 16, writing his controversial, feminist "Silence Dogood" letters, published anonymously in his brother's newspaper, The New England Courant.

3. As a teenager Ben Franklin became an expert swimmer. On his visit to London at age nineteen, Ben went on a boating excursion with his printer friends. During the trip he leaped into the Thames River and swam from Chelsea to Blackfriars, performing every kind of feat, under water and above. He had learned these feats in the Schuylkill River at home in Philadelphia. He was so expert that he seriously considered opening a swimming school.

---

[90] Adams, John (Charles Francis Adams ed.), (1997), *The Works of John Adams, Vol. II, The Diary* (1850), reprinted in Commager, H.S. and Nevins, A., (1939), *The Heritage of America.* Maier Pauline, American Scripture: *Making the Declaration of Independence.*

4. At the age of twenty-two, Ben Franklin was the owner of the Pennsylvania Gazette newspaper. His printing company printed the paper money for both Pennsylvania and Delaware.

5. As a young man in his twenties, Ben Franklin was elected clerk of the Pennsylvania Assembly, and he used his printing company to print their laws and other business. He was made postmaster of Philadelphia, which helped him circulate his newspaper.

6. Ben Franklin taught himself to read French, Spanish, Latin, and Italian. His passion for self-improvement extended to public projects; he organized the first fire company in the colonies, made designs for paving and lighting Philadelphia streets and for expanding the city watch to a force of police.

7. Ben Franklin, at the age of twenty-one, established the colonies' first circulation library for all interested citizens. The Library Company of Philadelphia, as it was called, housed not only books but also specimens of natural history and scientific apparatus. There were stuffed snakes, a dead pelican, and a collection of fossils.

8. Ben Franklin was already over forty-five years old when he started his experiments in electricity. In 1747 he was given a gift of his first experimental apparatus - a glass tube, over three feet long, as big around as a man's wrist, with instructions for its use in obtaining electric sparks.

9. In his first five years of conducting electricity experiments, Ben Franklin did not make much use of higher mathematics, since he was notably deficient in the subject. Rather, all his early experiments were done by hand, by trial and error, with simple objects as tools: glass tubes and tubes of resin, a gun barrel, corks, iron shot, and wax plates.

10. Ben Franklin's "single fluid theory" showed that a given body possessing a normal amount of electric fluid was called *neutral*. During the process of charging, the fluid was transferred from one body to the other; the body with the deficiency being charged *minus* and the body with the excess charged *plus* . But no fluid is lost.

11. Ben's "single fluid theory" led to the electron theory in 1900: electrons move about conductors much as a fluid might move. Nobel Prize winner and physicist, Robert A. Millikan, called Ben's experiment that led to this theory "probably the most fundamental thing ever done in the field of electricity".

12. Ben Franklin had to invent electricity terminology as he went along in his experiments. A scholar who traced Ben's vocabulary found at least twenty-five electrical terms which he was the first to use: examples -- *armature, battery, brush, charged, condense, conductor, plus* and *minus, positively* and *negatively.*

13. Ben Franklin became so absorbed in his electricity experiments that he sold his printing business to concentrate on his experiments. There is little doubt that he could have amassed a fortune had he stayed in business, but Ben enjoyed his simple style of living and he had no ambition for outward display of wealth.

14. Ben Franklin had a horror of debt, which he looked on as a kind of slavery: a man could thereby sell his freedom. Ben had seen his friends go down to ruin because of careless business practices. With money a man bought not only independence but he bought time, that most precious commodity, to use at his pleasure. For years Ben spoke quite seriously of founding an international organization to be called The Society of the Free and Easy -- meaning free of debt and, it followed, easy in spirit.

15. Ben Franklin was nearly killed by his early experiments with lightning; he survived only because he luckily didn't receive a strong enough charge. Twice he was knocked senseless - once when he attempted to treat a paralyzed man with electric shock, and another time preparing to kill a turkey by electric shock. In both cases Ben managed to take the whole charge through his hands and arms. He described the feeling as an "unusual blow throughout my whole body from head to foot... after which the first thing I took notice of was a violent quick shaking of my body, which gradually remitting, my senses as gradually returned".

16. Ben Franklin was the chief delegate to the Albany Congress of 1754, the first major conference to discuss a confederacy of the colonies. Upon his return from Albany, NY, Ben wrote a pamphlet called "Short Hints Towards a Scheme for Uniting the Northern Colonies". Several weeks before the Albany Congress, Ben's newspaper, the Pennsylvania Gazette, had printed the now famous drawing of a snake broken into eight pieces (eight colonies), each piece labeled with initials: "**NE., NY., NJ., P, M, V, NC, SC**". "**JOIN OR DIE** ", the caption read.

17. Ben Franklin organized the first volunteer fire company in 1736: The Union Fire Company. He wrote articles telling citizens how to prevent fires, stressing that an "ounce of prevention is worth a pound of cure" and he even told them to carry coals from one floor to another in a closed warming pan. Otherwise, he said, "scraps of fire may fall in to the chinks, and make no appearance until midnight, when your stairs being in flames, you may be forced (as I once was) to leap out of your windows and hazard your necks to avoid being over-roasted".

18. In 1751 Ben Franklin organized the first insurance company in the colonies; fire was the number one adversary. The full name was Philadelphia Contributorship for the Insurance of Houses from Loss By Fire. It was called a *mutual insurance plan* , "whereby every man might help another, without any disservice to himself".

19. The famous Ben Franklin invention, the Franklin Stove, was actually called the Pennsylvania Fireplace. It was first marketed in 1742 by Ben's friend, Robert Grace. Ben could have used the stove to make a fortune, but he consistently refused any personal profits from the enterprise. Ben's payment was the satisfaction that this stove warmed the houses of America more safely and effectively than before the stove's invention. He also was pleased that his invention would allow better ventilation and greater fuel efficiency.

20. In 1751 Ben Franklin was instrumental in founding the first hospital in America. He raised ten thousand pounds from the Pennsylvania Assembly and a matching amount from the public. He was the first scientist to realize the importance of fresh air in curing disease and aiding general health. James Parton, an early Franklin biographer, called Ben "the first effective preacher of the blessed gospel of ventilation". Parton added, "He spoke and the windows of hospitals were lowered; consumption [a lung disease] ceased to gasp and fever to inhale poison".

21. Ben Franklin, in 1761, invented the first original musical instrument created in America. It was known as the glass harmonica, or *armonica* as Ben called it. It became enormously popular in the eighteenth century, and music composed specifically for it was created by such luminaries as Mozart and Beethoven. Franklin also taught himself the violin, harp, and guitar; he even composed a string quartet, "Simplicity", that stressed easy playing.

22. Ben Franklin had long wanted to develop an Academy where the curriculum would focus on English composition and grammar, as well as a broad range of practical knowledge in science and mechanics. The school opened in 1751 with one hundred students. It was first chartered as both Academy and College in 1755, and, in 1791, was officially named the University of Pennsylvania, as it exists today. Ben, who had less than two years of schooling himself, was the clear and unchallenged ancestor of a major university.

23. During the Revolutionary War, Ben Franklin was in France, trying to get as much help for our new nation as possible. Even though France was officially neutral, France loaned America millions of dollars, let volunteers enlist, and permitted American warships to use its harbors. Hundreds of French military officers beseeched Ben to gain commissions in the American army.

24. When Ben Franklin returned to Philadelphia in 1785 from his service in France, guns fired and church bells rang to welcome him home. Upon his return he was made president of Pennsylvania's Supreme Council, a position like today's governor. Because he was in ill health, he had been determined to

avoid further public service. But he couldn't resist the call for his counsel. "My country's folk", he joked, "have taken the prime of my life. They have eaten my flesh and seem resolved to pick my bones".

25. In 1789, George Washington took the oath of office as president of the newly constituted United States. "Our grand machine has at length begun to work", said Ben Franklin. "I pray God to bless and guide its operations. If any form of government is capable of making a nation happy, ours I think bids fair now for producing that effect. But after all, much depends upon the people who are to be governed".

26. After the first Congress adopted the Bill of Rights as the first ten amendments to the Constitution, Ben Franklin wrote that he was pleased that it had done its work "with a greater degree of temper, prudence, and unanimity than could well have been expected, and our future prospects seem very favorable".

At the same time, the violent convulsions of the French Revolution appalled him, even though he hoped in the end that it would establish a good constitution for France. Two of his best friends had died, one assassinated and the other guillotined.

27. At his death in 1790, Ben Franklin was buried in Christ Church Burial Ground. A crowd of twenty thousand people came, the largest Philadelphia had ever seen. In one of his last letters -- to David Hartley, a British friend, Ben wrote: "God grant that not only the love of liberty, but a thorough knowledge of the rights of man, may pervade all the nations of the earth, so that a philosopher may set his foot anywhere on its surface, and say, 'This is my country'.".

28. In addition to the busybody, Franklin stove, and glass harmonica, Ben Franklin's inventions include:
    o The library stepstool, a chair whose seat could be lifted and folded down to make a short ladder
    o Mechanical arm for reaching books on high shelves (still used in many grocery stores)
    o The rocking chair (when he fitted the legs of his armchair with curved pieces of wood)
    o The "writing chair" -- a type of chair with an "arm" on one side to provide a writing surface (still used in many classrooms)
    o The odometer, used to measure distance along colonial roads used by the postal service
    o A new kind of ship's anchor
    o A candle made from whale oil that made a clear white light and lasted much longer than tallow candles.
    o A pulley system that enabled him to lock and unlock his bedroom door from his bed
    o An improved streetlight by fitting it with four panes of glass and piercing the top and bottom to allow for ventilation
    o Bifocal spectacles -- Ben thought of the idea when he was eating dinner and he noted that if he could see the food on his plate clearly he could not see the face of the person sitting across from him. With bifocals, he could use one pair of glasses for two purposes. [91]

Roger Sherman was smart and very measured in what he would say though he said a lot. He was 55 years old in 1776. James Madison noted that Sherman delivered no less than 138 speeches to the Constitutional Convention in 1787. Jefferson said of him, "Roger has never uttered a foolish word in his life." Although we don't know exactly how tall he was, he has been described as "tall and awkward." Sherman was an expert on monetary policy, having written a scholarly essay on "monetary theory." Because of his knowledge about monetary policy, Sherman was the founder

---

[91] Hollywood, Bill. (2014), *The Ben Franklin Busybody*. PO Box 2606, Cinnaminson, NJ 08077.

who, perhaps better than anyone else, had European banker's number. He knew who they were by name. Sherman understood that European banker's piece d' resistance would be to garner control of this project called the United States of America by commandeering its monetary policy.

Robert Livingston was 28 years old in 1776. He was born in New York City. The city was nothing like the New York City we know today. He was described as "[T]all and commanding, of patrician dignity. Gentle and courteous in his manners, pure and upright in his morals, his benefactions to the poor were numerous and unostentatious." [92]

He was a lawyer who was friends with Napoleon Bonaparte. Livingston negotiated the Louisiana Purchase from France, no doubt a result of his close association with Napoleon. Livingston had brown hair. Livingston thought like a lawyer and is responsible for much of the precise legal language found in the Constitution.

George Washington was a towering man for his time, standing almost 6'4" tall. In 1776 he was 44 years old. He had suffered from Smallpox as a child. As a result, his face was badly pockmarked. He was a soft-spoken man. If ever there were the living embodiment of Teddy Roosevelt's advice to "speak softly and carry a big stick," it would have been George Washington. Some historians believe that Washington's personal timidity was the result of having been raised by a domineering mother. I add parenthetically that another of America's great generals, Dwight David Eisenhower, was also raised by a powerful mother; a mother, by the way, who was a devout peace activist.

Washington proposed marriage twice and was rejected both times. I can't over emphasize the importance of having one's marriage proposals rejected, not once but twice. Marriage proposals were seldom turned down in Washington's day, and for it to have happened twice to him constituted a major blow to Washington's ego and sense of self. Before Washington became the man we revere today, he would have been what I have described as a "deselected male." Washington was "deselected" by women because of his poor dental health, bad skin and soft spoken and shy manner. These traits made it difficult for women to think of Washington as a viable mating choice. So much for judging a book by its cover, wouldn't you say?

George finally married the wealthiest widow in Virginia, Martha Dandridge Custis. Martha Washington had an interesting history that is worth recounting here because it provides great insight into General Washington. The Valley Forge Historical Society wrote this about Martha.

> "At the age of eighteen, Martha was married to Daniel Parke Custis. He was wealthy, handsome and twenty years older than her. Martha set up housekeeping on the Custis plantation, while her husband managed the estate, which encompassed over 17,000 acres. Her husband adored his young, pretty bride and pampered her with the finest clothes and gifts imported from England. They had four children, two died in infancy. John Parke, called "Jacky" and Martha, called "Patsy" were their two surviving children. In 1757, when Martha was twenty-six, Daniel Parke Custis died after a brief illness. Jacky was three and Patsy was less than a year old.
>
> Passing on without a will, Martha was left with the duties of running the household, the estate and raising her children. (Fatherless children were usually "raised" under the auspices of a guardian, even if the mother survived — which meant that another male, primarily a relative, took care of the estates of the children). Her early education proved quite helpful in the task. Her husband's former

---

[92] Lossing, Benson J. (1883), *Eminent Americans: Comprising Brief Biographies of Leading Statesmen, Patriots, Orators and others, Men and Women, Who Have Made American History*. New York: John B. Alden, Pages 105-106.

business manager stayed on to help with the operation of the plantation and she consulted with lawyers when she felt it was necessary.

Sometime later, Martha met a young colonel (several months younger than her) in the Virginia Militia at a cotillion in Williamsburg. **This young colonel fought for the British in the French and Indian War. His desire was to become a commissioned officer in the Royal Army, but the British never considered it. His name was George Washington.**

Martha fell in love and George found her quite attractive. (That she had a good disposition and inherited wealth were an added bonus to the relationship). He had had a crush on a pretty neighbor, Sally Fairfax, but when she married another, he knew he must find a suitable wife for himself.

Martha married George on January 6, 1759. The marriage changed George from an ordinary planter to a substantially wealthy landowner. He had resigned his commission in the militia and so, George, Martha, Jacky (4), and Patsy (2) moved into the enlarged and remodeled Mt. Vernon. Martha was careful and conscientious in running her home, although she and her husband did not pinch pennies when it came to caring for their home. Her children were denied nothing. She pampered and lavished attention and expensive gifts on them.

They lived well at first, but subsequent bad crop returns over a number of years began to take their toll on their finances. They continued their style of living, however, and the constant stream of visitors to entertain did not help their sagging bank account.

When the children were eight and six years of age, a Mr. Walter Magowen was hired as their tutor. At the age of twelve, Patsy had an epileptic seizure and as her condition worsened, she could no longer study. Mr. Magowen left for England soon after Patsy became ill and Jacky was sent to Boucher School in Caroline County (Boucher was moved to Annapolis in 1770). He was an indifferent student, interested more in having fun than being studious. A proposed trip for Jacky was refused by his stepfather because he felt Jacky was too immature, and their finances couldn't handle the expense. He was sent to King's College in New York instead. While there, he met Eleanor "Nelly" Calvert and they got engaged. Soon after he had left for New York, Patsy died at the age of 17. Martha was devastated, but told Jacky to remain in school. By December, Jacky wanted to return to Mt. Vernon, and on the way, on February 3, 1774, Jacky and Nelly were wed at Nelly's home Mt. Airy in Maryland, before heading further south.

Around the same time, the political unrest in the colonies was becoming more vocal. The colonists were being burdened with an inordinate amount of taxes and levies. Some of the friends and acquaintances of Martha and George, people who were visitors to their home, were soon to become the Founding Fathers. Martha herself was considerably torn. Her friends and family were split on both sides. Her son's in-laws were loyalists as well as some of their neighbors. George, however, felt it was his duty to assume some role of leadership at the urging of some of his fellow patriots. He began by working on recruiting and training an armed force. Militia were organized by state. Realizing he would have to be away from home, he asked Jacky and Nelly to stay at Mt. Vernon with Martha, which they did.

George Washington soon became the Commander-in-Chief of the Continental Army and he took charge of his army at Cambridge, Massachusetts in the winter of 1775. Martha, Jacky, Nelly, and some friends traveled two weeks to be with him there for Christmas. Martha stayed with him until June of 1776, but the others returned home soon after Christmas. She wouldn't see him again until March of 1777, where the army was encamped at Morristown for the winter. The General was feeling ill and his wife was there to nurse him. He sent her home when the fighting got closer.

At Mt. Vernon, Martha gathered her family to get the smallpox inoculation...an iffy project because you could contract the disease and die anyway. Martha would not rejoin her husband until February of 1778, where she joined him at Valley Forge. There she entertained some of the officers and the other wives who shared winter quarters there.

Jacky was becoming restless at home, and volunteered to become an aide to his stepfather. He was enlisted only a few days when he died on November 5, 1781 of "camp fever." Jacky was the last of Martha's children and she was quite distraught. George told her to stay at Mt. Vernon instead of being with him that winter. By this time, Jacky and Nelly had six children: Eliza Parke Custis, Martha Parke Custis, Eleanor Parke Custis, a set of twins who died and George Washington Parke Custis. Nelly was in poor health after the birth of her own Nelly and as a result, the young baby was sent to Mt. Vernon to be nursed. With the birth and death of the twins and the subsequent birth of George Washington Parke Custis, he joined his sister at Mt. Vernon.

The war ended on November 25, 1783, when the British left their last stronghold. Washington said farewell to his troops at Fraunces Tavern in New York, shopped for gifts for his grandchildren in Philadelphia and resigned his commission in Annapolis (temporary home of Congress). On Christmas Eve, he rode into Mt. Vernon." [93]

Washington suffered from periodontal disease. By the time he was elected President he had lost most of his teeth. When you see portraits of Washington, see if you can spot the cotton balls Washington stuffed into his cheeks to fill them out as he sat for hours while the painter captured his image on canvas. During battle, Washington would often lead his troops despite severe toothaches. By the way, his teeth were not made of wood, but lead filled natural material made from Walrus and Elephant tusks, in addition to Hippopotamus teeth shaped into human form.

James Madison stood about 5'4" tall and weighed less than 100 pounds. He was so diminutive that he could not meet the physical requirements to join the Continental Army. When he was only 25 years old he drafted Virginia's State Constitution in 1776. Virginia's State Constitution was a very important document because it was Madison's prose in that document that served as the template for the U.S. Constitution. His nickname was "diminutive Jimmy." He served as Jefferson's Secretary of State and, as previously noted, wrote the First Amendment to the Constitution, the "Freedom of Speech" Amendment. Madison was very close to Jefferson, so much so that Jefferson named one of his guest rooms at Monticello after Madison. While visiting Monticello for the research part of this book the accruements of Madison's guest room reminded me of a very personalized space that reflected Madison's personality, and the rest of Monticello. This suggests to me that Jefferson had accepted the distinct personality of his friend and permitted him to manifest that personality by personalizing one of Jefferson's guest rooms.

America's founders were tough, aristocratic, smart and fiercely independent. But more than anything else, these men one and all understood the archetypal enemy, not merely their British enemy. What may be surprising to many of my readers is the fact that America's founders were reluctant warriors. Jefferson bemoaned the fact that he had been forced into making a devil's choice of sorts, namely, the loss of his soul by remaining a British subject or going to war. Shadow men invariably force their victims to make a devil's choice. The bargain shadow men strike or force upon honorable men is an either/or choice: Fight them or lose your soul by going along to get along.

As you learned from the Valley Forge Historical Society, Martha Washington, and her family were like most other families in the Colonies, they were divided in their loyalties between the

---

[93] National Center for the American Revolution, Valley Forge Historical Society (2011), *Martha Washington.*

American idea and the British Crown. One interesting factoid is that the British had turned down George Washington when he applied to become an officer in the British Army. Colonists possessed conflicting loyalties. On the one hand they had a strong loyalty to the crown, but on the other hand, they possessed an equally strong drive to be free from oppression. The genesis of the American idea, the notion of freedom, from the European's perspective, illustrated the validity of the "law of unintended effects or consequences," the direct result of establishing a British colony so far away from the motherland.

Crossing the Atlantic took months. Once on the other "side" of the Atlantic you may as well have been living on another planet. The British became absentee owners who behaved as though they were in charge despite their absence, and technically speaking, they were in charge. What the British did not understand, however, is that **freedom is a state of mind** that needs to be treated very gently lest one arouse freedom's passion. You will learn from this book that shadow men ALWAYS arouse freedom's passion because they never, ever, know when to cease and desist vacuuming freedom of choice from other human beings. This is the reason that shadow men and their agents have spent so much time and effort gelding Americans and their natural passion for freedom and the exercise of free will.

Goethe's masterpiece *Faust* captured the archetypal nature of evil that tried to impose itself upon the Colonies. In 1672, Goethe gave voice to how archetypal shadow men think. If shadow men would talk honestly, this is what they would say:

> *"I am the spirit that negates.*
> *And rightly so, for all that comes to be*
> *Deserves to perish wretchedly;*
> *'Twere better nothing would begin.*
> *Thus everything that that your terms, sin,*
> *Destruction, evil represent—*
> *That is my proper element."* [94]

America's founders were intimately familiar with Goethe's masterpiece *Faust*. Undoubtedly, Jefferson understood what he and his fellow rogues were up to when they set about to "once and for all" hobble and shackle not only their oppressors in their time, but oppressors who would use the machinery of a government to oppress others in the future. Our founders learned from Goethe this principle, if they should be so fortunate to do the impossible, and successfully shackle tyrants by virtue of their Constitution, they and future generations had better be ever vigilant, to wit:

> *"Who holds the devil, let him* **hold him well,**
> *He hardly will be caught a second time."* [95]

I would ask the reader to re-read that last quote from Goethe. As you read it a second time appreciate that there are forces active, right at this very moment, to undo what America's rogue worthies, the men we refer to as America's founders, created and willed to those of us living today.

Shadow men have been actively scheming to undo what America's founders gave to us since it became clear that this idea called "America" would come to fruition. The premeditated assault upon the idea of America, using weaponized psychology as its slayer of choice, began in the 1920's but reached its stride in the late 1950s-60s. Ever since that time the premeditated assault upon the idea of America has only grown stronger and more pervasive.

---

[94] Johann Wolfgang von Goethe, Faust - Part One.
[95] Ibid.

If shadow men hate America's founding documents, what does that suggest to any critical thinker about the importance of those documents? Does it suggest that perhaps, just perhaps, they need to be protected and used for their intended purpose lest they whither away?

America's Constitution **is a document of principles** that is comprised of all the "holding mechanisms" designed from the ground up to shackle and turn the tables on all shadow men, then, now and in the future, once and for all.

Permit me to reiterate this point: To understand our founder's vision of America, the American idea, one must escape the boundaries of BOTH progressive and conservative prisms through which American history has been filtered. And as I will address later in this chapter, any racial prism through which America's history is filtered must be disabled for the truth to emerge.

The infallible prism, memorialized by such nonsense as "I cannot tell a lie" and "Chopping down a cherry tree," along with Howard Zinn's Communist inspired history of America where "the evil European white man sets about to rape and pillage the virgin lands and its peace loving people of the North American Continent," [96] are simply in error, simply wrong.

Its founders understood America's genesis as the beginning of an archetypal battle that transcended the men and the issues of the day. The shot that should have been heard only in the colonies near Concord and Lexington was heard "round the world" because these reluctant warriors we call our founders dared to stand before the ultimate triumvirate, The Royals, The Bankers, and The Anglican Clergy to speak these words: "We declare ourselves and our land to be free of your control." [97]

The Royals then, as now, were so arrogantly secure in their castles that these foolish colonial rogues who comprised America's founders were perceived as rather like a summer cold, i.e., at worst a transitory nuisance. The Anglican clergy of the Church of England doubled down on their well-practiced art of condemning America's founders as violating God's laws. But when one actually lives in God's country and knows God by experience, mere mortals dressed like the official impresarios of the Royals are less persuasive than they may have been led to believe by their fawning parishioners and their bosses back in London.

One such Anglican minister loyal to the Crown was Samuel Seabury.

---

[96] Zinn, Howard. (1980), *A People's History of the United States.* Harper Collins, New York, New York.
[97] *The Shot Heard Round the World* was originally from the opening stanza of Ralph Waldo Emerson's "Concord Hymn" (1837), and referred to the first shot of the American Revolutionary War. According to Emerson's poem, this pivotal shot occurred at the North Bridge in Concord, Massachusetts, where the first British soldiers were killed in the battles of Lexington and Concord.

Anglican Minister Samuel Seabury.

Seabury was horrified that this thing that called itself the Continental Congress dared to challenge the "word of God." Seabury condemned our founders as having been overtaken by what he called, "preposterous pride."

"Seabury followed his father into the Anglican ministry and in 1766 settled in the parish of Westchester, New York. A defender of religious orthodoxy, he was greatly alarmed by the appearance of the First Continental Congress and their attempts to halt imports from Great Britain. In Letters of a Westchester Farmer and other writings, Seabury charged Congress with producing "a venomous brood of scorpions to sting us to death." **Seabury had a religious explanation for the patriots' rash words and actions: "Preposterous pride! It defeats the end it aims at" and cheated people from the capacity "to learn prudence from our own misconduct."** *He attributed the urge for independence to emotionalism, a lack of reason: "The words independency and colony convey contradictory meanings." Colonies, by definition, were dependent, not free.*

Seabury was arrested late in 1775 and held prisoner in New Haven, Connecticut, for six weeks, refusing to admit authorship of his Loyalists tracts. He then returned to British-controlled New York City, where he remained during the war. Late in 1776 he recalled that he had responded to the "present unnatural rebellion" by endeavoring "to stem the torrent of popular clamor, to recall the people to the use of their reason, and to retain them in their loyalty and allegiance." He remained in the United States after the war and eventually became a loyal citizen." [98]

It was not the Royals, nor their religious handmaidens, who truly understood the depth and breadth of the threat represented by America's founders. It was the financiers and their investment bankers who immediately recognized these upstarts as representatives of their **archetypal enemies**.

---

[98] TAHPDX, Portland State University, U.S. Dept. of Education. (2011), *Great Decisions in U.S. History.*

Financiers, in association with their empowering shadow men who had the bigger piece of the action had, after all, financed this adventure that had surprisingly morphed into this idea named "America."

The success of this "new" endeavor bestowed upon the heirs of those who first landed on Plymouth Rock a desire for autonomy from their greedy masters. America's founders were physically separated by virtue of the Atlantic from those whose name appeared on America's "pink slip." But it wasn't the physical separation, important though it was, that proved to be the determining factor; it was the separation of spirit, a chasm greater than the Atlantic Ocean that fueled the American Revolution.

Both sides in this battle understood the other as their archetypal foe, not just men at odds over specific issues limited to their particular time in history. Historians have traditionally rendered the American Revolution down to specific conflicts, e.g., tax acts, stamp acts, molasses taxes, along with any number of specific points of friction between the Crown and the American rogues. And though their points are no less important, historians underestimated the fundamental psychological discordance in play. The American experiment pitted servitude by virtue of social class and history against the revolutionary notion of a God given right to be free from the shackles of class and provenance. It was, scientifically speaking, a battle of archetypal foes of grand proportion. It was a battle of equal opportunity and merit versus opportunity born of class or chosen status. It was good v. evil.

What did European financiers, investment bankers and their business dynasties have to do with the Colonies, you may ask? Permit me to respond with a question: Who do you think paid for the development of the Colonies? Bankers, NOT Queen Isabella, financed Christopher Columbus. A financier by the name of Luis de Santangelo advanced the sum of 17,000 ducats, approximately 50,000 pounds back in the day, to finance Columbus' August 3, 1492 voyage.

You may recall from your American history lessons that the Mayflower and its "Pilgrims" landed on Plymouth Rock in 1620. What you most likely were never taught is that in order to make that trip the adventurers/investors (The terms the men and women who made the trip used to describe themselves) had to indebt themselves to their English financiers in order to fund their trip.

> *"Fraught with risk, the Mayflower project endured a long period of trial, experiment and error. Deeply in debt to their backers in London, and chronically short of supplies to keep their feet shod, their muskets loaded and their small boats afloat, they needed a commodity to send back to England to be swapped for silver coins or used to redeem their IOU's. They eventually found it in the quantities they needed, up here in Maine. They bought it from the people who lived in the country below the watershed in what we now call Quebec and The United States. This was where the moment of maturity occurred. The place where they passed across an emotional frontier, form the line that separates insecure ambition from likely success."[99]*

In late December in 1606, some 12 years *before* the Mayflower landed on Plymouth Rock, 105 adventurers/investors departed England for the "new" world in three ships. The ships were named *The Susan Constant, The Discovery* and *The Godspeed*. Christopher Newport commanded the ships on a grueling 4 month long trip across the Atlantic. 105 men and women landed near Chesapeake Bay on April 26, 1607.

The Susan Constant, The Discovery, The Godspeed and *The Mayflower* voyages were business ventures. The adventurers/investors earned a place on these ships by purchasing shares of stock in something

---

[99] Bunker, Nick. (2010), *Making Haste from Babylon: The Mayflower Pilgrims and Their World: A NEW HISTORY*. Alfred A. Knopf, Toronto, Canada.

called *The Virginia Company*. This company was subsumed under The Merchant Adventurers Investment Group. The Merchant Adventurers had been around since the 15th Century.

In 1621, one year after the Mayflower landed on Plymouth Rock, another ship made the voyage to the new world as part of the same business venture. This vessel was named, aptly enough, *The Fortune*. *The Fortune* arrived off Cape Cod on November 9, 1621 and arrived in Plymouth Bay at the end of the month. The ship only stayed at Plymouth about three weeks unloading its cargo. *The Fortune* departed for England on December 13, 1621.

To give you a sense of the dangers associated with crossing the Atlantic, on January 19, 1622, The Fortune was overtaken and seized by a French warship. Passengers and crew were held under guard in France for about a month. The French seized *The Fortune's* cargo. *The Fortune* finally arrived back in England on February 17, 1622." [100]

Before *The Virginia Company* funded these various treks across the Atlantic, Sir Walter Raleigh tried to exploit the riches of the North American Continent, on behalf of Queen Elizabeth, by sailing to the new world in 1580. Raleigh's ship landed on what would now be the North Carolina Coast. This failed adventure became known as the Lost Colony after disease and famine killed a large number of these early adventurers, which scuttled the mission.

Raleigh was born a commoner but managed to catch the eye of Queen Elizabeth who, true to her shadow man's sexual proclivities, found Walter to be an attractive and suitable plaything she could use for her carnal pleasures. She knighted him for his Royal performances in her boudoir, and thus, he became *Sir* Walter Raleigh. I would ask the reader to compare the truth about Raleigh and the Queen as just presented versus what you were probably taught. If your mental image of Sir Walter Raleigh is that of a man who laid his jacket across a puddle of water for the benefit of Queen Elizabeth, please stand corrected, as historians insist this event never occurred.

Raleigh lays down his coat for Queen Elizabeth (This never happened).

Another reward bestowed upon this commoner turned sexual courtier took place when Elizabeth funded his adventure to the "new" world. Raleigh, of course, promised the Queen that all of the gold and other riches he expected to find in the new world would become Elizabeth's riches

[100] Charles Edward Banks, (2006), *The English Ancestry and Homes of the Pilgrim Fathers: who came to Plymouth on the "Mayflower" in 1620, the "Fortune" in 1621, and the "Anne" and the "Little James" in 1623* (Baltimore: Genealogical Publishing Co.

upon return. Eventually, as Goethe was yet to warn, Raleigh was destined to disappoint his shadow man/benefactor and she had him gleefully beheaded. This only goes to prove the limits of what chivalry and sexual performance can buy you.

Of all the motives that drove the adventurers and investors to the new world, none was more important than the financial independence motive. No doubt the adventurers/investors had their personal motivations to make the trip, but to believe that any of them labored under the belief that they were escaping the control of the Anglican Church or its Monarch makes better fiction than truth. If anything, the adventurers/investors would have reasoned that by further indebting themselves to the King's financiers, they would fall under greater control of the Monarchy and its Anglican clergy. What these men wanted was a piece of land they could call their own, all the while remaining loyal British subjects. In one sense, coming to the new world represented an exercise in upward social mobility. As Englishman John Locke had argued, man was entitled by God to life, liberty and property. It was the American rogues who rewrote Locke's words to read "life, liberty and the pursuit of happiness."

Wealthy investors created *The Virginia Company* and expected to make millions of pounds of profits from it. These men functioned similarly to investment bankers, as one might find on Wall Street, only this "Wall Street" was located in London in an area known as "Canary Wharf." No business venture, of course, was created without the permission of the King, and so it was here. The King gave his permission to *The Virginia Company* to sell stock under the auspices of a Royal Charter.

Proceeds from the sale of stock financed the ships, supplies and paid to find and equip the deck hands. A single share of stock in *The Virginia Company* cost 12 pounds 10 shillings. That was a lot of money to a commoner, equaling about six month's wages. *The Virginia Company* engaged in a very sophisticated PR campaign in order to convince people to become an investor. They printed pamphlets, put on plays, persuaded Anglican clergy to give positive sermons about the virtues of taking a risk in the "new" world. Do you think the Anglican clergy would have encouraged those first adventurers/investors to buy tickets had they thought for a moment that these men and women were trying to escape their control?

Approximately 1700 people purchased shares. Anyone with enough money could purchase shares. The largest single investor was Lord de la Warr, aka, Thomas West. Not surprisingly, West not only purchased the largest block of shares, but also the title of the first governor of Virginia in 1610, a post he held for eight years. In addition to these marketing schemes, company executives created lotteries in London and surrounding areas. These lotteries promised the winner up to £ 5,000 sterling. The lotteries became so successful (raising more than £ 29,000 before they ended in 1621), that they eventually became the primary source of investment income for *The Virginia Company*.

The first CEO of *The Virginia Company* was its treasurer, Sir Thomas Smythe. Stockholders were promised that after a given period of time, after the bulk of the riches they expected to find and develop had been transferred to the King, a little plot of land could be homesteaded to the adventurer/investor. *The Virginia Company* demanded of laborers (not investors) that they had to work for the Company for no less than seven years for a minimal wage. After seven years, they would be released from service, with the *possibility* of being granted their own little plot of land.

The King, true to his shadow man's personality, intended *The Virginia Company* to increase the land over which he had control. The King planned for the natives living in Virginia to be converted to the King's brand of Christianity. This plan of conversion was not about spreading the word of the Gospel, per se, it was about using the Church of England, a subsidiary of the King, as a means to psychologically control the natives for the benefit of the Monarch. The reasoning was impeccable, if not ethnocentric, "it worked in the British Isles and its Indian colonies; therefore, it will work in the new world."

The Virginia Company, by and through the King, gave the men and women explicit directions on what to do and how to behave. What follows is the actual text of the directions and guidelines each adventurer/investor had to follow once he/she landed in the new world:

"As we doubt not but you will have especial care to observe the ordinances set down by the King's Majesty and delivered unto you under the Privy Seal; so for your better directions upon your first landing we have thought good to recommend unto your care these instructions and articles following.

When it shall please God to send you on the coast of Virginia, you shall do your best endeavour to find out a safe port in the entrance of some navigable river, making choice of such a one as runneth farthest into the land, and if you happen to discover divers portable rivers, and amongst them any one that hath two main branches, if the difference be not great, make choice of that which bendeth most toward the North-West for that way you shall soonest find the other sea.

When you have made choice of the river on which you mean to settle, be not hasty in landing your victuals and munitions; but first let Captain Newport discover how far that river may be found navigable, that you make election of the strongest, most wholesome and fertile place; for if you make many removes, besides the loss of time, you shall greatly spoil your victuals and your caske, and with great pain transport it in small boats.

But if you choose your place so far up as a bark of fifty tuns will float, then you may lay all your provisions ashore with ease, and the better receive the trade of all the countries about you in the land; and such a place you may perchance find a hundred miles from the river's mouth, and the further up the better. For if you sit down near the entrance, except it be in some island that is strong by nature, an enemy that may approach you on even ground, may easily pull you out; and if he be driven to seek you a hundred miles [in] the land in boats, you shall from both sides of the river where it is narrowest, so beat them with your muskets as they shall never be able to prevail against you.

And to the end that you be not surprised as the French were in Florida by Melindus, and the Spaniard in the same place by the French, you shall do well to make this double provision. First, erect a little stoure at the mouth of the river that may lodge some ten men; with whom you shall leave a light boat, that when any fleet shall be in sight, they may come with speed to give you warning.

Secondly, you must in no case suffer any of the native people of the country to inhabit between you and the sea coast; for you cannot carry yourselves so towards them, but they will grow discontented with your habitation, and be ready to guide and assist any nation that shall come to invade you; and if you neglect this, you neglect your safety.

When you have discovered as far up the river as you mean to plant yourselves, and landed your victuals and munitions; to the end that every man may know his charge, you shall do well to divide your six score men into three parts; whereof one party of them you may appoint to fortifie and build, of which your first work must be your storehouse for victuals; the other you may imploy in preparing your ground and sowing your corn and roots; the other ten of these forty you must leave as centinel at the haven's mouth. The other forty you may imploy for two months in discovery of the river above you, and on the country about you; which charge Captain Newport and Captain Gosnold may undertake of these forty discoverers. When they do espie any high lands or hills, Captain Gosnold may take twenty of the company to cross over the lands, and carrying a half dozen pickaxes to try if they can find any minerals. The other twenty may go on by river, and pitch up boughs upon the bank's side, by which the other boats shall follow them by the same turnings. You may also take with them a wherry, such as is used here in the Thames; by which you may send back to the President for supply of munition or any other want, that you may not be driven to return for every small defect.

You must observe if you can, whether the river on which you plant doth spring out of mountains or out of lakes. If it be out of any lake, the passage to the other sea will be more easy, and [it] is like enough, that out of the same lake you shall find some spring which run[s] the contrary way towards the East India Sea; for the great and famous rivers of Volga, Tan[a]is and Dwina have three heads near joynd; and yet the one falleth into the Caspian Sea, the other into the Euxine Sea, and the third into the Paelonian Sea.

In all your passages you must have great care not to offend the naturals [natives], if you can eschew it; and imploy some few of your company to trade with them for corn and all other . . . victuals if you have any; and this you must do before that they perceive you mean to plant among them; for not being sure how your own seed corn will prosper the first year, to avoid the danger of famine, use and endeavour to store yourselves of the country corn.

Your discoverers that pass over land with hired guides, must look well to them that they slip not from them: and for more assurance, let them take a compass with them, and write down how far they go upon every point of the compass; for that country having no way nor path, if that your guides run from you in the great woods or desert, you shall hardly ever find a passage back.

And how weary so ever your soldiers be, let them never trust the country people with the carriage of their weapons; for if they run from you with your shott, which they only fear, they will easily kill them all with their arrows. And whensoever any of yours shoots before them, be sure they may be chosen out of your best marksmen; for if they see your learners miss what they aim at, they will think the weapon not so terrible, and thereby will be bould to assault you.

Above all things, do not advertize the killing of any of your men, that the country people may know it; if they perceive that they are but common men, and that with the loss of many of theirs they diminish any part of yours, they will make many adventures upon you. If the country be populous, you shall do well also, not to let them see or know of your sick men, if you have any; which may also encourage them to many enterprizes.

You must take especial care that you choose a seat for habitation that shall not be over burthened with woods near your town; for all the men you have, shall not be able to cleanse twenty acres a year; besides that it may serve for a covert for your enemies round about.

Neither must you plant in a low or moist place, because it will prove unhealthfull. You shall judge of the good air by the people; for some part of that coast where the lands are low, have their people blear eyed, and with swollen bellies and legs; but if the naturals be strong and clean made, it is a true sign of a wholesome soil.

You must take order to draw up the pinnace that is left with you, under the fort: and take her sails and anchors ashore, all but a small kedge to ride by; least some ill-dispositioned persons slip away with her.

You must take care that your marriners that go for wages, do not mar your trade; for those that mind not to inhabite, for a little gain will debase the estimation of exchange, and hinder the trade for ever after; and therefore you shall not admit or suffer any person whatsoever, other than such as shall be appointed by the President and Counsel there, to buy any merchandizes or other things whatsoever.

It were necessary that all your carpenters and other such like workmen about building do first build your storehouse and those other rooms of publick and necessary use before any house be set up for any private person: and though the workman may belong to any private persons yet let them all work together first for the company and then for private men.

And seeing order is at the same price with confusion, it shall be adviseably done to set your houses even and by a line, that your street may have a good breadth, and be carried square about your market place and every street's end opening into it; that from thence, with a few field pieces, you may command every street throughout; which market place you may also fortify if you think it needfull.

You shall do well to send a perfect relation by Captaine Newport of all that is done, what height you are seated, how far into the land, what commodities you find, what soil, woods and their several kinds, and so of all other things else to advertise particularly; and to suffer no man to return but by pasport from the President and Counsel, nor to write any letter of anything that may discourage others.

Lastly and chiefly the way to prosper and achieve good success is to make yourselves all of one mind for the good of your country and your own, and to serve and fear God the Giver of all Goodness, for every plantation which our Heavenly Father hath not planted shall be rooted out." [101]

Shadow men from Spain and France all had essentially the same idea, as did their English intramural competitors. Each had their sights set on a direct route to trade with the Orient. Ambitious Europeans envisioned they would find a river that traversed east to west the entirety of the North American Continent and take them to the shores of the Pacific Ocean. The benefits envisioned, the result of finding this route and settling the "new" world, were staggering. Benefits included developing new industries from the land (lumber, tobacco, fur, mining) of which the surplus could be sold to the Orient. Should the Colonies take hold and become as successful as imagined, they would represent a new market for goods and a new source of revenue from taxes of all color and stripe.

The costs associated with settling the Virginia colonies eventually became too much for *The Virginia Company*. Despite all the clever marketing the company ran an ever-growing deficit. This meant that stockholders (similar to bond holders) could no longer be paid in pounds, so the company promised them land in lieu of money. In 1618 Sir Edwin Sandys replaced Smythe as treasurer. Eventually, *The Virginia Company* went Bankrupt, partially the result of the mismanagement of funds by Company leaders who pocketed any excess cash for themselves. Sound familiar?

When word got out about the 1622 massacre of settlers at the hand of the locals, interest in coming to America to find one's fortune dried up. King James I sent his agents to investigate the Company and the Virginia Colony. As a result of his investigations, James I revoked the Company's charter. In 1624, Virginia became a royal colony, with the colonists directly answerable to and under the control of the Monarch's privy council.

With regard to the massacre in 1622, lest there be no mistake, Native Americans living in Virginia had their own shadow men who took the form of Chiefs and blood-line family dynasties. The United States National Park Service's historians had this to say about the Native Americans encountered by the adventurers/investors who landed on Plymouth Rock:

"When the English arrived in Virginia in 1607 and created the first permanent English settlement in North America at Jamestown, they did not encounter an uninhabited land. An

---

[101] University of Groningen. (2012), *American History: Instructions for the Virginia Colony 1606.*

estimated 50,000 Virginia Indians had called what is now the Commonwealth of Virginia home for more than 12,000 years. The tribes the English encountered first, and most often, belonged to the **powerful Powhatan Chiefdom***. The land occupied by the Powhatan Indians encompassed all of Tidewater Virginia, from the Potomac River in the north to south of the James River, and parts of the Eastern Shore. This area, which they called Tsenacommacah, was about 100 miles long from north to south and about 100 miles wide from southeast to northwest. Before the arrival of foreigners, and their unknown diseases, the Powhatan Indians were estimated to have numbered 25,000.*

By 1607, the Powhatan Chiefdom numbered approximately 15,000. **Chief Powhatan, whose given name was Wahunsunacock, was the mamanatowick (paramount chief) of the Powhatan Chiefdom.** *In the sixteenth century,* **he** <u>**inherited**</u> **six tribes from his mother or someone related to her; Powhatan society was matrilineal so descent was passed through the mother's line.** *By 1607, the Powhatan Chiefdom had more than 30 different tribes, each of which had its own chief (weroance/weroansqua). All had been gained* **through marriage alliance or coercion and were "ruled" by and had to pay "tribute" to Powhatan.***"* [102]

The founder of Jamestown, John Smith, probably had a more realistic view of the natives living in the Jamestown area. Recall that it was Smith who was captured by the King, or Chief of the Powatan natives and was just about to be mercilessly killed when the 11 year-old daughter of the Chief, not yet accustomed to ritualized executions, pleaded for Smith's life. The eleven year-old's father reluctantly acceded to her wishes. In 1622 Smith would write in his *New England Trials*: "God made Pocahontas, the King's daughter the means to deliver me."

All human beings tend to stratify into three major groupings, 1. Shadow men; 2. Shadow men's representatives and their on-site agents, and 3. The masses. The naïve who unconsciously soothe their P.C. nerves by embracing comic book-like depictions of peaceful Native Americans, living among one another in an egalitarian-collectivist utopia full of rainbows, moccasins, dream catchers, peace pipes and rhythmic dance, have deluded themselves in service to their own soothing virtual reality at the expense of the unnerving and non-politically correct real world truth.

The Powhatan chiefs were shadow men who had earned their rightful place at the top of the stratification heap by and through violence, coercion and matriarchal bloodlines. In this respect, they were virtually identical to their European shadow men counterparts, save for the matriarchal bloodlines. The European adventurers/investors were alien commoners who found themselves among people who were no strangers to violence and turf wars. I remind the reader that Native Americans are not "native" to the North American Continent. So-called Native Americans emigrated here, like everyone else. In the instance of so-called Native Americans, they made their way across the Bering Straits and happily fought their way to dominance over the locals on the North American Continent. None of those original "natives" survived, not even on reservations, so we know very little about them except for the fact that America's future "natives" who crossed the Bering Straits killed each and every last one of the natives living in America.

---

[102] National Park Service. (2014), *Historic Jamestown: The Powhatan Indian World.*
See: Gleach, Frederic W. (1997), *Powhatan's World and Colonial Virginia: A Conflict of Cultures.* Lincoln: The University of Nebraska Press.

Consider this, as you simultaneously recall your history lessons that depicted peaceful Native Americans bringing foodstuffs to the hungry Europeans as an act of peace and multiculturalism, only to be betrayed and killed by white men:

> *"The Indian Massacre of 1622 took place in the English Colony of Virginia, on Friday, March 22, 1622. Captain John Smith related in his History of Virginia that braves of the Powhatan Confederacy "came unarmed into our houses with deer, turkeys, fish, fruits, and other provisions to sell to us." [103] Suddenly the Powhatan grabbed any tools or weapons available to them and killed any English settlers who were in sight, including* **men, women and <u>children</u> of all ages.** **Chief Opechancanough led a coordinated series of surprise attacks of the Powhatan Confederacy that killed 347 people, a quarter of the English population of Jamestown."** [104]

There is little doubt in this forensic scientist's mind, nor the historians who have studied this blood bath, that the Mamanatowick premeditated this massacre against the "new" Europeans using feigned overtures of peaceful trade in order to take advantage of the trusting European aliens whose mere presence threatened his absolute control and wealth.   Shadow men never, ever, share. The indigenous shadow men wanted **every square inch of North America for themselves**. They had eradicated their predecessors and they were intent upon removing ANY competing group who would challenge their control, including other competing "native" tribes.   Simply put, they were unwilling to peacefully coexist with their fellow native Americans and certainly not the aliens from Europe.

North of Virginia, the Massachusetts Native Americans were named the Wampanoag tribe.

> *"<u>Right</u>* **before** *the Pilgrims landed in 1620, the Wampanoag Indians saw their population greatly reduced due to disease. One interesting fact that you may not know is that the tradition of Thanksgiving was adopted from the Wampanoag Indians interaction with the Pilgrims. However,* **Chief Metacomet, sometimes known as King Philip, declared war on the pilgrims. The growing number of English were displacing the Wampanoag Indians and converting them to their faith.** *(Christianity was changing the power matrix of the Native's power structure.) Overall, King Philip felt the English were having negative affects on the ways of his tribe. The war only lasted a year, but it was the bloodiest of the Indian Wars, with most of the Wampanoag Indians and their allies, the Narraganset, being killed."* [105]

Before the arrival of the Plymouth adventurers/investors the Wampanoag found themselves in a perpetual and never ending war with their intramural Native American competitors.   Like all people, the shadow men of each tribe were dedicated to consuming more of everything though there was enough for all, to wit:

> *"The Wampanoags had suffered a series of losses, of land, spirit and numbers (killed, maimed & massacred)* [106] *in the decade* **<u>before</u>** *the Pilgrims landed.* **The Tarrantine War resulted**

---

[103] James Mooney, (1907), *The Powhatan Confederacy, Past and Present,* American Anthropologist 9, no. 1 (Jan. – Mar., 129–52.

[104] Hoffer, Peter. (2000), *The Brave New World: A History of Early America.* JHU Press. p. 132. ISBN 0-8018-8483-7.

[105] Indians.org. (2014), *Wampanoag Indians.*

[106] The term "numbers" is a euphemism for killing, maiming and massacring. One group of Native American shadow men wanted the coastal areas inhabited by other Native Americans, brothers and they used violence to take it.

in the Micmac tribes taking the coast from the Penobscot tribes. After their victory, the Micmac began attacking the Wampanoag. The Pequot tribes moved into Connecticut and began to harry them there. Those tribes who traded with the Europeans during this time also succumbed to diseases as epidemics occurred. In some of the Wampanoag tribes as many as ninety percent of the people died. Tribes and tribal groups within the Wampanoags reorganized with the population decline. Where there had been ten groups, they reorganized in some places as one. The Wampanoags were now forced to submit to the Narragansett, an inland rival. The Narragansett had begun to demand tribute (a tax on their fellow native Americans) from the Wampanoags. With the arrival of the Europeans, Massasoit, Head Sachem of the Wampanoags, hoped that they would aid them in overcoming the Narragansett's oppression.

In 1621, Massasoit signed over about 12000 acres to the Pilgrims. The Narragansett became suspicious of the alliance between the Wampanoag and the English. However, before the Narragansett could react, they were attacked by the Pequot. When Massasoit became ill in 1623, the English nursed him back to health. The Plymouth Colony continued to grow and in 1632, when the Narragansett had finished their war with the Pequot and Mohawk, they attacked Massasoit's village of Sowam. With English aid, the Wampanoag's drove off the Narragansett." [107]

I suspect that this history is new to many readers, especially those multitudes who have been taught by anti-American revolutionaries. The reality I've presented here is consistent with known patterns in human behavior. People share a common genotype, thus behavioral profile. Men and women tend to compete with one another, but when times are tough they tend to form alliances. Choice Theory, a set of behavioral principles rooted in economics, would have predicted exactly happened in early America between and among the Natives and the Europeans. The fact that indigenous peoples found European Christian settlers much more reasonable than their fellow shadow men who led other indigenous peoples should not surprise anyone schooled in the science of human behavior or the intramural conflicts between and among Native Americans long preceded by the influx by Europeans.

As previously documented, and as noted by Aldous Huxley, human beings tend to stratify into high, middle and low demarcations. Shadow men, whether they call themselves Kings, Queens, Chiefs, Presidents, Potentates, Sheiks, Brahma, what have you, are insatiable consumers of other people's wealth, land and, by definition, freedom. Why this should have ever been imagined to have not been the case when it came to Native Americans BEFORE the white man arrived is a study in how powerful mind control artists have successfully brainwashed modern Americans. The mind control artist's client's needed to portray Native Americans in a way that served their political agenda of subversion of the American idea. Moreover, the emotional needs of the European masses (self-punishing guilt) that had been inculcated into them, trumped common sense and documented historical fact. The Oxford Companion to U.S. History wrote this about the peaceful Native Americans converted to a Christian, non-violent way of life:

"Among most Indian groups east of Mississippi River on the eve of European contact— including the Iroquois and Cherokee—warfare served both social-psychological and demographic functions. Indians waged war against one another to help members of their group cope with the grief experienced at the loss of a loved one or to avenge the death of a relative. Known as "mourning

---

[107] Hicks, Jeanne. (2011), *Wampanoag*, in Ancestry.com

wars," **these conflicts were intended to acquire captives who would in turn either be ceremonially tortured to death or adopted into the group**

> *[W]ars on the Plains and in the Southwest differed from those in the Eastern Woodlands in that these primarily broke out between peoples pursuing two distinct lifestyles—nomadic and horticulturist. While such groups often forged symbiotic relationships, e.g., exchanging crops for buffalo meat, these contacts sometimes degenerated into nomadic raids on villages.[108]*

S. C. Gwynne, Pulitzer Prize winning author of *Empire Of The Summer Moon: Quanah Parker and the Rise and Fall of the Comanche, the Most Powerful Indian Tribe in American History*, has written:

> *'No tribe in the history of the Spanish, French, Mexican, Texan, and American occupations of this land had ever caused so much havoc and death. None was even a close second [T]he logic of Comanche raids was straightforward:* **All the men were killed, and any men who were captured alive were tortured; the captive women were gang raped. Babies were invariably killed."** [109] (Emphasis Added)

I make reference to the Comanche because the truth as portrayed by the media entertainment complex should come with a free copy of George Orwell's 1984. For those who don't know, The Lone Ranger's sidekick & trusty companion was a Comanche named Tonto. Compare Gwynne's Pulitzer Prize winning history of the Comanche tribe with the images that more than likely have embedded themselves into your psyche, to wit:

Clayton Moore/Jay Silverheels: The Lone Ranger and Tonto (1950's TV Series).

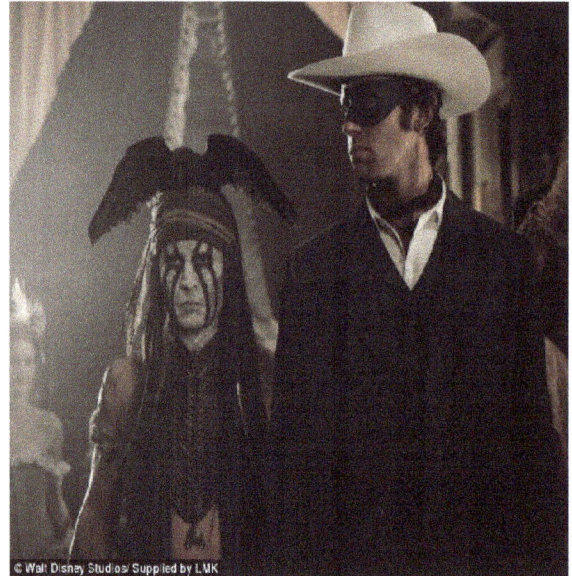

Armie Hammer/Johnny Depp: The Lone Ranger.

This book is not an academic exercise in apologetics for any one person's or group's bad behavior, whether it is a criticism of human sacrifice as practiced by some Native Americans before

---

[108] The Oxford Companion to American Military History. (2000), by Oxford University Press, Inc.
[109] Gwynne, S.C. (2010), *Empire Of The Summer Moon: Quanah Parker and the Rise and Fall of the Comanches, the Most Powerful Indian Tribe in American History.* Scribner, New York, London, Toronto, Sidney.

Europeans arrived on the continent or aggressive proselytism of Christianity by Europeans or the effect European culture had upon Native American's existent way of life or vice versa. My point is singular: Cartoonish depictions of good and bad always fail to integrate the truths about all people, especially the shadow men who have always been with us no matter what you call them.

The English were not the only settlers of the new world. Cooperation between Squanto and the English adventurers/investors was a product of Squanto's personal history at the hands of the Spanish and the Wampanoag's need to barter their survival skills for English assistance against their intramural Native American competitors, e.g., the Narragansett.

The cooperation between the stockholders in *The Virginia Company* and the Wampanoag was, like all human interactions, much more complex and layered than any two-dimensional history you may have been taught. I am more comfortable as a forensic scientist constructing a history from known facts that comport with known patterns in human behavior than a history that is nothing more than a series of psychological projections consciously or unconsciously purposed to idealize or demonize either the colonists or the Native Americans of their time. What is incontrovertible is that natural selection pressures were intense and impacted everyone involved in this new venture. Only the very strong survived the journey across the Atlantic and only the stronger yet overcame tremendous hardship to establish colonies in this "new" world.

Over the next hundred years the children, grand children and great grand children of these very first adventurers/investors became the civilization the English referred to as "The Colonies." They were a tough breed that had earned their intimate understanding and appreciation for what they had overcome in order to experience the fruits of their labor. These fruits they were willing to share, but only up to a point. Their freedom, however, was not negotiable. That point was made an issue by the greed, avarice and oppression of those who long ago financed their great, great grandfather's and grandmother's trip to what was then the "new" world. A place they now called their home.

The shadow men back in England took a different view of "The Colonies." The adventurers/investors were merely off-site subjects of the Crown, essentially chattel. The Royals had never forgotten that it was they, by and through their various charters given to wealthy investment banker types and their companies, that had financed the upstarts now successfully exploiting the riches of the "new" world. The "Colonies" were a plume du chapeau for the English Royals and, more importantly, an ever growing and reliable source of income. And with most major world events, money was key.

Economic conditions in England were not good at the end of the 17th Century, which made the Colonies even more important to the debt ridden Royals. Why so much debt? France had surprised its English archrival with a series of stinging defeats. Most notably, the crushing defeat at Beachy Head convinced the British that they were going to lose their war with France unless they took drastic steps to strengthen their military, and that takes a lot of money.

Britain regrouped its war effort under King William III with plans to build the world's largest and most powerful navy. As you will learn, however, King William did not have the funds to finance his naval project and he had already taxed his citizens to the breaking point.

The lead up to the American Revolution can be traced to economic conditions within Britain and its intramural battle with proxies for the Roman Papacy, France, Spain and Portugal, for world domination. The creation of the Bank of England in 1694 under King William, aka "William of Orange" and Queen Mary was the direct result of debt incurred by Britain's long and costly war with France under Louis "Quatorze." (Louis XIV).

Please keep in mind Napoleon's Monetary Axiom as you contemplate the lead up to the American Revolution: *Great wealth attracts thieves and manipulation.* Also, keep in mind that Jefferson and his fellow revolutionaries knew very well the history I am about to recount to you.

The rivalry between shadow men in Europe, notably the Papacy under Clement VII and King Henry VIII, set the stage for the animus between Anglican shadow men and their Roman rivals which, when all was said and done, nearly bankrupted Britain. William of Orange presided over one of these wars with Catholic France that would result in the creation of The Bank of England in 1694. The BBC's historians created a scholarly review of William of Orange in 2014. We quote from their original work in what follows:

> *"William was born on November 4, 1650 in The Hague. The young William was groomed to lead the powerful House of Orange and to become a 'Stadtholder', or head of state of the Dutch Republic. He learned to be astute and distrustful from an early age.*
>
> *William became a hero to his people in 1673 when he drove the invading Catholic forces of Louis XIV of France out of most of the Dutch Republic.* **Brought up to believe he was an instrument of God**, *William could be impatient with others. This trait is evidenced by his behaviour in the chambers of the Dutch government.* [110]

To understand what Jefferson understood, we must go back to the reign of Henry VIII. The British Monarch asked for an annulment of his marriage to Catherine of Aragon, a request Pope Clement VII denied. This is the same Pope that was busy issuing his own "new" world charters (Papal Bulls) that gave rights to Spain and Portugal to explore the North American Continent. The expeditions were envisioned for the joint benefit of both the Pope and the shadow men in Spain and Portugal who were, along with the British, after the riches of the "new" world. At one time, the British and the Pope functioned as joint masters of control over the British. That all changed with the reign of Henry VIII.

Henry VIII and his wife, Catherine of Aragon, were Roman Catholic followers. Henry and Catherine had been married for 23 years without the couple producing a son to carry on Henry's bloodline. True to his shadow man personality, Henry began looking for a new wife who could bear him healthy sons. A young and sexy Anne Boleyn caught his eye. Henry knew the Pope would never give him a divorce, but Henry reasoned that considering the source of the request, the Pope would probably, at the very least, give him an annulment of his marriage to Catherine.

Pope Clement denied Henry's request for one very important reason. And no, not because Catholics looked unkindly upon divorce, though that was and is true. Catherine's nephew, Emperor Charles V of Spain, had laid siege to Rome and was, for all intents and purposes, holding the Pope as prisoner. The Pope was a target because of the Catholic Church's massive wealth under the control of the Pope, thanks in part to The Knights Templar, who were by now enemies of the Papacy. The increasing power of Protestantism and Napoleon's Monetary Axiom fueled what came to be known as the "Sack of Rome."

> *"The sack of Rome began on May 6, 1527 when an army of Spanish Catholics and Lutherans beholden to Charles V and led by Charles III marched into Rome rebelliously, a city the troops held in a state of siege for nine months. When marauding, unpaid troops entered the city, they were bent on plundering and proceeded to loot and pillage ceaselessly for eight days, inflicting harsh treatment upon those who were directly associated with the Roman Catholic Church, most notably priests, monks, and nuns. The rampaging invaders raped nuns as well as female residents of Rome.*

---

[110] British Broadcasting Corporation (BBC). (2004), *History: King William III.*

They destroyed many of the city's most valued and beautiful frescoes and smashed priceless statuary. This was clearly a battle that largely resulted from the growing ascendancy of Protestantism in northern Europe.

Pope Clement VII, protected by his cadre of Swiss Guards, fled the Vatican, just one step ahead of the invaders, taking refuge in the castle of Sant' Angelo. Many of Pope Clement's guards were killed. The invaders from the north charged through the streets, humiliating the Romans in every possible way. They mocked them by dressing their leader in papal garb and leading him around the streets of the Vatican on a donkey. They ravaged the sacred tomb of Saint Peter and stole its riches. One soldier plundered the head of the lance that was supposed to have punctured Christ's side as he hung dying on the cross. The soldier then attached the lance head to his own weapon.

Pope Clement VII, the illegitimate son of Giuliano de' Medici, was orphaned at an early age. He was raised in the household of Lorenzo de' Medici, whose son, Leo X, was the boy's cousin. When Leo became pope in 1513, overlooking his cousin's illegitimacy, he named Clement archbishop of Florence and made him a cardinal. In this capacity, Clement was regarded as one of the most effective personages in the papal court. He served through Leo's papacy, which ended with Leo's death in 1521. He continued to serve through the papacy of Adrian VI, who was an unpopular pontiff and served less than two years before his death in 1523. When Clement was elected pope on November 19, 1523, Italy was immersed in a struggle between Francis I, king of France, and Charles V, king of Spain and Holy Roman Emperor.

Clement attempted to appease Charles V, but he had to make a choice eventually. Clement was forced to take sides, casting his lot with Francis and joining the League of Cognac with him in 1526, thereby infuriating Charles V. Francis was a strong Catholic, whereas Charles V clearly veered toward the Protestantism that was sweeping through northern Europe.

Clement fully expected Francis to provide troops to help protect the Vatican. This, however, did not happen. Francis, deeply in debt, could not afford to deploy troops to Italy when they were most needed to defend the Vatican in 1527. From the time Clement became pope to the spring of 1527, wars racked Italy and destroyed much of the country. The troops of Charles V gathered in Milan. Charles III, governor of Milan and a close ally of Charles V, was their leader. Francis I was unwilling and unable to assist the pope, who was seeking a truce with Charles V, but this was impossible because Charles's troops were becoming rebellious; they had not been paid for several months. Hungry for plunder, they marched south toward Rome and arrived there May 6, 1527. The sack of Rome ensued.

The carnage was considerable. During the occupation of the city, more than two thousand bodies were disposed of in the Tiber River and another ten thousand were buried in Rome and its environs. The losses on both sides were substantial. Many of the invaders succumbed to the plague that swept through Rome in the summer of 1527. The occupation continued until the following February. Pope Clement surrendered shortly after the invasion began and was a prisoner of the invaders until December 6, 1527. Upon his release, which was negotiated by paying Charles 400,000 ducats and surrendering several cities to him, Clement fled to Orvieto and then to Viterbo, staying in these cities for most of the next two years, essentially evicted from the Holy See. Clement eventually reached an accord with Charles V and acknowledged him as the Holy Roman Emperor, making official in the eyes of the Church the title that Charles had been granted through inheritance in 1519. Charles returned many of the spoils of the invasion, said to have a combined value of more than 4,000,000 ducats, to the Vatican.

The sack of Rome marked the end of Rome's distinction as the unofficial capital of the Renaissance world, although the city recovered with remarkable speed from the northern invasion.

Some historians think that the sack of Rome marked the end of the Renaissance altogether. Certainly, the age of Leonardo da Vinci and Michelangelo had passed, but the sixteenth century advanced in art and music nonetheless. One could say that the sack of Rome marked the end of the High Renaissance.

More significantly, Charles V's invasion challenged the authority of the Roman Catholic Church and marked a considerable advance for Protestantism. In 1533, Clement had to make the delicate decision about whether to grant King Henry VIII of England an annulment of his marriage to Catherine of Aragon in a manner the Church could sanction. His decision was as significant in the annals of Protestant advancement as was the sack of Rome.

Keenly aware that Catherine was the aunt of Charles V, who had a decided interest in Henry's petition, Clement denied the request, which caused Henry to withdraw from the Roman Catholic Church. The Church soon excommunicated him, leading to the formation of the Protestant Church of England. Without the sack of Rome and without Clement finding it necessary to consider how Charles V would react to his decision about the annulment, the pope might well have acceded to Henry's request, which would have had a profound effect on the course of European history." [111]

Pope Clement VII reasoned that Catherine was desperate to get away from the STD infected (syphilis and God only knows what else) and morbidly obese Henry as much if not more than Henry wanted a younger wife. The Pope calculated that Catherine would persuade her nephew to end the siege of Rome in order to sweeten the deal with the Pope if at first he said "no" to the request for an annulment. The Pope underestimated the depth and breadth of Henry's psychopathology and the effect of saying "no" to a megalomaniac.

The masses back then, as now, had no understanding of what was really going on in the shadows that resulted in their blood being shed for this or that campaign against constructed religious or national rivals. Rivals then, as now, were the handiwork fabrications of the mind control artists of the day. So it was that the English commoner's hatred of the Papacy was fabricated.

True, few like powerful people who tell you how to live. True, the Pope would, at times, behave like a grand master of control. But that is not what caused the war with Louis XIV and wasn't really the reason that we have Christians called "Protestants" (protesters) today. Henry VIII did not like being told "no" by anyone, including the Pope. Henry took a fledgling rebellion against the Pope and turned it into something much, much bigger.

Henry VIII retaliated against the Pope by a royal edict that came to be called "The Acts of Supremacy." Henry pulled this edict right out of thin air in response to the Pope's refusal to give him an annulment from Catherine. The Acts of Supremacy was empowered with a series of confiscatory raids on Papal owned property and interests. Pay close attention to the fact that Henry, like all shadow men, understood that confiscating money was the way to gain leverage and power over any rival or enemy.

Henry VIII wrested control from the Pope as punishment for saying "no" and made the English monarch head of the church, thereby establishing the Church of England. Just like that, the Church of England was born, not from religious inspiration but as an act of retaliation against another seat of authority. The Anglican clergy were, like all religious agents, spun off as subsidiaries of the King or Queen in control. Prior to the breakup, Rome had been so wealthy and powerful

---

[111] Moose, Christina J. (Editor) (2005), *The Renaissance and Early Modern Era*. Volume 2. 1534-1560: *The Sack of Rome*. Salem Press. Pasadena, CA/Hackensack, New Jersey.

that the Anglican monarchs had struck a deal with Rome that recognized the Pope as a distinct power, not just a subsidiary, joint ruler of the people.

While the masses labored under the delusion that God had spoken to King Henry and told him to get rid of the evil Pope, the truth was less noble but more logically understandable from a forensic and clinical perspective. Just imagine, one day you are a devout Catholic, living the life of a Catholic for public consumption, then one day the Pope doesn't give you what you want. Within a split second you retaliate and as your second act of retaliation your agents sell the masses a new institution named The Church of England. This is the exact same Church of England that would try to dominate the Colonies in service to then King George III. Keep in mind that we are covering this time period in great detail because the events of this period were the progenitors of America's founders.

Beginning in 1536, some 825 Catholic monasteries throughout England, Wales and Ireland were dissolved and Catholic churches were confiscated. When Henry VIII died in 1547, all monasteries, friaries, convents of nuns and shrines were destroyed or dissolved. When Mary I of England took the throne she reunited the Church of England with Rome with more than a little encouragement from the Papacy. Against the advice of the Spanish ambassador, Queen Mary persecuted Protestants during her reign in what have been called the "Marian Persecutions."

Queen Mary set the stage for a revival of hatred against Catholics because the masses that followed Henry into Protestantism found themselves being terrorized under Mary. Mary was followed by Elizabeth I and, upon encouragement from revolutionaries, she, once again, enforced Henry's Acts of Supremacy. This meant that Catholics were forbidden to become members of certain professions, hold public office, vote or educate their children. Executions of Catholics under Elizabeth I surpassed those of Queen Mary. And no doubt the masses that had been persecuted under Mary rejoiced. Britain tried to enforce the no Catholic rule in all of its territories. The forbearers to what would become America were steeped in this religious turmoil.

The roots of some of today's political rivalries can be traced to this period in history. For example, penal codes were enacted in Ireland against Catholics as part of England's purge of all things Roman Catholic. The Irish resisted this move. This is because the Irish associated Catholicism with nationhood and national identity. Catholicism provided the Irish that degree of autonomy from the English they craved.

The Irish have, historically, felt a great deal of ambivalence when it came to England's control over it. The same can be said of Scotland. The Irish resisted English efforts to eliminate the Catholic Church and, in so doing, set the stage for the rift between Northern and Southern Ireland, The I.R.A. The vestiges of this rift are seen today in organizations like Sinn Fein, et al. Scotland's effort to become independent from England is but one remnant of this period of history.

While the masses labored under the false belief that their blood had been shed and their passions had been invigorated for religious and patriotic reasons, the blood they shed and the passions they felt originated in nothing noble or religious. The masses shed their blood, in part, because of King Henry's payback vendetta against the Roman Papacy because Clement VII didn't give the King permission to jettison Catherine of Aragon for a much younger Anne Boleyn.

And speaking of Anne Boleyn, she did, indeed, become Henry's second wife and the mother of Elizabeth I. Anne was dark-haired and physically attractive. She was reputed to have lots of energy and was both funny and charming. She had been educated in Europe, largely as a lady-in-waiting to Queen Claudé of France. The French connection made her subsequent beheading as ordered by King Henry even more horrific in the eyes of not only British citizens but the French, as well.

King Henry, true to his shadow man personality, was a viper of a man and a living testament to the evils of any social construct that formally elevates any man above his fellow man for reasons of "royalty" or "chosen" status, both of which redact merit from the equation of social class.

This social construct's (Royalty) ignoble legacy was ever-present in the mind of Jefferson and his worthies. Living in the Colonies meant that the power of the throne was an ocean away. The British masses, on the other hand, despite their superior numbers, had been born into a society that forged their average man status into shackles they wore with pride as British subjects and as protesters of the Catholic Church, i.e., Protestants. These are exactly the same shackles that the Colonists refused to wear.

> King Henry the Eighth,
> to six wives he was wedded.
> One died, one survived,
> two divorced, two beheaded.

With this contextual background in place, let us return to our recounting of the lead up to the American Revolution. The battle between France and Britain explains why the French assisted the Colonists during the American Revolution. The war with France is also a significant reason for Britain's debt crisis, a crisis that evolved into a need to pillage the colonies to make up this debt.

> *In 1685, James became King James II. Many in Protestant England were deeply suspicious of the new Catholic monarch. When his wife gave birth to a son in the summer of 1688 it confirmed their worst fears of a possible Catholic monarch. This meant that James II's Protestant daughter, Mary, wife of William of Orange, was no longer next in line to the throne. Alarmed by the situation, a group of James's Protestant opponents secretly invited William to invade England and oust his father-in-law.*

> *William's mighty invasion force landed in Devon in November 1688. Many Englishmen supported William and, after some prominent English nobles defected to the invader, James II chose not to fight. He was subsequently captured and then allowed to escape to exile in France.*

> *Early in 1689, the English Parliament formally offered William and Mary the throne **as joint monarchs**, an event known as the 'Glorious Revolution'. William III of Orange was now William III of England and Ireland, and William II of Scotland. The new monarchs could not rule with the same direct power as their predecessors. They accepted Parliament's 'Declaration of Rights', later called 'Bill of Rights'. This restricted the king's power and marked an important transition towards the system of parliamentary rule that exists to this day.*

> *In March 1689, James landed in Ireland with French troops supplied by William of Orange's sworn enemy, Louis XIV. James planned to use Ireland as a base from which to invade England and recover his throne.*

> *In response William raised a huge invasion force, the largest Ireland had ever seen. In July 1690 he decisively defeated James at the Battle of the Boyne. James fled once again to France. The victory is still commemorated every year in Northern Ireland on July 12 by the Orange Order, named for William of Orange.*

> *Defeating Louis XIV of France remained William's focus throughout his life. In 1689 he had brought Britain into the League of Augsburg against France, transforming it into the 'Grand Alliance'. For the next eight years he was often away fighting, leaving his wife to rule in his absence. **In 1694 William set up the Bank of England in order to fund his war against Louis XIV.** Under William's leadership, the diverse Grand Alliance held together and in 1697 Louis XIV relinquished much of the territory he had won by conquest.*

In 1694 William's wife Mary died of smallpox. Inconsolable with grief, he fainted at her bedside. He continued to rule alone. Then in February 1702, William's horse stumbled on a molehill at Hampton Court and he was thrown, breaking his collarbone. His health, which had never been strong, deteriorated rapidly. He died on 8 March.

When courtiers undressed the king they found he was wearing Mary's wedding ring and a lock of her hair close to his heart.

William had no heir and his death brought an end to the House of Orange.

The supporters of James II, who had died in exile the year before, did not mourn him and toasted the mole who made his horse trip as 'the little gentleman in the black velvet waistcoat'. [112]

In 1694, England was only 83 years away from having to fight the American Revolution.

In 1694, this practice of creating money out of thin air was effectively legitimized with the founding of the Bank of England. It was not the first bank to be founded (Coutts was founded in 1690), but the nature of its creation was central to the role that banks went on the play in the supply of money.

In 1694, England was still a predominantly rural country. Most people still grew their own food, built their own homes, collected their own firewood for fuel, drew their own water from wells and frequently made their own clothes. Money was not the necessity that it is today for most people, **but it was still needed in large amounts when the nation went to war.**

The then King (William III) needed money to fight his war against the French. Both the King's capacity to tax and his authority were limited, so the quickest and easiest way to acquire his needs was to borrow.

A consortium of six London goldsmiths, lead by one **William Paterson, were given royal authority to create the first 'joint-stock' bank on the condition that they lent the King £1.2 million in gold at 8%. This was the start of the National Debt.**

More importantly, however, they were given the authority to create £1.2 million in paper money for private lending. This paper money was theoretically backed by the gold, but as that had been lent to the King, it meant that the same sum of money was lent out twice over! The validity of this practice was never tested in a court of law, as it remained a matter that was hidden from the general public. Even today, the banks like to draw a veil over their activities. [113]

The lesson here is that, once again, greed and avarice underlay much of the strife of this imperfect world. Debt, secondary to misadventures and personal grudges and the ever-present need to consume other's wealth is the baseline state of affairs found among shadow men. History loves to focus upon the onstage players, casting these actors as two-dimensional entities; thus, insuring that the men behind stage can continue to run the world as they so desire without the public's discernment.

Let's look more closely at the adventurers/investors who landed on Plymouth Rock and who have become the focus of ideologically driven recitations of history. Were they the violent renegades who raped and pillaged their way across the North American Continent, a la Howard Zinn's history? Put in context with what was occurring on the European Continent and the rest of the world, a very good case can be made that the Colonists were more civilized and restrained than

---

[112] Ibid.
[113] Money Reform Party. (2004), *The Bank of England.*

their fellow humans living on the North American Continent, across the Atlantic and in the Middle/Far/Near-East.

I would be remiss were I not to interject at this point a very brief review of what was going on in the Middle-East during roughly the same time frame as when Henry VIII was busy purging the vestiges of the Roman Papacy from England and its territories. This is a book about shadow men, and this chapter is about the American idea that came to fruition in a sea of shadow men. Then, as now, shadow men do not limit themselves to borders or international boundary lines. True, it was exponentially much harder to traverse the globe in the 18th century compared to today, but technological barriers were not perfect and shadow men have always found ways to reach across continents and oceans. As you read this brief overview, consider the origins of the strife consuming modern day Middle-Easterners. Also keep in mind that America's founders were well aware of what I am about to share with you:

"In the early sixteenth century, the accomplishments of Sultan Selim I included the annexation of Egypt, Palestine, and Syria. The reign of his son, Süleyman I (called "the Magnificent" by Europeans), is remembered as the golden age of Ottoman power and grandeur. In his early campaigns, Süleyman captured Belgrade (1521) and Rhodes (1522), defeated the Hungarians (1526), and laid siege to Vienna (1529).

The expansion of the empire was due in part to its military organization, to the relative weakness and disunity of its opponents, and to its practical policies for governing a large and diverse empire. From the mid-1300's, well-paid professional soldiers called Janissaries included volunteers, war captives, and Christian youths from various parts of the empire. These recruits were converted to Islam, trained with the strictest discipline, and not allowed to marry until they retired from the service.

Despite the Ottomans' reputation for despotism, they allowed a great deal of local autonomy, as long as taxes were paid and order was maintained. In an intolerant age, the Ottomans permitted religious freedom for Christian sects and Jews (called millets), although non-Muslims paid special taxes and were not allowed to serve in the army or hold positions in the central government.

Pay close attention to how the Ottomans are treated by this particular recitation of history. The tenor of this recitation is that the Muslims were so gracious and kind to their Christian subjects. Christians were vanquished and killed, those who were not killed were considered "Millets," that word is akin to the racial epithet "Nigger." Christians were forced to pay a tax for their infidel status and if they did not they were beheaded.

After 1502, the newly founded Safavid Dynasty of Persia (now Iran) became a significant threat to Ottoman interests in southwestern Asia. In 1514, Sultan Selim I, determined to restrain the Safavids, attacked their forces. Prevailing in several battles, he extended the Ottomans' eastern frontier. This began a long-standing rivalry between the two imperial powers. Although the major issue was dynastic hegemony, differences in religion added to the bitterness of the rivalry. The founder of the Safavids, Shah Ismāʿīl I, recognized the Shiite form of Islam as the state religion, whereas the Ottomans were committed Sunni Muslims, often claiming the title of caliph (or suc- cessor to the prophet) after their conquest of Egypt. Both sects viewed the other's religious doctrines as heretical.

The area that Europeans called Mesopotamia (meaning "between the Tigris and Euphrates Rivers") was the main frontier separating the Ottoman and the Safavid Empires. Mesopotamia therefore became the theater for most of the fighting between the two dynasties. Although almost all Mesopotamians were Muslims, they spoke dialects of the Arabic and Kurdish languages mostly, and they resented external rule by either Turks or Persians. Fragmented into a variety of warring tribes and independent villages, however, the Mesopotamians were in no position to defend themselves against their powerful neighbors.

While Süleyman was busy leading campaigns in the Mediterranean and the Balkans, he was almost powerless to deal with the situation in the east, more than 1,000 miles away. Thus, the Safavid Empire was able to expand its holdings and make additional political alliances. In 1532, Shah Tahmasp I acquired influence over the town of Bitlis in eastern Anatolia, which had been within the Ottoman sphere of influence.

After making a temporary peace with the Habsburg Empire, Süleyman in 1534 gave orders for his army to consolidate eastern strongholds and stop Persian advances. Although it was customary for the sultan to lead the troops into battle personally, Süleyman appointed his trusted vizier, Ebrahim Pala, as commander of an invading army of about 100,000 troops."[114]

As you can see, the Middle East, like the rest of the earth, has a long and inglorious history of turmoil. Should we travel to the Asian continent, and time would permit, we would find a consistent pattern emerging similar to other parts of the world. I'm going to insert a very brief timeline of Japan and China at this point for the reader to contemplate our central thesis about conflict being the norm among various factions of shadow men across the planet.

JAPAN

- 1600: at the battle of Sekigahara, Tokugawa Ieyasu, a friend of Hideyoshi and Nobunaga, defeats the other contenders to the leadership of Japan
- 1603: the emperor appoints Ieyasu as shogun, who moves his government to Edo (Tokyo) and founds the Tokugawa dynasty of shoguns
- 1603: the Tokugawa Shogunate divides the subjects into five hereditary classes of decreasing importance (lords, samurai, farmers, artisans, merchants)
- 1614: Ieyasu bans Christianity from Japan
- 1615: Ieyasu captures Osaka and destroys the Toyotomi clan
- 1633: the shogun Iemitsu forbids travelling abroad and reading foreign books
- 1638: the shogun Iemitsu forbids ship building
- 1639: Iemitsu restricts interaction with foreigners to Nagasaki
- 1641: Iemitsu bans all foreigners, except Chinese and Dutch, from Japan (the Dutch remain off the coast of Nagasaki)
- 1650: with peace, there evolved a new kind of noble, literate warrior according to bushido ("way of the warrior")
- 1700: kabuki and ukiyo-e become popular
- 1707: Mount Fuji erupts
- 1790: Neo-Confucianism becomes the official state philosophy [115]

CHINA

- 600: the Chinese empire is the largest nation in the world
- 1616: Nurhachi unifies the Jurchen (Manchus) and creates the state of Jin/Qing in northeastern China

---

[114] Moose, Christina J. (Editor); Thomas Tandy Lewis, (2005), *The Renaissance and Early Modern Era.* Volume 2. 1534-1535: *Ottomans Claim Sovereignty over Mesopotamia.* Salem Press. Pasadena, California/Hackensack, New Jersey.
[115] Scaruffi, Piero (2011), *Timeline of China and Korea.*

- 1620: A 15-year old boy ascends to the Ming throne and the eunuch Wei Zhongxian/ Wei Chung-hsien is the de facto ruler of China
- 1622: The Jesuit Johannes-Adam Schall moves to China and becomes the favorite astronomer of the emperor
- 1623: A military coup installs the "Westerners" in Korea
- 1625: The Qing move their capital south to Mukden
- 1626: Spain begins colonizing Formosa/Taiwan
- 1626: Nurhachi dies and the empress Abahai/ Xiao Lie Wu is forced to commit suicide, while power shifts to his eighth son Hong Taiji
- 1628: A peasant, Li Zicheng/ Li Tzu-cheng, starts a rebellion against the Ming
- 1636: Qing emperor Hong Taiji changes the name of his people from Jurchen to Manchu ("pure")
- 1637: the Manchus invade Korea and Korea becomes a vassal state of the Manchus
- 1642: Holland seizes Formosa/Taiwan from Spain
- 1643: Qing emperor Hong Taiji dies and is succeeded by Dorgon, regent for Hong Taiji's six-year old son Fulin,
- 1644: Li Zicheng/ Li Tzu-cheng, who controls northwestern China, sacks Beijing and overthrow the Ming, and general Wu Sangui asks the Manchu for help
- 1644: the Manchus, led by Dorgon, invade northern China and take Beijing, establishing the Qing dynasty, while general Wu Sangui and two other generals create their own states in the south
- 1650: Koxinga (Kuo Hsing Yeh), refusing to submit to the Manchus, founds a pro-Ming kingdom in the South China Seas
- 1658: Koxinga retreats to Formosa/Taiwan with more than 1,000 scholars and artists
- 1661: Koxinga expels the Dutch from Formosa/Taiwan
- 1661: Kangxi, still a child, ascends to the throne of the Manchu/Qing but real power is in the hand of prime minister Oboi
- 1663: Tainan is declared capital of Formosa/Taiwan
- 1668: Chinese immigration to Manchuria is banned by the Manchus
- 1669: Kangxi throws Oboi into jail and assumes real power
- 1673: Wu Sangui and the other two states in the south rebel against the Qing
- 1681: Wu Sangui is defeated by the Qing
- 1683: Koxinga's grandson Zheng Keshuang cedes Formosa (Taiwan) to the Manchus
- 1685: Guangzhou opens to foreign trade
- 1689: China signs a border treaty with Russia (first bilateral agreement with a European power), the treaty of Nerchinsk, to settle the border between Russian Siberia and Chinese Manchuria, declaring Outer Mongolia a neutral land (partition of the steppe world between Russia and China)
- 1696: The Qing defeats the barbarian Galdan of Eastern Turkestan, supported by Tibet, at the battle of Urga
- 1699: Britain opens a trading post in Canton
- 1708: Jesuit missionaries draw the first accurate map of China
- 1715: East India Company opens offices in Guangzhou
- 1722: Qing emperor Kangxi
- 1723: Yongzheng becomes Qing emperor
- 1724: Yongzheng persecutes the Jesuits

- 1724: Yongjo becomes emperor of Korea
- 1727: Russia and China sign the treaty of Kyakhta, defining their border and granting Russia a trading post in Kyakhta
- 1728: France establishes a trading post in Canton
- 1729: the emperor issues a decree banning the sale of opium
- 1736: Yongzheng dies and his fourth son Qianlong becomes emperor
- 1750: Dream of the Red Chamber
- 1757: China invades eastern Turkestan
- 1760: all foreign trade is confined to Guangzhou
- 1766: The Qing send troops to Burma
- 1776: Yongjo dies and his grandson Chongjo becomes emperor of Korea
- 1777: The corrupt Heshen becomes influential on the Qing emperor
- 1785: Korea bans Christianity because it disapproves of ancestor worship
- 1787: the Qing send troops to quell a rebellion in Taiwan
- 1790: The Qing send troops into Nepal [116]

No matter where you go on earth, then or now, shadow men and their agents are busy fighting, stealing, killing, raping and pillaging. And why is this so? Because shadow men possess an unholy and insatiable appetite for more power, more control.

What is different today, if and when it is different, is that sophisticated Fabian strategies of control have replaced more overt and brutish methods. The cast of characters in this perpetual turmoil is always the same, regardless of race, color or creed. The common denominators are the personalities of the shadow men and the witless masses that end up shedding their blood and losing their freedoms for reasons of which they are oblivious, but are convinced are right.

Moving back to the "new" world, 20 or so years before the American Revolution, we find some very interesting economic data points. Keep in mind that shadow men and the governments they create are obsessed with accumulating more power, more wealth. Governments are pathologically committed to ever-increasing regulation, taxation and control. Groupthink comes to dominate all governments, sooner or later, whether created with good intentions or despotism. These tendencies are exacerbated by governments that have accumulated debt, and yet, continue to lavishly spend. Take a look at the financial situation of the time around the American Revolution:

- British national debt in 1755: £72,289,67342
- British national debt in 1763: £122,603,33643
- British national debt in 1764: £129,586,789 (**this was money that the British government borrowed from banks and investors**, and it would be the equivalent of tens of trillions of dollars today) [117]
- Value of annual British imports to the North American colonies in the 1720s: just under £200,000 [118]
- Value of annual British imports to the North American colonies in the 1770s: nearly £885,00046

---

[116] Ibid.

[117] Edmund S. Morgan and Helen M. Morgan. (1995), *The Stamp Act Crisis: Prologue to Revolution* (Chapel Hill, NC: The University of North Carolina Press, 21; Eric Foner, Give Me Liberty! An American History (New York: W. W. Norton, 2006), 151.

[118] Jack P. Greene, (1998), *Pursuits of Happiness: The Social Development of Early Modern British Colonies and the Formation of American Culture* (Chapel Hill: University of North Carolina Press, 91.

- Average annual increase in the gross national product (GNP) of British North America between 1650 and 1770: 2.7% [119]
- **Total number of times the gross national product (GNP) of British North America multiplied between 1650 and 1770: 25** [120]
- Number of regular troops the British maintained in North America after the French and Indian War: 10,000 [121]
- Annual cost for maintaining those troops: over £200,000 [122]
- Average annual amount that royal customs collectors amassed in 1763, when George Grenville took office as Lord of the Treasury: £1,800 [123]
- British America's most valuable exports in the early 1770s, in order of total value: sugar, tobacco, wheat, rice [124]

King George III declared that the Colonies belonged to the crown. The investment bankers chartered by the King laid claim to North American profits, which were increasing day by day. The Crown was in dire financial straits due to war, imperialistic overreach and the financial drain built into the institution of the Crown. The British in Europe were content with supporting the Royals, no matter what, but the Colonists had grown weary of the Crown's overreaching, especially given that the Colonies were becoming aware that they could be a self-sustaining enterprise.

The English were not the only one's who had their eye on the "new" world. All of Europe's shadow men had the same general idea, exploit the "new" world for their benefit. **Native American shadow men had exactly the same idea**. With all of these shadow men competing for the dominant role in the "new" world, it was only a matter of time before they began to battle one another in open conflict. For example, the "Seven Year War," also known as the French and Indian War, was nothing more than a turf battle between shadow men.

The war involved shadow men from Austria, England, France, Great Britain, Prussia, and Sweden. Fighting occurred in Europe, India, and North America. In Europe, Frederick the Great, King of Prussia was so powerful that Sweden, Austria, and France joined forces against him. In the "new" world it was primarily two old rivals, The English and the French. These two powerhouses also had their sights set on the Caribbean and India. The English ultimately defeated France, but at such a cost and so much debt that it nearly bankrupted the English government.

*The French and Indian War, as it was referred to in the colonies, was the beginning of open hostilities between the colonies and Great Britain. England and France had been building toward a conflict in America since 1689. These efforts resulted in the remarkable growth of the colonies from a population of 250,000 in 1700, to 1.25 million in 1750. Britain required raw materials including copper, hemp, tar, and turpentine. **They also required a great deal of money, and so they provided that all of these American products be shipped exclusively to England (the Navigation Acts).** In an effort to raise revenue and simultaneously interfere with the French in the Caribbean, a 6 pence tax on each gallon of molasses*

---

[119] Ibid, pg. 182.

[120] Ibid, pg. 182.

[121] Edmund S. Morgan and Helen M. Morgan, (1995), *The Stamp Act Crisis: Prologue to Revolution* (Chapel Hill, NC: The University of North Carolina Press, 22.

[122] Ibid, pg. 22.

[123] Ibid, pg. 23.

[124] Jack P. Greene, Pursuits of Happiness. (1998), *The Social Development of Early Modern British Colonies and the Formation of American Culture* (Chapel Hill: University of North Carolina Press, 144.

*was imposed in 1733 (the **Molasses Act, soon followed by The Sugar Act**). Enforcement of these regulations became difficult, so the English government established extensive customs services, and vice-admiralty courts empowered to identify, try, and convict suspected smugglers. These devices were **exclusive of, and superior to, the colonial mechanisms of justice.***

*The colonies were wholly interested in overcoming the French in North America and appealed to the King for permission to raise armies and monies to defend themselves. Despite sincere petitions from the royal governors, George II was suspicious of the intentions of the colonial governments and declined their offer. **English officers in America were also widely contemptuous of colonials who volunteered for service.** A few of the men who signed **the Declaration had been members of volunteer militia who, as young men, had been dressed down and sent home when they applied for duty in service to the Crown.** Such an experience was not uncommon. It led communities throughout the colonies to question British authorities who would demand horses, feed, wagons, and quarters — but deny colonials the right to fight in defense of the Empire, a right which they considered central to their self-image as Englishmen.* [125]

It is fascinating that when some well-known Colonists attempted to demonstrate their loyalty to the Crown, by joining King George's Military, they were rejected. The Royals and their agents are physical manifestations of this peculiar notion in human affairs that they are "better than" the common folk. And make no mistake about it, the Colonists were relegated by the elite of the day into the role of commoner.

The Crown's Military was part of the cadre of elite who ruled the commoners in the Colonies. People who believe they are superior after redacting merit from their evaluation metric, those who believe they are chosen or who belong to any of the elitist labels that men have created across cultures to denote higher status, behave in ways that are exploitive by definition. The same men who were rejected as "not worthy" to join the King's Military, are the same men who would rebel and defeat these red jacket wearing elites who sorely underestimated the commoners who would eventually have enough of their superior attitude and declare a meritocracy.

The psychology of hubris is so important to world affairs that the failure of historians to focus upon it is both fascinating and an egregious oversight. He who believes he is chosen, an elite, knows better than, etc., after redacting merit from the equation, wields group power over the people that forces the masses to either take up the sword or lose their soul to their oppressors.

Elites invariably create governments that institutionalize their divine right to exploit the masses. It matters not what underling ideology created the government apparatus that endowed itself with the right to impose its will into every detail of its citizen's lives. Any government that wields such power over the people becomes a "Royal" government, sooner or later. America's founders implicitly understood this.

This is why the British Crown was the perfect template from which America's founders could design a counterpoint template for a government that would inherently resist the tyranny of future men to convert it to a device of oppression. England's hubris got them into trouble in India and their problems there played a big part in the American Revolution. Britain not only had to defend its turf in the "new" world but also had its hands full in India. Britain's economic viability had

---

[125] Independence Hall Association (2014), U.S. History.org. *The French and Indian War, 1756-1763.*

become inextricably linked to the success of The East India Company. Problems in India meant the Colonies became even more important to Britain's economic survival.

East India Company Headquarters, London, England. By Thomas Walton.

"Britain was fighting a war in India in order to maintain the integrity of the East India Company. The company received a Royal Charter from Queen Elizabeth in 1600, [126] *six years before the Virginia Company received its charter. Wealthy merchants and those aristocrats close to the crown owned the Company's shares.* [127] *The government owned no shares and had only indirect control. The crown's interest was to be found in the revenues generated by the company and its role as a mercenary operation that extended the British Empire to India.*

The East India Company evolved to rule large areas of India by virtue of its own private armies. [128] *The Company grew to account for half of all the world's trade. The company's stock in trade was the import/export of cotton, silk, indigo dye, salt, saltpetre, tea and opium. For all*

---

[126] Birdwood, Sir George. (1893), The Register of Letters etc. of the Governor and Company of Merchants of London trading into the East Indies, 1600–1619.

[127] Baladouni, Vahe (1983). "Accounting in the Early Years of the East India Company." The Accounting Historians Journal 10 (2): 63–80. Retrieved 13 November 2012.

[127] Farrington, Anthony (2002). Trading Places: the East India Company & Asia, University of Toronto.

intents and purposes, the company was one and the same when it came to the British Empire in India." [129]

The Indians were not always receptive to the British Merchants. Company rule solidified in 1757 after the Battle of Plassey and lasted until 1858 when, following the Indian Rebellion of 1857, the Government of India Act 1858 led to the British Crown to assume direct control of India in the new British Raj. Notice that just as it did with the Virginia Company, the royals eventually dissolved the Merchant's association and took direct control.

> *"The Company saw the rise of its fortunes, and its transformation from a trading venture to a ruling enterprise, when one of its military officials, Robert Clive, defeated the forces of the Nawab of Bengal, Siraj-uddaulah, at the Battle of Plassey in 1757. A few years later the Company acquired the right to collect revenues on behalf of the Mughal Emperor, but the initial years of its administration were calamitous for the people of Bengal. The Company's servants were largely a rapacious and self-aggrandizing lot, and the plunder of Bengal left the formerly rich province in a state of utter destitution. The famine of 1769-70, which the Company's policies did nothing to alleviate, may have taken the lives of as many as a third of the population. The Company, despite the increase in trade and the revenues coming in from other sources, found itself burdened with massive military expenditures, and its destruction seemed imminent. State intervention put the ailing Company back on its feet, and Lord North's India Bill, also known as the Regulating Act of 1773, provided for greater parliamentary control over the affairs of the Company, besides placing India under the rule of a Governor-General.*
>
> *It was that debt that caused the escalation of tensions leading to the Revolutionary War. Parliament was desperate to obtain two objectives; first, to tax the colonies to recover monies expended on the battle over North America, and second to restore the profitability of the East India Company in an effort to recover monies spent on the battle over India."* [130]

As always, shadow men are never satisfied with what they have and must lay claim to more and more of its citizen's money. The Jamestown/Yorktown Foundation had this to say about economics around the time of the American Revolution:

> *"By the 1770's, Great Britain had established a number of colonies in North America. The American colonists thought of themselves as citizens of Great Britain and subjects of King George III. They were tied to Britain through trade and by the way they were governed. Trade was restricted so the colonies had to rely on Britain for imported goods and supplies. There were no banks and very little money, so colonists used barter and credit to get the things they needed.*
>
> *Following the French and Indian War, Britain wanted to control expansion into the western territories. The King issued the Proclamation of 1763 prohibiting settlements beyond the Appalachian Mountains. Colonists who had already settled on these lands were ordered to return east of the mountains.*
>
> *In 1765 Parliament passed the Quartering Act that said the colonists needed to find or pay for lodging for British soldiers stationed in America. With the French and Indian War over, many colonists saw no need for soldiers to be stationed in the colonies.*

---

[130] Sweeney, Richard J. (2004), *Constitutional Conflict and the American Revolution*. McDonough School of Business: Georgetown University.

Britain also needed money to pay for its war debts. The King and Parliament believed they had the right to tax the colonies. They decided to require several kinds of taxes from the colonists to help pay for the French and Indian War. These taxes included the Stamp Act, passed in 1765, which required the use of special paper bearing an embossed tax stamp for all legal documents. Other laws, such as the Townsend Acts, passed in 1767, required the colonists to pay taxes on imported goods like tea.

Many colonists felt that they should not pay these taxes because they were passed in England by Parliament, not by their own colonial governments. They protested, saying that these taxes violated their rights as British citizens. The colonists started to resist by boycotting or not buying, British goods. In 1773 some colonists in Boston, Massachusetts demonstrated their frustration by dressing up like Indians, sneaking onto ships in the harbor, and dumping imported tea into the water. This was called the Boston Tea Party. The British took action by closing the Boston port. A similar but smaller tea party took place in Yorktown, Virginia in 1774." [131]

What the thoughtful reader may recognize at this point in our chapter is that all of the ingredients necessary for a perfect storm of rebellion had been put into place in the year before the war for independence. Capricious control over the Colonies had reached a fever pitch, concurrent with the Crown's economic fortunes, which were under attack on multiple fronts.

Returning to our opening narrative that examined the five men chosen to draft The Declaration of Independence, we can begin to see that The Declaration of Independence is an eloquent articulation of just how invasive shadow men's control has to get before a critical mass of freedom loving citizens reaches their breaking point.

America was designed from its inception to not only protect the colonists from tyrants (those who exercise opprobrious control) but to protect future Americans from the progeny and kindred spirits who dominated our ancestors. **Our founders recognized that all governments tend to devolve into controlling machines manned by control freaks that are, in turn, simply agents of powerful forces living in the shadows.**

The reader may find it interesting that the first person to articulate a detailed analysis of just how bad things must get before an outright rebellion occurs was not Thomas Jefferson or one of his American compatriots, but Englishmen John Locke. In fact, it was Locke's Second Essay, published in 1693, which formed the basis for Jefferson's narratives as memorialized in The Declaration of Independence. Then, as now, citizens tend to deny, rationalize, adapt, retreat, compensate or live the life of a serf until they reach their breaking point. What follows is Locke's elegant narrative on the subject:

"Secondly: I answer, such revolutions happen not upon every little mismanagement in public affairs. Great mistakes in the ruling part, many wrong and inconvenient laws, and all the slips of human frailty will be borne by the people without mutiny or murmur. But if a long train of abuses, prevarications, and artifices, all tending the same way, make the design visible to the people, and they cannot but feel what they lie under, and see whither they are going, it is not to be wondered that they should then rouse themselves, and endeavor to put the rule into such hands which may secure to them the end for which government was at first erected..." [132]

Locke's Second Essay mentions "train of abuses, prevarications and artifices. " Recognize that Locke's listing of abuses is comprised of types and sub-types of control. The breaking point for

---

[131] Ibid.

[132] John Locke. (1693), *Concerning the true extent and end of civil government.* Second Essay, Chapter 19.

Locke, and for Jefferson, as well, occurred when they became aware of the fact that everything their overseers were doing was *designed to destroy their God given right to freedom.* Freedom is just another word for the absence of opprobrious control. It is that revelation that served as the impetus to no longer submit to shadow men government's will and served to motivate their battle cry of Independence from their overseer's control.

What follows is Thomas Jefferson's Declaration that describes his breaking point and that of his compatriots. Rather than a declaration of independence, think of it as a declaration of his and his countrymen's intent to no longer submit to control. It is a reaffirmation of their RIGHT to be free as God intended:

> *"Prudence, indeed, will dictate that Governments long established should not be changed for light and transient causes; and accordingly all experience hath shown, that mankind are more disposed to suffer, while evils are sufferable, than to right themselves by abolishing the forms to which they are accustomed. But when a long train of abuses and usurpations, pursuing invariably the same Object evinces a design to reduce them under absolute Despotism, it is their right, it is their duty, to throw off such Government, and to provide new Guards for their future security."* [133]

Here we see Jefferson articulate man's self-defeating tendency to go along to get along ("mankind are more disposed to suffer while evils are sufferable") under the thumb of controllers. He also noted that at some point, however, governments tend to become agents of despotism REGARDLESS of their original intent or design; and it is at that point that despite man's ability to suffer, declares ENOUGH! Importantly, Jefferson ended our quoted passage from The Declaration of Independence by telegraphing what this "new" government was all about,

"Provide new Guards for their (Your) future security."

In other words, Jefferson and his compatriots intended to erect firewalls to the archetypal (not merely British) despots over them and those who would undoubtedly appear at some time in the future to control you, the reader of this book. The controllers Jefferson helped to defeat are back, but this time they are armed with a much more sophisticated armamentarium.

America's founders understood control better than almost any other group of people then or now. This is because of two things: 1. America's founders were comprised of men who possessed a burning passion to be free of control, and 2. America's founder's had the best teacher on planet earth when it came to educating them on the insidious, devious and pervasively rancid personalities who aspire to control their fellow man.

I repeat Goethe's dire warning about second chances should one be so fortunate to defeat the devil,

> *"Who holds the devil, let him hold him well,*
> *He hardly will be caught a second time."*

The devil did break loose sometime in the 20th century and the question that is yet to be answered is this: Can 21st Century Americans prove Goethe wrong? 21st Century America is under siege by the progeny of the same shadow men who attempted to destroy America during its infancy. Only this time they have equipped themselves with mind control technology, that is functionally more powerful than any army. Americans living today have been intentionally separated from an understanding of who they are and where they came from. The rule, not the exception today, is that Americans have been brow beaten to feel ashamed of their provenance. This is particularly true when referencing America's youth and black Americans.

---

[133] Thomas Jefferson. Declaration of Independence, 1776.

African Americans who were brought here by slave traders have been denied an accurate and factually based understanding of the fact that the people who were behind the slave trade were not the founders of the United States. I gently remind the reader that mind control is insidious, in that, when applied with scientific precision, as it has been, can turn historical facts on their head.

Once again, I remind the reader that all sophisticated mind control strategies, including those used on African and white Americans, alike, have built in failsafe mechanisms that prevent their deconstruction. Nevertheless, I am going to try to deconstruct the insidious mind control strategies used against African and white Americans. These mind control strategies were designed to make black Americans dependent upon the state, and thus, under the state's control, by exploiting *the fact of* slavery. Similarly, the politicians who fomented this dependency on the part of black Americans insured their own continued employment every time they reinforced victimhood and dependency upon the state. My last sentence will undoubtedly energize the forces of mind control to destroy the messenger of that simple truth. Simply put, the careers and fortunes of men and women who make their living exploiting the lies I am about to debunk would go up in smoke.

Black and white Americans have been denied a justifiable pride in America, not because of the fact of slavery but because of the lies and half-truths about slavery inculcated into students as if they were the truth. I want you to keep something in mind if you choose to read the rest of this chapter.

> *Excuses or apologies that are purposed to mitigate the fact of or the consequences of slavery are not tolerable to me. I'm after the truth and it is my considered opinion that my readers have not only been denied the truth they have been lied to when it comes to the issues surrounding slavery in America and the rest of the world. If you read something in the following narratives that makes you feel differently about the historical fact of slavery, then do not attribute that change in feeling to me, but to your reaction to the facts. My purpose in what follows is to simply provide data that was probably kept from you.*

Virtually all, if not all, of America's founders were opposed to slavery though some had slaves working for them. This inconsistency is not what it may appear to be. **America's founders intended to free all slaves and make their freedom a part of the Declaration of Independence, and certainly the Constitution**. In taking this revolutionary position, America's founders WERE THE FIRST HUMAN BEINGS ON EARTH TO OPENLY DECLARE, BY AND THROUGH A FORMAL INSTRUMENT OF GOVERNMENT, THAT SLAVERY WAS ANTI-CHRISTIAN AND INTOLERABLE TO ANY CIVILIZED MAN.

That particular revolutionary proposition-the abolition of slavery in principle, for its time and in context, was regretfully judged to be too dangerous to add to an already risky endeavor, i.e., over throwing the most powerful nation on earth. Furthermore, and more importantly, there were intense political and psychological pressures put on America's founders who had fully planned to free each and every slave as part of the Declaration of Independence. Who pressured these anti-slavery American rogues?

Slave traders, who were not white Christians for the most part, funded and promoted a campaign to frighten and threaten America's founder's into believing, that should they free the slaves before the British had been defeated, that revolutionary act would put the entire proposition of a free America, and their plans to free the slaves, at risk. Virtually no black American has been permitted to learn about the existence of the powerful forces that were intent upon stopping the first men on planet earth, America's white founders, to free blacks from the bondage of slavery.

And who were some of the men who lobbied and threatened America's white founders? African warlords, that is, African shadow men whose fortunes were inextricably linked to capturing then selling their fellow Africans, lobbied hard against abolishing the institution of slavery. In fact, African and Muslim warlords met with British leaders, in part, to have them put a stop to these white rogues in the colonies that were intent upon ending slavery in their country. [134]

Slavery in America is always framed as a black and white issue by historians who are often times unwitting agents for those men living in the shadows who do not want readers to get a feel for the context, a world view, of slavery. Since Americans are typically ethnocentric, both white and black children and adults just assume that when the subject of slavery is brought up, you are necessarily talking about white people enslaving blacks. But that is patently and undeniably wrong.

Slavery's origins preceded written history. It may be a new concept to some readers, both white and black, that slavery is not a "black" or "white" issue. Rather, slavery is an ignoble example of the evils of shadow men. It is the "elitist" personality-type, and the governments those personalities always seem to capture in their control net, that created the institution of slavery. The institution of slavery has very deep roots and has a very, very long history that preceded the American idea by thousands of years. The name, itself, "Slavery," comes from the word "Slav" because so many Slavs, that is, white people, were exploited as chattel, that is, "slaves." Virtually all of the exploitation of "Slavs," by the way, was at the hands of darker skinned people, i.e., their slave masters.

In the earliest written records on earth slavery is treated as an established institution. The Code of Hammurabi in 1760 BC, for example, prescribed death for anyone who helped a slave to escape or who sheltered a slave fugitive. The Christian Bible mentions slavery as an established and ingrained, **but anti-Christian**, institution. Slavery was endemic to every ancient civilization and society and involved *every* racial group, especially Africans. In fact, the majority of African states practice slavery to this day. Ancient civilizations that had slavery as an ingrained part of their culture included The Sumer, Ancient Egypt, Ancient China, the Akkadian Empire, Assyria, Ancient India, Ancient Greece, the Roman Empire, the Islamic Caliphate, the Hebrew kingdoms in Palestine, and the pre-Columbian civilizations of the Americas. Yes, Native Americans were deeply committed to slavery as an institution.

However, despite slavery's deeply ingrained roots, slavery was NOT revered nor supported **by America's founders**. Supreme Court Chief Justice John Jay noted that there had been few, if any, serious efforts to dismantle the institution of slavery anywhere on planet earth prior to America's founding fathers. Thomas Jefferson specifically noted that separation from Great Britain would be necessary before the Colonists could rid themselves of the institution of slavery. **Benjamin Franklin stressed that every effort on the part of the Colonies to end slavery had been thwarted or reversed by the British Crown using physical force, economic sanctions and psychological threats.**

True to their word, as soon as the Colonists had separated from Britain, many of America's founding fathers released their slaves despite threats and dire warnings from vested interests who threatened to bring the entire country to its knees if anyone dared to free slaves. America's most vocal founders vehemently opposed to slavery included: John Dickinson, Caesar Rodney, William Livingston, George Washington, George Wythe, John Randolph, Richard Bassett, James Madison, James Monroe, Bushrod Washington, Charles Carroll, William Few, John Marshall, Richard Stockton, Zephaniah Swift, and many, many more.

---

[134] DuBois, W. E. B. (1896), *The Suppression of the African Slave-Trade.* Cambridge: Harvard University Press.

Benjamin Franklin and Benjamin Rush founded **the world's first** antislavery society two **years before the American Revolution in 1774.** Supreme Court Justice John Jay was president of an anti-slavery group in New York. Refer back to William Livingston, one of the five men assigned the task of drafting the Declaration of Independence, here is what Mr. Livingston said about slavery:

> *"I would most ardently wish to become a member of it [referring to Justice John Jay's anti-slavery group in New York] and... I can safely promise them that neither my tongue, nor my pen, nor purse shall be wanting to promote the abolition of what to me appears so inconsistent with humanity and Christianity... May the great and the equal Father of the human race, who has expressly declared His abhorrence of oppression, and that He is no respecter of persons, succeed a design so laudably calculated to undo the heavy burdens, to let the oppressed go free, and to break every yoke."* [135]

While black African national shadow men, without exception, were dedicated to protecting and insuring the continuance of the institution of slavery in 1776, including enslaving their own race for profit, back in the Colonies, America's most famous General, George Washington, was arguing for slavery's abolition:

> *"I can only say that there is not a man living who wishes more sincerely than I do to see a plan adopted for the abolition of slavery."* [136]

George Washington was not alone in his feelings about slavery. John Adams had this to say about slavery:

> *"[M]y opinion against [slavery has always been known... [N]ever in my life did I own a slave."* [137]

Charles Carroll, one of Jefferson's "worthies" had this to say on the subject of slavery:

> *"[W]hy keep alive the question of slavery? It is admitted by all to be a great evil."* [138]

John Jay, President of The Continental Congress, Chief Justice of the U.S. Supreme Court and Governor of New York, said this about slavery:

> *"That men should pray and fight for their own freedom and yet keep others in slavery is certainly acting a very inconsistent as well as unjust and perhaps impious part."* [139]

Richard Henry Lee was President of The Continental Congress and a Signer of the Declaration of Independence. Lee, like his fellow "worthies," was no supporter of slavery:

> *"Christianity, by introducing into Europe the truest principles of humanity, universal benevolence, and brotherly love, had happily abolished civil slavery. Let us who profess the same religion practice its precepts... by agreeing to this duty."* [140]

A short seven years after the passage of America's Constitution in 1787, delegates from all over the Colonies met in Philadelphia. These white men had as their goal the permanent abolition of

---

[135] United States Army Center of Military History (1987), *Soldier-Statesmen of the Constitution.* Brig. Gen. William A. Stofft, Chief of Military History. Washington, D.C.
[136] Ibid.
[137] Ciiaelks C. (1854), *The Works of John Adams, Second President of the United States.* Little Brown and Company, Vol. IX pp. 92-93. In a letter to George Churchman and Jacob Lindley on January 24, 1801.
[138] Rowland, Kate Mason (1898), *Life and Correspondence of Charles Carroll of Carrollton.* Vol. II, pg. 231. G.P. Putnam's Sons, New York and London:
[139] Johnston, Henry P. Editor, (1891), *Correspondence and Public Papers of John Jay:* In a letter to Dr. Price, Richard. September 27, 1785. Vol. III, pp. 168-169. G.P. Putnam's Sons, New York and London.
[140] Carey, H.C. and Lea, I. (1825) *Memoir of the Life of Richard Henry Lee and His Correspondence With the Most Distinguished Men in America and Europe: The first speech of Richard Henry Lee in the House of Burgesses.* Vol. I, pp. 17-19. William Brown, Philadelphia, PA.

slavery as an institution. Benjamin Rush, signer of the Declaration of Independence, said this to the convention:

> "*Domestic slavery is repugnant to the principles of Christianity... It is rebellion against the authority of a common Father. It is a practical denial of the extent and efficacy of the death of a common Savior. It is an usurpation of the prerogative of the great Sovereign of the universe who has solemnly claimed an exclusive property in the souls of men."* [141]

Every racial group on earth has, at one time or another, embraced and protected the institution of slavery, including, debt-slavery, punishment for crime, the enslavement of prisoners of war, child abandonment, and the birth of slave children to slaves. [142]

It is remarkable that America's founders, all of whom were white, were the first men on earth to create a government that was ideologically opposed to an institution that was so entrenched, so ingrained into the fiber of every nation on earth. Slavery was and is so ingrained into the world's fiber, that not only does slavery exist today, it flourishes, especially on the African Continent, where blacks enslave other blacks, a practice well established a thousand years BEFORE any white man set foot on the African Continent.

How fascinating it is, then, that if you ask American citizens, slavery is simply assumed to be a creation of white men with all of their victims being of African origin. It was a mere 75 years after the Constitutional Convention that slavery was totally outlawed in America. **The fact that slavery flourishes in the 21st Century among people living in parts of Africa, but not in America, is a testament to the worthies who founded America.** [143] It borders on criminal, that rather than being revered for their bravery as they confronted the entrenched love of slavery in every culture on earth, America's founders have been castigated by agents for shadow men who find it all too easy to brainwash the masses who are all too willing to believe their lies and half-truths.

For those people who have been so thoroughly brainwashed, and I have concluded that those who fit into that group comprise the vast majority of Americans, that they cannot see any good in America because of the fact of slavery, are simply ignorant of the world context within which America's founders created their enterprise. In addition to the ignorant, a cabal of men, both black and white, have made fortunes and created a life's career out of promulgating lies and half-truths about slavery. While those who are merely ignorant may alter their beliefs after learning the truth, I have no such illusions regarding those men and women who would have no career and no income were the truth to be told. I expect this cabal, more than any other group, to become the most vociferous and vicious among this book's detractors. I remind the reader that predictive validity is the best and most powerful validity.

So who or what kept the slave trade up and running long after it was outlawed and declared to be morally reprehensible by America's founders? The answer may surprise you. International slave merchants, shippers, corporate agriculture operations and African shadow men were behind the

---

[141] Poulson, Zachariah Jr. (1794), p. 24. "To the Citizens of the United States:" Minutes of the proceedings of a Convention of Delegates from the Abolition Societies Established in Philadelphia : Printed by Zachariah Poulson, Jr. number eighty, Chesnut-Street, eight doors below Third-Street, MDCCXCIV.

[142] Harris, W. V. (1999) Demography, Geography and the Sources of Roman Slaves, The Journal of Roman Studies.

[143] Elizabeth Donnan, 4 Volumes, 'Documents Illustrative of the History of the Slave Trade to America' Washington, D.C. 1930, 1935 Carnegie Institute of Technology, Pittsburgh, Pa.

organized push back in favor of keeping slavery as an institution. America and Britain were dedicated to ending slavery, **not so with** *any* **of the African nations ruled by black shadow men, who not only profited from slavery but counted on it for their very survival as shadow men.** The slave traders also had a life's blood financial interest in keeping slavery alive and well.

African tribal governments taxed the slave trade, even if they were not actually involved in capturing then exporting their fellow Africans. The mere thought of losing tax and tariff revenue was unthinkable to them. As mentioned earlier, but worth repeating, African warlords, chiefs and tribal government officials were so concerned about these white rogues in America who would threaten their slave industry, that they sent official emissaries to London to lobby against the abolition of slavery. African warlord shadow men were not about to allow the cash that came rolling in from the slave trade to end, especially by a group of rogue whites living in the colonies.

The comic-book fairytale portrait of white people making raids on peaceful African villages, where families of royal lineage were separated, brutalized and shipped to America was fabricated for the most part by the agents of shadow men to use the fact of slavery as a way to mind control both black and white people. Africans were brutalized and millions died, but NOT, as a rule, at the hands of white American Christians and certainly not by America's founders. The fact of the matter is, Africa was known as "The White Man's Graveyard." This is because of deadly threats from predator animals, disease, terrain and African warlords or African tribesmen. So who captured black people on the African continent in order to enslave them? African shadow men were well practiced at raiding an intramural competitor's village. <u>Such raids are such a part of Africans and African culture that the practice of raiding adjoining villages continues unabated to this day.</u>

*"**The slave trade in Africa flourished** <u>long before</u> **the introduction of Europeans.** Africans would enslave people for different reasons. According to the memoirs of an Italian born French slave trader, Captain Theodore Canot (also spelled Canneau) there are five principles for the enslavement of Africans by other Africans. The first reason for slavery was the prisoner of war. War between rival communities over land or for other fractions left people who were captured. These people were mainly adopted into the new culture, in order to increase the power of the dominant society; they were not only used for labor purposes.*

War between communities was not the only means of fighting that caused slavery. The second principle concerns fighting between family members. If a household becomes too upset by a certain member of the family, the remaining members have the option to sell the troublemaker into slavery. This in turn would solve the familial problem, as well as enable profit for the family and the individual. The family gains wealth and goods, as the individual is able to learn how to control oneself as well as gain a sense of responsibility.

Debt proved to be another main resource for the buying and selling of people in Africa, which is the third principle. "In Africa, where coin is not known, the slave is made a substitute for this commodity, and in each district a positive value is given him which is passed for currency and legal tender." There are cases of parents having to sell their kin because they were in such debt, as well as people selling themselves into slavery for a certain amount of time. These were not uncommon forms that shaped the familiar frame of African tradition.

The fourth principle of African slavery, according to Captain Canneau, contained those "inculpated with witchcraft, the Crim Con [criminal conviction] cases (not few in Africa), orphans of culprits, vagabonds who dare not to return to their tribes, and unruly sons." This shows a more focused rationalization to the enslavement of others, rather than just random selection. However, some of these are not acquired through choice but rather by birth, which proves to be a correlating perquisite to the American slave system.

Finally, Conneau states that gamblers were the fifth principle to the evolution to slavery. This however, was evident after the introduction of Europeans. The gamblers mainly focused on trading for their own personal gain, which will be discussed later. Nonetheless, Africans take chances on selling each other in order to try to make their life situation better. A primary example of this is the selling of a handicapped child in order for the father to buy a new wife in hopes of having a 'normal' offspring." [144]

African tribal chiefs, in cahoots with international slave merchants, dominated the slave trade. One shipping magnate, in particular, Aaron Lopez, owned and operated at least 50% of the slave trade vessels involved in the Transatlantic slave trade. Lopez fought tooth and nail against America's founders who were intent upon eradicating slavery in America.

Aaron Lopez

The historical record memorialized Aaron Lopez' importance to the economy of slavery. It was Lopez and his colleagues, Arabs and African warlords, who were directly and mostly responsible for the brutality and inhumanity directed at millions of Africans. Historians know of Aaron Lopez' involvement because he signed bills of landing, port clearances and penned other receipts, all of which documented his dominant role in the slave trade. Lopez owned or controlled more than 80 sailing vessels. He was an important public figure in Newport, Rhode Island, no doubt because of his connections and wealth. Recall that it was Rhode Island that had refused to join the union of the colonies and was, therefore, targeted by Muslim leaders to be their point of operation in the Americas. Lopez was a philanthropist in Newport, often financing projects that furthered his dreams. For example, he established the beautifully designed Touro Synagogue, the oldest Jewish synagogue in America. [145]

---

[144] Conneau, Captain Theophilus. (1976), *A Slaver's Logbook or 20 Years Residence in Africa: the original manuscript by Captain Theophilus Conneau.* New Jersey: Prentice-Hall, 1976. Commentary by: Melissa B. McLean: Slavery, Africa, Europe, and Jamaica. The Dread Library (2014).
[145] Cowley, Malcolm. (1928), *Adventures of an African Slaver.* Published by Albert and Charles Bori, New York, New York.

Name of ship	Owners
Abigail	Aaron Lopez, Moses Levy, Jacob Franks
Crown	Issac Levy and Nathan Simpson
Nassau	Moses Levy
Four Sisters	Moses Levy
Anne & Eliza	Justus Bosch and John Abrams
Prudent Betty	Henry Cruger and Jacob Phoenix
Hester	Mordecai and David Gomez
Elizabeth	Mordecai and David Gomez
Antigua	Nathan Marston and Abram Lyell
Betsy	Wm. De Woolf
Polly	James De Woolf
White Horse	Jan de Sweevts
Expedition	John and Jacob Roosevelt
Charlotte	Moses and Sam Levy and Jacob Franks
Caracoa	Moses and Sam Levy

The Most Prolific Transatlantic Slave Ships and Their Owners.

Africans captured their own people and sold them to international merchants. The vast majority of slaves were transported to South America and the Caribbean where, unlike North America, slavery was widely promoted and accepted by the masses and political leaders. Portuguese shipping moguls sometimes hired mercenaries, in order to cut out African warlords, who captured Africans on the West Coast of Africa, though this was not the favored way of procuring slaves for transport to South America or the Caribbean because it was costly and inefficient. The "locals" knew their country better than alien mercenaries and that knowledge made raiding local villages very efficient. Simply put, African shadow men were well practiced at capturing their fellow Africans.

Tribal chiefs who relied upon the slave trade for their income and station in life would capture young men and women from neighboring villages. Those men and women they did not kill or use for their own sexual pleasure or work were sold to international slave merchants who were willing to share in their profits from slavery. These international merchants pushed their human product mostly to South America, in particular Brazil and the Caribbean. In North America, on the other hand, there were relatively **few farmers** who were able to afford slaves and, concurrently, not opposed to slavery because of the Christianity and/or because they followed the lead of America's founders. Massive agri-corps are a modern artifact. The vast majority of farms during this time were family operations. So how many farmers could afford to buy slaves and take care of them you might ask? Your mental pictures of slavery, no doubt created by shadow men's public relation's agents, are inaccurate if you think that the vast majority of white Christian American families had poor black souls doing their labor for them while they sat back drinking lemonade and liquor while raping their female slaves and using a whip on their male slaves.

According to data in the official U.S. 1860 census, fewer than **385,000 individuals or about 4.8% of southern whites, even less in the North, owned one or more slaves.** [146] [147] **This rather paltry percentage of slaveholders in America makes forensic sense because only wealthy landowners could afford to buy and keep slaves. Slaves were expensive to buy, costly to keep healthy and "owning" slaves in a Christian country where its political leaders and local ministers found the institution of slavery to be an abomination against God made slavery an unpleasant and costly endeavor.**

The vast majority of Americans (80%) living in 1860 were rural Americans. They were **family farmers who operated their farms on a shoestring budget, only able to survive** with the help of members of their own family. Slaves were for rich, non-principled, non-Christian people. According to the Texas Historical Society and The National Bureau of American Negro Slavery, this is what slaves cost:

- Average cost of an unskilled slave (of any age, sex, or condition) in 1860 =
- $ 800 ($21,300 in 2009 dollars)
- Cost of a prime field hand (18-30 year-old man) in 1850 = $ 1,200 ($34,000 in 2009 dollars)
- Cost of a skilled slave (e.g. a blacksmith) in 1850 = $ 2,000 ($56,700 in 2009 dollars)
  [148] [149]

One way to put these costs into context is to compare the costs of "purchasing" a slave to the wages earned by white Americans. The following table lists wages for various professions and activities from 1860 to 1880 in America.

[146] Behrendt, Stephen D., Richardson, David and Eltis, David. W. E. B. Du Bois Institute for African and African-American Research, Harvard University. Based on "records for 27,233 voyages that set out to obtain slaves for the Americas." Stephen Behrendt (1999), "Transatlantic Slave Trade". Africana: The Encyclopedia of the African and African American Experience. New York: Basic Civitas Books. ISBN 0-465-00071-1.

[147] Engerman, Stanley L., Sutch, Richard, and Wright, Gavin. (2003), SLAVERY: Historical Statistics of the United States Millennial Edition. University of California Project on the Historical Statistics of the United States. Center for Social and Economic Policy, U.C. Riverside.

[148] Texas State Historical Society (2009), *Slavery*.

[149] Evans, Robert Jr. (1962), *The Economics of American Negro Slavery*: Aspects of Labor. National Bureau of Economic Research. Princeton University Press. ISBN: 0-87014-305-0.

Facts & Figures:
Income and Prices 1860 - 1890

1860

Occupation	Income
Bricklayer	$ 1.53/day
Firemen	$ 1.33/day
Farm Labor	$ 0.88/day

Product	Price
Cotton Sheeting (Yard)	$ .082
Sugar (Pounds)	$ .096

1870

Occupation	Income
Bricklayer	$ 3.97/day
Firemen	$ 1.73/day
Farm Labor	$ 1.50/day

Product	Price
Cotton Sheeting (Yard)	$ .140
Sugar (Pound)	$ .135

1880

Occupation	Income
Bricklayer	$ 2.68/day
Firemen	$ 1.37/day
Farm Labor	$ 1.25/day

Product	Price
Cotton Sheeting (Yard)	$ .081
Sugar (Pounds)	$ .099

150

Gerald Moore conducted an analysis of farm income in one Southern state, Tennessee, in particular, Wayne County, Tennessee. This one southern county is representative of the South of this era. Here is what Mr. Moore's analysis found:

> *The assets for Wayne County farms in 1860 were calculated by summing the values of land, personal property, farm machinery, and livestock. The median for 1,123 farms was $1,420, and two thirds of these farms reported assets of $440-5,600. Income was calculated by summing the sales from homemade items, slaughtered animals, and fruit orchards. No income was reported by a few farms and some data are illegible for others. Among the remaining 975 farms, the median income was $150, and two thirds of these farms reported annual sales of $62-300. There was almost certainly additional income from the sale of crops and things not included in the census, such as cattle hides (worth $3.30 each in the manufacturing census), eggs, and feathers. Also, many farms earned money from the sale of fence rails, charcoal, tanbark, barrel staves, wheel spokes, wood shingles, or firewood. Crop production costs are unknown, but, before the days of machinery*

---

150 Historical Statistics of the United States. Colonial Times to 1970; Value of a Dollar 1860 – 1999.

162

and commercial fertilizers, these costs were low. Large farms used paid or slave labor, but small farms depended upon family labor. Considering all of these factors and ignoring the value of family labor, average farm profit might have been a little more than the median income ($150/yr) shown by the census.

Ignoring the value of family labor, the median ratio of assets/profit on 975 farms in the census of agriculture for 1860 might be about 9.5. If so, the investment represented by the farm assets was earning an average annual profit of 10% in 1860. If family labor was worth $10-20/mo, on the other hand, the average investment return was minimal or negative. Nevertheless, the farm families in 1860 had earned and saved enough to buy their land and to accumulate the other assets in the census. And one history says that many families spent no more than $50/year for supplies." [151]

The facts I have just presented are incongruent with what mind control artists have used to brainwash black and white Americans in order to energize their various political and ideological strategies. Remember, men whose names you undoubtedly know live well, eat at expensive restaurants and live in mansions because they have made a career of exploiting half-truths and pandering to people they continually reinforce to be perma-victims the direct result of having relatives who were enslaved by the white man.

If anyone dares to provide context for the factual record, as I have just done here, that person is viciously attacked as either favoring slavery or as someone engaged as a slavery apologist. And, of course, such a person is plastered with the Scarlett Letter of "Racist." Such accusations and attacks are merely PSYOPs designed to protect the underlying lies and the false images ingrained into every American's psyche by shadow men and their agents. Such PSYOPs are designed to energize the useful idiots to attack the threat to shadow men's lies. As if I need to write this, but I will, nonetheless, **"Even one slave is one too many slaves from my point of view."**

Slavery is the result of mankind's willingness to exploit disparities in power between and among people, and has little or nothing to do with race, per se. Consistent with that analysis, I'll refer to the work of Henry Louis Gates, an African-American history professor who teaches at Harvard University and Larry Koger, author and researcher on black slaveholders in America. These men, by the way, are not the exception. African-American scholars will attest that what professor Gates has concluded is accurate. The existence of black slaveholders is undisputed. But even those people who consider themselves to be informed on the subject, do not realize how many free blacks held other poorer blacks as slaves in antebellum America.

Those among you who have not studied African American history may have heard of professor Gates within another context. Professor Gates was one of the participants in President Barach Obama's "beer summit" during his first term as President. Professor Gates had been wrongly targeted as a home invader in his own home because, according to professor Gates, he is a black man. The white police officer, President Obama and professor Gates met, discussed the event and parted ways, according to the participants, as friends.

Professor Gates was interviewed on CSPAN. During that interview professor Gates said the following:

---

[151] Moore, Gerald K. (2002), *THE 1860 CENSUS OF AGRICULTURE, WAYNE COUNTY, TENNESSEE.* THE USGenWebProject.

"This is the dirtiest secret in African American history. **A surprisingly high number** of free Negros in the South owned Slaves." [152]

Of course, to be in a position to own slaves in a white country, when you are black, means that whites had not enslaved these black men. In 1860, for example, William Ellison, a black man, was the *largest* slaveholder in all of South Carolina. [153] Just let that indisputable fact sink in. Thus, any number of freed black men naturally viewed enslavement as part of doing business as a free man, that is, IF you could afford to buy and keep slaves AND your religion did not disapprove of the institution. Against all of this, America's white founders, and their kindred spirits in Britain and some parts of Canada, stood alone in their opposition to slavery when virtually the entire world embraced slavery as just a part of life, **including many free black men**. Always remember this: Mind control artists are so good at brainwashing the masses that even after learning the truth, those who have been brainwashed will not let go of the mind control beliefs deeply and purposefully embedded into their psyche. If you are one who can let go, consider yourself blessed. Our point is merely that the perpetrators of the abominable and horrendous slave trade have been misidentified and those who opposed slavery, when the entire world supported it, have not received their due.

No man or woman should ever forget that right at this very moment as you are reading this sentence, 38 out of 54 nations in Africa have an active slave trade. The slavers are black and the slaves are black. Many slavers are Muslim. All men and women, regardless of race, color or creed, should actively fight modern day slavery. Perhaps 21st Century citizens, especially progressive minded citizens, who often think of themselves as part of a global community, can show the same degree of bravery and moral strength as America's founders did when they opposed the institution of slavery when the **entire world** was against them.

To add yet another layer to this most interesting issue, consider these facts: Americans, by virtue of the fact that they were Christians and white, were routinely taken as slaves, themselves, by Africans living in the Barbary States. Never heard of this fact? Permit me to tell you about this little known history of white Americans being enslaved by Muslim Africans. What follows is derived from a speech given by the brilliant scholar Michael B. Oren, Senior Fellow at The Shalem Center, Columbia University.

In 1775, the year before the revolution, America was becoming a maritime merchant powerhouse. Its ships routinely traveled the globe carrying cargo from the new world to the whole of Europe. Pirates were everywhere in those days. But thanks to the British Navy, the "Colonies'" ships were protected. Britain's Navy, the most powerful in the world, consisted of approximately 800 ships.

America's maritime routes included the West Indies extending east to the Mediterranean. America's ships traveled from Gibraltar to the Levantine and Anatolian coasts. By the 1770s, Mediterranean countries were buying 20% of all American exports. American vessels numbering over 100 set sail for all points east. The Colonies shipped about 100 hulls annually.

But all was not well. America faced a serious threat from Muslims located in North Africa. This area was known as the al-Maghreb, or "the West." Four countries in particular posed a serious threat to America: Morocco and the three semi-autonomous Ottoman provinces or regencies of

---

[152] CSPAN. Quoted Verbatim from: An interview with Professor Henry Louis Gates. https://www.youtube.com/watch?v=4a8EhhbTs0A

[153] Koger, Larry. (1995), *Black Slaveowners: Free Black Slave Masters in South Carolina, 1790-1860.* McFarland Publishing, Jefferson, North Carolina.

Tunis, Algiers and Tripoli (that is, present day Libya). All four of these Muslim countries were pirate kingdoms, known to Jefferson and his worthies as the "Barbary States."

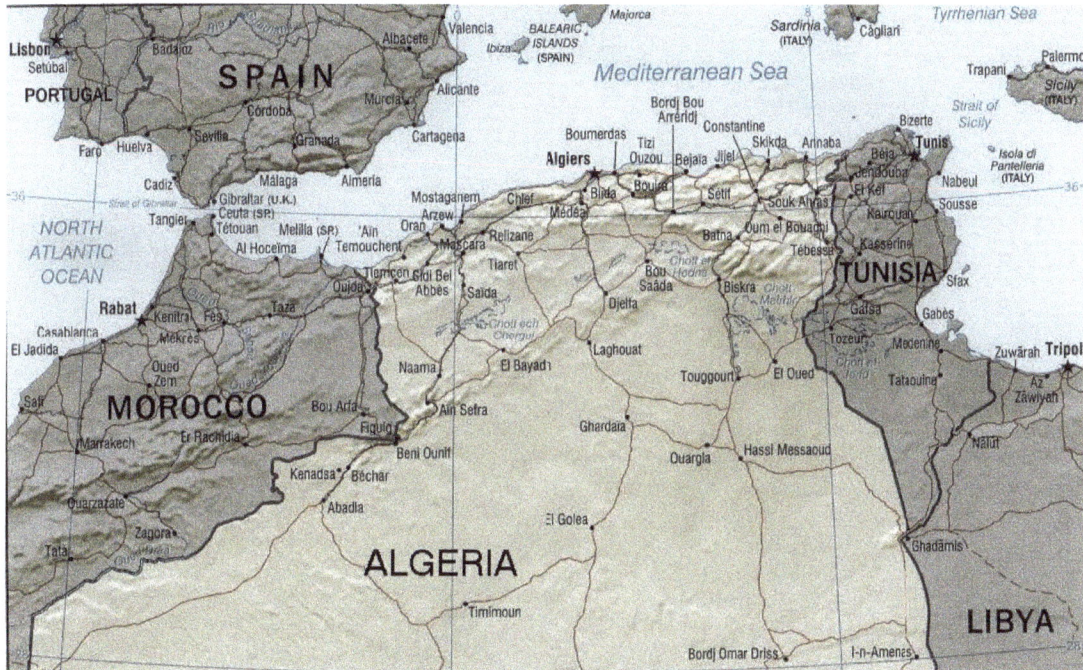

The Barbary Coast States.

The Arab slave traders preexisted the transatlantic slave trade by hundreds of years. Southeast Africa was a rich source of slaves and concubines for the Arabs. [154] It has been estimated that Muslims uprooted at least 150 million Africans and 50 million slaves from non-African nations. These numbers make the trans-Atlantic slave trade look miniscule. Scholars estimate the total number of Africans brought to early America as slaves to be approximately 600,000 men and women. A total of 12 million Africans were brought to the Americas. Most of these slaves ended up in the Caribbean and South America, in particular, the country of Brazil. Compare those numbers to the 200 million men and women uprooted, enslaved then transported by Arab Muslims.

Muslims made it their business to force African slaves to convert to Islam. Even after their conversion, however, Africans were still considered to be more akin to animals than people. Again, many African warlords and kings got rich from opening their countrymen up for exploitation by the Arabs. When it came to the Muslim slave trade, unlike those relatively few who made it to North America where many slaves lived long lives, often longer than whites living in America's big cities, slaves taken by Muslims died quickly if they were male and once the women taken as slaves showed any signs of aging, they were killed. I ask the reader to study the following photograph carefully to see if you can identify the races of the people pictured.

---

[154] Kissling, H. J., Barbour, N., Trimingham J. S., Braun, H., Spuler, B., Hartel, H., and Bagley, F.R.C. (1997), *The Last Great Muslim Empires*, Brill Academic Publishing.

Getty Images: British colonial official with Islamic/African slave traders in Zanzibar.
On the far right is Hamad bin Mohamed bin Jumah bin Rajab bin Mohamed bin Said al-Murghabi, more commonly known as Tippu Tip. He was the most notorious Islamic slaver. al-Murghabi died in 1905.

Muslims were not only instrumental in developing the slave trade, but from the thirteenth to the seventeenth centuries, Muslim pirates preyed upon European mariners and their goods. Muslims took tens of thousands of prisoners and forced them into slavery. White Christian Europeans were sold, shackled, beaten and forced by Muslims to work in the mines on land or the galleys of their pirate ships.

Muslim men placed an especially high value upon European women because of their light complexions. White women were prized commodities and often warranted premium prices when sold into slavery to be used in African Muslim harems. These infidel women were forced to perform sex acts whenever their African masters demanded.

Muslims, as taught in the Qur'an and in the Hadiths, were permitted to ransom their slaves, although the going rate for redemption was invariably cost prohibitive. [155] The lives of white American and European slaves was brutal and mercifully short, unlike their black counterparts in America who had life spans that were virtually identical if not longer than their white counterparts living in America's biggest cities.

---

[155] Hadith |hə'dēTH|, noun (pl. same or Hadiths), A collection of traditions containing sayings of the prophet Muhammad that, with accounts of his daily practice (the Sunna), constitute the major source of guidance for Muslims apart from the Qur'an.

Barbary Coast Pirate, by:
Francesco Mola Pier.

Mulai Ahmed er Raisuli, the last of the
Barbary Pirates (old era), 1650.

Slaves living in America were viewed as expensive chattel to be taken care of. On the other hand, white European slaves were infidels and, therefore, unable to work, charm or manipulate their way into the good graces of their masters. Once they were beaten or worked to death they were simply replaced.

What follows is a comparative table of life spans for various populations gleaned from records of mid-19th Century America:

U.S. White – 40
England and Wales, 1838-1856 – 40
Holland, 1850-1860 – 36
France, 1854-58 – 36
U.S. Slave – 36
Italy, 1885 – 35
Austria, 1875 – 31
Chile, 1920 – 31
Manchester, England, 1831 – 24
New York, Boston, and Philadelphia, 1830 – 24 [156]

The facts on lifespan do not comport with race merchants. The facts of the matter is, a slave working on a farm in Virginia would likely live longer and be healthier than a white person living in New York, Boston or Philadelphia.

The first recorded incident of a pirate attack upon a colonial vessel took place in 1628, only eight years after adventurers/investors landed on Plymouth Rock. We know from official records

---

[156] Fogel, Robert William and Engerman, Stanley L. (1974), *Time on the Cross: The Economics of American Slavery.* Little Brown and Company.

that of the 390 English captives ransomed from Algiers by Muslim pirates in 1680, eleven were residents of New England and New York.

What the reader should be recognizing is that America's founders were well acquainted with Islam's imperialistic and warrior culture. And for those who have labored under the belief that America's battles with Islam are a modern artifact, secondary to America's ill-fated incursion into the Middle East under G.W. Bush, nothing could be further from the truth. In fact, our earliest settlers, long before The War for Independence, knew all too well about the imperialistic nature of mainstream, run-of-the-mill Islam.

None other than Captain John Smith, founder of Jamestown, was a battle-hardened soldier who had faced Islamic Jihadists many times before coming to America in 1607. If this information is new to you, thank the authors of your history books and your teachers who may have found what I am about to recount to you to be politically incorrect. Historian and scholar Charles Dudley Warner wrote the following in 1881, long before there was such a thing as political correctness and before shadow men had targeted public schools to be their new indoctrination camps.

"At age 21, John Smith joined the ranks of Austrian Hapsburg Earl of Meldritch, being assigned to the General of Artillery, Baron Kisell. Smith marched with German, French, Austrian and Hungarian troops to fight the Muslims, who had captured Budapest and were invading Lower Hungary, Wallachia, Moldovia, Romania and Transylvania near the Black Sea. In 1600-1601, during the campaign of Romanian Prince, Michael the Brave, John Smith introduced ingenious battle tactics. When Muslims were besieging the garrison at Oberlymback, Smith devised a method of signaling messages with torches and using gunpowder to create diversions. The resulting victory earned him the rank of captain with a command of 250 horsemen. Fighting with the Duc de Mercoeur at the siege of Alba Regalis, Smith devised makeshift bombs. Earthen pots filled with gunpowder, musket shot and covered with pitch were catapulted into the city, contributing to the Muslim evacuation. Muslims had captured the city of Regall, located in a pass between Hungary and Transylvania, "the Turks having ornamented the walls with Christian heads when they captured the fortress." Smith fought under General Moyses, serving the Prince of Transylvania, Sigismund Bathory, to lead a campaign to regain the city. During a lull in the fighting, the bashaw (officer) of the Turks put out a challenge. In a "David and Goliath" style contest, the 23-year-old John Smith was chosen to fight. He defeated the bashaw, cutting off his head. To avenge the bashaw's death, another Muslim challenged Smith and lost his head. This happened a third time, resulting in Smith being awarded a "coat-of-arms." General Moyses, with Captain John Smith, soon recaptured Regall, then Veratis, Solmos and Kapronka. At Weisenberg, Prince Sigismund Bathory conferred on John Smith a shield-of-arms with "three Turks' heads." John Smith continued in the regiment of Earl Meldritch, fighting in 1602 for Radu Serban to defend Wallachia against invading Turkish Muslims. In the battle, the Earl of Meldritch was killed along with 30,000 soldiers. John Smith was wounded and left for dead: Smith among the slaughtered dead bodies, and many a gasping soul with toils and wounds lay groaning among the rest, till being found by the pillagers he was able to live, and perceiving by his armor and habit, his ransom might be better than his death, they led him prisoner with many others. At Axopolis, Smith was sold with other prisoners at the slave market to Bashaw Bogall, "so chained by the necks in gangs of twenty they marched to Constantinople." There, Smith was pitied by Bashaw Bogall's mistress, who sent him to her brother, Tymor Bashaw. Unfortunately, Tymor "diverted all this to the worst cruelty," stripped Smith naked, shaved him bald, riveted an iron ring around his neck, clothed him in goat skins and, as slave of slaves, was given only goat entrails to eat. Following a beating while he was thrashing in a field, Smith seized the opportunity and killed his master. He hid the body in the straw, put on his

master's clothes, took a bag of grain and rode off toward Russia. After 16 days he reached a Muscovite garrison on the River Don, where the iron ring was removed from his neck. With their help he found his way through Poland back to his troops in Transylvania. After being released from service with a large reward, John Smith traveled through Europe to Morocco in Northern Africa to fight Muslim Barbary pirates in the Mediterranean." [157]

One can only imagine the terror that sailors felt when Britain withdrew its protection of America's merchant vessels when war with Great Britain became a fait accompli. Britain knew of the threat posed by Muslim pirates and the Crown knew of America's intent to abolish slavery. What sweet payback it was for the English Crown to teach these colonist rogues a lesson about taking unpopular moral stances that would threaten Britain's control.

The British armada, numbering 800 navy ships, that once protected America's merchant fleet, was now its mortal enemy. With virtually no navy to speak of, the United States couldn't even protect its own coast, much less its merchant vessels thousands of miles from their homeport. American merchant ships and their crews were vulnerable from the moment they left their moorings in the colonies and virtually helpless on the high seas.

The French Navy assisted the fledgling country long enough for it to survive the War for Independence. By the time the shooting stopped in 1783, America had only one functional Navy vessel. As a comparison, the imperialistic Muslim countries of North Africa outnumbered the American Navy by 100 to 1. For example, Algiers, alone, had approximately 50 navy vessels.

How bad was Muslim piracy? Over a two-year period (1783 -1785) Muslim countries commandeered three American merchant vessels. The crews were captured and paraded down the streets of Fez and Algiers. The Muslim population standing on the sidelines that watched the spectacle threw rotten vegetables and the entrails of slaughtered animals at the Christian infidels. The local Pasha (Muslim shadow man) was reported to have told the captured Americans: "I'll make you eat stones you Christian dogs." The Americans, now white slaves of North African Muslims, were sold to the highest Arab bidders to be worked and abused until they died, which usually did not take long.

One fascinating cultural note made by Mr. Oren is that among rank and file colonists, i.e., the masses, the Middle East held a special place in their imagination. In fact, after the Bible, the most popular book among the colonial masses was a collection of Persian stories entitled: *A Thousand and One Arabian Nights.* The reality, when compared to the imagined Middle East as depicted in this popular book, like today, is a chasm as wide as an entire ocean.

The Arab pirates were close to crippling America's foundling economy because of their ruthless attacks on American merchant vessels. Increasing insurance rates and the loss of business was having its effect on the new country. Arab pirates were so ravenous that none other than Benjamin Franklin's ship was nearly seized by Algerians on his way back from England. When John Jay sailed to Britain, he had to make the journey in a European flagged vessel so as to not be captured and sold as an infidel white slave by Muslims.

America tried its best to garner the continued assistance of the French, but Paris soon recognized that as much as they wanted to help the colonies, the colonies had the potential of becoming an economic powerhouse competitor, so assistance was denied; thus, once again leaving

---

[157] Warner, Charles Dudley. (1881), *Captain John Smith (1579-1631) Sometime Governor of Virginia, and Admiral of New England. A Study of His Life and Writings.* Holt, New York.

the Americans all on their own. With little recourse, some Americans concluded that it would be less costly simply to pay the ransom of the Arab states commandeering American's ships than to take military action.

In 1786 none other than John Adams met with shadow man 'Abd al-Rahman al-'Ajar in order to work out a "deal." Then, as now, Adams learned a sobering fact about true believer Pashas of Barbary's Muslim theo-political states. Adams was simply told that the Barbary States had declared war on the United States and that the price of ending that conflict would be a cool $1 million. Back then, $1 million dollars was about 1/10 of America's total yearly budget.

No sooner had the War for Independence ended than the young country found itself besieged by a cabal of Muslim countries residing in Northern Africa. Europe had chosen to negotiate with pirates, essentially paying ransoms when Muslim pirates were able to circumvent their defenses. Thomas Jefferson offered another solution, a solution born out of having just defeated the most powerful force on earth, the British. Jefferson argued that America must form its own powerful navy IF it intends to do business on the high seas. Jefferson believed that the "temper," as he called it, of the American people, made them inherently resistant to blackmail. The American idea was rooted in independence from tyranny, an archetypal tyranny, anywhere and at anytime. Jefferson reasoned that American men would prefer building a naval armada rather than cave to the Muslims residing on the Barbary Coast. He figured correctly, but not until America learned its lesson the hard way.

Jefferson, as we have previously documented, was an expert on the psychology of tyrants, in whatever form they may take now or in the future. Thus, Jefferson was convinced that tyrants would never fulfill their obligations under any treaty. Jefferson demonstrated his keen understanding of the shadow man's mind when he noted that the more Americans paid the tyrants their blackmail bounty, the more they would sense America's weakness and demand even more next time. Jefferson's proposals constituted America's first tangible foreign policy. He termed our new approach to foreign affairs as having "an erect and independent attitude" when it came to dealing with foreign nations who wished us harm. This meant no payoffs, no caving, no weak-kneed responses. It meant for this new policy to have teeth, America would have to embark upon creating a Naval force that would be unequaled among all other nations.

Jefferson in fact obtained and studied a copy of the Qur'an in order to better understand the maniacal motivations of people who were viciously attacking America's vessels and taking American's hostages and making the women sex slaves and the men short-lived slaves, despite the fact that Islam had had no direct contract or conflicts with America. The rewriting of history to comport with the politically correct police, one that would have students believe that President Jefferson possessed a Qur'an because he respected and honored Islam, borders on insanity and or criminal intent.

Dr. Samuel L. Blumenfeld has written that Jefferson specifically queried Sidi Haji Abdul Rahman Adja, the Tripolitan ambassador to Britain, as to why Muslims were so hostile to America. The response from Adja was the same response made by experts on Islam since the 7th Century BCE right up today:

> *"It was written in their Koran that all nations which had not acknowledged the Prophet were sinners, whom it was the right and **duty** of the faithful to plunder and enslave; and that every*

mussulman (Muslim) who was slain in this warfare was sure to go to [P]aradise.'[158] (Emphasis Added).

It is fascinating that Congress opposed Jefferson's prescient advice about how to deal with Muslim tyrants. As a result, in the summer of 1786, Congress instructed Jefferson to join Adams in London for one more try at negotiating with Tripoli's envoy, 'Abd al-Rahman. Just like Jefferson had predicted, the overture for peace was met with the back of the Pasha's hand. 'Abd al-Rahman arrogantly repeated his demand for $1 million. Just like in today's world where lessons learned over 200 years ago must be relearned, the Pasha gave a speech that should remind every American infidel where we stand in the world when it comes to Islam, 2015:

> *"[I]t was ...written in the Quran, that all Nations who should not have acknowledged their [the Muslims'] authority were sinners, that it was their right and **duty** to make war upon whoever they could be found, and to make Slaves of all they could take as prisoners, and that every Mussulman who should be slain in battle was sure to go to Paradise."* [159] (Emphasis Added).

Adams continued to believe that peace through negotiation was the better route when compared to confrontation. "We ought not to fight them [the Barbary States] at all unless we determine to fight them forever. This though, I fear, is too rugged for our people to bear." Jefferson was not persuaded by his fellow worthy that negotiation was the correct path to take. He insisted that the American people would rather fight if only given the option.

Congress chose Adam's approach, and again ordered Adams and Jefferson to negotiate a resolution, this time with Morocco. Morocco's sultan, Sidi Muhammad, was willing to suspend assaults on American merchant vessels for a mere $20,000 dollars. (millions of dollars today) In return for that ransom, the sultan would grant the U.S. consular privileges in Tangiers. That consular outpost remains, to this day, and is America's oldest foreign embassy.

Unfortunately, but predictably, other Muslim states viewed the deal with Morocco as an invitation to become even more aggressive with the new country. As a result, in 1787, pirates seized eleven American vessels and the Algiers Navy took hostage 121 American sailors. The Pasha of Algiers demanded a $1 million ransom for his American prisoners. George Washington upon learning of this demand said, "Would to Heaven we had a navy to reform those enemies to mankind or crush them into non-existence."

It was none other than James Madison, author of the First Amendment to the Constitution, joined by John Jay and Alexander Hamilton, who wrote about the importance of cooperation between the states, in part, to defeat the enemies of freedom, the Islamic nations of Northern Africa. These writings, of course, came to be known as The Federalist Papers.

It was Hamilton, the same Hamilton who defended Zenger in his libel case involving British governor, William Cosby, who pointed out that America was inherently a seafaring nation. America, therefore, could not survive without a navy. And to do that, it needed a central command of that navy. Madison made a persuasive case that only a unified *United* States could defeat "the rapacious demands of pirates and barbarians."

Author Peter Markoe, a Philadelphian, wrote a book entitled *The Algerine Spy in Pennsylvania*. In that book Markoe documents how Muslims located on the Barbary Coast viewed the American idea of freedom. Markoe wrote about a Muslim spy name Mehmet. Mehmet was a spy for Algiers. He had been sent to America to spy on her defenses. Mehmet was struck by the amount of economic

---

158 Blumenfield, Samuel L. *Thomas Jefferson's Qur'an.* In: Defeat the Third Jihad. September 10, 2010.
159 Frank Lambert (2005), *Jefferson's War: America's First War on Terror 1801–1805*, by Joseph Wheelan.

and individual freedom possessed by Americans. Mehmet described American's freedoms as an Achilles' Heel, of sorts, that could be exploited by his Muslim benefactors, "[T]otally ruined by disunion and faction, the states may be plundered without the least risk and their young men and maidens triumphantly carried into captivity." To further demonstrate how weakness of spirit was viewed then and now, Mehmet opined that Rhode Island could be converted into a local base for Algerian operations, the equivalent of an "Ottoman Malta." Why Rhode Island? Because Rhode Island was the only colony that boycotted the Continental Convention to form the United States, believing that, in part, the other states were preparing for war. Recall that slave magnate Aaron Lopez lived in Newport, Rhode Island and was an important shaper of public opinion.

In March of 1789 the Constitution was ratified. It empowered the central government to make war and to "provide and maintain a navy" (Article 2, Section 2). **Thus, thanks to the Barbary Muslims who had declared war on the brand new country, America made its first archetypal decision to double down on the idea that the American idea would give no quarter to an enemy**. Still, despite America's stated refusal to submit to tyranny, nothing was done to actually build an American Navy. Like all matters of substance, including America, herself, it began with an idea. America would have to have its nose rubbed in Islamic Millet before teeth were put into the idea of giving no quarter to any enemy.

By the end of 1793, the Algerian ransom demand had risen to $2 million. American ships had been driven out of the Mediterranean. Americans were disgusted with their government's impotence, as reported in their free press that reported the butchery of the Barbary States. Poems and novels, along with plays were read and performed that ridiculed America's leaders for their impotence in the face of terrorists on the high seas.

On March 27, 1794, Washington signed into law a bill authorizing an outlay of $688,888.82 for the building of six frigates. This marked the birth of the United States Navy. America's desire for peace, however, would overrule Jefferson's prescient teachings when it came to how to deal with tyrants. And on September 5, 1795, America signed a Treaty of Amity and Friendship with Algiers. In return for releasing American prisoners, the Algerian ruler was promised a long list of gifts -- "25 chests of tea of 4 different qualities, 6 Quintal of loaf sugar refined and some elegant penknives. Some small guilt thimbles, scissor cases, a few shawls, with roses, curiously wrought in them in" The blackmailers bounty was worth more than $650,000, a far cry from the $2 million dollar figure previously demanded.

Remarkably, and foolishly, the U.S. also agreed to provide Algiers with cannons, gunpowder and a 36-gun made-in-America warship. As soon as word got out to the other Muslim nations in the area, they wanted their bounty from the new country. Tunis and Tripoli got similar deals paid to Algiers. And the lesson learned? By 1800, the United States was paying out 20% of all its federal revenues to North Africa as blackmail ransom.

Adding insult to injury, proving once again that Islam was answering to a higher power than presidential overtures and negotiated peace settlements, the American warship, the George Washington, captained by William Bainbridge, was forced at cannon-point to transport Algiers's goods, including 150 sheep, 25 cows, five horses, four each of antelopes, tigers and lions, to Istanbul.

On assuming office in 1801, the new President Thomas Jefferson made a list of his foreign policy priorities. The Barbary issue was his number one priority. **On May 14, 1801, Libya became the first foreign state to formally declare war against The United States of America.** The new President was in no mood to appease the enemy. Jefferson responded by sending three separate squadrons against Tripoli. Each expedition proved more disastrous than the one before it. In spite of some early victories against pirate vessels, an American landing party was ambushed, with fifteen killed—the first American servicemen to be killed in action overseas—and then the pride of the fleet, the USS Philadelphia, commanded by an inept William Bainbridge, foundered on a reef and all 308 of its crewmembers were imprisoned by Tripoli. Need is the mother of invention.

Enter one William Eaton. Eaton was a veteran of the Continental Army who fought under General Anthony "Mad" Wayne. Eaton was a tough, man's man who was a natural born soldier. It was as if God looked down on America and concluded, that she needed to be saved from her own patience and peaceful nature. God sent an avenger in the personage of Eaton. In 1799 Eaton was appointed America's first consul to Tunis. Eaton was told by his superiors to appease the Barbary pirates. It would be hard to imagine a more unsuitable character to carry out such an order.

What followed next was that Eaton appeared to go through the motions of appeasement, but right from the get-go he took it upon himself to end, once and for all, the tyranny of Muslim pirates. Eaton was the living embodiment of that American temperament that Jefferson had written about. Eaton wrote these prescient words that modern Americans would do well to heed:

> "How art thou prostrate! Are we then reduced to…bartering our national glory for the forbearance of a Barbary pirate?"

Eaton then described the nature of tyrants anywhere and everywhere, and what civilized men must confront sooner or later:

> "There is but one language which can be held to these people, and this is terror."

Eaton came up with a plan to land 1,000 marines in Tunis who would set their sights on the capital. Secretary of State Madison rejected Eaton's Tunis plan. Not to be dissuaded, Eaton proposed a military solution to the problems in Tripoli. Eaton took a page out of the Fabian playbook when he proposed staging a coup by the exiled brother of Tripoli's Pasha. Once the coup was successful, Eaton proposed installing a pro-American government in Libya. Eaton's plan, in what is now Libya, may have constituted America's first plan to effectuate regime change. What Eaton had not factored into his equation is that his civilian commanders had just fought a war against a government that was well practiced at regime change and were in no hurry to become like the British. As a result, Madison rejected, once again, Eaton's plan. Madison reminded Eaton that the United States had a policy of non-interference in the internal affairs of other states.

Despite having his plans now dashed twice by Madison, Eaton would not be knocked off course to rid America of the tyrants along the Barbary Coast. Eaton warned his civilian leaders that unless something was done the Muslim pirates would soon start raiding U.S. shores. Eaton said the following in a cryptic tone:

> "Muslims are commanded by Allah to abduct women and young boys. Americans might as well start dressing as slaves."

In one of the first recorded acts of an American military leader's patriotic insubordination, Eaton decided that he had to take matters into his own hands, in order to save the United States from its civilian leaders who failed to grasp the true nature of Islam and who had allowed their more peaceful side get in the way of victory. Eaton tracked down the exiled brother of the Pasha in Tripoli. He found Hamid in Egypt. What he did next is either an example of force majeure or stark insubordination, perhaps both. Eaton took only nine Marines, accompanied by a mercenary force of 400, and did the seemingly impossible, he marched 500 miles over the African desert and attacked Tripoli's second-largest city, Darna. Eaton took the Muslim soldiers defending the town by surprise. From all reports the fighting was vicious, as it always is, when dealing with men who would just as soon die for Allah rather than be defeated at the hands of the infidels.

Eaton was critically wounded in the fighting. Nevertheless, he and his band of only nine Marines and mercenary troops not only took the city, but then set about to march on Tripoli. What happened next is a lesson in human behavior and, in particular, a lesson on how to deal with Muslim theo-political states. The Pasha of Tripoli took measure of Eaton and his indelible spirit, and decided that perhaps the Philadelphia prisoners should be released and that the deal previously offered by Jefferson, upon reflection, would be the wiser choice to make.

Jefferson and Eaton, two kindred spirits, formed an informal pact with one another, and in December of 1805, Jefferson reported to Congress that, "the states on the coast of Barbary seem generally disposed at present to respect our peace and friendship." But in true Jeffersonian and Eatonian form, Jefferson sent naval commander Stephen Decatur, along with a fleet of warships, into the harbors of Tripoli, Tunis and Algiers. Once in the enemy's harbors, with old glory waving proudly, Jefferson laid down the law, you have a choice, he said, between "powder and balls" on the one hand, or signed treaties foreswearing piracy. In a surprise to everyone except Eaton and Jefferson, all three Muslim states signed the accord. [160] History would record that by the time of Thomas Jefferson's death, the United States was a recognized naval power, capable both of protecting its shores as well as of maintaining a permanent squadron in the Mediterranean.

With this history in mind as documented by Mr. Oren, and context in place, let's revisit the American slavery issue. While the following analogy is not perfect, not taking action on an issue one knows to be wrong and immoral, whether legal or not, is something that today's successful African American citizens should review in their own mind because it may help them gain a better understanding of how entrenched institutions, like slavery, despite the fact that people find such practices to be immoral, have a way of perpetuating themselves.

For instance, as I stated earlier, slavery is alive and well on the Continent of Africa in the 21st Century. Christian girls, some as young as 10 years old, are not infrequently stolen by their Muslim captors and forced, actually sold in many instances, into slavery. This is certainly immoral but in some places where Sharia law is the rule of law, it is not illegal. I repeat, we are talking about female children in most cases of abduction.

American blacks who are multi-millionaires, even billionaires, do nothing tangible to stop their "blood" back in Africa from engaging in slavery and what amounts to organized pedophilia rings in the name of Islam.[161] America's black politicians refuse to stop these pedophilia rings with tangible action even though they find it abhorrent. This is because the problem seems too big, too systemic, too politically incorrect to confront, especially since, according to these same people, other more pressing issues must be dealt with (sound familiar?). True, the issue belongs to another nation, but considering the fact that early America had not even come into existence when the fight to end slavery was started by white Americans, demonstrates how good men can, at the very least, take a stand.

African culture in America has historically glamorized the role of the pimp. Certainly I do not assert that black pimp culture is the exact equivalence of the transatlantic slave trade. The point I am making is that injustice and exploitation can very easily exist and flourish right under our noses because such practices are part of a cultural fabric.

---

160 Oren, Michael B. (2005), *The Middle East and the Making of the United States, 1776 to 1815.* In a speech delivered at Columbia University. (Professor Oren is a Senior Fellow at The Shalem Center at Columbia University).

161 The author uses the term "blood" not in a pejorative sense, but as blacks often use the term to refer to their racial brothers and sisters.

Pimps control a stable of young girls and exploit them. Cash from this *glamorized slave trade* business among segments of the African American Community is used to buy fine jewelry, cars, houses and clothes. Why don't successful and wealthy black Americans, along with black politicians, put a stop to this, especially since it is widespread, often glamorized and right under their nose, in their own community?

And for those of you so thoroughly brainwashed or out of touch with reality who doubt that being a black pimp, i.e., modern day slave holder, is not glamorized and woven into the culture of black Africans living in America, then perhaps this will help change your mind. What follows is an article that appeared in USA Today. It was written by a black man:

"This fall, not too long after kids go back to school, a new animated movie will appear in theaters across the country. It is the latest in a genre of films that use the voices of well-known actors to bring life to a series of drawings. Labeled a comedy, this movie is nothing to laugh about.

It is the story of a 9-year-old pimp. That's right, I said pimp — as in one of those degenerates who peddle female flesh for a living. Lil' Pimp, as this film is called, is the cinematic manifestation of a pop-cultural attempt to glamorize this repugnant lifestyle.

In the twisted world of this movie's story line, the young pimp is a good guy, and the mayor of its imaginary city is sleazy. Not surprisingly, the voices of several of the characters belong to some of rap music's raunchiest acts.

Rap music has a love affair with pimps. And it is the broad appeal of rap artists who glorify pimping that has likely convinced Hollywood that there's a profit to be made in a movie about a pre-pubescence boy "who hustles his ho's around the neighborhood."

For years, rap artists have spiked their salacious lyrics with talk of these bottom feeders.

But recently some have gone from talking about pimps to acting like them. In their latest video — titled P.I.M.P. — rappers 50 Cent and Snoop Dogg prance before the camera in the flashy, gaudy attire of a pimp.

Their video is just the latest in what has become a steady stream of rap songs that celebrate pimps as hot-dressing, slick-talking, women-running men and ignore both the cruelty and criminality of the profession.

"I think it (rap artists' infatuation with pimps) has sort of dumbed-down rap music and its constituency," said DeVone Holt, whose book Hip-Hop Slop: The Impact of a Dysfunctional Culture, will be published next month. "They've surrendered their authentic artistic traits and settled for the less-demanding challenge of selling sex. That probably takes the least amount of talent when you're selling sex because you're just appealing to folks' natural desires."

Holt, 30, who grew up on a steady diet of rap music, said that it's not what it used to be. "The traits that drew me to hip-hop are the same ones that are drawing kids today," Holt said. "Hip-hop and rap music are a rebellious music, a rebellious culture. But in the days when I grew up listening to it, hip-hop and rap rebelled against oppressive institutions. Today, they just rebel against traditional values."

More to the point, a growing number of rap performers are trying to redefine the culture by turning one of society's dregs — the pimp — into an acceptable lifestyle. In his recent music video titled Pimp Juice, rapper Nelly gave cameo roles to Max Julien, an aging actor who played a pimp in the 1973 movie, The Mack, and a one-time, real-life pimp named Bishop Don "Magic" Juan.

Snoop Dogg not only sings about pimping, he said he wants to be a pimp. A former Los Angeles-area gang member, Snoop says he has given up his gang-bangin' days for pimping because pimps live longer.

Now that's dysfunctional. Like too many rappers, Snoop has a big bankroll and low self-esteem. Rather than aspire to be something more than his great musical skills helped him to escape, Snoop wants to emulate the high-living style of a lowlife. While Snoop's immense talent has lifted him out of the ghetto, it hasn't taken the ghetto out of him.

"If it's wrong to call a woman a b—— with $2 in your pocket," Holt said of the language pimps regularly use to describe women, "it's wrong to call a woman a b—— with $2 million in your pocket."

He's right. Rap stars who glamorize the pimp lifestyle deserve our disdain. And movie producers who try to profit, hopefully, will lose their shirts." [162]

The horrific costs, both physical and emotional, to the women who are exploited as slaves by the black pimp (slave) culture in America is virtually ignored by America's highest office holders in the land. For example, one musician who has extolled and glamorized the "pimp" culture is a Hip Hop performer who goes by the name of Jay-Z.

Jay-Z (far left), Unknown, President Obama, Beyoncé (far right).

Jay-Z, Beyoncé & President Obama.

JAY-Z LYRICS

"Big Pimpin' (Extended)"
(feat. U.G.K.)

[Jay-Z]
Uhh, uh uh uh
It's big pimpin baby..
It's big pimpin, spendin G's
Feel me.. uh-huh uhh, uh-huh..
Ge-ge-geyeah, geyeah
Ge-ge-geyeah, geyeah..
You know I - thug em, fuck em, love em, leave em
Cause I don't fuckin need em
Take em out the hood, keep em lookin good
But I don't fuckin feed em
First time they fuss I'm breezin
Talkin bout, "What's the reasons?"

---

[162] USA Today. (2013), By: DeWayne Wickham. *Rappers' glorification of pimps deserves disdain*, June 6.

I'm a pimp in every sense of the word, bitch
Better trust than believe em
In the cut where I keep em
til I need a nut, til I need to beat the guts
Then it's, beep beep and I'm pickin em up
Let em play with the dick in the truck
Many chicks wanna put Jigga fist in cuffs
Divorce him and split his bucks
Just because you got good head, I'ma break bread
so you can be livin it up? Shit I..
parts with nothin, y'all be frontin
Me give my heart to a woman?
Not for nothin, never happen
I'll be forever mackin
Heart cold as assassins, I got no passion
I got no patience
And I hate waitin..
Hoe get yo' ass in
And let's RI-I-I-I-I-IDE.. check em out now
RI-I-I-I-I-IDE, yeah
And let's RI-I-I-I-I-IDE.. check em out now
RI-I-I-I-I-IDE, yeah
[Chorus One: Jay-Z]
We doin.. big pimpin, we spendin cheese
Check em out now
Big pimpin, on B.L.A.D.'s
We doin.. big pimpin up in N.Y.C.
It's just that Jigga Man, Pimp C, and B-U-N B
Yo yo yo.. big pimpin, spendin cheese
We doin - big pimpin, on B.L.A.D.'s
We doin.. big pimpin up in N.Y.C.
It's just that Jigga Man, Pimp C, and B-U-N B
[Bun B]
Nigga it's the - big Southern rap impresario
Comin straight up out the black bar-rio
Makes a mill' up off a sorry hoe
Then sit back and peep my sce-nawr-e-oh
Oops, my bad, that's my scenario
No I can't fuck a scary hoe
Now every time, every place, everywhere we go
Hoes start pointin - they say, "There he go!"
Now these motherfuckers know we carry mo' heat than a little bit
We don't pull it out over little shit
And if you catch a lick when I spit, then it won't be a little hit
Go read a book you illiterate son of a bitch and step up yo' vocab
Don't be surprised if yo' hoe stab out with me

and you see us comin down on yo' slab
Livin ghetto-fabulous, so mad, you just can't take it
But nigga if you hatin I
then you wait while I get yo' bitch butt-naked, just break it
You gotta pay like you weigh wet wit two pairs of clothes on
Now get yo' ass to the back as I'm flyin to the track
Timbaland let me spit my pro's on
Pump it up in the pro-zone
That's the track that we breakin these hoes on
Ain't the track that we flow's on
But when shit get hot, then the glock start poppin like ozone
We keep hoes crunk like Trigger-man
Fo' real it don't get no bigger man
Don't trip, let's flip, gettin throwed on the flip
Gettin blowed with the motherfuckin Jigga Man, fool
[Chorus Two: Bun B]
We be.. big pimpin, spendin cheese
We be.. big pimpin, on B.L.A.D.'s
We be.. big pimpin down in P.A.T.
It's just that Jigga Man, Pimp C, and B-U-N B
Cause we be.. big pimpin, spendin cheese
And we be.. big pimpin, on B.L.A.D.'s
Cause we be.. big pimpin in P.A.T.
It's just that Jigga Man, Pimp C, and B-U-N B.. nigga
[Pimp C]
Uhh.. smokin out, throwin up, keepin lean up in my cup
All my car got leather and wood, in my hood we call it buck
Everybody wanna ball, holla at broads at the mall
If he up, watch him fall, nigga I can't fuck witch'all
If I wasn't rappin baby, I would still be ridin Mercedes
Chromin shinin sippin daily, no rest until whitey pay me
Uhhh, now what y'all know bout them Texas boys
Comin down in candied toys, smokin weed and talkin noise
[Chorus Two]
[Jay-Z]
On a canopy my stamina be enough for Pamela Anderson Lee
MTV jam of the week
Made my money quick then back to the streets but
Still sittin on blades... sippin that ray...
Standin on the corner of my block hustlin
Still gettin that cane
half what I paid slippin right through customs
It'll sell by night its extra white...
I got so many grams if the man find out
it will land me in jail for life
But im still big pimpin spendin chesse

with B.U.N. B, Pimp C, and Timothy
We got bitches in the back of the truck, laughin it up
Jigga Man that's what's up

This song glamorizes beating women, sexually exploiting them, holding them as slaves. And yet, apologists, **both white and black,** are never at a loss to rationalize why modern day slavery in black America, in the form of the glamorized pimp culture, is too ingrained in black American culture to eradicate. Some even go so far as to explain black pimp culture as a vestige of white slavery. Such delusional apologetics are nonsensical. Black slavery, as is documented by dozens of historical studies, preceded the introduction of the white man by thousands of years and continues, unabated, to this day.

What is incontrovertible is that black slavery did end in America and that the principles created and memorialized by America's founders have made it possible for the Africans living in America to have exponentially greater success, freedom, health and opportunity than the Africans who remained in Africa where, as I and others have documented, tribal warfare, slavery, institutionalized rape and butchery is epidemic outside of white, South Africa.

Here is an article from the progressive L.A. Times that provides an overview of how bad black Africa is when it comes to human rights, i.e., slavery. The reader should appreciate that when a progressive newspaper covers a story like this, you know the situation is bad, very bad.

Now remember, this article was written in the 21st century, NOT 18th Century America. Also, keep in mind that what you are about to learn PRECEDED European colonization in Africa.[163] In the 18th Century, America's founders had already decided that slavery should be ended for moral (Christian) reasons. **Millions of black Africans living in Africa have not yet reached that point of spiritual and moral development, as America's founders did over 200 years ago, to wit:**

"JOHANNESBURG, South Africa -- African countries dominate a new global index on slavery, with 38 of the 54 nations where the scourge is at its worst found on the continent. The Global Slavery Index, released Thursday, estimated that nearly 30 million people remain enslaved globally, millions of whom are in Africa.

Mauritania has the poorest record, with some 150,000 people in a population of 3.8 million held captive, many of whom inherited their status from their parents.

Other African countries with particularly high prevalence of slavery are located in West Africa: Benin, Ivory Coast, Gambia, Gabon and Senegal.

West Africa has a somber place in the history of transatlantic slavery as the departure gateway for slaves seized in raiding expeditions before they were shipped to the New World. Today children are trafficked around the region and forced into domestic service, farm labor or sexual exploitation.

"In 2013, modern slavery takes many forms, and is known by many names," the report said. "Whether it is called human trafficking, forced labor, slavery or slavery-like practices (a category that includes debt bondage, forced or servile marriage, sale or exploitation of children including in armed conflict), victims of modern slavery have their freedom denied, and are used and controlled and exploited by another person for profit, sex or the thrill of domination."

---

[163] Kwokeji, Ugo G. (2011), *Slavery in Non-Islamic West Africa, 1420-1820.* In David Eltis and Stanley Engerman. The Cambridge World History of Slavery, Volume II. pp. 81–110.

In many African countries, children are sold into labor by poor rural parents, sent to Koranic schools where they are forced to beg on the streets by imams, or recruited as unpaid porters or child soldiers by armed militias. Girls are often married off young and denied an education, or forced to be sex slaves, porters and cooks by armed groups. More than 16% of slaves are in sub-Saharan Africa, according to the report.

"Ongoing conflicts, extremes of poverty, high levels of corruption and the impact of resource exploitation to feed global markets all increase the risk of enslavement in many African countries. Child and forced marriages are still tolerated in the context of informal or 'traditional' legal systems in many countries," the report said.

In Mauritania, as many as 20% of the population is enslaved, according to a nongovernmental organization there interviewed by the Walk Free Foundation. A 2013 U.S. report on human trafficking gave a similar estimate.

Slavery in Mauritania goes back generations and is deeply entrenched, though the country has banned the practice and signed international conventions against slavery and child labor.

Adults and children from slave castes in Mauritania are usually illiterate, unaware of their rights and enslaved in domestic labor and as cattle herders, regarded as the property of their masters. Slaves can see their children sold to other masters, or given away as gifts.

"Indoctrination to ensure people in slavery accept their situation of ownership is a key feature of slavery in Mauritania, with understandings of race and class, as well as some religious teachings being used to justify slavery," the Global Slavery Index report said. "Without access to education or alternative means of subsistence, many believe that it is God's wish for them to be slaves."

The report called on Mauritania to conduct a nationwide investigation into continuing forms of slavery, end impunity for slaveholders and do more to support slaves leaving their masters and to help them mount legal action for compensation.

In Ivory Coast, many children work without pay in fishing, farming, building, domestic service and the cocoa industry, one of country's major exports. Up to 800,000 children work on small family farms with working conditions "akin to the worst forms of child labor," according to the report.

The United States is ranked 134th in terms of prevalence of slavery, with nearly 60,000 estimated to be in modern slavery.

The Walk Free Foundation was founded last year by an Australian mining magnate, Andrew Forrest, to campaign against slavery and fund programs to eradicate the practice. One of its campaigns focuses on pressing companies to ensure their production and supply chains are free of developing-world slaves.

Former Secretary of State Hillary Rodham Clinton said the report was not a perfect measure of global slavery but was a good starting point.

"I urge leaders around the world to view this index as a call to action, and to stay focused on the work of responding to this crime," she said. [164]

For some readers this chapter's content has challenged every "given" you thought you knew about America and the men who founded it. For the person who has been beguiled by the unconscious burdens placed upon you as an American, and this includes both black and white citizens, I trust that you have learned that two-dimensional treatments of American history,

---

[164] Los Angeles Times. *Slavery still haunts Africa, where millions remain captive.* By: Robyn Dixon. October 17, 2013.

whether filtered through a left or right prism miss the mark. If the reader has concluded, after reading this chapter, that he or she has been told half-truths or sold a bill of goods, then you have learned a valuable lesson regarding shadow men and have taken the very first step toward regaining your freedom. For those of you who, after reading this chapter, are motivated to undermine all that you have learned, realize that your motivation to do so is a classic illustration of the effects of brainwashing. I know how hard it must be to realize that much of your education and perhaps your life's very essence has been built upon half-truths told to you by shadow men and their agents who wanted you to do and feel exactly what you have been doing and feeling. Stating the obvious, if you are one of these people, you'll do what you want to do, regardless of the truth of the matter.

CHAPTER 11: DEMOCRACY - TYRANNY USING THE MASSES

Josiah Ober, an expert in the classics at Stanford University, said this about the term democracy:

> "[A]ncient critics of **popular** rule sought to rebrand Demokratia as the equivalent of a tyrannical "polloi-archia" – as the monopolistic domination of government apparatus by the many who were poor...
>
> **[P]lacing democracy on a par with oligarchy**, as little more, in principle or practice, than the monopoly over established governmental offices by, respectively, the many (poor) and the few (wealthy), is to accept fifth-century anti-democratic polemics as an accurate description of political reality."(Emphasis Added) [165]

As far back as ancient Greece, it was fully understood that the seemingly "fair" notion of rule by "common people" (demos) can, and almost certainly will, result in tyranny by the masses using the cudgel of popularity and majority rule as its mechanism of tyranny. Greek Philosopher Plato preceded many other great thinkers who cautioned us about the perils and pitfalls of democracy:

> "In democracy, the lower class grows bigger and bigger. The poor become the winners. Diversity is supreme. People are free to do what they want and live how they want. People can even break the law if they so chose. This appears to be very similar to anarchy." [166]

Democracy is not merely "another path," it is the favored way for shadow men to rule over the masses by deluding the masses into believing that "they" are in control. Why? Because democracy just seems fair and makes sense to the literal and concrete mind. As a matter of indisputable fact, democracy can *easily* be used to subordinate the most intelligent and productive citizens of a town, region or country by imposing "popular will" upon them.

> **This functional equivalence between shadow men control and democratic or majority rule is because it has been demonstrated, time and time again, that shadow men can easily manipulate the masses to do their bidding under the guise of democratic rule and by massaging the herd instinct with little or no awareness on the part of the masses, i.e., demos.**

Since the term "democracy" has attached to it any number of halo-valenced protections, no one, especially the victims of the demos, dare say anything to the contrary lest they be accused of being an elitist or, to use the term made fashionable by Marx and Engels, a member of the bourgeoisie.

The common people (demos) are revered as collectively wise and righteous. "I trust in the American people" is a thought that has been expressed in one form or another by every populist American politician that ever ran for office. Expressions of this elevation of the demos to Solomon-like wisdom can be seen when a politician who is running for the highest office in the land is complimented as "He is the kind of fellow you'd like to have a beer with." Pandering to the demos may take the form of wearing a plaid shirt and jeans when campaigning in Iowa, eating Polish

---

[165] Stanford University. By: Josiah Ober. *The original meaning of "democracy:" Capacity to do things, not majority rule.* September, 2007.

[166] Cahn, Steven M. (2002), *Classics of Political and Moral Philosophy*, Oxford University Press, with reference to the words of Plato.

sausage in certain areas of the Northeast or speaking with a down-home twang when delivering a speech to Southerners.

We know as a matter of fact that popular opinion is NOT inherently wise. How do we know this? For popular opinion to inherently be wise, it must then be true that majority voters have always made the wise choice at the ballot box. We know that can't be true because if it were true it would mean that the best candidate always wins and that simply is not true. If one asserts that democracy is, by definition, "right" because it is the majority's will, then that would connote infallibility to the decisions of the masses popular opinion.

Is it really necessary for me to list the disastrous regimes that came to power with overwhelming popular support under democratic rule? Is it really necessary for me to itemize the collective wisdom of the masses as denoted in their trust in "blood letting" and Asafoetida bags? Both of these medical treatments were popular and widely accepted as proper medical care by the masses in their day. Before we continue, contemplate the utter stupidity of citing popular opinion in polls designed to prove that one view or another is the wiser choice.

Popular opinion as expressed using a democratic model has never worked well over the long haul. The examples are too numerous to recount. Slavery was an example of democratic rule in the vast majority of countries and cultures at one time. The feudal lord-serf system of economy back in its day was popular. Adolph Hitler was famously popular, as was Mao Tse Tung, Joe Stalin and Uganda's cannibal leader Idi Amin Dada. The list of popular, but stupid, miscreant or vicious leaders is almost endless. This inherent flaw in democracy is the reason that *the founders of America established it as a Constitutional Republic, __NOT__ a democracy.*

To be perfectly clear, not only was America never designed to be a democracy, it was never conceptualized nor intended to function as a "representative democracy," though that term is often paired with America's system of governance as though it is true. The word "democracy" is nowhere to be found in America's Declaration of Independence. **It is ironic that my last point regarding American's popular misconception of it being designed as a democracy proves my point about the fallibility of popular opinion.** While America uses limited parts of a democratic model to do the legitimate business of government, e.g., we elect our politicians and they, in turn, pass laws using majority rule. That is where the similarities end.

A Constitutional Republic relies upon a Constitution that sets clear parameters or limits, if you will, for what government can do and be, regardless of what popular opinion might support or what politicians empowered by the masses may wish to impose upon it. Popular opinion was recognized by agents of the British government as fertile soil to till. America's founders knew this and fully intended to erect firewalls to a pure democracy. A number of mind control experts have built their careers upon managing popular opinion, i.e., the demos. One of the most notable among these experts is Edward Bernays.

Edward Bernays is considered to be the father of modern public relations and a preeminent expert on and purveyor of propaganda and mind control. Bernay's special expertise encompassed group psychology and mass attitude modification among the demos. His uncle, Dr. Sigmund Freud, wrote the seminal book on the subject of group behavior entitled *Group Psychology and Analysis of the Ego.* [167] Freud's book was the first work to scientifically dissect the various phenomena that take place in groups and to provide a theoretical framework from which manipulation could take place.

---

[167] Freud, Sigmund. (1922), *Group Psychology and Analysis of the Ego.* Boni and Liveright.

Bernays justified his admitted *social engineering of consent*, [168] as he called it, by stating that the demos naturally behave irrationally and dangerously the result of their herd instinct. Bernays demonstrated his expertise in mind control by successfully stampeding "the herd" to adopt any number of "new" attitudes and behaviors about whatever he had been paid to change.

For example, Bernays, along with his colleagues, Carl Byoir and John Price Jones, manipulated public opinion to support America's involvement in World War I. President Woodrow Wilson (The President who presided over the establishment of The Federal Reserve Act in 1913) viewed Bernays as a valuable national resource. In fact, Bernays was invited by President Wilson to attend the Paris Peace Conference in 1919 as his personal guest.

One of Bernay's cohorts involved in the coercion of consent involving WWI was songwriter George M. Cohan. Here is a flyer of a Broadway Anthology put together by Bernays that lists George M. Cohan, among other popular show business personalities of the time:

The

Broadway Anthology

BY

EDWARD L. BERNAYS

SAMUEL HOFFENSTEIN

WALTER J. KINGSLEY

MURDOCK PEMBERTON

NEW YORK
DUFFIELD & COMPANY
1917

Copyright, 1917
BY DUFFIELD & COMPANY

VAIL-BALLOU COMPANY
BINGHAMTON AND NEW YORK

EDWARD L. BERNAYS

ACCIDENTS WILL HAPPEN
THE BARITONE
PATRIOTISM
THE PILLOW CASES
BETTER INDUSTRIAL RELATIONS
THE PRIMA DONNA
PRESS STORIES
THE DISTRIBUTION OF CREDIT
TEARS
PHOTOGRAPHS

SAMUEL HOFFENSTEIN

THE THEATRE SCRUBWOMAN DREAMS A DREAM
THE STRANGE CASE OF THE MUSICAL COMEDY STAR
THE STAR IS WAITING TO SEE THE MANAGER
THE JESTER
IN A CAFE
TO A CABARET SINGER
IN THE THEATRE

WALTER J. KINGSLEY

LO, THE PRESS AGENT
FIRST NIGHTS
THE DRAMATIST
TYPES
GEORGE M. COHAN
DAVID BELASCO
LO, THE HEADLINER

George M. Cohan's seemingly patriotic song, "Over There," got the public (demos) all worked up over Germany and helped to motivate a war-weary American public to enter World War I. If you have ever hummed this tune or sang this song please appreciate the fact that you were parroting a clever PSYOP that motivated men to fight and die in a war they knew little or nothing about.

Lyrics to "Over There" by George M. Cohan

Johnnie get your gun, get your gun, get your gun

Take it on the run, on the run, on the run

Hear them calling you and me

Every son of liberty

Hurry right away, no delay, go today

Make your daddy glad to have had such a lad

Tell your sweetheart not to pine

To be proud her boy's in line.

---

168 Bernays, Edward L.; Cutler, H.W. (1955), *The Engineering of Consent.* University of Oklahoma Press.

CHORUS (repeated twice):
Over there, over there
Send the word, send the word over there
That the Yanks are coming, the Yanks are coming
The drums are rum-tumming everywhere

So prepare, say a prayer
Send the word, send the word to beware
We'll be over there, we're coming over
And we won't come back till it's over over there.
Over there.

Johnnie get your gun, get your gun, get your gun
Johnnie show the Hun you're a son of a gun
Hoist the flag and let her fly
Yankee Doodle do or die
Pack your little kit, show your grit, do your bit
Yankees to the ranks from the towns and the tanks
Make your mother proud of you
And the old Red White and Blue.
CHORUS (repeated twice):
Over there, over there
Send the word, send the word over there
That the Yanks are coming, the Yanks are coming
The drums are rum-tumming everywhere

So prepare, say a prayer
Send the word, send the word to beware
We'll be over there, we're coming over
And we won't come back till it's over over there.
Over there.

To our knowledge, neither Bernays nor any of his show-business cohorts were sufficiently motivated to actually go to war and personally fight in Europe. Their job, as they defined it, was to motivate the masses to fight and die, not actually do the fighting themselves. In 1936, as a "thank you" for helping the government garner a willing fighting force for an unpopular war, Cohan was awarded the Congressional Gold Medal for writing "Over There."

When the powers that be in the government and their overlords realized their paid agents could motivate a war-weary and reluctant public into supporting an unpopular war, thus transforming something unpopular, into something popular, they behaved like precocious adolescents who had just discovered the more pleasurable parts of their body.

The Ph.D.'s and other group psychology experts behaved like supplicant genies when approached by government operatives to modify the masse's thoughts, feelings and behavior, "your wish is my command." Not only did government have, for all intents and purposes, an unlimited budget; but also, the human behavior experts discovered that by working for the government they could do what they had always wanted to do, experiment on their fellow man and exercise their psychological expertise doing work for an appreciative and powerful client, all the while getting paid handsomely for their efforts.

Bernays either invented or made popular what advertisers, press agents and public relations departments consider de rigueur these days. Here is a representative sample of some of the handiwork of Edward Bernays. As you read about Bernays, keep in mind that I am recounting to you propaganda technology that is now some 90 years old. Keep in the back of your mind the technology of a 1917 horseless carriage when compared to a 2015 luxury automobile. Propaganda has advanced in a similar, if not even more, dramatic fashion than have automobiles.

Bernays perfected the art of the fake news PSYOP in order to make advertising or mind control, appear as though it was news. You see this PSYOP prominently on display in every major search engine home page where visitors are purposefully duped into clicking on an ad that looks and feels like a news story, but is not. Newspapers do this as a matter of course. The "Nightly News" is a favorite format within which this particular PSYOP can, and often is, strategically placed. The engineered news story is manipulative and duplicitous, by definition, and relies upon the relatively poor attention and acuity of the masses along with a media entertainment complex that will do most anything for a dollar or to help their owner's achieve their desired effect.

We human beings are highly suggestible creatures. Go into any full movie theater and try this trick. Start coughing repeatedly and I virtually guarantee you that you will ignite a coughing epidemic throughout the theater as patrons unconsciously copy your cough. You can also yawn in a group of people and watch the yawning contagion take hold. Laughing is also contagious. This is why producers of sit-coms have, since the 1950's, used "laugh tracks" [169] to make whatever they were broadcasting funnier than it otherwise might be without a laugh track.

Here is one of Bernay's classic PSYOPs using subtle suggestion and mind control strategies. This particular PSYOP was the predecessor of and blueprint for the modern PSYOP known as "The War on Women." Bernays was hired by the maker of Lucky Strike Cigarettes to overcome the stigma attached to women smoking cigarettes. In the 1920's, women were only allowed to smoke in designated areas, if at all. Although rarely enforced, if women violated the prohibition against smoking in public, they could be arrested.

BARRED FOR WOMEN; POLICE ENFORCE LAW

Head of Aldermen Never Heard of It, but Author Says Hylan Signed Ordinance.

PENALTY FOR PROPRIETORS

Consternation Along Rialto as Detectives Order Cigarettes Put Out.

Ten Days or $5 to $25 Fine If They Permit Transgressions—Some Hotel Men Approve.

1920's New York City Newspaper Stories

---

[169] Laugh Tracks were recordings made of actual audiences in the 1950's, 60's and 70's that were particularly effusive in their laughter. These old recordings were dubbed over countless television sit-coms in order to "suggest" when and how much to laugh.

Bernays chose, of all things, the 1929 Easter Parade in New York City to manipulate women using dramatic suggestion. In a Machiavellian display of blatant manipulation of women, Bernays hired beautiful women who were provided Lucky Strike cigarettes to smoke as they rode on a beautiful Easter float. Not only did Bernays show beautiful women (all women want or have wanted to be beautiful) smoking Lucky Strike Cigarettes, but also, in a devious display of his social engineering acumen, labeled the float "Torches of Freedom." By labeling the float "Torches of Freedom," Bernays implied, through suggestion that, women were being held in bondage and dominated by men who frowned upon their smoking. And how to break those bonds of patriarchal domination? Why, smoke a Lucky Strike Cigarette, of course.

Bernays insured that his Easter Parade drama was presented as "news," i.e., a spontaneous display of independence on the part of feminist women who just happened to be breaking the law and, at the same time, breaking the bond of male domination by smoking Lucky Strike Cigarettes.

Then, as now, the press was so easily duped into reporting this event as a spontaneous event, that no one was the wiser. Did it work? You bet. Bernays helped to speed up women's adoption of the bad habits of men until the point where by the late 20th century women were suffering the ill effects of smoking at the same rate as men. Although not exclusively responsible for women taking up smoking, Bernays certainly sped it up. Bernay's, using his clever cigarette/feminist PSYOP, has ravaged the lives of millions of women and cost the economy of the United States untold billions in health care costs, while making the American Tobacco Company rich in the process.

The Lucky Strike campaign was the first major exploitation of women in the marketplace using sophisticated (for its day) PSYOPs. Women were targeted because they represented an undeveloped market. Please pay close attention to some of Bernay's other mind control PSYOPs we will present to you, as they will serve you well in understanding how shadow men, by and through their mind control agents, manipulate the masses.

Bernays was hired by pork producers to manipulate the public's view of "heavy" breakfasts, e.g., bacon and eggs. In the 1920's and before Bernay's socially engineered breakfast behavior, the average American breakfast consisted of toast, coffee or tea. Bernays concocted a manipulative survey and sent it to a group of physicians as the first step in his devious PSYOP. Bernays understood that when it comes to any survey, the nature of the question and how it is asked virtually guarantees the nature of the answer.

For instance, if you want to dupe the public into supporting a high-speed rail boondoggle, you ask this question: Wouldn't it be wonderful if you could travel from San Diego to San Francisco in an hour and a half on a luxury bullet train? The vast majority of people will say yes to that question. But if you inquire of voters about how they may feel about a high speed bullet train using objective questions, you get the exact opposite response, e.g. "Are you willing to have your taxes raised to build a high speed rail system that will service a limited number of business travelers who want to go from San Diego to San Francisco on a train in roughly the same time and cost it takes to fly there now?

Bernays framed his survey to physicians this way, and I paraphrase: "Which is better, no breakfast or a breakfast consisting of bacon and eggs?" Once Bernays got the responses he knew he would get, he sent the results to another group of 5,000 physicians. He simultaneously sent out a press release. (Once again, to the dupes in the press) It wasn't long before bacon and eggs became THE stereotypical mainstay breakfast in America. After all, the herd instinct had been triggered with advice from doctors, that is, doctors who had been manipulated by the nephew of one of the greatest psychoanalysts of all time.

Shadow men crave wealth and power. Untapped demographic markets represent an irresistible "opportunity" for shadow men to increase their wealth; thus, their control. Referring back to Bernay's Lucky Strike Campaign, the tobacco companies profited, to be sure, *but they're not the real power behind the exploitation of women.*

The financiers attached to these engineered deals made out like bandits because they lent the money to develop more land for more tobacco plants for more fertilizer for more cigarette processing and packaging plants for more advertising, etc. But it's not even the capitalists in the food chain who really drove the exploitation of women. It was the unseen banking barons who, as we have demonstrated, own the machinery of money. And above these men are bastions of power and wealth that had their eyes on the untapped market of women and finally discovered a way to exploit this untapped market. Thanks to Dr. Freud, his nephew and an ever-growing number of researchers in the field of mind control, shadow men finally had at their disposal an effective method to exploit the female gender *without so much as one iota of awareness on the part of Americans.*

Not only did women not resent being exploited, **they welcomed it**. "It is my right to smoke just like a man." "No one is going to tell me what to do." "If a man can do it so can I." "Men who don't want me to smoke are dominating me and I won't have it." "This is a war on women and I'll show you." Are you beginning to see how devious PSYOPs can be?

Mind control artists never, ever permit their intended victims to know the truth. Recall that mind control artists have always identified their victim's vociferous support for their own demise as the best compliment they can receive. Bernay's 1929 exploitation of women's desire to "be like men" was copied in the 1960's with a Virginia Slims Cigarette campaign, that used advertising copy that reminded cigarette addicted women: "You've come a long way baby." By the dawn of the 21st Century women's rate of lung cancer, heart disease and blood clots were rivaling those of men. You certainly have "come a long way baby."

In the 1950's, the female demographic was ripe for the picking, and it wasn't just smoking cigarettes this time around. From shadow men's perspective, economics is a zero sum game. And as you may recall from our chapter on the psychology of banking, there was something very troubling about the late 1940's and 50's that caused shadow men concern.

Men and women, when paired in a committed marriage, were wealth magnets. For the first time in the recorded history of man, the average working man and woman who had married and formed a family were accumulating wealth. Increasing wealth means more power and independence from outside control. With ever-increasing wealth (please refer back to our chapter on banking to refresh your memory on the economy of the 1950's) came ever-increasing power. Wages were increasing, working conditions were improving and these little industrial units called traditional nuclear families were creating islands of power and wealth. It was becoming obvious to shadow men that they were losing control over the masses.

A conversation in at least one important think tank located in New York City, in the late 1950's, took place that sounded very much like the following, and I paraphrase:

"Social mobility is getting out of hand for both Negro and Caucasian traditional families living in America. Our advisors inform us that a solution is available to mitigate this problem that involves the industrial unit used by the masses to facilitate their upward social mobility. This industrial unit is the nuclear family.

We have an untapped labor market numbering approximately 50% of the population of the United States that is comprised of females. This untapped market represents one of the bulwarks in the masses' industrial unit. Imagine for a moment if we could dissolve the existent social fabric of the country and thereby, over the next 50 years, double the workforce by encouraging women to enter the workforce.

If our efforts are successful, we can almost double the number of workers without increasing the number of jobs available to those workers. As a result, wages will go down. If we can encourage BOTH men and women to work outside the home, we can double the prices of housing, cars, items of necessity and discretion, virtually everything. If our efforts are successful, we will be able to industrialize the raising of the masses' children because it will take two parents working to earn the wages it now only requires one to make. This will provide us direct control over the masses' children. Our political arms will embrace the idea of increased tax revenue that will come rolling in the result of women having entered the work force. Deconstructing the nuclear family will create a new wealth generating center in the form of a cottage industry centered around childcare, but more importantly, will allow us to program the masses' children to accept our "new" system of thinking, feeling and behaving that will nullify the industrial unit of the nuclear family and committed relationships.

Of particular concern are the Negroes. Negroes are assimilating into the fabric of America very rapidly and, before long, will come to possess economic power and independence from our control. But if our consultants are accurate, we can socially engineer a new order. In order to accomplish this we must dissolve the existent culture and the masses' industrial unit. When we are successful, and we are assured by our behavioral experts we will be successful, we will once again gain absolute control over the masses."[170]

By the late 1960's the handiwork of the mind control artists who had cut their teeth on the Lucky Strike Campaign were operating at full speed in service to dissolving America's traditional culture, and in particular, what social engineers of the day termed the "industrial unit" of the average man and woman i.e., the traditional nuclear family.

Permit me to address what human behavior experts refer to as "process." My colleagues in the behavioral sciences created a number of protective PSYOPs involving the subjects I am about to reveal to you. These protective PSYOPs are designed to insulate their social engineering handiwork from disclosure, should someone (like me) ever attempt (like I am now) to lift the cloak on what they created. Think of these protective PSYOPs as triggers that will explode the bomb if anyone tries to disarm their social engineering handiwork. So let's return to the content part of this book and explore the truth. We'll soon see if I can disarm my colleague's strategically placed firewalls and explosive failsafe mechanisms. My success in my efforts to deprogram you, the reader, will be dependent upon you and you alone.

The masses and the pundits who cover this general subject ASSUME, and take for granted, that the feminist movement of the 1960's was a spontaneous, grass roots movement. **Nothing could be further from the truth.** Whenever we examine the behavior of the masses, we keep in mind the relative ignorance of any one individual's understanding of the powerful forces that drive any social movement. Individuals are motivated to do things for personal reasons. I'm sure, for example, that the women who rode on Bernay's "Torches of Freedom" float in the 1929 Easter Parade, happily smoking Lucky Strike Cigarettes, had their own reasons to participate in Bernay's PSYOP that were divorced from the motivations of Bernays and the American Tobacco Company. It could have been merely a job, a fun opportunity to ride in the Easter parade. It could have been an opportunity to model or to garner attention from the crowd or it could have been all of these things, together.

---

[170] Anonymity requested from an elderly man with a guilty conscience who wishes to protect his final years without retribution for having told the truth.

People are egocentric, this means that people erroneously think that their personal reasons to join a movement or participate in a PSYOP trump the motivations of the social engineers who made the individual's motivation possible in the first place. Apologists invariably cite to the personal motivations of the individuals being socially engineered, as if to prove that the overarching motivations of shadow men are invalid. Again, **nothing could be further from the truth.**

Clinical psychologists have chronicled any number of personality characteristics among the group calling themselves "feminists" that predisposed them to become feminists. All of these motivations were personal, but did NOT create nor fuel the feminist movement.

> **Notwithstanding what rank and file "feminists" believe, along with the general public, the social revolution termed "feminism" was funded, promoted and *imposed* upon America and Western Europe by agents of shadow men who plotted the demise of the traditional nuclear family unit in order to increase their wealth and control over the masses.**

Permit me to insert here that as you learn about how shadow men imploded the traditional nuclear family in America, that their shadow man families, their traditional values, their culture, their religions, were left intact and remained immune from their skullduggery directed at those under and not of them.

Multinational corporations and Marxist revolutionaries joined forces to create and promote feminism for the masses. If those two entities strike you as strange bedfellows, it is probably because you fail to see the common denominator shared by these two vested interests.

From the multinational corporation's perspective, women represented a huge untapped profit center. This is the exact same motivation used by the owner of Lucky Strike Cigarettes, The American Tobacco Company, to encourage women to take up smoking. The fact of the matter is, multinational corporations realized that the profit potential was breathtaking if only women could be convinced to join the same rat race disproportionately populated by men.

Just as with Lucky Strike Cigarettes, The American Tobacco Company could not just come out and say, " I want to sell cigarettes to the other 50% of the population in order to become even richer." Likewise, if you are agents of shadow men, you can't come out and say, "women are an untapped market, a commodity to exploit if only we could change their cognitive and emotional mindset."

Never mind that multinational corporations knew perfectly well that the health of women would be utterly destroyed if they were successful in subverting women, or that consumer prices would double across the board, homes would no longer be affordable without long and indentured mortgages, no longer would children have a mother or father to spend significant time with them, no, of course not (these were positive outcomes from shadow men's perspective). The so-called women's movement was not about women in the least. Feminism was about MORE MONEY AND CONTROL FOR SHADOW MEN. Of course, and as stated earlier, rank and file "feminists" have personal motivations to do what it is they do, but the feminist movement and the transformation of an *entire* culture were NOT the result of a grassroots movement in the same way that women smoking cigarettes was NOT an expression of freedom, as in "Torches of Freedom. " It was, in fact, the exact opposite.

> **Feminism was the end result of an invisible hand socially engineering women's attitudes in service to dissolving the wealth generating power and autonomy of the average man and woman, and transferring that wealth and control into the hands of shadow men and their agents.**

A cabal using PSYOPs honed by the progeny of Bernays invented "feminism," the movement, not feminists, per se. Every unhappy woman with a domineering father or brother gladly joined so called feminists because that gave them a way to vent their anger. Lesbians and their gay male counterparts joined in because they now had a way to bite back at those in the heterosexual community who treated them badly. Feminism gave Masculine Protest [171] women a means by which they could project their own psychopathology onto the general population. But these sub-groups were in the minority. Besides the inherent greed-logic that should convince you of the validity of who was and is behind "feminism," I am going to reference here the work of an iconoclastic filmmaker who dared to expose the truth on how feminism, the movement, came to be.

Aaron Russo was a famous Hollywood mogul who passed away in 2007. He was a director, producer and ultimately a documentary filmmaker. Russo was, for most of his career, a card carrying progressive. He was a member of Hollywood's "in crowd." Russo's show business career began as a music promoter/club owner in the late 1960's. Russo's wildly popular music venue named *The Kinetic Playground* in Chicago, Illinois, featured the who's who of the music business, e.g., The Grateful Dead, Iron Butterfly, Jefferson Airplane, Janis Joplin, Led Zeppelin, Rotary Connection, and The Who. Russo also worked as singer/actress Bette Midler's manager from 1972 to 1979, along with managing the very successful jazz ensemble Manhattan Transfer. Russo produced such Hollywood blockbusters as "The Rose" starring Michael Douglas; "Trading Places" with Eddie Murphy and "Wise Guys" starring Danny DeVito and Harvey Keitel. Six of Russo's movies were nominated for Academy Awards and two of his films received Golden Globe Award nominations.

In the 1990's Russo decided to strip himself of the airs and graces of politically correct Hollywood. Russo no longer had the need to prove himself or to bow to the powers that be in order to make a living in Hollywood. Russo produced a documentary film entitled *America, Freedom to Fascism*. In that documentary, Russo disclosed, for the first time, that he had been approached, as were other power brokers in Hollywood, to become part of the Public Relation's Arm for a cadre of elite families (shadow men). Russo said that Nicholas Rockefeller, of the famous Rockefeller family, had confessed to him how the Rockefeller family, along with other elite multinational interests, had created, then financed, the feminist movement, to wit:

> "Rockefeller said a number of elite families created and financed the women's liberation movement so they could tax another half of the population and so that the children would be trained by them in government schools rather than in the context of the family unit." [172]

Russo's independent recounting of Nicholas Rockefeller's stated motivation for sponsoring the feminist movement corroborates our independently researched transcript from an actual meeting in New York where the plot was hatched to create feminism, the movement.

The Rockefellers were only one of many elite families who financed mind control agents to brainstorm how to socially engineer a culture that would provide to them even greater wealth and control over the demos. Their scheme was simple: Dissolve the traditional nuclear family, and the best way to do that, is to brainwash women to abandon their families for self-expression in the

---

[171] **Masculine Protest**: A tendency attributed especially to the human female in the psychology of Alfred Adler to escape from the female role by assuming a masculine role and by dominating others; broadly : any tendency to compensate for feelings of inferiority or inadequacy by exaggerated overt aggressive behavior.

[172] Russo, Aaron. *Freedom to Fascism*. (2006), Aaron Russo Productions.

capitalist marketplace. I'll interject at this point that women being captive to the family unit in the role of homemaker was **not**, nor has it ever been, the issue.

The wealth producing traditional nuclear family unit could have been protected had the cultural norm been: "the parent most capable of making a living" is the parent who worked outside the home while the remaining parent, man or woman, managed the nuclear family unit, including rearing, educating and helping to develop the family' human and material fortunes. Had freedom of choice become the social norm, the average man and woman could have maintained their material and human security while embracing freedom of choice. Of course, that didn't happen and now we have neither material or human security for either men or women. You'll learn more about this later in this chapter.

Earlier I stated that not only were multinational corporations fomenting the feminist movement, but that Marxist/Communist revolutionaries were, likewise, vested in promoting feminism. Let's test the validity of that statement and test the provenance of that idea by quoting the so-called brain trusts behind the feminist movement. Catherine MacKinnon [173] wrote the following retrospective in 1989:

> *"Feminism, Socialism, and Communism are one in the same, and Socialist/Communist government is the goal of feminism."* [174]

Marx and Engels writings corroborate Professor MacKinnon's thesis:

> *"Although Marx and Engels were not the instigators of the anti-family trend among socialists, they—especially Engels—contributed mightily to it. A Prussian agent reported back to Marx's brother-in-law, the Prussian Minister of the Interior, that the German communists in London, with which Marx was associated, were 'so unusually dangerous for the state, the family and the social order' Engels thrust the issue into the foreground shortly after Marx's death by publishing The Origin of the Family, Private Property, and the State (1884), a work that, according to Engels, Marx had wanted to write and that reflected Marx's views. In 1895 Clara Zetkin, a leader of the socialist women's movement in Germany, praised this work as 'of the most fundamental importance for the struggle for liberation of the entire female sex'. Not only did Engels' book exert influence in the late-nineteenth century, but also it has enjoyed a renaissance among contemporary socialists and feminists, though it has probably received as much criticism as praise, even among socialist feminists."* [175]

Another leading feminist writer by the name of Robin Morgan [176] said this:

> *"We can't destroy the inequities between men and women until we destroy marriage."* [177]

---

[173] Prof. MacKinnon's scholarly books include: *Sexual Harassment of Working Women* (1979), *Feminism Unmodified* (1987), *Toward a Feminist Theory of the State* (1989), *Only Words* (1993), *Women's Lives, Men's Laws* (2005), *Are Women Human?* (2006), and the casebook *Sex Equality* (2001/2007).

[174] MacKinnon, Catharine A. (1989), *Toward a Feminist Theory of the State*. First Harvard University Press.

[175] Weikart, Richard. *Marx, Engels and the Abolition of the Family.* (1994) In: *History of European Ideas. Vol.* 18, No. 5., pp. 657-672. Elsevier Science Ltd.

[176] In the late 1960s Robin Morgan was a founding member of radical feminist organizations such as New York Radical Women and W.I.T.C.H. She founded or co-founded the Feminist Women's Health Network, the National Battered Women's Refuge Network, Media Women, the National Network of Rape Crisis Centers, the Feminist Writers' Guild, the Women's Foreign Policy Council, The National Museum of Women in the Arts, the Sisterhood Is Global Institute, GlobalSister.org, and Greenstone Women's Radio Network. She also co-founded the Women's Media Center with activist Gloria Steinem and actor/activist Jane Fonda.

[177] Morgan, Robin. (1970), *Sisterhood is Powerful*. Pg. 537.

A very interesting article appeared in New York's Village Voice in 1979. It chronicled a shadowy relationship between none other than Feminist Poster Child, Gloria Steinem and The Central Intelligence Agency (CIA):

"At Random House on March 15, 1976, "Feminist Revolution" was just another women's book in production. It consisted of a multifaceted analysis of the women's liberation movement edited by members of Redstockings, an early radical feminist group. A self-published edition released the previous fall had stirred up controversy with its indictment of liberals, lesbian pseudo-leftists, and foundation grant feminists. 5000 copies had sold out.

Part of the book-some say the most interesting part-was titled "Agents, Opportunists and Fools." It attempted to link the CIA and the corporate establishment to several individuals and institutions connected with Ms. Magazine... Feminist Revolution had passed an initial libel reading by Random House's legal department on March 2nd, and a contract was signed in the office that March morning. 20,000 copies of the book were scheduled to hit the stores in June.

That afternoon, an unannounced visitor appeared in the citadel of the free press. A presumably angry Gloria Steinem asked to see Random House president Robert Bernstein. She was there to hand-deliver a letter from her attorney threatening to sue for libel unless the chapter on the CIA was removed from the book.

No one knows what Steinem and Bernstein said in their private meeting, and it may have been just coincidence that, within weeks Random House was blitzed with similar threats from other people and groups mentioned in the CIA chapter: Clay Felker, Women's Action Alliance, Warner Communications, Franklin Thomas, the Overseas Education Fund of the League of Women Voters, and Katherine Graham.

But, in any case, publication of Feminist Revolution was delayed nearly 3 years; the printing run was cut to 12,500, despite 13,000 advance orders; and when the book was finally released last month, the chapter on Gloria Steinem and the CIA had been deleted in its entirety.

[I]n 1967 both the New York Times and the Washington Post carried interviews with Steinem in the wake of Ramparts' expose of CIA funding of the National Student Association and other organizations. Steinem was the founder and director of one of those groups, Independent Research Service, for which she had solicited and obtained CIA money to carry out covert operations at Communist youth festivals in Vienna and Helsinki in 1959 and 1952. Unlike most of the other principals in the scandal, who had repudiated their past work with the agency and turned over information to the press, **Steinem defended her secret deal with the CIA, calling the undermining of the youth festivals "the CIA's finest hour."** [178]

---

[178] Beal, Dana; Nichols, Grace and Conliff, Steve. (1983), *1983 Youth International Party Information Service. Blacklisted News, Secret History: From Chicago, '68, to 1984.* Bleecker Publishing, POB 392, Canal St. Station, New York, NY 10012. ISBN 0-912873-00-0.

Gloria Steinem: Flashing the Eye of Horus Symbol.

The C.I.A. states the following:

"CIA's mission is to collect information related to foreign intelligence and foreign counterintelligence. By law, the CIA is specifically prohibited from collecting intelligence concerning the domestic activities of U.S. citizens. By direction of the President in Executive Order 12333, as amended, and in accordance with procedures approved by the Attorney General, the CIA is restricted in the collection of intelligence information directed against U.S. citizens. Collection is allowed only for an authorized intelligence purpose; for example, if there is a reason to believe that an individual is involved in espionage or international terrorist activities. The CIA's procedures require senior approval for any such collection that is allowed, and, depending on the collection technique employed, the sanction of the Director of National Intelligence and Attorney General may be required. These restrictions on the CIA, or similar ones, have been in effect since the 1970s." [179]

From the very beginning of the feminist movement, before it appeared on the average person's radar, Marxists/Communists, multinational corporations, on behalf of their shadow men overseers, engaged in clandestine scheming that, as we have documented, involved America's premier intelligence agency, the C.I.A.

The sketchy nature of these relationships is the direct result of agent's concerted efforts to keep as much of their subversion efforts secret as humanely possible. A public conditioned to believe in the tooth fairy while rejecting as nonsense the mere notion of coordinated subversion of their lives, i.e., "conspiracy," has brought us to this point in human history where the victims become advocates for the victimizers, daring and/or ridiculing anyone to say anything to the contrary.

Bernays learned from his uncle Freud that people in groups do things they would never do when alone. Mob psychology manifests everywhere and hasn't changed over the millennia except in one very important way. Mobs used to be local phenomena. In today's world, mobs are not only precipitated by local events but can take shape around events anywhere the media-entertainment complex broadcasts. This underlying tendency on the part of man to join a mob is the mechanism

---

[179] Central Intelligence Agency. (2014), https://www.cia.gov/library/publications/additional-publications/the-work-of-a-nation/items-of-interest/frequently-asked-questions.html

by which vested interests can create, out of thin air, a modification of man's mind. Thanks to the herd instinct, massaged and nurtured by the media entertainment complex, an entire culture can be turned inside out. To understand how the media-entertainment complex can facilitate the creation and behavior of groups turned into mobs, we'll next examine the dynamics of group psychology.

According to Bernays, and those who preceded him, man has a herd instinct that resides in his genetics. Instincts are primitive motivational forces that circumvent reason and tend to operate independently and reflexively. Instincts function much like certain neural circuits that operate in a self-enclosed pathway, generally routed through the spinal cord, and are not routed through the CNS. One such circuit that all of us should be familiar with is the pain-reflex response circuit.

If you have ever stepped on a sharp object, e.g., a tack, you can attest to the fact that long before you could ever cognitively register an awareness of pain and think of a response to make the pain go away, your reflexive circuitry did the job for you.

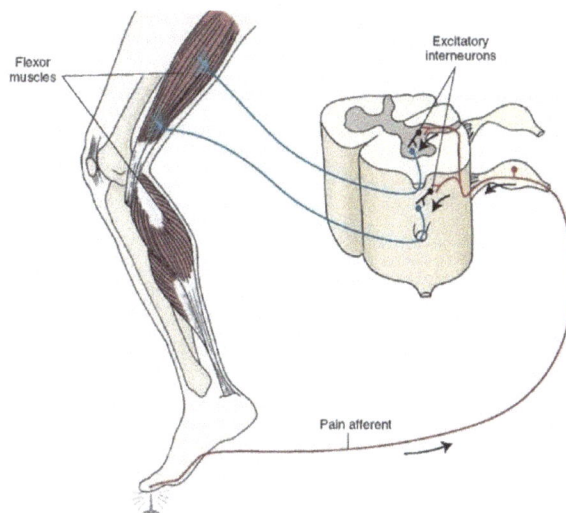

Flexor (withdrawal) Reflex.
A noxious stimulus (in this case stepping on a thumbtack) applied to the skin or deeper structures stimulates free nerve endings, and the resulting impulses are conducted through small-diameter myelinated afferent fibers and unmyelinated afferent fibers. These fibers make polysynaptic connections with at least three to four excitatory interneurons. The result is that ipsilateral flexor muscles contract, ipsilateral antagonist extensor muscles relax, and the person withdraws the limb in response to the noxious stimulus.

The withdrawal reflex is a good **metaphor** for the triggering of instincts that motivate humans to behave in otherwise irrational ways and not in their own best interest. For example, much of sexuality is instinctual as is "that feeling" of belonging that comes from being part of a group.

Groups are like raindrops in that they must form around something. In the case of the raindrop it is usually a speck of dirt. Group members share some important characteristic(s) with other members. The most primitive groups share an acute passion, that is, everyone in a crowd shares a passion (fear, rage, indignation, sexual arousal). Once the crowd "shares" in the passion, whatever it may be, the group turns into a crowd and depending upon the nature of the passion, the crowd may turn into a mob. Once the crowd forms, it becomes a functionally autonomous group that may be completely separated from the mind control agents who started it. Groups can form around physical characteristics, e.g., race.

Think of modern day Halloween when contemplating how the origins of a group activity can become functionally autonomous from its later version. When Halloween began it was named "All Hallows Eve." It truly was a scary time because people once believed that on All Hallows Eve the dead would rise from their graves and evil spirits would rule the night. Man created lighted and carved gourds and pumpkins to scare away the evil spirits. Today, we carve pumpkins because it is tradition and because trick or treating is fun. So it is with crowds and political/social movements.

Mobs are irrational when viewed from the outside by someone who does not share the passion or physical identity glue that holds the group together. It is irrational for sport's fans to go on rampages after their team wins a championship. But this mob behavior is not uncommon and has, for instance, appeared all over the world after any number of sporting events. These mobs set fires, ransack stores, overturn police cars. From the outside, the mob's thuggish members appear as though they have lost their mind. As a matter of fact, they have, they've lost their rational mind and have relinquished control to their herd instinct. If you sense that feminism, for example, is more like a cult and functions like a mob at this point in history, you would be right. This is because of mob psychology.

In 1898 a researcher at Indiana University, located in Bloomington, Indiana, studied something he called "social facilitation." He studied a phenomenon that he observed where cyclists not in direct competition with one another made their way around I.U.'s track and field circuit faster when in pairs or when they were part of a group of cyclists than when they rode alone.

What Dr. Norman Triplett had really stumbled upon was the herd instinct that Edward Bernays would use to engineer the public's consent. Not only did Triplett uncover a herd instinct, he discovered a "facilitation effect." [180] If we're studying cyclists the effect means the cyclists peddle faster. If we are studying aggressive behavior then others become more aggressive when in groups. If we are studying people who are angry, then put them in groups and they become even angrier. And to make the phenomenon of social facilitation even more fascinating, it occurs, just like the withdrawal reflex, without one iota of conscious awareness or input. Can you begin to see how Bernays rationalized his manipulation of the masses for their (our) own good? Here is what Edward Bernays said about his work:

> *"The conscious and intelligent manipulation of the organized habits and opinions of the masses is an important element in democratic society.* **Those who manipulate this unseen mechanism of society constitute an invisible government, which is the true ruling power of our country. ...We are governed, our minds are molded, our tastes formed, our ideas suggested, largely by men we have never heard of.** *This is a logical result of the way in which our democratic society is organized. Vast numbers of human beings must cooperate in this manner if they are to live together as a smoothly functioning society. ...In almost every act of our daily lives, whether in the sphere of politics or business, in our social conduct or our ethical thinking, we are dominated by the relatively small number of persons...who understand the mental processes and social patterns of the masses. It is they who pull the wires which control the public mind."* [181] (Emphasis Added)

The economic and control benefit of social engineering is the key to understanding why shadow men remake entire cultures. When the family model of mating and procreation was utterly blown

---

[180] Triplett, N. (1898).], *The dynamogenic factors in pacemaking and competition.* American Journal of Psychology, 9, 507-533.
[181] Bernays, Edward L. (1928), *Propaganda.* Ig Publishing, Brooklyn, New York.

up in the 1960's, as Russo, myself and others have documented, it was replaced by an industry that has now grown into a multi-billion dollar business. This industry employs hundreds of thousands of people whose raison d'être is to meddle in other people's lives, especially the lives of the traditional nuclear family. The industrialization and warehousing of children takes the form of day care, extended school hours, nannies, caretakers and the ever-present department of social services worker.

Erin Pizzey is founder of Chiswick Women's' Aid, the **first ever** refuge in the world for victims of domestic violence. She is a lecturer and advocate, and has authored books on domestic abuse, including the seminal "Prone to Violence." Her latest effort is her autobiography, titled "This Way to the Revolution." She is also an Editor-at-Large and adviser for A Voice for Men on domestic violence policy.

Pizzey's credentials, when it comes to helping abused women, are beyond reproach. Pizzey is also a fascinating historical figure in the women's liberation movement because she was there in the very beginning and saw it develop. When Pizzey saw what was happening to her therapeutic movement by the operatives of shadow men intent upon establishing what would come to be known as the women's liberation movement, she rebelled. In retaliation for her speaking out, shadow men's agents killed her beloved dog, threatened her with death and set about to marginalize this brave woman who set up the first battered women's shelter. Pizzey described how she was targeted for eradication by shadow men's agents at the International Conference on Men's Issues in 2014:

> *"Now, in the beginning, I was booted out of the Women's Movement, and I've still got the letter banning me (the liberation movement) from all the collectives, because I stood up and said, if this is your intention in these huge collectives to say that the family is a dangerous place for women and children, I, for one, do not believe you. Anyway – you have nothing to do with women – there has never been a Women's Movement. It was not a Women's Movement. It wasn't about women. It was about a handful of powerful Marxist women turning on men of the Left, and brilliantly deciding they would create a billion-dollar industry."* [182]

Pizzey represents yet another independent, and exceptionally reliable and knowledgeable source, that corroborates our investigative work regarding the plot hatched in New York City to create feminism, the movement, and later attested to, independently, by Aaron Russo in Hollywood. Pizzey saw the writing on the wall before anyone else from ground zero. And as she describes it, what she predicted was so unbelievable 40 years ago, no one would believe her warnings.

> *"In America – I came to America in the early Seventies, and I could see what was happening: exactly the same thing. The women were scribbling Title-whatever-it-was [editorial note: Title IX], to get the money to create the Empire, on the backs of very fragile women and children. And this is going on 40 years, it's going on and it's getting bigger and bigger and bigger. And I stood back, then, and I was begging: I was saying to people, "This is a fraudulent movement, listen to what I'm saying!" And nobody would say anything; because for a long time, the media, the courts, the agencies, certainly the universities, were preaching this doctrine which was in essence a feminist-Marxist doctrine that eviscerated men off the scene. [W]omen would be putting their children, one of the demands was 24-hour nurseries; women would become the earners, men would become dispensable. And it sounded so laughable 40 years ago, nobody would believe me!*

---

[182] Erin Pizzey. Speech given to The International Conference on Men's Issues. June 27, 2014.

Now I sit here, and I don't think there's anybody in this room who doesn't believe me." [183]
(Emphasis Added)

Pizzey, now in her 70s, does not mince words when it comes to whom she blames. Pizzey was the first insider of the so-called women's liberation movement who became a whistleblower. Pizzey saw her battered women's shelter, the first of its kind, and her therapeutic efforts, commandeered by a Marxist-multinational corporation cabal. Her punishment was violence directed at her and her family, going so far as to kill her beloved dog. But none of this stopped Pizzey's speaking out, to wit:

"And we need to name names – and first on my list is Hillary Clinton. And I accuse her of being one of the leaders of this fraudulent movement; followed by Germaine Greer, by Harriet Harmon, by – Betty Friedan's dead – but all the whole lot of them. And we need to go after them! We cannot allow this to continue. And if we don't stop it, I don't see a future for marriage, for love, or for anything. And that question about marriage: I see men's point of view. Why on earth would you take a risk that has a 90% chance of stripping you of everything you have, particularly your children?" [184]

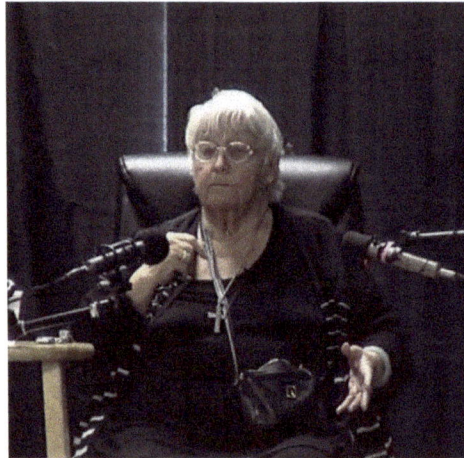

Erin Pizzey, speaking to an audience at the International Conference on Men's Issues, June 27, 2014.

Look at the data regarding which gender is responsible for physical altercations between men and women. It is time for another process time out. I am about to provide to you unassailable data that should make you question **everything** you thought you knew about domestic violence.

Professor John Archer from the University of Central Lancashire in the UK has conducted a number of meta-analytic reviews of studies of domestic violence and found that **women are as**

---

[183] Ibid.
[184] Ibid.

likely to use domestic violence as men, but women are twice as likely as men to be injured or killed during a domestic assault. [185]

University of Florida researcher and criminologist Angela Gover has studied domestic violence and gender. "We're seeing women in relationships acting differently nowadays than we have in the past. The nature of criminality has been changing for females, and this change is reflected in intimate relationships as well." In a survey of 2,500 students at University of Florida and the University of South Carolina between August and December 2005, more than a quarter (29 percent) reported physically assaulting their dates and 22 percent reported being the victims of attacks during the past year. **Thirty-two (32) percent of women reported being the perpetrators of this violence, compared with twenty-four (24) percent of men.** [186]

"According to a 2010 national survey by the **Centers for Disease Control and U.S. Department of Justice,** in the period from December 2010 to December 2011, <u>more men than women were victims</u> of intimate partner physical violence and over 40% of severe physical violence was <u>directed at men</u>. Men were also more often the victim of psychological aggression and control over sexual or reproductive health. Despite this, few services are available to male victims of intimate partner violence." [187]

This study was funded by the Centers for Disease Control and U.S. Department of Justice. The survey was entitled: The National Intimate Partner and Sexual Violence Survey (hereinafter NISVS). It was released in December of 2011. The study found that 5,365,000 men and 4,741,000 women were victims of intimate partner physical violence. [188] Dear reader, 5 million is a larger number than is 4 million.

Let's look at a study done a decade earlier. The National Violence Against Women Survey (NVAWS) estimated that 1.2 million women and 835,000 men were victims of intimate partner physical violence in the preceding 12 months. [189] Even those data, contrary to popular opinion, demonstrate that when it comes to domestic violence, males are often the victims of violence at the hands of female partners. The data inform that male violence against women has been declining while violence against men by women has been on the increase. [190] Corroborative data of this trend include work done by Statistics Canada, conducted in 2006 and 2011. Those studies found that 45.5% of the victims of present or former spousal violence were men. [191] Despite these and other supporting data that nullifies assumptions regarding strongly disparate patterns of domestic violence

---

[185] John Archer, Abigail J. V. Thornton, Nicola Graham-Kevan. Nonviolent Offending Behavior: A Comparison of Self-Reports, Victims' Reports, and Third-Party Reports. Journal of Interpersonal Violence, May 2012 vol. 27 no. 8 1399-1427.

[186] Gover, Angela. *Women more likely to be perpetrators of abuse as well as victims.* University of Florida. Published July 13, 2006.

[187] Hoff, Burt, H., JD. (2012), National Study: *More Men than Women Victims of Intimate Partner Physical Violence, Psychological Aggression.* University of Phoenix School of Criminal Justice and Security.

[188] Black, M.C. et al., (2011), *The National Intimate Partner and Sexual Violence Survey*: 2010 Summary Report. Centers for Disease Control, Atlanta, Georgia.

[189] (Tjaden, P. G., & Thoennes, N., (2000), The National Violence Against Women Survey.

[190] C.f. Straus and Gelles, (1988); Straus, (1995); Catalano , (2005) and Truman, (2011).

[191] Statistics Canada (2011), *Family Violence in Canada: A Statistical Profile Catalogue.* January, Catalogue No. 85-224-X, pp. 7-8, Ottawa, ON; Statistics Canada (2006), *Measuring violence against women: Statistical trends 2006.* October, Catalogue No. 85-570-XIE, Ottawa, ON.

based upon gender, it is a fact that the term "domestic violence," itself, is just assumed by the public and government agents to be a term that describes male against female violence.

Perception is reality when it comes to manipulating man's herd instinct. The money governments spend on battered women's shelters, counseling, etc., simply take for granted that the male is always the aggressor. Given the data that clearly point out that domestic violence is an equal opportunity and bi-gender phenomenon, and given that equality between the genders is not only the social engineer's mandate but is also the law, why is it that government and its proxy social services institutions, including family courts, just assume and take for granted that men are the aggressors when the term "domestic violence" is spoken? **Could it be that social engineers have broadened their attack on men and the traditional nuclear family using a contrived definition of domestic violence as a cudgel in its arsenal against men?**

Bert Hoff, J.D., took note of how men are treated in a domestic violence system that just assumes males are the aggressors:

> *There has been little research on responses to male victims of intimate partner violence, in part because agencies refuse to fund such research. For example, the U.S. Department of Justice solicitation of proposals for Justice Responses to Intimate Partner Violence and Stalking (p. 8) stated "What will not be funded: Proposals for research on intimate partner violence against, or stalking of, males of any age or females under the age of 12." In the few studies done, many men report that hotline workers say they only help women, imply or state the men must be the instigators, ridicule them or refer them to batterers' programs. Police often will fail to respond, ridicule the man or arrest him. (Cook 2009)(Douglas and Hines, 2011)[192]*

The American Judges Association has stated the following:

> *"Domestic and sexual violence, including stalking, come before the courts in large numbers of cases.* **Domestic violence cuts across all racial, ethnic, economic class, religious, and educational lines.** *Despite many legislative and public policy reforms, domestic violence remains a substantial social problem in the U.S. and around the world. Recent statistics support this disturbing reality."[193]*

Did you notice what was missing in the aforementioned listing of demographic variables that cut across domestic violence? "Gender" was missing from the *"Domestic violence cuts across"* statement. With bias like this coming from judges, that is, the men and women who adjudicate allegations of domestic violence, is it any wonder that men are presumed guilty before they enter the courtroom?

Our point is not to place blame for domestic violence solely upon either gender, nor is it to say that there is absolute equivalency between the genders on this or any other issue. Our point is that the dissonance between perception and reality is a symptomatic of socially engineered gender bias that is consistent with and part of the attack upon the father and male role within the nuclear family in 21st century America. And even more profoundly, while we are forced to dissect male and female behavior to get to the bottom of these PSYOPs, gender, per se, has little or nothing do to with the motivations of those behind the social engineering of male and female roles.

---

[192] Hoff, Bert H. J.D. (2011), *National Study: More Men than Women Victims of Intimate Partner Physical Violence, Psychological Aggression.* Professor Hoff teaches at University of Phoenix School of Criminal Justice and Security.

[193] The American Judges Association (2014), http://aja.ncsc.dni.us/pdfs/domestic-violence-the-courtroom.pdf

The wholesale assault upon the nuclear family and traditional mother and father roles, as we have documented, resulted in an economic redistribution of wealth tsunami, wherein money migrated from the traditional nuclear family unit into the hands of financiers, bankers and a cottage industry comprised of divorce lawyers, domestic violence counselors, "battered women" shelters, child protective services, day care facilities and workers, professional nannies, nurseries in workplaces and a myriad of other beneficiaries of the handiwork of shadow men's social engineers. Shadow men and their proxies schemed to redistribute wealth from the traditional family unit to themselves, all the while protecting their own traditional nuclear families! They accomplished this redistribution tsunami using a similar approach taken by Edward Bernays when he persuaded women to take up smoking in the name of liberation and freedom from gender inequality.

And speaking of the cottage industry created by the proxies of shadow men when they imploded the traditional nuclear family, consider the data about who takes care of America's children. The industrialization of childcare was a desired fringe benefit of the mass redistribution of wealth scheme that "liberated" women from caring for their own flesh and blood. Please read that last sentence again.

YOU GET WIC, FOOD STAMPS ,WELFARE ,CHILD SUPPORT , MEDICAID AND FREE HOUSING?

CALM DOWN YOU'RE NOT A SINGLE PARENT AND YOU'RE NOT DOING IT ALL ON YOUR OWN!

Child Care
an Important Part of American Life

Families rely on a patchwork of child care services to meet their work and family needs. Data from the Survey of Income and Program Participation (SIPP) helps us understand child care usage among families.

32.7 Million
Children in Care Arrangements

In 2011, 32.7 million children were in a regular child care arrangement while their parents worked or pursued other activities outside of the home.

12.5M
Preschoolers
(ages 0–4)

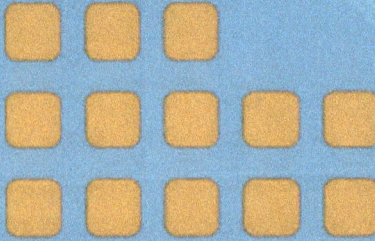

20.2M
Grade Schoolers
(ages 5–14)

61%
A greater percentage of preschoolers participated in child care compared to grade schoolers.

50%
Percentage of grade schoolers who participate in a regular child care arrangement.

One block represents approximately one million children in a regular care arrangement.

Who's Minding the Kids?

Increases in the number of working mothers and the desire to provide young children with educational opportunities have driven up the demand for various types of child care. Relatives regularly provide care for preschoolers.

Relatives	27%
Organized facilities	25%
Parents	22%
Other nonrelative	13%
Other	13%

◄ **One in five** relatives who provided care was a grandparent.

49% Parents and relatives make up half of all preschool child care arrangements.

DEFINITIONS

Relatives—grandparents, siblings, and other relatives.

Organized Facilities—day care or child care centers, nursery schools, preschools, and Head Start programs.

Parents—fathers who provided care while the mother worked or mothers who provided care while working.

Other nonrelative—in-home babysitters, neighbors, friends, and family day care homes.

Other—school, self care, and no regular arrangement.

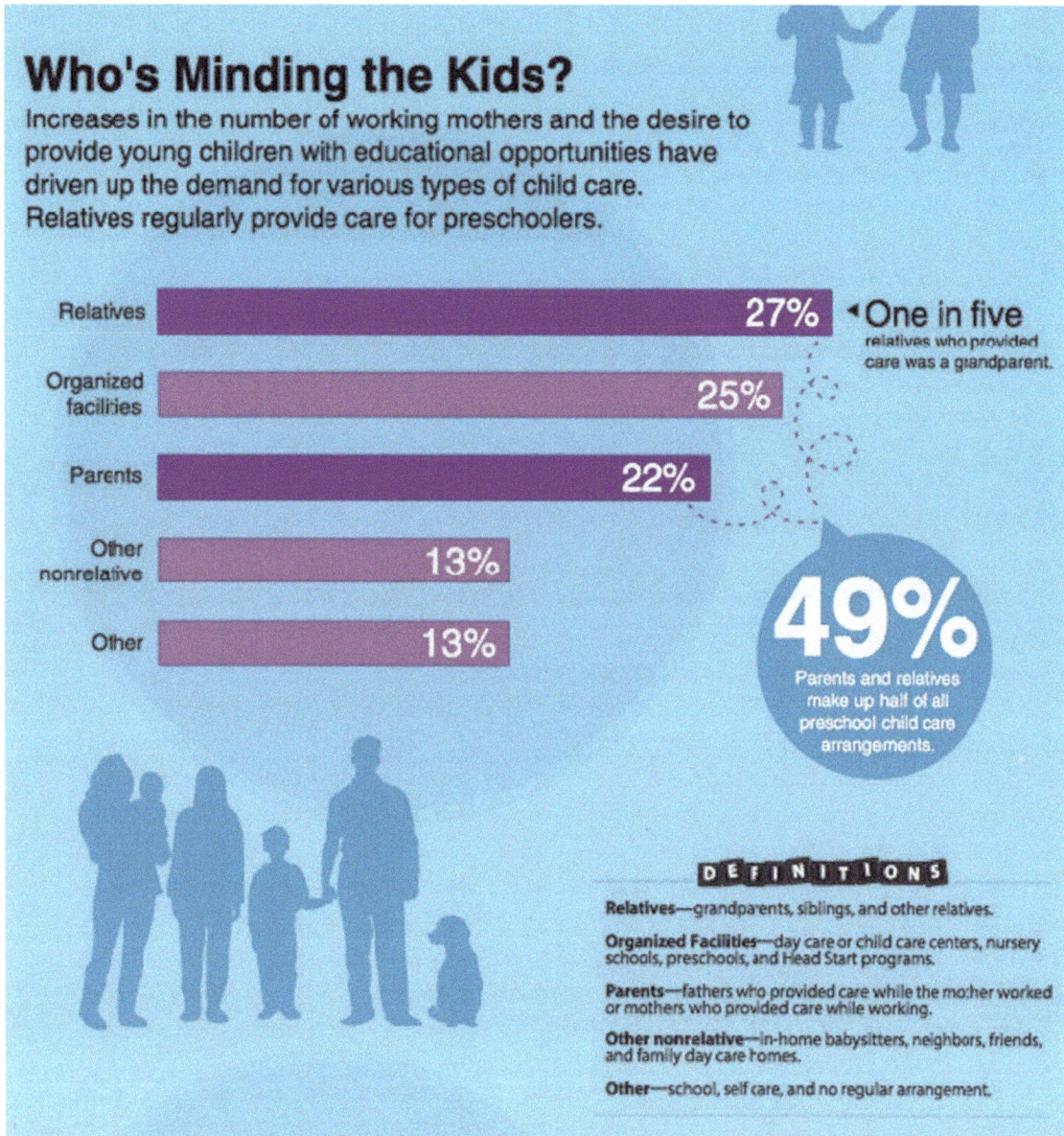

Child Care Aware of America provided this overview of the child-care industry in America, 2012:

"Nearly 11 million children under age 5 in the United States are in some type of childcare arrangement every week. On average, the children of working mothers spend 35 hours a week in childcare. About one-third of these children are in multiple childcare arrangements so their parents can meet the need for childcare during traditional and nontraditional working hours.

The number of parents losing jobs, working part time, taking pay cuts or working two or more jobs reflects the reality associated with the weak economy of the last few years. Parents are forced to make difficult decisions about the care of their children.

As this report shows, the average annual cost of full-time care for an infant in center- based care can range from about $4,600 in Mississippi to $20,200 in the District of Columbia, and from about $4,000 in Mississippi to $12,350 in the District of Columbia for an infant in a family child care home. It is not much better for the annual cost of care for a 4-year-old. Center-based care ranges *from about $3,900 in Mississippi to $15,450 in the District of Columbia and from about $3,850 in Mississippi to $9,600 in New York state for care in a family child care home.*

Anecdotal evidence from Child Care Resource and Referral agencies (CCR&Rs) across the country as well as newspaper stories, throughout the states, shows families are struggling to make ends meet. This financial insecurity leads some parents to decide to remove children from organized child care and make do with whatever arrangements they can find and/or afford. Unlike a mortgage or rent or a car payment, childcare is an area where parents seek to find savings – and keep their fingers crossed that all will go well.

Ironically, in a weakened economy, the stress placed on families makes quality child care settings even more important to the healthy development of children. The quality of childcare has a lasting impact. A National Institute of Child Health and Human Development (NICHD) report found that high-quality child care leads to more positive outcomes even during the teenage years. Children who received high quality care in the first few years of life scored higher in measures of academic and cognitive achievement when they were 15 years old and were less likely to misbehave than those who were enrolled in lower quality childcare. Even 10 years after children left childcare, experiences in quality settings were still related to higher academic achievement.

It is essential for America's future economic prosperity that our children receive quality, developmentally appropriate care. However, as working families struggle with the costs of childcare, they also find that the availability of the quality of care varies greatly.

Child Care Aware® of America and individual state and local CCR&Rs support parents as they make tough decisions about child care. CCR&Rs work within every state to help families find access to affordable, quality child care. CCR&Rs are uniquely positioned within communities to not only work with parents, but also with child care providers and state and local governments to strengthen the quality of care.

In the United States, about 90 percent of the cost of childcare is assumed by parents. **This is supplemented by more than $10 billion in government money that is spent annually by the states for childcare. For the most part, funding for child care comes from the Child Care and Development Block Grant (CCDBG), the Temporary Assistance for Needy Families (TANF) program, the Social Services Block Grant (SSBG or Title XX) and state funds."**[194]

Once again, we see the American taxpayer picking up the tab for shadow men's redistribution of wealth scheme when cash-strapped parents can no longer make ends meet.

Sociologists who study the impact of the destruction of the traditional nuclear family unit have gathered data on a construct they refer to as "Family Belonging and Rejection." According to The Marriage and Religion Institute,

"The Index of Family Belonging is a measure of the proportion of American adolescents who have enjoyed stable intact family lives-with both birth parents-throughout their childhoods. It is calculated from data provided by the American Community Survey of the U.S. Bureau of the Census and is strongly associated with measures of child well-being."

Data from 2008-2010 found that less than half of 17 year-olds (45%) in America grew up in an intact nuclear family where both birth parents were serving in the roles of parents. The remaining

---

[194] Child Care Aware of America. (2012), *CHILDCARE IN AMERICA 2012 State Fact Sheets.*

55% of 17 year-olds in America grew up in a household where one parent or the other had initiated a divorce and all that accompanies divorce, e.g., alimony, custody, visitation, etc. [195] [196]

MARRI's researchers, Potrykus and Fagan, reported the following societal consequences the result of the dissolution of the traditional nuclear family in America:

"Influence of family intactness on need & dependency

Family intactness is the most important factor (or shares the place of greatest importance) in determining an area's dependence on welfare programs that target organic poverty:

- *Receipt of food stamps,*
- *Temporary Assistance for Needy Families and state welfare transfers,*
- *Supplemental Security Income transfers, and*
- *Prime-age adult public healthcare recipiency.*
- *Family intactness has the second-largest influence on overall diminishment of prime-age female, and child, poverty.*
- *Family intactness has the strongest attenuating influence on teenage out-of-wedlock birth, itself a source of economic hardship.*

Influence of family intactness & family size on education & income

- *Family intactness is very influential on high school graduation rates. It influences high school graduation rates more than does the fraction of adult college graduates in an area.*
- *Family intactness and the fraction of adult high school graduates in an area have similar beneficial influences on prime-age male employment rates.*
- *The ratio of children to adults in an area (larger families) has a large, positive influence on prime-age male employment, and it has the largest consistently positive influence on earnings of prime-age males in the area.*

Low importance of race & ethnicity

Once family intactness, high school dropout levels and other demographic factors are taken into account, the fraction of blacks or Hispanics in an area rarely has a strong detrimental influence on the outcomes studied.

- *The fraction of the population that is Hispanic is normally a beneficial influence or shows no precise impact and has an adverse influence on less than one fourth of the outcomes studied*
- *The fraction of the population that is black has an adverse influence on approximately half of the outcomes measured and is otherwise a beneficial or indeterminate influence."* [197]

The authors go on to conclude that all the government programs in the world are incapable of mitigating the disaster wrought upon American traditional nuclear families by shadow men and their

---

[195] American Community Survey of the U.S. Bureau of the Census, 2008-2010.

[196] Potrykus, Henry, PhD & Fagan, Patrick, PhD. (2013), *U.S. Social Policy Dependence on the Family, Derived from the Index of Belonging.* Religion Research Institute (MARRI).

[197] Ibid.

agents. After looking carefully at the data, the agents who orchestrated this redistribution of wealth scheme, wherein wealth was taken from traditional nuclear families and routed to financiers, bankers, various cottage industries and government, may be more accurately named: "Weapons of Mass Destruction."

The traditional nuclear family unit had served as the bulwark in traditional American life. This was true for all races and ethnicities. The traditional nuclear family was the means by which traditional American values were passed on to future generations. An intact traditional nuclear family unit negated dependence upon the state for economic and psychological sustenance. In fact, after WWII, for the first time in the history of the world, **the average man and woman of all races** were accumulating wealth within the confines of the traditional nuclear family unit, that is, before it was systematically and with malice aforethought imploded.

The traditional American family unit made wealth accumulation possible for the common man. If financiers, bankers and the beneficiary agents of shadow men have as their ultimate goal the confiscation of the wealth generated by the common man, and the autonomy (freedom from control) it afforded them, then something had to be done to obliterate the wealth generator that was the traditional nuclear family unit. If one's goal is to increase dependence upon the state, thereby transforming the state from its purely managerial role into a surrogate father and mother which citizens first look to in order to satisfy their needs and wants, the traditional nuclear family unit had to be dissolved. **And who do you think would ultimately control the apparatus of the all-powerful state? Shadow men!**

The logic used by shadow men is impeccable. By undermining the father figure and promoting independent mothers, they removed the bulwarks from the traditional nuclear family structure. Once women were encouraged to separate from her family the father was soon to follow. Once children, by necessity, became wards of the childcare industry and government programs, their bond with their birth parents weakened. Commitment within the nuclear family was all but destroyed and both genders abrogated their marriage vows. I remind you and cannot over stress this fact: Shadow men left their traditional nuclear families untouched by the lethal virus they unleashed on those not like them.

Both fathers and mothers had to work in order to make ends meet post implosion. Wealth accumulation became a thing of the past. Prices were raised on durable and discretionary goods such that it now took two dedicated workers to support financiers, bankers and the struggling family's monthly nut. It now took two people working full time to make the same amount of money that just one breadwinner brought home in the 1950s. With the other 50% of the population flooding the work force, consumer prices inflated while wages flattened or retreated. With no time left after work for the family unit, our culture's lexicon changed to reflect this social upheaval. The term "family time" was replaced with, for example, "quality time." Discipline became an uncomfortable act on the part of parents because when one's time is limited to "quality time" with their own children, the natural tendency is to be lenient and permissive; rather than be a mentor, teacher, disciplinarian, that is, parent. As discipline waned and teachers were persuaded to encourage artificially high self-esteem, children became independent agents, navigating the adult world with immature bodies and minds.

Single mothers as a demographic entity transitioned from unfortunate anomaly to nominal paradigm. And in a perverse shift in perception, single motherhood became something to revere and brag about. By the 1990's, the descriptor "single mother" became a badge of honor displayed as though one were displaying an Olympic gold medal, as opposed to what it really is, a harbinger of problems, not only for the single mother, her children and her absent birth and surrogate father, but for society and the American taxpayer.

Single motherhood, as we have documented, is a demographic marker that has been proven to be the BEST predictor of who will suffer economic hardship. Economic hardship means, in a welfare state, that single mothers will, more often than not, become dependent upon the state for their survival. And of course, where does the state get its money? Why, from hard working Americans who not only must take care of their own family obligations, but also strangers who were jettisoned from the only stable model of wealth accumulation ever proven to work, the traditional nuclear family unit. As you continue to learn, begin to ask yourself this question: What punishment would fit the crimes committed by shadow men and their agents?

The collateral damage to women's mental and physical health, the result of this redistribution of wealth scheme, is far reaching and makes women's adoption of smoking seem minor. It wasn't just women's physical and emotional health that suffered. Emily Thomas, writing for the Huffington Post, looked at the data regarding the trends in incarceration rates based upon gender. What Ms. Thomas reported on should give one pause:

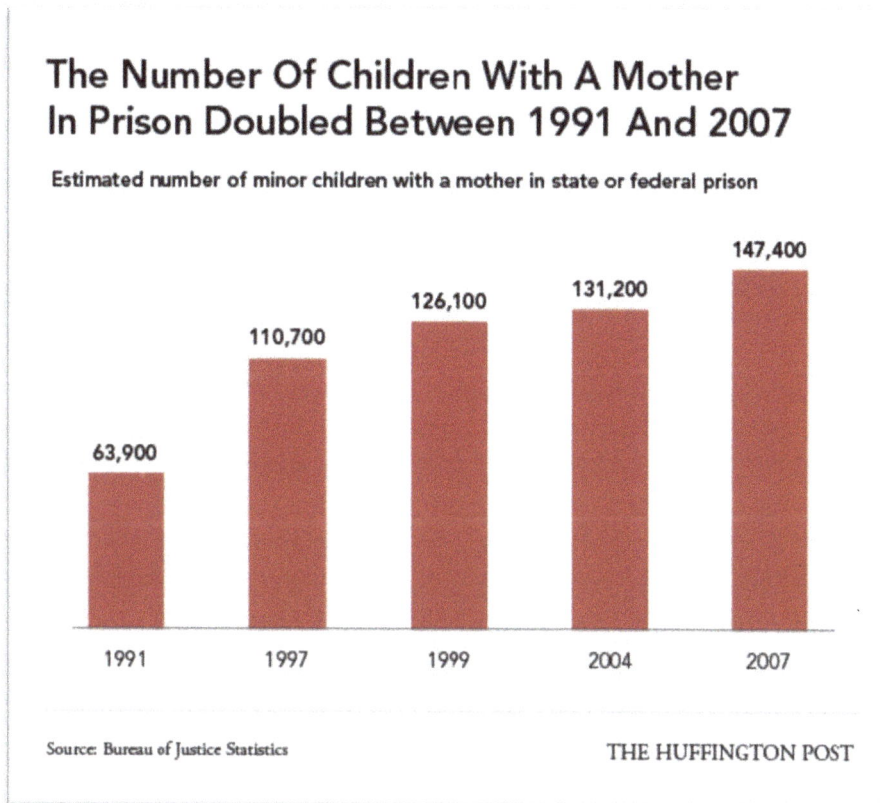

The Number Of Children With A Mother In Prison Doubled Between 1991 And 2007

Estimated number of minor children with a mother in state or federal prison

1991	1997	1999	2004	2007
63,900	110,700	126,100	131,200	147,400

Source: Bureau of Justice Statistics

THE HUFFINGTON POST

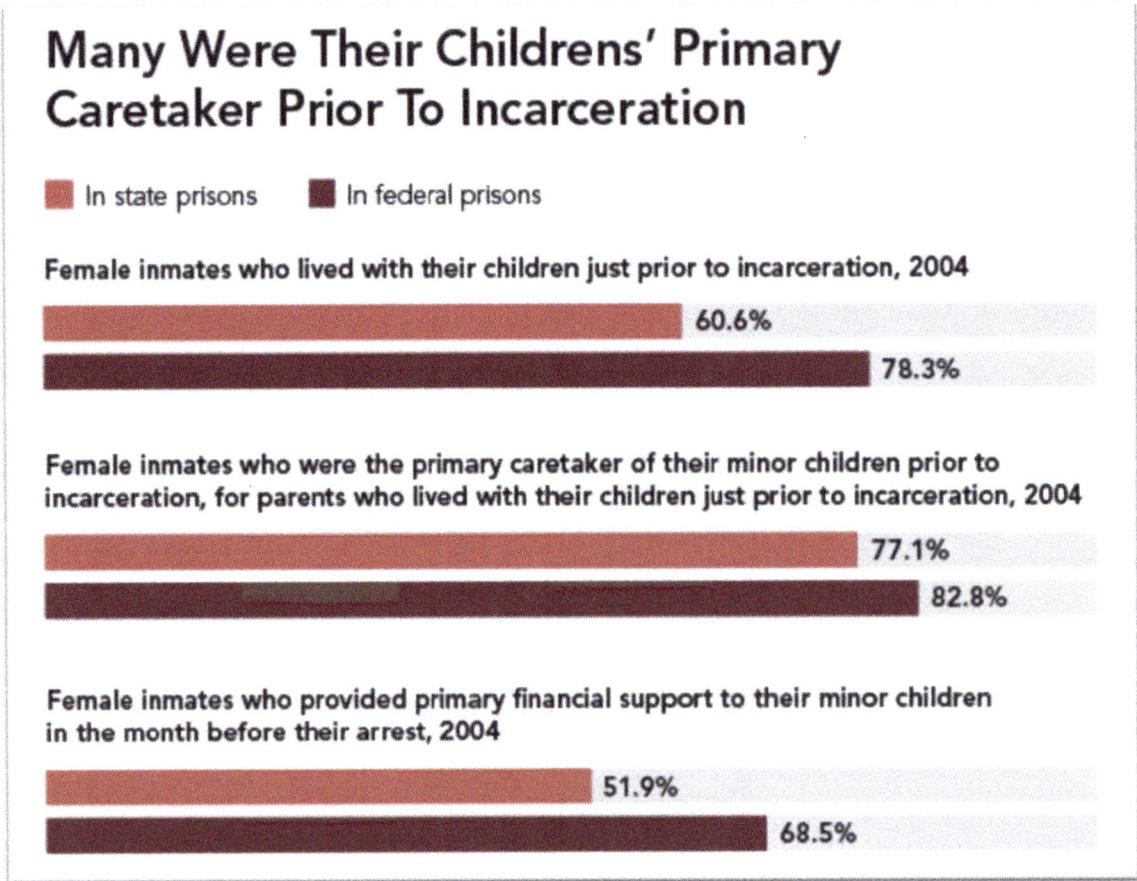

Many Were Their Childrens' Primary Caretaker Prior To Incarceration

■ In state prisons   ■ In federal prisons

Female inmates who lived with their children just prior to incarceration, 2004

60.6%

78.3%

Female inmates who were the primary caretaker of their minor children prior to incarceration, for parents who lived with their children just prior to incarceration, 2004

77.1%

82.8%

Female inmates who provided primary financial support to their minor children in the month before their arrest, 2004

51.9%

68.5%

198

The shadow men who caused women's dependency upon the state were assured that the single mother demographic would vote their political agents into office. The "honorables" who promised to support single mothers with taxpayer-funded entitlements and handouts would come to count on a loyal and ever-growing voter base in order to keep their jobs.

Were the destruction of the nuclear family unit not so devious and manipulative, one would have to marvel at shadow men's brilliance. Not only did shadow men confiscate wealth from the traditional nuclear family, but also, the financial shortfall, created by their theft, was shifted to and paid for by hard working taxpayers. The taxpayer funded model for single mothers, mirrors the one used by banking interests when their fortunes went bust in 2008-the American taxpayer paid for their mess when all was said and done.

The PSYOPs chosen to accomplish dissolution of the traditional American family unit utilized a number of Edward Bernays inspired PSYOPs. These particular PSYOPs initiated in the late 1960s were similar to the strategies used by Bernays to increase piano sales. What did Bernays do to increase piano sales? Bernays didn't pitch pianos, per se, he associated himself with single-family home architects and persuaded them to make the music room a common feature in American home

---

198 The Huffington Post. (2014), *The Number Of Women Behind Bars Is Skyrocketing, And Here's The Upsetting Result.* Reported by: Emily Thomas, July.

design. Once people had a music room what, pray tell, do you think Bernay's target audience filled those music rooms with? Why, pianos, of course.

Chess is a game that serves as the perfect metaphor for how America's nuclear family unit was imploded. Chess rewards the player who can plan several moves in advance. The first chess move made in a 10-move sequence, for example, may appear to simply be a simple move of a pawn, nothing more. Not until the opposition player's King is threatened near the final move of the sequence, does the devious 10-sequence strategy reveal itself for what it is. By then, of course, it is too late.

Bernays used a limited 2-move sequence PSYOP when he plotted to increase piano sales, e.g., First Move: Create Music Rooms, Second Move: Sell Pianos. As Bernay's approach evolved, it became more common for mind control artists to increase the number of steps involved in executing any one particular PSYOP. With each successive complication (step addition) to these PSYOPs, one submerges deeper and deeper to the point where almost anyone, even bright non-intelligence agent experts, monitoring surface behavior, have no idea what is lurking deep below the sea. Like a nuclear submarine that does its work deep below the surface, cruise missiles seemingly appear out of nowhere to wreak havoc on the enemy. Those of us who are familiar with the intelligence business, find it very difficult to make average people understand that they are no match for their adversaries; thus, they should adopt a wary humility, not confident arrogance.

The conscientious reader of this book will be conflicted between, on the one hand, a desire to preserve free will and freedom of choice for all men; but on the other hand, a fear born of the recognition that man's nature can so easily be molded that if not purposefully molded for good then it will be molded for bad.

Earlier we stated that virtually all men underestimate the degree to which he or she is vulnerable to mind control. Permit me to put this particular underestimation into context. People tend to overestimate their intelligence. People tend to overestimate the physical attractiveness of their children. Women, when first married, tend to overestimate the potential of their husband. Men tend to overestimate their manliness. Fishermen tend to overestimate the size of the fish they catch.

A mantle of psychological defenses protects man's soothing, but patently false, beliefs about who is really in control. These protectors of any number of false beliefs are very strong and resist most attempts to break through them. "It can't happen to me" is but one example of how defenses protect us from a reality check. Should one attempt to break through these defenses, like I am doing in this book, that person is, more often than not, met with anger and resistance. Challenge a person's sacred cow beliefs and be prepared to suffer their wrath. Approach a mob throwing rocks at the police and try to calm them down using reason and see what happens. This problem is equally distributed among all political parties and party affiliations.

This is why Bernays and every other mind control artists, past and present, deluded their victims into believing that they were in control, that they made the choice to do this or that. Bernay's victims actually believed in what Bernays had molded them to think, feel and do. Tell someone who is so deluded, a voter for example, that he has been duped and is being played for a fool. Get back to me with their response, that is, if you are still able to communicate.

The shadow men who run this world know all of the things I have been discussing in this chapter. Believe me when I tell you that I have only scratched the surface of the surface. The subject area of mind control using group psychology has such depth and breadth that most Ph.D.'s are experts in only one sliver of the entire data set.

America's Constitutional Republic has been all but taken over by mind control artists who have employed strategies that make Edward Bernay's techniques look like child's play. Central to shadow men's Fabian inspired strategies is to exploit the sacrosanct notion of democracy to create a tyranny of and by the masses. To make matter worse, the handmaidens of the shadow men in control, i.e., the politicians, are using taxpayer's money to subvert a system that was designed to protect against such tyranny. Alexis de Tocqueville wrote the following in the mid-1800's after visiting America:

> *"The American Republic will endure until the day Congress discovers that it can bribe the public with the public's money."* [199]

Bernays recognized that people project parental needs upon authority figures, including those men and women we call politicians.

An authority figure may, indeed, protect the welfare of the masses as would a good parent. But no authority figure should ever be trusted unless that person is virtuous. The quality of virtue must be factored into the expert/authority figure equation before you should trust any authority figure, especially a politician.

Bernays understood the masses need and want a surrogate father or mother figure to metaphorically embrace them so as to "make a scary world all better." The most important thing an average man or woman unconsciously wants from a leader is a mirage that matches the ideal parent/lover image that resides in the deepest crevices of their mind.

Ever wonder about why politicians appear on television to "console" a distraught citizenry after a natural disaster? Surely you do not think that without the President's signature or some other affirmative act on his or her part relief would not be forthcoming to the victims, do you?

All of the procedures and guidelines for FEMA assistance, as well as assistance from state and local governments, for example, are virtually pro forma when it comes to approval. In fact, I cannot think of one instance where disaster relief was not already gearing up by the time the president, governor, senator, congressman or other political figure appeared in the media to reassure and console the masses. Theoretically, I suppose, a governor or President could intervene and attempt to stop relief efforts from any number of independent agencies on the scene of a devastating disaster, but that has never happened and it never will for obvious reasons. When the degree of disaster is such that it is not clear whether or not an area or event should be classified as a "disaster area," then politicians may have more discretion. In those instances, however, disaster relief is generally not so pressing.

The politician (father or mother figure) always appears after some frightening event in various staged dramas to console the masses. For purely psychological reasons, the masses are assured when they see a President flying over, for example, a flood ravaged city or a Hurricane disaster in his helicopter. The masses are assured when the surrogate father or mother figure tours the disaster area, hugs victims and passes out food. All of this is concocted drama designed to assuage a public's fears but makes no logical sense, other than fulfilling the psychological needs of a frightened populace.

If you ask the boots on the ground, the people who are actually doing the caretaking at a disaster scene, they will tell you that the presence of the President, for example, makes their job much harder because of the logistical nightmare of any presidential visit that is imposed upon an already chaotic environment.

---

[199] Alexis de Tocqueville, (1851), *Democracy in America.* New York: A. S. Barnes & Co.

The public projects upon a father or mother figure, that he/she will magically make things all better. The projection is one of a frightened child to an all loving and caring parent. It is that way because that is where the need originated and the vast majority of people never emotionally grow out of the need. Bernays not only exploited man's nature, but he and others socially reengineered man's nature and his environment in order to make him even more susceptible to mind control. Welcome to 1984.

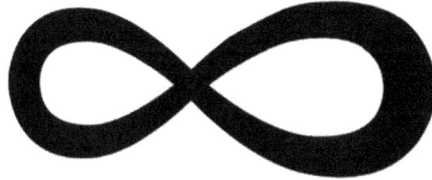

CHAPTER 12: ON AND BACKSTAGE PSYCHOLOGICAL OPERATIONS

I am now going to share with you as much inside information as is legally allowable regarding tangible PSYOPs. The reader may read between the lines, but I suggest that only those readers who are not prone to paranoia, and who have the ability to think critically, should do so.

It has been known for a very long time that an enemy that operates behind the curtain, an enemy that cloaks its true intentions by assuming the role of a patriot, is the most dangerous of all enemies of free men. An enemy that reveals itself in an honest display is an enemy that awakens man's instinctual drive to remain free. Not so with the traitor, the mole or the treasonous leader who is popular. The great Roman thinker Cicero had this to say on this very subject:

> *"A nation can survive its fools, and even the ambitious. But it cannot survive treason from within. An enemy at the gates is less formidable, for he is known and carries his banner openly. But the traitor moves amongst those within the gate freely, his sly whispers rustling through all the alleys, heard in the very halls of government itself. For the traitor appears not a traitor; he speaks in accents familiar to his victims, and he wears their face and their arguments, he appeals to the baseness that lies deep in the hearts of all men. He rots the soul of a nation, he works secretly and unknown in the night to undermine the pillars of the city, he infects the body politic so that it can no longer resist. A murderer is less to fear."* [200]

The United States Military acknowledges the existence of its own dedicated PSYOP forces. Here is how the U.S. Army describes its PSYOP mission:

> *"PSYOPS or Psychological Operations: Planned operations to convey selected information and indicators to foreign audiences to influence their emotions, motives, objective reasoning, and ultimately the behavior of foreign governments, organizations, groups, and individuals. The purpose of psychological operations is to induce or reinforce foreign attitudes and behavior favorable to the originator's objectives. Also called PSYOP. See also consolidation psychological operations; overt peacetime psychological operations programs; perception management. (Source: U.S. Department of Defense)*
>
> *Psychological Operations are a vital part of the broad range of U.S. political, military, economic, and ideological activities used by the U.S. government to secure national objectives. PSYOP is the dissemination of truthful information to foreign audiences in support of U.S. policy and national objectives.*
>
> *Used during peacetime, contingencies, and declared war, these activities are not a form of force, but are force multipliers that use nonviolent means in often violent environments. Persuading rather than compelling physically, they rely on logic, fear, desire or other mental factors to promote specific emotions, attitudes or behaviors. The ultimate objective of U.S. military psychological operations is to convince enemy, neutral, and friendly nations and forces to take action favorable to the United States and its allies.*

---

[200] Grant, Michael, Translator, (1971), *Selected Works by Marcus Tullius Cicero.* Penguin Classics, New York, New York.

Psychological operations support national security objectives at the tactical, operational and strategic levels of operations.

Strategic psychological operations advance broad or long-term objectives. Global in nature, they may be directed toward large audiences or at key communicators.

Operational psychological operations are conducted on a smaller scale. They are employed by theater commanders to target groups within the theater of operations. Their purpose can range from gaining support for U.S. operations to preparing the battlefield for combat.

Tactical psychological operations are more limited, used by commanders to secure immediate and near-term goals. In this environment, these force-enhancing activities serve as a means to lower the morale and efficiency of enemy forces.

Both tactical and theater-level psychological operations may be used to enhance peacetime military activities of conventional and special operations forces operating in foreign countries. Cultural awareness packages attune U.S. forces before departing overseas. In theater, media programs publicize the positive aspects of combined military exercises and deployments.

In addition to supporting commanders, psychological operations provide interagency support to other U.S. government agencies. In operations ranging from humanitarian assistance to drug interdiction, psychological operations enhance the impact of actions taken by those agencies. Their activities can be used to spread information about ongoing programs and to gain support from the local populace.

Psychological operations units of the U.S. Army are language and culturally oriented. The 4th Psychological Operations Group (Airborne) at Fort Bragg, N.C., the only active Army psychological operations unit, constitutes 26 percent of all U.S. Army psychological operations units. The remaining 74 percent, split between the 2nd and 7th Psychological Operations Groups, are in the Army Reserve."[201]

U.S. Army PSYOP Insignia.

---

[201] U.S. Army Special Operations Command.

Here is a sampling of declassified operation patches I am personally familiar with that have been used to commemorate various PSYOPs over the years:

The reader will take note of the fact that the U.S. Military stresses that its charter to conduct PSYOPs is limited to foreign lands and foreign governments. Similarly, the Central Intelligence Agency has a specific edict against engaging in any of its various and sundry intelligence activities, including psychological operations, on domestic soil. As I have previously documented, for example, Gloria Steinem has acknowledged that the CIA helped to fund her feminist agenda and her magazine "Ms."

The CIA justifies its engagement in its various intelligence activities, including PSYOPs, on domestic soil and upon and in cooperation with American citizens, e.g., Gloria Steinem, by an exception to their charter that recognizes that foreign interests can operate on American soil and American citizens may, by and through their activities, further the interests of the agency. It is that pooling of partially salt (foreign) and partially fresh (domestic) water that creates a unique eco system in which agencies like the CIA can operate without technically violating their charter.

Every country on earth has its own PSYOPerators financed by their government. Here is a representative listing of a few of the more sophisticated intelligence agencies I am personally familiar with: The former USSR had the KGB. The Russian Federation relies upon Federal Security Service (FSB) – Федеральная служба безопасности; The Federal Protective Service (FSO) – Федеральная служба охраны; The Main Intelligence Directorate (GRU) – Главное Разведывательное Управление and its Foreign Intelligence Service (SVR) – Служба Внешней Разведки. Iran has the remnants of SAVAK in the form of Ministry Of Intelligence and Security (MOIS), sometimes called VEVAK. Israel has Mossad (הַמוֹסָד). Canada has its Canadian Security Intelligence Service – Service Canadien du Renseignement de Sécurité (CSIS/SCRS). China has its Ministry of State Security (MSS)國家安全部. Cuba has its Dirección de Inteligencia (DGI) (Directorate of Intelligence). France has its Central Directorate of Interior Intelligence (DCRI) – Direction Centrale du Renseignement Intérieur. Germany has the Federal Intelligence Service (BND) – Bundesnachrichtendienst. The Republic of Korea relies upon its National Intelligence Service (NIS). And finally, surprising to some observers, even Christmas Island has the Foreign Security Directory (FSD) (external), the State Department of Investigation (SDI) (internal) and the National Defense Institute (Military). To be sure, every country, both big and small, has its own intelligence services, each with its PSYOPs division, each comprised of human behavior experts who plot, scheme and use weaponized versions of psychological principles in order to change minds and, therefore, change behavior.

Yuri Bezmenov, a former KGB operator who defected to the United States in the 1970's, has stated that only about 15% of the KGB's budget was allocated to physical operations. Bezmenov has said that 85% of the KGB's budget went to what he terms "active measures." Here is an excerpt from a speech Mr. Bezmenov made in 1985 laying all of this out:

> *"Ideological subversion is the process which is "legitimate" — overt and open — you can see it with your own eyes. All you have to do, all American mass media has to do is to unplug their bananas from their ears, open up their eyes and they can see it. There is no mystery...there is nothing to do with espionage. I know that espionage and intelligence gathering looks more romantic...it sells more to the audience...for the advertising, probably. That's why your Hollywood producers are so crazy about James Bond type of thrillers.*
>
> *But in reality, the main emphasis of the KGB is not in the area of intelligence at all. According to my opinion, and the opinion of many defectors of my caliber, only about 15% of time, money and manpower is spent on espionage as such. The other 85% is a slow process which we call either ideological subversion or active measures — Активные мероприятия in the language of the KGB — or psychological warfare."*

As I have emphasized throughout this book, PSYOPs are clandestine by their nature. This is because when PSYOPs circumvent the conscious mind and rational analysis, they can avoid detection and be more effective. PSYOPs can be cloaked in darkness or they may be hidden in plain sight. Both versions of clandestine operations are effective, but the versions hidden in plain sight are the most difficult to deconstruct and are often most effective.

Governments spy on one another and run PSYOPs on their intramural rivals and friends alike. Anyone in the know is aware of this fact. Revelations made in 2013 by whistleblower Edward Snowden, regarding the extent of the NSA's intelligence gathering operations, were only surprising to the American public and other world citizens who lack discernment or knowledge. People "in the know" were already aware of the extent to which the U.S. Government, by and through the NSA, spied on its own and foreign citizens.

The NSA has only recently become known to the average American citizen. But in the 1970s the NSA was the subject of a Congressional investigation body that was known as The Pike Committee. The Pike Committee's examination of the NSA, known during that time as "No Such Agency," revealed that even back then (1975) the NSA was gill netting Western Union messages, AT&T phone records and even absconding with the snail mail of everyday citizens. [202]

It will come as a surprise to some readers that America spies on its friends and the favor is more often than not returned. More of a surprise to some is that our allies have run PSYOPs on America that resulted in the loss of life. One such event in America's history is what has come to be known as the Lavon Affair. [203] One of things you learn after studying spies and spy agencies is that their projects are almost always given clever names. The Lavon affair was not an exception to this rule. The Lavon project was code named "Operation Suzannah."

In 1954, Dwight David Eisenhower was President of the United States. Eisenhower, as the former head of allied forces, understood war like few other presidents of the 20th century or since. Israel was desirous of involving America into its ongoing battle with Egypt, but Eisenhower was

---

[202] The Pike Committee was as Congressional investigation into intelligence activities. It was headed by Congressman Otis Pike (D) New York. Pike's Committee was the successor to the Nedzi Committee, headed by Congressman Lucien N. Nedzi, (D) Michigan. President Gerald Ford empowered the Nedzi and Pike Committees, along with the Senate's version, headed by Senator Frank Church, (D) Idaho.

[203] Weiss, Leonard. *The Lavon Affair: How a false-flag operation led to war and the Israeli bomb.* Bulletin of the Atomic Scientists, Vol. 69, page(s): 58-68, July 2013.

reluctant. Persuasive overtures by the Israeli's fell on deaf ears in the White House. The Israeli's would not take no for an answer, however.

Israeli agents engaged a PSYOP known as a false flag event (FFE). Mossad agents working in Egypt planted bombs in various embassy buildings, including a United States diplomatic facility. Mossad agents planted evidence that they knew would implicate Egyptians as the bombers.

The PSYOP nearly worked, but one of the bombs planted by Mossad agents detonated before the Israeli operators had vacated the scene of the crime. Egyptian security forces captured one of the Israeli agents on scene. Through interrogation and further investigation, other Israeli PSYOPerators were captured. Israel's response to their failed PSYOP illustrates how PSYOPs have built in protections that engage a second layer of PSYOP in order to protect the first PSYOP layer.

For example, Israel unequivocally declared that there was no spy ring. Moreover, Israel accused those who were daring to expose their skullduggery as "anti-Semites." That label, and its use as a powerful PSYOP protector, capitalizes upon the power of labeling theory. That particular PSYOP shield stopped many critics of Israel dead in their tracks.

The matter was eventually adjudicated and in the Israeli trial that followed, it was proven that Israeli agents had perpetrated the PSYOP in order to draw America into a war with Egypt. The person held responsible for this PSYOP was Israeli's Defense Minister Pinhas Lavon, hence the name " Lavon Affair. [204]

The United States used an unsophisticated PSYOP of a similar nature to the Lavon Affair to garner support for the Viet Nam war. According to Lieutenant Pat Paterson, USN,

> *"Questions about the Gulf of Tonkin incidents have persisted for more than 40 years. But once-classified documents and tapes released in the past several years, combined with previously uncovered facts, make clear that high government officials distorted facts and deceived the American public about events that led to full U.S. involvement in the Vietnam War."*
>
> *[C]ommander Stockdale was again in the action, this time alone. When his wingman's aircraft developed trouble, Stockdale got permission to launch solo from the Ticonderoga . He arrived overhead at 2135. For more than 90 minutes, he made runs parallel to the ships' course and at low altitude (below 2,000 feet) looking for the enemy vessels. He reported later, "I had the best seat in the house to watch that event and our destroyers were just shooting at phantom targets—there were no PT boats there . . . there was nothing there but black water and American firepower." [205] Captain Herrick also began to have doubts about the attack. As the battle continued, he realized the "attacks" were actually the results of "overeager sonar operators" and poor equipment performance. The Turner Joy had not detected any torpedoes during the entire encounter, and Herrick determined that the Maddox 's operators were probably hearing the ship's propellers reflecting off her rudder during sharp turns. 12 The destroyer's main gun director was never able to lock onto any targets because, as the operator surmised, the radar was detecting the stormy sea's wave tops.[206]*

President Lyndon Johnson used an Ericksonian style PSYOP [207] to motivate the American public (thru fear and jingoistic pride) to support an escalation of the Viet Nam war.

---

[205] Stockdale, Jim and Sybil. (1984), *In Love and War.* New York: Harper and Row.

[206] Paterson, Pat, Lieutenant USN. *The Truth About Tonkin.* Naval History Magazine, February, 2008, Volume 22, No. 1.

[207] Milton Ericson, M.D. was a psychiatrist who taught clinicians to use whatever occurred organically during an induced hypnosis session to further the induction, e.g., a telephone or doorbell ringing.

While the Gulf of Tonkin incident was not a pure false flag operation, like the botched Lavon Affair, it was a version of the same PSYOP. Both examples intended to arouse jingoistic pride and the desire to retaliate against an assault upon "the flag" that never actually occurred as portrayed. The underlying psychological principle that drives citizen's support for government's war, as evinced in both the Gulf of Tonkin and the Lavon Affair, were articulated most eloquently by Nazi propaganda guru, Hermann Goering:

> *"Naturally, the common people don't want war, neither in Russia nor in England nor in America, nor for that matter in Germany. That is understood. But the people can always be brought to the bidding of the leaders. That is easy. All you have to do is tell them they are being attacked, and denounce the pacifists for lack of patriotism and exposing the country to danger."* [208]

I don't want the reader to get the idea that government PSYOPs are predominantly comprised of false flag events. Nevertheless, America's history is replete with FFEs that served to trigger America's entrance into wars throughout our modern history. In each instance, the media entertainment complex was either unquestioning conduits of government propaganda or were actively involved in insuring the success of the FFE operation.

One FFE that involved a complicit media was the sinking of the USS Maine in Havana Harbor in 1898. 270 sailors were killed by a naval mine. President McKinley blamed Spain for the event. The sinking of the Maine provided the rationale and the impetus to initiate the Spanish American War that resulted in displacing Spain from Cuba. New York Journal publisher William Randolph Hearst used his newspaper and a technique that came to be termed "yellow journalism" in order to inflame the passions of his readers for a war against Spain. Whether Spain was responsible or not, the event was used as an Ericksonian PSYOP by William Randolph Hearst. The Lusitania sinking is yet another example of bootstrapping the motivation for war upon either a FFE or an Ericksonian PSYOP.

PSYOPs are routinely used by various agencies within the Federal government in order to achieve a goal or purpose. A PSYOP used by The Secret Service is the use of decoy presidential limousines in motorcades. Every time a clone presidential limousine is added to the president's motorcade, the probability of an assassin accurately choosing to attack the presidential limousine in which the president is riding is reduced by a numerical factor related to the ratio between the numerator (True Presidential limousine) and the denominator (Limousine Decoys).

Another example of the use of PSYOPs that make use of clones is the body double. Many world leaders in various parts of the world make use of body doubles. It is the body double that is placed in harm's way when the masses need the assurance of a leader's personal appearance but when the risks are too high for the real leader. PSYOPs directed at cult of personality leaders make use of body doubles, as well. Listed below is a sampling of some of the more interesting body doubles and their adventures:

---

[208] Goering, Hermann. (1947), Testimony Given During The Nuremberg Trials.

General Montgomery   Body Double: M.E. Clifton James

Clifton James was a native Australian who joined the British Army during World War II with aspirations to become an entertainer for Allied forces. The talent scouts in MI-5, that is, British Intelligence, immediately noticed James' uncanny resemblance to General Montgomery. The PSYOPerator's wheels began to turn. PSYOPerators flew James around Europe and held public events featuring Montgomery's double. All of this movement suggested to the Germans that Allied forces intended to invade the motherland using routes from Southern France.

James was so glib, and good at impromptu dialogue, that he was sent to parties in Gibraltar wherein he would pretend to get a little tipsy and then share his military plans in earshot of Nazis in attendance. James was flown to North Africa where he walked around in view of Nazi spies as he pointed out toward the Mediterranean as he both whispered to another General in on the plot and while giggling as though he had something up his sleeve. Well, the Nazis bought the PSYOP and shifted their troops from the North to the South, thus removing what would have been a much stronger force confronting the troops who landed on Normandy on D-Day.

A more recent body double was used by the Hussein regime to help protect one of Saddam's high profile sons, Uday Hussein.

Uday Hussein   Body Double: Latif Yahia

According to body double Latif Yahia, he was shot and stabbed at least 26 times by people mistaking him for Saddam Hussein's son Uday. Yahia says that he was almost killed by Desert Storm forces that were tasked with capturing or killing Uday.

Yahia wrote that his work as a body double began in 1988. While serving as an Iraqi soldier, Uday spotted him and approached him to become his "fiday," that is, body double. Yahia insists that he originally turned down the offer, after which Uday had him placed in jail under solitary confinement. Given some time alone to think about what his next move would be, he decided that being a "fiday" was not so bad after all. One of the more interesting stories told by Yahia is that a certain young woman known to both he and Uday found him, that is Yahia, to be the more attractive of the two look-a-likes; at which point Uday promptly shot Yahia. So much, I suppose, for the benefits of loyalty to the Husseins. The CIA helped Yahia escape control of the Hussein family in 1991 in return for him sharing his knowledge of the inner workings of the Hussein family.

Before we leave the Hussein family, one of the more interesting body doubles involved the fatay for Saddam, himself. What is interesting about this body double is that the CIA chose this fatay, not Saddam. A little background is in order here. World leaders who are what the intelligence community refers to as "cult of personality" figures, rely upon their persona and lifestyle as a big part of their cache. For example, the late North Korean leader Kim Jong-il was reputed to have made several holes-in-one the very first time he played golf. Kim was reputed to have no need to go to the bathroom, because unlike mere mortals, "Dear Leader" did not produce urine and feces. His public image was preened by images that resembled movie set stills from a John Wayne western. The public, as we have noted throughout this book, is predictably vulnerable to consuming such orchestrated depictions of their leaders and in return projecting great reverence upon them. The original shadow men were the first to tap into this phenomenon. Intelligence services of America and other countries cultivate the public's vulnerabilities regarding their cult of personality projections upon their leaders. So, what if one of these cult of personality leaders was seen doing things that were repulsive as opposed to awe inspiring? Enter the body double.

The CIA set about to find a body double for Saddam Hussein. The plan was to produce a video that resembled a home movie of Saddam having sex with a boy. The movie would then "miraculously" leak and make its way into the Iraqi public's consciousness. The PSYOP movie was envisioned to disrupt the public's childlike adoration and idealization of Iraq's bigger-than-life leader. For various reasons this particular PSYOP never came to fruition. However, a similar PSYOP was used on the late Osama bin Laden. CIA operators produced at least two home movies of a bin Laden look-alike drunkenly bragging about how many boys he had sex with. Osama's inner circle did not buy it and more than a few technical errors in the bogus film's production made it too obvious that the footage was not real.

An Egyptian by the name of Mohamed Bashir denies that he was a fiday for Saddam. Bashir denies either an Iraqi or American formal involvement in his role as a body double. He does, however, admit to being hunted by those seeking to cash in on the American's multi-million dollar bounty on Saddam. Bashir also recounted a rather interesting story about independent porn producers who attempted to kidnap him and/or pay him hundreds of thousands of dollars to play Saddam in a porn movie sometime in 2011. What is the truth about the porn movie? Permit me simply to say this, stranger things have happened.

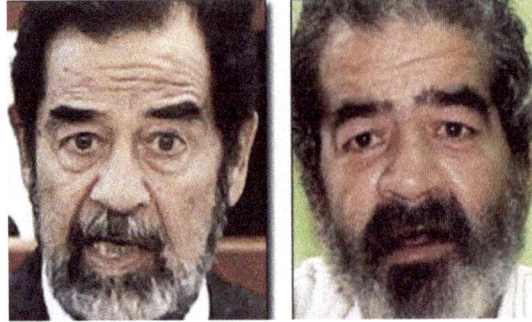

Saddam Hussein   **Body Double: Mohamed Bashir**

The reader should take note of the fact that the underlying psychological principle involved in body double PSYOPs is inextricably related to the masses' failure of discernment and average IQ, paired with the public's tendency to project upon its leader's a larger than life persona. Absent these three neuropsychological tendencies, much of the effectiveness of the body double PSYOP, in all of its permutations, would disappear.

Another PSYOP reliant upon the masses' failure of discernment and intelligence is the rumor PSYOP. Rumors are relatively easy to generate and only require an unwitting or complicit media to disseminate the rumor to the masses. Social media has made the dissemination of rumors unbelievably easy. Rumors are the gift that keeps on giving and serves their creators quite well.

Some rumors are termed "flagpole" rumors. This term derives from the allegory to running a flag up a flagpole to see if someone salutes it. Floating a rumor provides operatives another benefit, in that floating a rumor allows operators a dry run in order to see how the intended audience would respond should the rumor be widely disseminated. With reference to the intended audience, PSYOPerators are more interested, usually, in audiences not comprised of the public. This is because the intelligence community knows the discernment limits of the population at large and because the masses are so easy to manipulate, there is not much sport in it. On the other hand, using a well-crafted rumor to modify a world leader's behavior, that requires a great deal of finesse. The best rumor strategy, when dealing with world leaders, is to plant a rumor that confirms a pre-existing suspicion.

For example, some world leaders tend to be paranoid. This is especially true of dictators and those who are properly described as cult of personality leaders. If the intent is to undermine a rival's position with the leader, a strategically placed rumor can ruin a target rival's credibility.

I find it absolutely fascinating that the PSYOP of rumoring is a favorite tactic of BOTH pre-teen and teen girls and high-level CIA operatives! When any PSYOP has such widespread adoption, across gender, demographic and professional status, one must look to a flaw in human nature to understand why such a PSYOP, like rumoring, works so well. Again, our old friends, failure of discernment and the masses' gullibility related to their inefficient cognitive information processing appear to be the gifts that keeps on giving.

In addition to running the flag up the flagpole and undermining a rival's credibility, rumors strategically placed can bring down politicians, candidates, products, stock prices and almost anything one can imagine. High beta publicly traded companies, for example, are a favorite target of stock price manipulators who can stampede Lemming-like investors/stock holders with a strategically placed and well-timed rumor. Whether it is the health of the CEO of the company, a made-up defect in an upcoming product, a glitch in the company's supply chain or a suspiciously timed investment analyst's downgrade, the reason these rumors work is because human beings are not smart enough to recognize PSYOPs and are fearful that they might be true. Thus, we are forever being reminded of the raison d'être for this book. We have a saying in the intelligence community when it comes to rumors regarding anyone's health : "If we wait long enough we will always be right."

Character assassination is much preferred over a bloody assassination in today's intelligence community. It is relatively easy to start a rumor and then sit back as man's herd instinct takes over. It is relatively easy to assassinate **any** famous person's character because the famous person is more often than not the object of projections and fantasy on the part of the public. If the public figure is a man, then one can be assured that there will be more than a few women whose fantasies regarding their sexual attraction to the star or famous person are encouraged to morph into allegations of molestation, rape or other exploitation. The key to uncovering truth from fiction is to study what we in the intelligence community call "bumpers." Bumpers are events or things that immediately preceded the onslaught of disclosures that serve as the fodder for the character assassination. For example, if a person criticizes a powerful figure who has access to PSYOPerators, and shortly thereafter that person's character is assaulted, then it may be helpful to ask the next question we in the intelligence community always ask: "Why this, why now?" If one day you criticize a powerful person's policies and shortly thereafter a bevy of women seemingly come out of nowhere reporting that the star/powerful person criticizer, raped them, you may wish to take a step back and reconsider the drama being played out before your eyes.

Permit me to hasten to add that famous people, no matter how bad their behavior, can be protected and/or rehabilitated by a complicit media entertainment complex that disseminates the protective PSYOPs that can add a Teflon™ coating to any opprobrious character or behavior. The masses are so gullible that by simply not covering or giving airtime to undeniably bad or criminal behavior, the public goes on its merry way without so much as one iota of awareness that they are being "played."

The public has been made aware of any number of "official" PSYOP programs, each of which has mysterious names and are cloaked in intrigue. The people and groups who compile lists of such PSYOPs never quite explain why it is that they were able to identify programs that if they were what they are alleged to be, they would have never known about them. I am more interested in why the public appears to be fascinated by such programs. Sexy and intriguing does not necessarily mean an effective PSYOP. Many of the early experiments on hypnosis and drugs, for example, were studies that explored the limits of hypnotic suggestion and psychotropic medications, but never truly came to fruition.

Perhaps no other covert program that explored mind control, drugs and hypnosis was as famous as MK-ULTRA. MK-ULTRA was created in 1953. The goal of this effort was to learn how to program or deprogram, as it were, a subject's memory and cognitive functions. In 1964 MK-ULTRA morphed into MK-SEARCH. MK-SEARCH can be thought of as MK-ULTRA on steroids. The 1964 group conducted experiments that were highly risky to test subjects. Studies were performed on prisoners, patients suffering from a terminal illness and others who were described as "mental defectives." Then came operation "Artichoke" which was a sub-division of MK-ULTRA and then "Project Monarch."

Monarch focused upon multiple personality disorders (MPDs), both in terms of what these rare psychological presentations were and how to re-create MPDs in the lab using induced trauma. Monarch wanted to know if agents could use lab created alternative personalities to do things that most people would not do willingly. Another cloak and dagger drug experiment involving LSD and mind control was coined: Operation Midnight Climax. In 1979, writer John Marks wrote the book:

The Search for the Manchurian Candidate. Much of what Marks wrote in his book has been confirmed in declassified CIA documents.

Three or more CIA operations were run in the San Francisco/Bay Area. One operation was housed at 225 Chestnut Street on Telegraph Hill in San Francisco. The Chestnut Street operation ran from 1955 to 1965. Telegraph Hill was strategically chosen because it was a short trip to North Beach's bars and hangouts. Ladies of the evening, paid by the government to lure clients to Chestnut Street house/lab, spiked cocktails with LSD and then gave them to unwitting "johns." Climax houses were equipped with two-way mirrors along with recording devices, some of which masqueraded as electrical outlets.

To set the proper mood, the walls of Telegraph Hill were adorned with photographs of women in various provocative poses. What kind of agents did this type of work? One agent was George H. White who had been trained to break up heroin and opium drug trafficking operations located in the Far East. It was White who came up with the intriguing name, Operation Midnight Climax.

The upshot of all of these programs, including MK-ULTRA, Artichoke, Monarch, Operation Midnight Climax, et al. was this: While interesting and useful in certain situations where U.S. and international law is inapplicable, the utilitarian value of using targeted drugs and/or any combination of hypnosis and induced trauma **is unnecessary and too messy** to garner compliance or make people do your bidding and/or compromise a target.

The same behavioral outcomes can be achieved in a much more parsimonious manner, for example, by simply finding sociopaths who are willing to carry out missions by rewarding them with money or other tangible and intangible benefits. The pesky problem of covering the agencies' tracks when utilizing a sociopath is as simple as terminating the command of the sociopath who, despite knowing the risks, is almost always more than willing to engage the mission because like all sociopaths, he believes that he is the one exception to the rule, meaning, he won't be double crossed by the originators of the plan nor be terminated. Intelligence agencies also recognized that tremendous leverage can be exercised against an otherwise reluctant sociopath if blackmail is used strategically, thus, negating the need for narco-hypnosis.

The rule in blackmail is this: The greater the compliance required, the more heinous the underlying defect in character or behavior must be that is used to effectuate the blackmail. Thus, if a person is to be placed in a position of great power and authority, that person can only be made to comply with the program's director if, and only if, a hidden defect of monumental proportions is used to blackmail the operator. What would constitute something of such severity? It would be something that if revealed would make the operator a target of a likely successful felony conviction or brought up on articles of treason if we are talking about a politician in high office. Thus, high-level agents who are controlled using blackmail always connote a high stakes game of chicken between the agency and their target. Thus, rather than being the worst choice for a political leader, from shadow men's perspective, a fatally flawed character constitutes the BEST choice to be the political front man or agent in disguise.

The psychology in such instances of high-stakes blackmail is fascinating because of this fact, one that we have made reference to earlier in this book, the bigger the lie the easier it is to garner the public's belief in that lie. The fact of a Manchurian Candidate controlled by blackmail and the "candidates" own psychopathy is inconceivable to a child-like public that lacks discernment. The public would more likely believe in a screenwriter's vision of a Manchurian Candidate, a person hypnotized and/or under the influence of mind control because that is immeasurably more sexy and spy-like when compared to the way it is really done. So yes, many of the mysterious and cloak and dagger type programs some paranoid and not so paranoid bloggers and broadcasters discuss are or were real. But no, much more parsimonious and effective methods supplanted these intriguing but inefficient methods.

No discussion of military/governmental intelligence programs would be complete without examining "Operation Paperclip." In some sense, Operation Paperclip is the beginning of the story. After the end of World War II in 1945 and into the early part of 1946, President Harry Truman and elite members of America's intelligence community recognized that a wealth of human talent in Hitler's intelligence services and military technology labs were looking for a new home.

The Allies had first hand knowledge of German's cutting edge military and mind control technology and had been advised of some breathtaking scientific advancements, in beta testing back in Germany. Nazi or no Nazi, Hitler's talent pool was too good to put on trial, execute or put in jail. Truman also knew that every other government had the same idea as the Americans, namely, "Hitler's talent pool was too good to pass up."

Convinced that German scientists could help America's postwar efforts, President Harry Truman agreed in September 1946 to authorize "Project or Operation Paperclip" (OP), a program to bring selected German scientists to work on America's behalf. In the spring of 1947, The War Department's Joint Intelligence Objectives Agency (JIOA) submitted dossiers of former German scientists for review by the Secretary of State and Department of Justice. The summary analysis of the dossiers concluded that the men were ardent Nazi supporters. Since Truman had specifically instructed agents involved with Operation Paperclip to exclude die hard Nazis, this posed a problem.

The head of the JOIA, Bosquet Wev, argued that America should overlook Nazi's war crimes. He stressed that if the targets of Operation Paperclip were left in Germany they would likely end up in either the Soviet's hands or some other intramural competitor with America. By 1947 it was becoming obvious that Stalin was intent upon increasing the USSR's power and influence in the world. Wev went on to argue that the national security risks associated with not employing former Nazis should be avoided at all costs.

CIA director Allen Dulles met with Nazi Intelligence Chief Reinhard Gehlen. Gehlen was a James Bond type figure that had infiltrated the Soviet's iron clad intelligence service. Dulles simply could not permit such raw German talent to go elsewhere. As a result, Gehlen was promised safe harbor. CIA's Dulles rewrote OP's target's dossiers in order to assuage President Truman's concerns. In a 1985, an investigator/writer by the name of Linda Hunt wrote in The *Bulletin of the Atomic Scientists*, that every one of the Germans brought to America had their dossiers "cleaned up." According to Hunt, President Truman was either kept out of the rewrite loop or was willingly oblivious to his agent's backstage work to cleanse Nazi collaborators of their most heinous crimes. Consistent with the proposition that President Truman and later Eisenhower were kept in the dark, Clare Lasby's book about Operation Paperclip made the point that President Truman honestly denied the existence of any program designed to whitewash Nazi collaborators. I mention this little walk down memory lane because Gehlen's men were the same people who created MK-ULTRA, ARTICHOKE, MONARCH, OPERATION MIDNIGHT CLIMAX, et al.

Agents provocateurs is yet another simple but effective PSYOP. This particular PSYOP is effective when the desired outcome is to undermine the credibility of a group, organization or gathering of people in opposition to the agencies' interests. This particular PSYOP can be traced back to the French Revolution. At that time Freemasons, working on behalf of intramural competitors within Louis XVI's palace, were tasked with stirring up trouble among the masses in order to cause King Louis trouble. Sara Barmak, writing for Quebec's Star, took note of agents provocateurs in modern times:

"A 1976 report by a U.S. Senate committee on government operations found that "[u]nsavory and vicious tactics have been employed" in the drive to collect intelligence from Americans, "including anonymous attempts to break up marriages, disrupt meetings, ostracize persons from their professions, and provoke target groups into rivalries that might result in deaths." Agents provocateurs weren't the sole preserve of the FBI, however. The shadowy figures have popped up in many key historical events, including the Russian Revolution, where imperial police used Yevno Azef, an embezzler, as a double agent to spy on socialist groups. Azef organized assassinations of key officials in the monarchy, which then justified arrests of his accomplices." [209]

If peaceful demonstrators are left to make their points with persuasive credibility, the group may be able to effectuate change. The introduction of an agent provocateur into the group can change that outcome.

The agent provocateur may carry a stupid, racist, inflammatory sign, making sure that the media focuses upon the sign. This tactic can be embellished to include an interview with a media accomplice wherein the agent gives an interview that speaks for the group in a way as to undermine its credibility. Other agent provocateurs can become violent, i.e., throwing things, being abusive to the local authorities, etc. Sometimes the agent provocateur can inflame members of "his" group using misdirection, disinformation, etc. Sometimes agent provocateurs can use hybrid PSYOPs to great advantage. For example, agents may incorporate rumors that are communicated to a group's leadership or media arm. The result is always the same; the media almost always look no deeper than the surface image their cameras pick up. And, if the rumor confirms the media's inherent bias, not only will the media not investigate the truth, but will, in fact, add fuel to the rumor fire. The media entertainment complex in America is well known in the intelligence community as being sympathetic to any event or person who undermines the credibility of any group that would limit the power of the federal government. As with most PSYOPs, and certainly when it comes to agents provocateurs, effectiveness relies upon the failure of discernment on the part of the public and in particular, the media. You may properly think of the media entertainment complex as nothing more than the PR arm of shadow men. Using agents provocateurs is not the exclusive purview of governments, of course, as corporate espionage can make use of this PSYOP with great effectiveness.

Government agencies have always had a keen interest in weapons and gadgets that could be used by agents in the field. These are the weapons and gadgets that men like Agent 007 use on screen, but are, in fact, real. What follows are a sampling of gadgets that have been used by agents employed by American, British and Soviet intelligence agencies. I'm going in back in history because it would be illegal to reveal to you CURRENT gadgets used in espionage today. See if you can identify the underlying psychological principle that all of these gadgets have in common:

British Intelligence Umbrella Dart Gun.

---

[209] The Star. *A Brief History of Agents Provocateurs.* By: Sara Barmak, August 25, 2007.

USSR Poison Dart.

Martini Olive Listening Device (USA).

Compass Hidden in Button (USA).

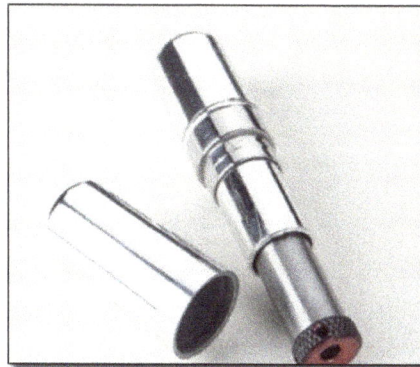

Lipstick Gun (USA).

Pocket Watch Gun.

Pen Gun (USA). [210]

If you reasoned that the psychological basis for all of these spy gadgets was related to subterfuge, you reasoned accurately. Mind controller's stock in trade is subterfuge. Objects that appear on the surface to be innocuous are really tools of death. **Whether shadow men and their agents are subverting minds, overthrowing countries, destroying and then remaking the mating habits of the masses, it is all carried out with a lie, a misdirection, a mistaken identity and always in the name of peace, justice and fairness or, in the case of spy gadgets, everyday innocuous things.**

The lipstick gun was not only real, it serves as the perfect metaphor for how shadow men go about their devious work to garner more and more control over the masses. Had the target on the business end of the lipstick case survived, undoubtedly he would have reported that, "I thought she was going to put on lipstick, instead, she shot me." "I thought he was simply carrying an umbrella because it looked like rain. The next thing I know, I'm lying here in this hospital bed." "I thought I was simply watching a clever TV show with an attractive ingénue named Marlo Thomas, the next thing I know I was a childless middle aged woman living alone and eating cat food."

---

[210] Cracked. *6 Real World Spy Gadgets Straight Out of the Movies.* By, Eric, A. September 29, 2011.

I'll leave you with a New York Times story that covered the 1975 Church Hearings on the CIA. In that hearing it was revealed that the CIA had developed a futuristic looking dart gun that could deliver a pin-prick dart, barely perceptible to the victim, that would deliver a cardio toxin that would cause the heart to go into cardiac arrest. Once the chemical had caused cardiac arrest, it would metabolize and disappear, without leaving a trace. Thus, no one would be the wiser.

Frank Church Showing Off C.I.A. Poison Dart Gun, 1975.

COLBY DESCRIBES C.I.A. POISON WORK

He Tells Senate Panel of Secret $3-Million Project That Lasted 18 Years

By NICHOLAS M. HORROCK
Special to The New York Times

WASHINGTON, Sept. 16 — The Central Intelligence Agency operated an 18-year, $3-million super-secret project to develop poisons, biochemical weapons and such devices as dart guns to administer them, the agency's director testified today.

William E. Colby, Director of Central Intelligence, told the Senate Select Committee on Intelligence that pursuant to a Presidential order the project, code-named "MK. Naomi," was halted in February, 1970.

Mr. Colby showed the committee a dart gun patterned on the Army's Colt semi-automatic pistol but electrically fired. He said it could shoot a dart 100 meters and was "almost silent."

The dart gun, brought before the committee at its request, was described in a C.I.A. memo as a "nondiscernible microbionoculator."

The committee made public C.I.A. documents showing that the agency had a vast array of poisons, including many that would cause deadly diseases, and systems for destroying crops.

The documents also showed that the C.I.A. had used the New York City subway system.

Continued on Page 27, Column 1

CHAPTER 13: GOOGLE IQ™

Author H.G. Wells foresaw advancements in mass communication technology and how one day those scientific wonders would make mass indoctrination possible for the first time in human history. Over a half century ago, H. G. Wells sensed the vast potentialities of these inventions when he wrote in the New York Times:

> *"Modern means of communication—the power afforded by print, telephone, wireless and so forth, of rapidly putting through directive strategic or technical conceptions to a great number of cooperating centers, of getting quick replies and effective discussion have opened up a new world of political processes. Ideas and phrases can now be given an effectiveness, greater than the effectiveness of any personality and stronger than any sectional interest. The common design can be documented and sustained against perversion and betrayal. It can be elaborated and developed steadily and widely without personal, local and sectional misunderstanding."*[211]

The Internet and other digital media conduits represent the quintessential manifestation of H.G. Well's prescient, if not idealistically naïve, warnings regarding technology and mass mind control. Keep in mind, however, that digital media and its content require a willing and supplicant audience before it can facilitate mass indoctrination. Just as a farmer tills the soil and prepares it for seeding, so has mankind been tilled and prepared for being continuously plugged-in to the means by which thoughts, feelings and behavior are controlled.

Napoleon's Second Axiom states:

The smarter man thinks he is, the easier he is to control.

Knowing this, mind control experts, in association with revolutionaries who had their own motives to enhance man's view of his own intelligence, joined forces to create what mind control artists refer to as, "artificially high self-esteem Sheeple." I reflect upon Commodore Oliver Hazard Perry's famous quote: "We have met the enemy and he is us."[212]

Shadow men, by and through their proxy agents, have convinced American children since the late 1960's that they are all budding geniuses (top 1% to 2% in intelligence of all human beings on earth). [213] To be sure, once shadow men initiated the artificially high self-esteem movement, a lot of well-intentioned secular humanists jumped on this feel good bandwagon. When the students of these "feel good" secular humanist school teachers and shadow men revolutionaries became adults, it began to dawn on them that their achievements never matched their potential, as promised to them by parents, teachers, counselors, media, advertisers, etc. This cognitive dissonance between the promises, vs. real world outcome, was exacerbated by an economy created by shadow men that made wealth accumulation almost impossible for the common man. Despite their disappointing real

---

[211] Bernays, Edward L. (1928), *Propaganda.* Ig Publishing, Brooklyn, New York.

[212] Cartoonist Walt Kelly (Pogo) is the person who added the word "us" part of the quote. The original quote, the one Kelly modified, came from Commodore Perry who used the word "our."

[213] Actuarial data have documented that 84% of ALL human beings possess either average or below-average intelligence.

world performance versus what they had been brainwashed to believe they were entitled to, their artificially high self-esteem remained, for the most part, intact. Thus, a state of cognitive delusion became the norm for Millennial America.

Socially engineering artificially high self-esteem became the only religious study that could be taught in America's public schools. Statists, in cooperation with shadow man-driven mind control agents, funded and promoted the artificially high self-esteem movement.

The widespread disconnect between poor discernment while being unaware of that lack of discernment has resulted in a body of research that has documented this disconnect. In fact, this phenomenon has a name: The Dunning-Kruger Effect, to wit:

> *"The Dunning–Kruger effect is a cognitive bias wherein unskilled individuals suffer from illusory superiority, mistakenly assessing their ability to be much higher than is accurate. This bias is attributed to a metacognitive inability of the unskilled to recognize their ineptitude. Conversely, highly skilled individuals tend to underestimate their relative competence, erroneously assuming that tasks which are easy for them are also easy for others."* [214]

One of the more insidious qualities of the Dunning-Kruger Effect is that the very quality that would permit discernment is missing in those who lack discernment. [215] This defect in cognitive functioning was recognized by shadow men and their agents and exploited by exacerbating the masses' lack of discernment by convincing them that rather than lacking discernment, they actually possessed it. A devious slight of hand was used that played upon the average man's lack of discernment in order to convince him that all knowledge and expertise was merely opinion; and as the masses were taught: Opinions are like anuses, everyone has one and all opinions are equal because that is only "fair."

A collateral benefit of the Google IQ™ phenomenon is related to the fact that among the masses there were always smart people who had not been compromised by shadow men or their agents. These gems, as they are known, provided the average man a fighting chance against the insidious PSYOPs directed at them. However, since the establishment of the Google IQ™ phenomenon, the average man no longer accepts that his opinion is any less important than is the opinion of the smartest among the masses. The Google IQ™ phenomenon, and the cultivation of artificially high self-esteem, removed that last layer of insulation between shadow men's mind control and the masses' victimization.

Many of the authors of public school children's textbooks, as well as their teachers, fit all of the criteria necessary to label them as Marxists. Many were, as a matter of public record, card-carrying, dues paying and acknowledged Communists. Marxists are expert at promoting the Dunning-Kruger Effect. Here is the bibliography of just one of the more famous teachers of public school teachers who, along with his wife, Bernadine Dohrn, transformed American public schools into indoctrination camps designed to subvert the American idea by replacing merit with The Dunning-Kruger Effect:

- *Education: An American Problem.* Bill Ayers, Radical Education Project, 1968, ASIN B0007H31HU OCLC 33088998
- *Hot town: Summer in the City: I ain't gonna work on Maggie's farm no more*, Bill Ayers, Students for a

---

[214] Kruger, Justin; Dunning, David (1999), *Unskilled and Unaware of It: How Difficulties in Recognizing One's Own Incompetence Lead to Inflated Self-Assessments.* Journal of Personality and Social Psychology 77 (6): 1121–34.
[215] Fuller, Geraint (2011), *Ignorant of ignorance?* Practical Neurology 11 (6): 365.

Democratic Society, 1969, ASIN B0007I3CMI

- *Prairie Fire: The Politics of Revolutionary Anti-Imperialism*, Bernadine Dohrn, Jeff Jones, Billy Ayers, Celia Sojourn, Communications Co., 1974, ASIN B000GF2KVQ OCLC <u>1177495</u>

- *The Good Preschool Teacher: Six Teachers Reflect on Their Lives*, William Ayers, Teachers College Press, 1989, <u>ISBN 978-0-8077-2946-5</u>

- *To Teach: The Journey of a Teacher*, William Ayers, Teachers College Press, 1993, <u>ISBN 978-0-8077-3262-5</u>

- *To Become a Teacher: Making a Difference in Children's Lives*, William Ayers, Teachers College Press, 1995, <u>ISBN 978-0-8077-3455-1</u>

- *City Kids, City Teachers: Reports from the Front Row*, William Ayers (Editor) and Patricia Ford (Editor), New Press, 1996, <u>ISBN 978-1-56584-328-8</u>

- *A Kind and Just Parent*, William Ayers, Beacon Press, 1997, <u>ISBN 978-0-8070-4402-5</u>

- *A Light in Dark Times: Maxine Greene and the Unfinished Conversation*, Maxine Greene (Editor), William Ayers (Editor), Janet L. Miller (Editor), Teachers College Press, 1998, <u>ISBN 978-0-8077-3721-7</u>

- *Teaching for Social Justice: A Democracy and Education Reader*, William Ayers (Editor), Jean Ann Hunt (Editor), Therese Quinn (Editor), 1998, <u>ISBN 978-1-56584-420-9</u>

- *Teacher Lore: Learning from Our Own Experience*, William H. Schubert (Editor) and William

- C. Ayers (Editor), Educator's International Press, 1999, <u>ISBN 978-1-891928-03-1</u>

- *Teaching from the Inside Out: The Eight-Fold Path to Creative Teaching and Living*, Sue Sommers (Author), William Ayers (Foreword), Authority Press, 2000, <u>ISBN 978-1-929059-02-7</u>

- *A Simple Justice: The Challenge of Small Schools*, William Ayers, Teachers College Press, 2000, ISBN 978-0-8077-3963-1

- *Zero Tolerance: Resisting the Drive for Punishment*, William Ayers (Editor), Rick Ayers (Editor), Bernadine Dohrn (Editor), Jesse L. Jackson (Author), New Press, 2001, <u>ISBN 978-1-56584-666-1</u>

- *A School of Our Own: Parents, Power, and Community at the East Harlem Block Schools*, Tom Roderick (Author), William Ayers (Author), Teachers College Press, 2001, <u>ISBN 978-0-8077-4157-3</u>

- *Refusing Racism: White Allies and the Struggle for Civil Rights*, Cynthia Stokes Brown (Author), William Ayers (Editor), Therese Quinn (Editor), Teachers College Press, 2002, ISBN 978-0-8077-4204-4

- *On the Side of the Child: Summerhill Revisited*, William Ayers, Teachers College Press, 2003, ISBN 978-0-8077-4400-0

The artificially high self-esteem movement is a feel good PSYOP with a much deeper and nefarious purpose. An elite group of social engineers purposefully designed the artificially high self-esteem movement to increase the malleability and vulnerability of the masses to mind control. These same social engineers, in explicit and implicit cooperation with multinational corporations, saw the benefit of making children think that they were smarter and more talented than they really were. To add to the effectiveness of this PSYOP, while self-esteem was being artificially raised, real educational standards were being lowered. Man's nature all but insures that he is almost always vulnerable to a well-placed compliment. And telling everyone that they are budding geniuses is a lie that feels really, really good to both the liar and the recipient of the lie.

No longer do we teach or accept as true the wisdom found in this principle: *Knowing how you arrived at the correct answer is at least, if not more important, than the answer itself.* Google has made it possible for this principle to be turned on its head. Google, when paired with the artificially high self-esteem movement, has undermined man's ability to know something more than factual information he or she can easily copy, cut and paste.

Google generated knowledge, with the exception of isolated factual information, e.g., how many continents are there? What is the mass of the earth? What is a good recipe for apple pie, promotes the delusion in its user that he is smarter and better educated than he really is.

Here is but one example that illustrates this phenomenon. One can do a Google search for the landing protocol of the Boeing 777 aircraft. The search results can then be inserted into a term paper, they can be quoted at a social gathering or they can be authoritatively inserted into a blog, etc. Does this mean the holder of this information knows *how* to land a Boeing 777 aircraft? No, of course not, and therein is the problem. I saw comedian Howie Mandel do the following at one of his live performances that illustrates the subject of this chapter.

Mandel, a high school kickout, played an emergency room physician on a TV show. During one of his standup performances broadcast on HBO, I saw Mandel **arrogantly** question a real emergency room physician who was sitting in his audience. Mandel **brashly** questioned the real doctor about various treatment protocols that had been written into one of the show's scripts that Mandel had memorized. The ER doctor didn't rattle off the answers like a parrot when challenged to do so by Mandel, but Mandel did regurgitate the text from the memorized script and demonstrated this to his fawning audience who applauded his display of his script memorization. The interaction between Mandel and the doctor did not come across as a joke and it certainly wasn't funny.

> **It was clear to me that Mandel really believed that parroting medical terms from a TV script was the equal of the knowledge possessed by the real emergency room doctor.**

How did we get to this point where a high school kickout comedian feels that he can compete with (actually know more than) a real doctor?

All of us know by now that we live in the "information age." Information is everywhere and easily accessible to anyone with access to the Internet and the ability to enter a search term(s) into your favorite search engine. Information that was once buried in the musty stacks at the university's library is now a few mouse clicks or finger swipes away, eagerly awaiting insertion into a school paper, speech tweet or casual conversation at a dinner party.

With all of this information at our fingertips, conventional wisdom is that we are all smarter and better educated, but is that true? Does having the results of a Google search mean you necessarily know something of substance? Regardless how you answer that question, there is one thing we do know, and that is the easy access to information has promoted the *belief* among the masses that they are smarter and know more than those who grew up without access to the Internet. I call the delusion of being smarter and better educated, after scrolling through the results of a Google search, *The Google IQ™.*

I set about to investigate this phenomenon. I wanted to know if beyond the ability to cut and paste quotes and the ability to repeat terms of art, do Google IQ™ people have the ability to extrapolate from the information their search engine spat out? I wanted to know if Google IQ™ers really had acquired generative knowledge or were they more like recorders who "played back" what their favorite search engine had displayed on their screen?

Think of Google IQ™ knowledge as having memorized the periodic table of elements; whereas, substantive or generative knowledge of the periodic table means that you can actually generate new molecular structures and predict rules for how existing molecules should react and behave with one another. As I stated earlier, recipes, number-based facts, e.g., "How high is the Empire State Building," that sort of thing, is not what I am talking about here.

I wanted to know if Google IQ™ people really did confuse the ability to parrot or cut and paste a term of art or repeat some narrative with substantive or generative knowledge, that is, the ability to understand a subject area that permits one to extrapolate new summary information. Can a Google IQ™ person, who memorizes A+B=C, turn around and deduce from that simple equation that IF A+B=C THEN B-A=C?

I took a group of 1970s liberal arts college graduates and compared them to a group of late 1990s liberal arts college grads. The 90's group comprised a demographic described as The Millennial Generation. Each test subject in both groups had studied chemistry in high school. No one from either group had gone on to work in a field that required them to apply their knowledge of chemistry. No one in either group considered themselves to be a "chemistry buff."

The first thing I did was to isolate the subjects from one another. I then asked each test subject to *estimate* what he or she thought the melting point would be for salt, e.g., high, medium, low. I then asked each test subject to tell me, how did you come up with your answer? Once the subjects had recorded their estimates, I then moved each subject to another room and provided them with access to the net and told them to find the melting point of salt.

Among the 1990's group, only 20% of them accurately estimated the melting point of salt to be high. The other 80% either guessed the right answer without any reasoning (just a pure guess) or guessed wrong using no underlying reasoning. Pure guesses, even if accurate, were not counted as correct answers.

Among the 1970's group, 40% of them accurately estimated the melting point of salt to be "high." This correct answer was twice that of the millennial test subjects. But more interesting was the fact that of those 40% who got the answer right, 15% of those people used generative knowledge to arrive at the correct answer. The other 25% told me they seemed to have remembered their teacher harping on the fact that salt was hard to melt or that it had a high melting temperature. As before, any correct answer arrived at by purely guessing was not counted as a correct answer.

The 1970's educated subjects who answered correctly **reasoned** during the estimation phase that the melting point of salt would be "high" because sodium (Na) was positively charged while chloride (Cl) was negatively charged, thus creating a strong bond that would only break at high temperatures. After both groups were permitted to Google "the melting point of salt," I found that 75% of the 1990s subjects parroted the term "ionic bond" but admitted, when asked, that they still didn't know why the melting point of salt would be "high" even after they Googled "what is the melting point of salt?" The 1970's test subjects reported after their Google search that the search had refreshed their memory and that the search results confirmed what they had been taught in school. Here is another interesting study that illustrates how potentially deluding and dangerous the Google IQ™ phenomenon is.

In 1990 a study was published in the American Journal of Respiratory and Critical Care Medicine. This study found that physicians trained before 1970 were significantly better at identifying heart murmurs by listening to the heart with a stethoscope than were new residents trained in the 1990s. The young doctors in the study pool were drawn from 31 training programs in internal medicine or family practice. Surprisingly, the 1990's trained physicians made the correct diagnosis of common heart abnormalities only 20 percent of the time after making a clinical examination of the patient's heart.

One of the authors of the study, Dr. Salvatore Mangione, stated that the young doctors should have been able to accurately identify at least 70 percent to 80 percent of heart murmurs simply by listening to the heart. Dr. Salvatore Mangione, and his co-author Dr. Linda Nieman, conducted their study to test the ***commonly held belief*** *among medical educators that doctors today are less skilled than they used to be at traditional tasks like examining patients and making diagnoses based on physical findings.* [216]

The results of the Mangione and Nieman research were due to both the Google IQ™ phenomenon and the fact that physicians have lost touch with the skill set necessary to diagnosis heart murmurs using a stethoscope because they rely heavily upon EKG and Echocardiogram studies.

To fully understand the Google IQ™ phenomenon and the Dunning-Kruger Effect, one needs to understand how America came to confuse the summary knowledge of facts and terms of art with substantive or generative knowledge. Before the 1970s, education in America consisted of teaching the predicate knowledge and methods of reasoning that would, when tilled by a creative and motivated mind, produce generative knowledge. What follows is a 1912 8th grade graduation test from Bullitt County, Kentucky. Our thanks go to Valerie Strauss of the Washington Post who published this test in 2012:

---

[216] Salvatore, Mangione, Nieman, Linda. (1999), *Pulmonary Auscultatory Skills During Training in Internal Medicine and Family Practice.* American Journal of Respiratory and Critical Care Medicine. Volume 159, Issue 4.

Arithmetic

1. Write in words the following:
   .5764; .000003; .123416; 653.0965; 43.37.   10
2. Solve: 3 5-7 plus 4, 5-8 plus 5-14—5 9-112.   10
3. Find cost at 12½ cents per sq. yd. of kalsomining the
   walls of a room 20 ft. long, 16 ft. wide and 9 ft. high,
   deducting 1 door 8 ft. by 4 ft. 6 in. and 2 windows 5 ft.
   by 3 ft. 6 in. each.   10
4. A man bought a farm for $2400 and sold it for $2700.
   What per cent did he gain?   10
5. A man sold a watch for $180. and lost 16⅔ %. What
   was the cost of the watch?   10
6. Find the amount of $50 30 for 3 yrs., 3 mo. and 3 days,
   at 8 per cent.   10
7. A school enrolled 120 pupils and the number of boys
   was two thirds of the number of girls. How many of
   each sex were enrolled?   10
8. How long a rope is required to reach from the top of a
   building 40 ft. high, to the ground 30 ft. from the base
   of the building?   10
9. How many steps 2 ft. 4 in. each will a man take in
   walking 2 1-4 miles?   10
10. At $1.62½ a cord, what will be the cost of a pile of
    wood 24 ft. long, 4 ft. wide and 6 ft. 3 in. high?   10

History.

1. Who first discovered the following places:—Florida, Pacific Ocean, Miss River, St Lawrence River?
2. Sketch briefly Sir Walter Rawleigh, Peter Stuyvesant.
3. By whom were the following settled:—Ga., Md , Mass., R. I., Fla
4. During what wars were the following battles fought:—Brandywine, Great Meadows, Lundy's Lane, Antietam, Buena Vista.
5 Describe the battle of Quebec.
6 Give the cause of the war of 1812 and name an important battle fought during that war.
7. Name 2 presidents who have died in office: three who were assasinated.
8. Name the last battle of the Civil War; War of 1812; French and Indian War, and the commanders in each battle.
9. What president was impeached, and on what charge?
10. Who invented the following.—Magnetic, Telegraph, Cotton Gin, Sewing Machine, Telephone, Phonograph.

William Foster,
Ed C Tyler,
J E. Magruder,   Bullitt County Board of Education.
F T Harned,
Ora L. Roby,
                        Chas. G. Bridwell, Truant Officer.

Civil Government

1. Define the following forms of government: Democracy, Limited Monarchy, Absolute Monarchy, Republic. Give examples of each.   10
2. To what four governments are students in school subjected?   10
3. Name five county officers, and the principal duties of each.   10
4. Name and define the three branches of the government of the United States.   10
5. Give three duties of the President. What is meant by the veto power?   10
6. Name three rights given Congress by the Constitution and two rights denied Congress.   10
7. In the election of a president and vice-president, how many electoral votes in each State allowed?   10
8. Give the eligibility of president, vice-president and Governor of Kentucky.   10
9. What is a copyright? Patent right?   10
10. Describe the manner in which the president and vice-president of the United States are elected.   10

Geography.

1. Define longitude and latitude   10
2. Name and give boundaries of the five zones.   10
3. Tell what you know of the Gulf Stream.   10
4. Locate Erie Canal; what waters does it connect, and
   why is it important?   10
5. Locate the following countries which border each other:
   Turkey, Greece, Servia, Montenegro, Roumania.   10
6. Name and give the capitals of States touching the Ohio
   River   10
7. Locate these cities: Mobile. Quebec, Buenos Aires,
   Liverpool, Honolulu.   10
8. Name in the order of their size three largest States in
   the United States.   10
9. Locate the following mountains: Blue Ridge, Hima-
   laya, Andes, Alps, Wasatch.   10
10. Through what waters would a vessel pass in going from
    England through the Suez Canal to Manila?   10

Physiology.

1. How does the liver compare in size with other glands
   in the human body? Where is it located? What does
   it secrate.   10
2. Name the organs of circulation.   10
3. Describe the heart.   10
4. Compare arteries and veins as to function. Where is
   the blood carried to be purified?   10
5. Where is the chief nervous center of the body?   10
6. Define Cerebrum; Cerebellum.   10
7. What are the functions (or uses) of the spinal column?   10
8. Why should we study Physiology?   10
9. Give at least five rules to be observed in maintaining
   good health.   20

If you belong to the 1960's "flower child," Millennial or Gen-X generations, you are likely to fail this test. This exam at the turn of the 20th century was a measure of generative knowledge taught as a matter of course to 8th graders in America's public schools. You may be wondering, what happened to America's public school system?

During the late 1960s the art of test taking preparation became a burgeoning cottage industry. This was the result of several factors, most important of which was a sociopathic-like ambition of parents to get their average children into the best schools and those schools reliance upon *standardized* test scores in evaluating prospective students. Parents had been brainwashed to believe that the environment could not only help their children reach their potential, which it can, but also that teachers and devices and books could actually make their children more intelligent, not merely better educated. After the 1960s the notion that intelligence had a significant biological component was redacted from common knowledge by shadow men's agents who found such truths as discordant with their desire to foment artificially high self esteem.

Summary knowledge was all that mattered on standardized tests, that is, regurgitate facts and voila, you get an "A." For those questions on standardized tests that required a modicum of deductive and/or inductive reasoning, test preparers, another burgeoning cottage industry of the day, taught techniques that circumvented actual reasoning with "gaming" the test in order to arrive at the correct answer.

One of the early markers of this cultural trend toward the regurgitation of facts and terms of art as a substitute for substantive and three-dimensional knowledge was the creation of Cliff's Notes. For those few of you who don't know, Cliff's notes became a lucrative business by boiling down almost any subject or book you can think of into crib notes or a "cheat" sheet.

Cliffs Notes sold 18,500 books in 1958, the year the company opened its doors, increasing to 2 million books by1965 and growing exponentially every year thereafter. Cliff's Notes marked a cultural transition that was a harbinger for what was to come.

In 2001, *The No Child Left Behind Act* (NCLB), was signed into law by President George W. Bush. The NCLB Act was predicated upon the belief that setting high standards and establishing measurable goals would improve public education. The NCLB Act requires states to develop assessments in basic skills to be given to all students commensurate with their grade level. But here is where it gets sticky, because if those states are to receive federal funding, students must perform at acceptable levels on standardized tests designed by each state for their students, enter teaching to the test.

Standardized test performance scores tied to federal funding galvanized the Google IQ™ phenomenon. Test performance became the specious, sine qua non of generative knowledge for purposes of the NCLB Act and, therefore, became the preferred measure of how effectively our public schools were educating our students because this time test scores were tied to monetary grants. The result of the NCLB Act has manifest with the conviction of countless school officials who were simply trying to get money from the federal government by good old-fashioned cheating on standardized tests.

"One of the largest school cheating trials in U.S. history drew to a dramatic close Wednesday with a jury finding 11 Atlanta elementary school teachers and administrators guilty of taking part in a racketeering conspiracy to illegally boost students' test scores. Some of the educators face up to 35 years in prison. Shock swept through the courtroom as the verdicts were announced, with defense attorneys for the majority of defendants rushing to seek bond for their clients.

"Now the rubber has met the road," Fulton County Superior Court Judge Jerry W. Baxter said, noting that throughout the trial he had tried to persuade defendants of the seriousness of the

charges. "They are now convicted felons, as far as I'm concerned. I don't like to send anyone to jail ... but they have made their bed and they're going to lie in it." Ten of the convicted educators were led out of the courtroom in handcuffs. One, who is pregnant and weeks from her delivery date, was allowed to remain free on bond." [217]

Teacher Diane Buckner-Webb with attorney Kevin Franks after a jury found her guilty in the Atlanta schools cheating trial. (Kent D. Johnson / Atlanta Journal-Constitution).

School Administrators, parents and, of course, students, either turned a blind eye, welcomed or set about to rationalize why teaching summary knowledge, as in test answers, was synonymous with generative knowledge. Summary knowledge is, by its very nature, limited knowledge. Once a Google IQ™er has the information they searched for they seldom can answer this simple question: Why is this so? They can't extrapolate from their search results nor can they critique the content of their search. **This inability to critique what they learn from the net creates an environment where the relatively ignorant publish to others, who are also relatively ignorant, with both parties believing that they know what they are talking about when, in fact, nothing could be further from the truth. Anyone with a keyboard can write anything and make it look authoritative, no matter how foolish or stupid or ill informed the content happens to be.**

What is the value of generative knowledge? Years ago, I sent my high school Latin teacher (Thelma Lou Parks) a thank you note after earning an "A" on a neuro- anatomy test in graduate school. Being able to seamlessly translate the Latin terms, for example, "dura mater," "pia mater," "pons" and "medulla oblongata" into English not only gave me a depth of understanding lost on today's Google IQ™ers, but it also helped me locate these neural structures in relationship to one another in the brain. After all, the "pia" or "soft" mater should reside below the "dura" or "hard" mother, right? The "pons" (bridge) focused my attention on those areas of the brain where two structures needed bridging. Google IQ™ that!

The Google IQ™ phenomenon has changed everything, even the law. As a forensic psychologist, I have spent a lot of time in courtrooms. Before Google, lawyers cross-examining experts relied upon other experts to help them formulate their questions directed a medical experts. These experts would coach the lawyer about the basis for the terms of art used in the subject matter before the court, the logic of certain medical procedures, engineering principles, what have you.

---

[217] Los Angeles Times. *Atlanta schools cheating scandal: 11 educators convicted of racketeering.* April 1, 2015, reported by Jenny Jarvie.

Experts always have an advantage in these types of lawyer/expert match ups when it comes to generative knowledge and the lawyers knew it. Were it not for the fact that the lawyers wrote the rules about questioning and what evidence could make its way before a jury, the lawyers wouldn't have had a chance when going head to head with a medical expert.

Today, however, lawyers rely upon Google to prepare their cross-examinations. Lawyers deluded by their inflated Google IQs™ enter courtrooms with search engine printouts and summary data. Lawyers parrot terms of art, data specifics and they *sound* like they know something, a la Howie Mandel. Nevertheless, the first time an expert chooses to go deeper than the summary terms so glibly parroted by the lawyer doing the questioning, the lawyer's Google IQ™ takes a nosedive. In my opinion, especially when it comes to medical malpractice lawsuits, the inflated Google IQ™ of lawyers actually encourages medical malpractice lawsuits because lawyers, like so many other lay people, confuse search engine results with generative medical knowledge.

Shadow men, by and through their proxies, government agents and their myriad of vested interests, hire the brightest mind control agents available. They fund, support, protect and insure that the masses don't have a fighting chance against their PSYOPs. We are about to enter that battle in an effort to see if we can't even the scales, even if just a bit, for my readers.

CHAPTER 14: HANDIWORK EXPOSED

I am now going to dissect some of the psychological operations that are reformatting brains in The United States. I could broaden my scope to the entire planet, but in as much that it is The United States that shadow men have focused their attention upon, our content will emphasize what is taking place in America. This is not to say, however, nor is it to minimize the fact, that shadow men and their mind control agents have always had their sights set on all of mankind.

I want to put a finer point on why shadow men have had a special interest in the USA. As we have learned, America's founders managed to escape the surly bonds of the shadow men of their day to become an outlier nation. Permit me to reiterate the confluence of factors that made that possible. America's founders were, perhaps like many of you, obsessively protective of their free will. America's founders were moral, brilliant and learned men, having studied the great thinkers that preceded them, with a particular appreciation for the writings of John Locke, Thomas Hobbes, Charles Montesquieu, Voltaire, Goethe and the writers who authored the books in the Christian Bible, among others. As we have addressed elsewhere, key parts of Jefferson's Declaration of Independence, were directly inspired by John Locke's Second Essay published in 1693. [218]

Modern day Americans have become purposefully and with malice aforethought separated from their founder's ideas that, ironically, made it possible for them to safely disengage their public mind from the evils of shadow men. **But now, as we move forward into the 21st century, the shadow men who have been around since time immemorial, the men who never went anywhere and who deeply resented the revolutionaries we refer to as our founding fathers, are back with a vengeance and they want what they paid for returned to them.**

Never forget that shadow men share a seamless lineage with the very first shadow men who cleverly used their superior intelligence and cunning to enslave their fellow man. Our founders gave you, me and everyone else living in the United States, a priceless gift. This gift is the *right* to be free from shadow men as a matter of Constitutional law. No one had successfully thumbed their nose at shadow men and gotten away with it before America's founders did it in 1776. Then, as now, only a minority of people living in the colonies boldly and bravely stood up to the shadow men rulers of the day, and the men and women who did were not respected by agents of their British shadow men foes, to wit:

> [T]he Americans had neither a standing army nor a navy; few among them were experienced officers. Britain possessed a professional army and the world's greatest navy. Furthermore, the colonists had virtually no history of cooperating with one another, even in the face of danger. In addition, many in the cabinet were swayed by disparaging assessments of American soldiers leveled by British officers in earlier wars. For instance, during the French and Indian War (1754-63), Brig. Gen. James Wolfe had described America's soldiers as "cowardly dogs." Henry Ellis, the royal governor of Georgia, nearly simultaneously asserted that the colonists were a "poor species of fighting men" given to "a want of bravery." [219]

Fighting The War for Independence was a costly and ultimately unsuccessful use of British force to change the minds of the men and women living in the "colonies." This is but one more

---

[218] John Locke. (1693), *Concerning the true extent and end of civil government*. Second Essay, Chapter 19.
[219] Smithsonian Magazine. *Myths of the American Revolution*. John Ferling, January, 2010.

example of why shadow men transitioned to a more Fabian approach to mind control rather than rely upon brute force to enforce their will.

I have analogized the 20th century technological advances in communication to the development of lightweight metals, carbon fiber and flight computers used in aeronautical engineering. Sir Isaac Newton mastered the understanding of how to go to the moon as early as 1610, but he did not have the technology to transform his knowledge into reality. Shadow men, unlike Newton, are now in possession of the technological and psychological knowledge necessary for them to realize their dream of world domination.

Shadow men have always had as their ultimate goal control over the minds of everyone living on earth. The fact that these ravenous men have always found ways to manipulate man's consent in one way or another is proof of their dedication to this project. But now, thanks to permanently plugged in and Google IQ™ plagued citizens, their ultimate dream of complete control is within their grasp.

I want to make clear that the problem is not with Google, per se, or any other search engine or library for that matter. Google has opened up an entire world of information to anyone with net access. The problem resides in our now constant companion of the masses' failure of discernment, insulated by the now epidemic Dunning-Kruger effect. To the average man, "having" the information is the equivalence of understanding that information. "Having" information permitted an easy way for the average man to be as educated as the people who generated the information produced in a search, or so the delusion goes.

All of the PSYOPs I will reveal to you in this chapter have been equipped with explosive protection shields. These shields are activated or triggered by what I am doing here, that is, by exposing the underling PSYOPs for which the shields were designed to protect. Once triggered, these shields are enforced by the PC police, who begin the process of attacking the threat by attaching to the source of the threat any number of stigmatized labels and all the other PSYOPs their mentors have taught them to use. PhD's modeled this genre of protection after man's immune system, specifically, how our immune system deals with threats from microbes. The enforcement agents that bring life to these protective shields are called the PC police.

The PC police are, themselves, a socially engineered construct. The PC police were consciously modeled after strategies developed by the Nazis. The PC police were designed to terminate the command of the threat by attaching an explosive-like semantic device to the source threat. The PC police function like automatons that have been programmed to attack and have no idea they are merely handmaidens in service to shadow men. PC policemen are like Manchurian candidates who come to life once exposed to a trigger word, phrase or image. So what can set these explosive PC Policemen off?

Anyone who dares to imply or assert, for example, that any two things, groups of people, cultures, almost anything, are different, i.e., better than or more dangerous, etc., will trigger the PC enforcers to destroy the threat. **This is because discernment of differences between good and bad is step one in regaining one's freedom of choice.** What I want the reader to recognize is that the behavior of the PC Police is of a curious nature. It is like a pre-programmed response, like a tic or an OCD ritual that "plays" once the PC Policeman is aroused. You'll notice that PC enforcers always repeat talking points and attach to their victims the same hackneyed list of labels. The labels function as preprogrammed responses to violations of political correctness.

Where do these pre-programmed labels come from? They were invented by shadow men's agents and then disseminated by programmers in the guise of public school teachers and actors who work in the media entertainment complex. These labels are repeated over and over and over, beginning in grade school classrooms throughout America and in the media entertainment complex, until they become embedded within the engrams of those who, because of their personality, become PC enforcers. The on-site, front line teachers have NO idea as to what they are actually doing. In this respect, teachers function as useful idiots.

Use the terms "right or wrong" in a declarative sentence and the Manchurian candidates will begin to attack, like someone who pokes at a beehive of Africanized Honey Bees. Make a declarative sentence about men or women that does not include an implied equivalency and, once again, you will immediately witness a response that looks very much like someone whose "on" button had just been pushed. Note that every PC enforcer response will be automatic, unthinking and like the response a doctor gets when he strikes your patellar tendon with a rubber hammer. PC enforcers have become so rabid in their enforcement efforts that many famous comedians refuse to book college campus shows. Two such performers who, as of 2015, no longer play colleges or universities, are Jerry Seinfeld and Chris Rock.

It is not just words or phrases that will trigger a PC enforcer's response. Images can have the same triggering effect. American flags, conservatively dressed men or women, white women or males in positions of authority, children depicted as quiet and well mannered, all of these images will trigger a response of condemnation, criticism, cryptic comment or blatant attack upon the publisher of the image.

Conversely, should these Manchurian, PC enforcer candidates be subjected to words and phrases that connote moral relativism, nihilism, anti-capitalist, existential philosophical notions, you will be rewarded with sex, companionship, a place to sleep or a ticket into their "groups" inner sanctum. Wear a Che Guevarra T-shirt, peace symbol, tie dyed garment or display a COEXIST symbol, marijuana leaf, pentagram, Eye of Horus or almost any other occult image, and you will be rewarded by agents of shadow men with sex, money, acceptance and status.

I am also going to reveal in this chapter low-level, but devious, PSYOPs designed to make you buy things. In as much that a library of books could be written on this general subject, I am going to limit my review to archetypal examples that illustrate key principles of some of the more popular PSYOPs in operation. So let's begin by exposing some low-level marketing PSYOPs.

The next time you see a commercial for almost any weight loss program or weight loss supplement, take note of the fact that there are two primary approaches to marketing weight loss. The first is what I call the "magic bullet" approach and the second relies upon classical conditioning and manipulation of desire to condition the viewer.

Recall that man is, by nature, a symbol monger. He trades in symbols. Images, words, sounds, colors, textures and light flashes, each of which talk to the brain in a language that only the brain truly understands.

People who want to lose weight love food. Obese people typically have a relationship with food that is best characterized as a love/hate relationship. Food functions as a substitute for any number of emotional needs. Food is comforting and hunger often reaches the point of craving. Obese people find it very difficult to deny themselves the comfort that food provides.

So what do you think you see most of in many diet commercials, that rely upon a system and not a magic bullet pill? You see food dominating the real estate of the TV screen, but it is not just any food, it is comfort food. What does comfort food mean? It often means fattening food. You mean that fattening food is the star in many weight loss commercials, and it is fattening food that is used to sell the diet? Yes, exactly.

In studying a cross section of weight loss commercials that sell a system as opposed to a magic bullet approach, I found something very interesting. The viewer's visual field is literally bombarded with a rapid paced display of every comfort/fattening food you can think of. The viewer is shown every desert imaginable, including chocolate cake, cheesecake and pies topped with whipped cream. Potatoes, bread and a cafeteria full of every high calorie food you can think of, including fried chicken, meatloaf, ham, yams and steak fills every square inch of the TV screen's real estate.

In addition to comfort foods, you will find photos and video of slimmer bodies sequentially interposed between visual images of comfort foods. The ads typically flash to the viewer sequential images of comfort food/slimmer bodies/comfort food/slimmer bodies, ad infinitum. This PSYOP relies upon Pavlov's classical conditioning model of modifying human behavior and is brilliant because the target is unconsciously made to pair two things they want: 1. Comfort foods for breakfast, lunch and dinner, and 2. A slimmer body.

Studies have demonstrated that photos of fattening foods hold a special attraction to obese people when compared to how naturally thin people react to photos of fattening food. This result is not surprising when one stops to consider that one of the reasons thin people stay thin is because food doesn't hold the same degree of allure that it does for obese people. Showing images of fattening food, as part of diet commercials, captures the attention of the target audience marketers have set their sights upon. It would be as if I wanted to target pedophiles in order to sell to them some miracle program that would cure them of their psychopathology, and to do that I chose to show them alluring photos of little children. It is no different when it comes to certain diet commercials.

Showing the slimmer bodied after photo/video has the same effect of seeing a car pass by that you would love to buy but can't afford. The weight loss program or product being sold will promise that one day soon you will have the money to buy that car, but first you must buy the diet program and/or product.

Weight loss commercial PSYOPs create hunger by displaying images of fattening foods then pair those images with photographs of thin people. The two sets of images are linked using a classical conditioning model. The running audio in many of these ads is remarkably similar to one another. The point is driven home with repeated phrases like "You don't need to deny yourself," "You don't have to go without," "You can enjoy your favorite deserts," "You can eat your favorite foods like fried chicken, meatloaf and baked potatoes." The running narratives address the psychological lynch pin often found in obese subjects, diets equate in their mind with denial and pain. Taking away chocolate cake, for example, is like withholding love for many obese people.

The next most popular PSYOP related to weight loss is what I call the "magic bullet" approach. This approach to weight loss is interesting because it promises an easy path to the ideal body by simply taking a pill or supplement. These TV ads are typically much shorter in duration and tap into man's belief in the miracles of modern science, that is, "we have a pill for everything and relief is just a swallow away." Pills, sprays, granules sprinkled on fried chicken, you name it, its is there for those who have been pre-sold on the false belief that complex problems can be solved by a "magic bullet." An interesting question to ask is this: Where did mankind get the idea that *any* complex and recalcitrant problem can typically be cured or fixed by taking a pill?

Pharmaceutical manufacturers are in the business of making medicines that are used to treat any number of maladies. Medicines that can be taken as a pill represent a user-friendly means by which man can do something easy to feel better. In addition, mankind is predisposed to want to believe that relief from what ails him is as easy as swallowing a pill or elixir. Snake oil salesmen have exploited this tendency to believe in a magic pill or elixir since time immemorial.

Have you ever wondered why your various screens and cellulose reading material are saturated with advertisements for medicines that you can't go out and buy without a prescription from your doctor? Billions of dollars are spent each year marketing prescription medicine to consumers. What is wrong with this picture? The key here is *prescription* medicine.

The viewer enticed to want one of these prescription meds must ask his doctor for the med. And if your doctor needs to be told by his patient, about what drugs to be administered, you have a bigger problem to deal with. Pharmaceutical manufacturers know full well that they are not selling prescription meds to consumers; they are reinforcing your natural tendency to believe in "magic pills." There is big money in promoting the belief that the pharmaceutical industry has a pill for everything.

By the way, have you noticed how the FDA mandated disclosure of side effects and contraindications are handled by these drug advertisement PSYOPs? While the almost endless list of frightening side effects and contraindications are read off to the viewer by a voice over artist using his or her most pleasant and mellifluous voice, images of pure happiness, health, vigor, vitality, peace and safety are displayed in rapid succession. So while the voice over artist is saying things like "may cause blindness, sudden death and worsen your symptoms," the actors on screen may be seen romping through a field like teenagers with boundless energy as though they have no cares at all. This PSYOP strategy of pairing good images with bad news we call reciprocal inhibition. The pleasant images inhibit the frightening meaning of the side effects and contraindications being read to you. Now let's move on to the PSYOPs designed to modify the social fabric of America in order to make you and your behavior more easily manageable by shadow men.

The next series of PSYOPs are examples of social engineering designed to destroy the importance of the father figure as a means to weaken the traditional nuclear family unit, i.e., the common man's mechanism of wealth accumulation. The next time you see a TV commercial, comedy or drama that incorporates a traditional nuclear family, pay close attention to how the genders are portrayed.

I became interested in this particular subject after noticing that, with few exceptions, fathers are portrayed as stupid, uncouth, rude, lazy, moronic, worthless, helpless and unattractive, in the American media. On the other hand, females in these PSYOPs are portrayed as leaders, wise, smart, attractive, well dressed and in charge. To illustrate just how bad fathers are portrayed these days, a Sprint commercial from 2014 cast the father as a rodent in a cage labeled "Dad."

Actual Stills from Sprint (Family Plan) Commercial
In this commercial paid for by Sprint we see a family portrayed in various role specific activities. Not only is the "father figure" portrayed as a non-human rodent, but the other males are portrayed in various unattractive roles. See this commercial here: https://www.youtube.com/watch?v=h5A1OsCsaz4

Besides commercials, sitcoms universally cast fathers as failures that are self absorbed, unhappy and disgusting people. The character Al Bundy, in the sitcom *Married with Children*, is a classic example of this pattern. Bundy is the brainchild of two transplanted East Coast writers named

Michael Moye and Ron Leavitt. Moye and Leavitt chose as their sitcom canvas a Midwestern family. Moye' and Leavitts' storylines portrayed the father, Al Bundy, in an unflattering light that reinforced any number of unattractive stereotypes of what middle-American nuclear families, especially white fathers, are like.

Al Bundy, *Married with Children*, Created by Moye and Leavitt (Fox Network).

Another example of how white fathers are portrayed is the cartoon character Peter Griffin. Peter is the father in the animated series *Family Guy*. Peter was created by Seth MacFarlane to represent his vision of what a nuclear family unit father is like. Peter Griffin is stupid, unattractive, particularly abusive (emotionally and physically) to his daughter, is condescending to his wife and is the foil of jokes at his expense, especially by the much wiser, smarter, better looking female characters in *Family Guy*.

Another animated character that illustrates the PSYOPs targeting fathers is Homer Simpson. Homer is dimwitted, uncouth and ineffectual in almost all situations.

(Left) Peter Griffin Father figure in *Family Guy*, Created by Seth MacFarlane & (Right) Homer Simpson, Father figure in *The Simpsons* Created by Matt Groening. (Fox Network).

The consistency with which men of almost all races are portrayed as stupid clowns, the butt of jokes or helpless without the ever watchful eye of a strong woman, should inform any student of PSYOPs that the traditional nuclear family is under assault, but by who? The answer is an unholy alliance between Marxist revolutionaries and multinational corporations, underwritten by shadow men who, by and through their PR agents in Hollywood and New York, intend to eradicate a respectable father figure in American life among the masses, thereby enabling shadow men to accumulate even more wealth and power. Never forget that shadow men and their top-level agent's nuclear families are off limits for ridicule.

Not all cultures are under assault. Midwestern and Southern family units, especially white Christian family units, are the favorite targets of shadow men, revolutionaries and their agents. Hollywood and New York based writers, producers and directors are quite selective when it comes to which racial/religious demographic they CHOOSE to ridicule, undermine and redistribute wealth from.

Larry David, writer and actor of the HBO series, *Curb Your Enthusiasm*, wrote one episode where he urinated upon a portrait of Jesus. Larry lost control of his urine stream after taking the prescription medicine Flomax ™. Christians saw the drops of urine on the portrait of Christ's eyes and concluded that Jesus was crying. Larry cast unattractive, uncouth and stupid looking actors to play the fools who mistook Larry's urine for Jesus' tears.

Larry David, HBO's Curb Your Enthusiasm

To put this attack on father figures, traditional nuclear family and Christianity in context, compare and contrast how father figures used to be portrayed by an earlier generation of shadow men. In the 1950's Robert Young played a strong, wise, generous, happy, loyal, good provider to a white, Christian, nuclear family in a sitcom entitled *Father Knows Best*. Even the name betrays the stark differences between today's portrayals of father figures compared to the 50's through the 80's.

Jim Anderson, *Father Knows Best*, Created by Ed James (NBC)

In the late 1960's Bill Bixby starred in *The Courtship of Eddie's Father*. Bixby played a widowed magazine editor by the name of Tom Corbett. Corbett was a wonderful father figure who parented under difficult circumstances. One of the enduring qualities of the lead character was his consistent and unwavering "putting his son's welfare first" as he dated various women. Notably, up until the

1980's, a single parent was "single" NOT by choice but by fate. Eddie's father was a widower, for example.

Bill Bixby, Still from The Courtship of Eddie's Father

The first TV show that glamorized and promoted the single lifestyle for women was a sitcom named *That Girl,* starring Marlo Thomas. Thomas is an interesting figure in that she is the daughter of the late conservative actor/comedian Danny Thomas. Marlo Thomas is married to progressive activist Phil Donahue. Marlo appeared on a Phil Donahue talk show in the 1970's when Phil was still doing his show from Dayton, Ohio. Donahue was married at the time. Soon after Thomas' appearance on his show, Donahue and Thomas began to date. Donahue divorced his wife of several years and then married Thomas. Both Donahue and Thomas are active in any number of progressive political action committees and champions of any number of collectivist inspired political movements.

That Girl's theme song is a classic example of how PSYOPs, when one pulls back their cloaking, become brazenly obvious. Marxist inspired revolutionaries, along with any number of multinational corporations that are ruled over by shadow men, were and are intent upon destroying the traditional nuclear family. In a classic Bernays-type attack on the nuclear family, the PR agents of these revolutionaries reasoned that if young women were conditioned to think that being single was "the thing to be" the masses would, according to herd instinct, follow suit. All that was needed was to ignite the fire. Study the lyrics of *That Girl's* theme song. The song was written by two men, named Hagen and Denoff:

Diamonds, Daisies, Snowflakes,
That Girl
Chestnuts, Rainbows, Springtime ...
Is That Girl
She's tinsel on a tree ...
She's everything that every girl should be!

Sable, Popcorn, White Wine,
That Girl
Gingham, Bluebirds, Broadway ...
Is That Girl
She's mine alone, but luckily for you ...
If you find a girl to love,
Only one girl to love,
Then she'll be That Girl too ...
That Girl!

Marlo Thomas as *That Girl (1960s)*

We see here the use of classical conditioning pairing, where being single is purposefully paired with any number of highly desirable foodstuffs and accruements favored by young women. Thus, psychologically being single becomes classically conditioned to white wine, popcorn, sable, bluebirds and Broadway, diamonds, daisies, snowflakes and rainbows. Just like the sound of the can opener that alerts the pet dog that he is about to be fed, living the single life sounds like bluebirds chirping in the Springtime, tastes like white wine, feels like you are wearing diamonds and it is like you look up into the sky and see a beautiful rainbow.

Picture the target audience comprised of white Christian masses sitting like unwitting test subjects in front of the box they erroneously believe is just a TV, as one meta-communication after another, composed of overt and subliminal anti-male, anti-family and adoration of self messages, are pumped directly into their central nervous system. *That Girl* was just the first of a never-ending series of similar "shows" that idealized the single lifestyle while subtly and not so subtly ridiculing family oriented commitment.

When girls and women are brainwashed to reject traditional values, the vacuum created is filled with hedonism, self absorption and behavior that looks eerily similar to anti-commitment males, including sexual promiscuity and all that goes along with it. The transformation from commitment within a traditional nuclear family to sexual libertine transformed people with dignity and values into consumers who served the role of shadow man plaything and rapacious consumer who is obsessed with their taste buds, gonads and expression of self.

Girls BEFORE social engineering 1950s-early 1960s.

Girls AFTER social engineering by agents of shadow men

The key here is that girls and women were targeted for sexual transformation because only females are capable of carrying a "new" child and giving birth to that child. As you will soon learn, shadow men long ago concluded that there were too many among the masses that were reproducing. And to think, the PR agents in Hollywood and New York got rich for transforming America from a self sustaining reproductive culture, characterized by commitment within the traditional nuclear family, into self absorbed sexual libertines who comprised a dying reproductive eco system.

If, for a moment, the reader can hold in abeyance her socially engineered prejudices about women's roles in American society, she can better understand how a reproductively self-sustaining culture and population were transformed into a dying, non-reproductively self-sustaining culture and population. Looking at this geopolitically, one eco-system, i.e., shadow men, set out to destroy a competing eco- system, i.e., certain threatening segments of the masses' population. If I may use this allegory, girls in America were transitioned from Home-Economics classes into classes in La Crosse in one short generation. Regardless of how you may feel about gender roles, La Crosse was not designed nor could it reasonably promote a reproductively self-sustaining population; whereas, Home-Economics classes prepared the student to fulfill the basic biological necessity of "nesting."

Acculturating nurturance was replaced with socially engineering warrior princesses who competed with men to see who could out masculine the other. Nascent warrior princesses were brow beaten to shed every trait, every predisposition that was part and parcel to being the only gender capable of carrying a child in her womb, feeding that child from her breasts and making sure that her genes prospered in not only her lifetime but in her offspring as well.

Traditional male gender roles have been under assault by the same competing eco-system right along with those of girls and women. Males have been subjected to an endless barrage of PSYOPs, all of which are designed to emasculate them, and in so doing undermine their reproductive viability and protector roles. Men have been brow beaten by social engineers to avoid displaying their masculinity in public, otherwise face social engineers' PC Police. Boys have been transitioned from celebrating their inherent maleness to a gender that is conceptualized as an imperfect female that must be fixed.

Just one example among thousands of these emasculating PSYOPs became transparent when male Arizona State and Temple University ROTC cadets were forced to march in red high-heel shoes in support of women's abuse awareness month. Built into this PSYOP was the fact that males are inherently abusive and that because of that they must be emasculated in public as if to genuflect to the power of women. By the way, studies show that male ROTC cadets are more likely to be protectors of women, not their tormenters and certainly not their abusers.

Arizona State ROTC cadet Wearing Red High Heel Shoes (Spring, 2015)

One of the last bastions of masculinity is the National Football League. Even there, social engineers have "pinked" players in a blatant act of emasculation and genuflection to females. As with all PSYOPs, the rationale for engaging an emasculation operation is cloaked in a halo-valenced cause. Should anyone dare to expose the underlying emasculation PSYOP protected by a halo-valenced cause, in the instance of the NFL, Breast Cancer Awareness Month, PC Police are awakened like a hibernating bear by the first warm day in spring. I'll draw the reader's attention to the fact that during Prostate Cancer Awareness Month, neither NFL players nor the league's officials are forced to modify their colors or insignias by their "owners" and the media entertainment complex.

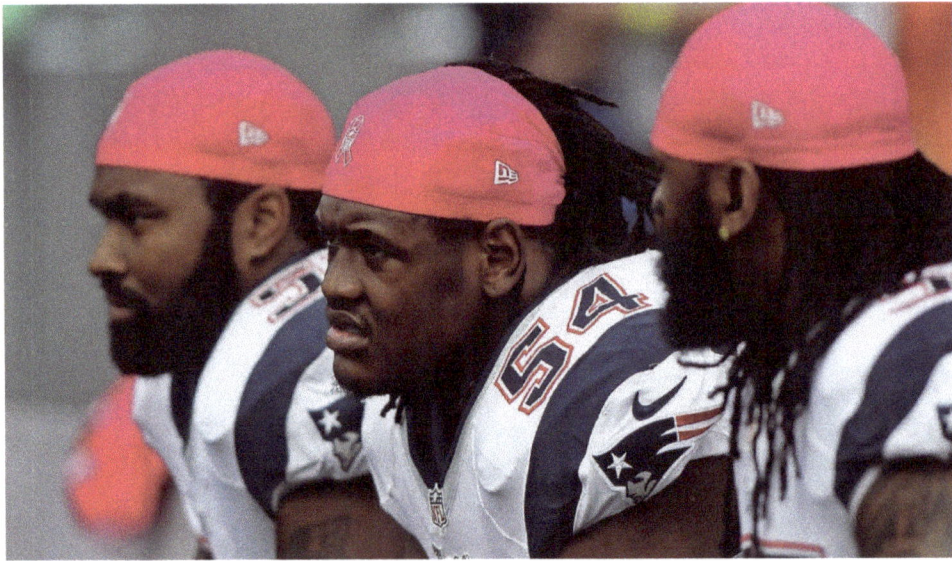

New England Patriot Players Wear Pink Hats

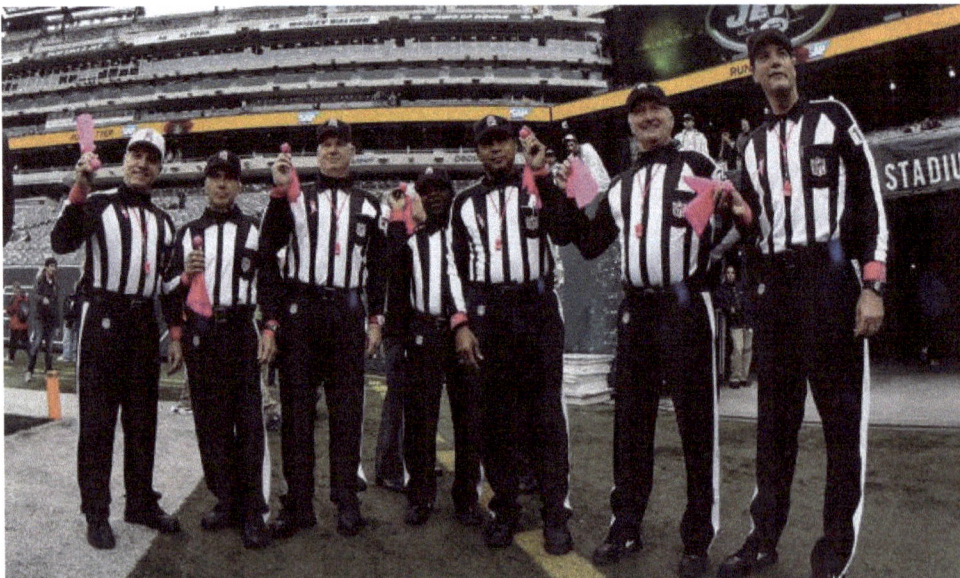

NFL Officials Show Off Their Pink Penalty Flags

By chronicling the transition from masculine movie stars of the 1950s and 60s to the movie stars of the new millennium, we can clearly see the impact of a half-century of mind control over the masses' sense of what it means to be a man. I could provide readers hundreds of examples, but will only provide one representative example of the emasculation PSYOP and how it has modified our male matinee idols.

Steve McQueen   **Russell Brand**

Socially engineered assaults upon the masses' eco-system included changes in biology, psychology and culture. Biology was changed by interrupting menstrual cycles, through the effect of extreme sports, or other intense physical activity, like La Crosse, for example, that resulted in any number of biological changes in the female. These changes included a cascade of deleterious pathophysiological syndromes and conditions, e.g., *The Female Athletic Triad*. This condition causes amenorrhea, eating disorders and loss of mineral density in bone. Women involved in extreme sports, including intense training as is sometimes encouraged beginning as early as junior high school, results in late onset of menarche and an increase in the male hormone androgen, produced in the females' adrenal glands. [220] Simply put, women who are victims of The Female Athletic Triad are incapable and/or reluctant to become pregnant for both biological and psychological reasons.

During this same time period, the late 1960's, writer Paul Ehrlick was a frequent guest on TV talk shows where he discussed the dire consequences to America and the rest of the world if the masses did NOT stop reproducing, i.e., reject the nuclear family/children model. His book *The Population Bomb* was an all out attack on the traditional American nuclear family. The book redefined the acts of having babies and making nuclear families as something evil and selfish. Ehrlick was a willing agent for the revolutionaries that had the American family in its crosshairs. Here are some of the blatant lies Ehrlick spouted to the test subjects who thought they had simply tuned in to watch The Tonight Show with Johnny Carson in the 1960's:

---

[220] Please see: Laura M Gottschlich, DO, Assistant Professor of Family and Community Medicine and Orthopedic Surgery, Medical College of Wisconsin; Consulting Staff, Family Medicine Residency Program, All Saints Hospital, Wheaton Franciscan Healthcare. *The Female Athletic Triad*. December 17, 2014. Medscape Continuing Medical Education.

255

Ehrlick often told late night talk show host Johnny Carson the following, with a degree of certainty that had the same effect upon young white American women of reproductive age as an air raid siren going off in the bedroom during sex. Ehrlick predicted with GREAT certainty that NOTHING can prevent famines in which *hundreds of millions* of people will die during the 1970s. He said that it was a CERTAINTY that the death rate would sky rocket. Ever the slick PR agent, Ehrlick changed the drop-dead decade from the 1970s to the 1980s in later editions of his book. So what happened?

The global death rate *declined SUBSTANTIALLY* since Ehrlick, on behalf of the agents of the shadow men, spouted his psychological sterilization project. It has decreased from 13/1000 during the time frame of 1965 to 1974 to 10/1000 between1985 to 1990. You may reason in support of Ehrlick: "Well, that is because Ehrlick helped to reduce population growth." Sorry, you're wrong. Here are the facts, the population of the world *has more than doubled* since Ehrlick's sterilization PSYOP was funneled into the American psyche. [221]Almost every demographic and racial group continued to reproduce with abandon except white middle to upper class women.

In 2012 Prince Phillip of England, big game hunter, father of four and founder of the World Wildlife Fund, said in a BBC interview that the greatest threat to conservation was human population growth. He went on to say that from where "he is," what else is there? When asked about his views on the solution to this "problem," he laughed and said: "Can't you guess." In 1988 his royal highness said this about over population in the human species in a book he penned entitled: *Down to Earth.*

*"I don't claim to have any special interest in natural history, but as a boy I was made aware of the annual fluctuations in the number of game animals and **the need to adjust the "cull"** to the size of the surplus population."[222]* (Emphasis Added)

Prince Phillip (Left), Founder of World Wildlife Fund, Standing Over His Trophy Kill. Also Pictured, Queen Elizabeth (Center).

---

[221] Dan Gardner (2010), *Future Babble: Why Expert Predictions Fail – and Why We Believe Them Anyway.* Toronto: McClelland and Stewart.
[222] HRH Prince Phillip (1988), *Down to Earth.* Pg. 8.

So how does it feel to know that those who rule over you, those people financially supported and revered by you, have concluded that YOU and your genetic reference group need to be "culled?" Let me help the reader who may not fully understand the meaning of the word "cull." Here is the definition from American Heritage Dictionary:

> **CULL:** *verb [with obj.] (usu. be culled)*
>
> *select from a large quantity; obtain from a variety of sources: anecdotes culled from Greek and Roman history.*
>
> • *reduce the population of (a wild animal) by selective slaughter: he sees culling deer as a necessity | (as noun culling) : kangaroo culling.*
>
> • *send (an inferior or surplus animal on a farm) to be slaughtered.*
>
> • *literary pick (flowers or fruit): (as adj. culled) : fresh culled daffodils.*
>
> *noun*
>
> *a selective slaughter of wild animals.*
>
> • *[usu. as modifier] an inferior or surplus livestock animal selected for killing: a cull cow.*

Nowhere does Phillip reference the breeding habits of his self anointed elite peers, and certainly not his own bloodline. "HRH" Phillip is unequivocally dedicated to the culling of the masses and when it suits him killing beautiful Tigers. Phillip is not alone. American financial baron, founder of Cable News Network (CNN), and prolific reproducer, Ted Turner, a man who has at least five children, has argued for mandated limitations on the masse's ability to reproduce. Tim Graham, writing for News Busters, notes that:

> *"When he was bothered on the street about his ideal population number for Earth, Turner insisted he would like to reduce the world's population by five billion people, imposing a policy mandating a "one child family...for 100 years." 'I think two billion is about right,' Turner said as he walked briskly away. Last year, the number of people in the world reached seven billion." [223]*

The world's richest man, Microsoft founder Bill Gates, spoke to an invitation only event of TED in 2010. TED stands for Technology, Entertainment and Design. It's organizations feature cutting edge developments in these three fields. Gates said the following:

> *"First we got population. The world today has 6.8 billion people. That's headed up to about 9 billion. Now if we do a really great job on new vaccines, health care, reproductive health services, we lower that by perhaps 10 or 15 percent." [224]*

The logical minds in attendance at the 2010 TED conference in Long Beach must have wondered why Gates listed vaccines in his list of items of those things that would keep a lid on human population growth. Vaccines prevent disease and the untimely deaths that sometimes occur due to vaccine preventable diseases. Successful vaccines would then, logically, increase the breeding population. Does Mr. Gates know something about his vaccination programs that the rest of us do not know?

Mark Snyder complied the following quotes from members of the self- anointed and legacy elites and/or their agents that have aligned themselves with limiting the breeding habits of the masses. The list was current as of 2013:

---

[223] News Busters. *Still Crazy: Ted Turner Favors Global One-Child Policy for 100 Years.* By: Tim Graham, June 9, 2012.
[224] TED Conference. Long Beach, CA. *Innovating to Zero.* A speech by William Gates, 2010.

1. UK Television Presenter Sir David Attenborough: "We are a plague on the Earth. It's coming home to roost over the next 50 years or so. It's not just climate change; it's sheer space, places to grow food for this enormous horde. Either we limit our population growth or the natural world will do it for us, and the natural world is doing it for us right now"

2. Paul Ehrlich, a former science adviser to president George W. Bush and the author of "The Population Bomb": "To our minds, the fundamental cure, reducing the scale of the human enterprise (including the size of the population) to keep its aggregate consumption within the carrying capacity of Earth is obvious but too much neglected or denied"

3. Paul Ehrlich again, this time on the size of families: "Nobody, in my view, has the right to have 12 children or even three unless the second pregnancy is twins"

4. Dave Foreman, the co-founder of Earth First: "We humans have become a disease, the Humanpox."

5. CNN Founder Ted Turner: "A total world population of 250-300 million people, a 95% decline from present levels, would be ideal."

6. Japan's Deputy Prime Minister Taro Aso about medical patients with serious illnesses: "You cannot sleep well when you think it's all paid by the government. This won't be solved unless you let them hurry up and die."

7. David Rockefeller: "The negative impact of population growth on all of our planetary ecosystems is becoming appallingly evident."

8. Environmental activist Roger Martin: "On a finite planet, the optimum population providing the best quality of life for all, is clearly much smaller than the maximum, permitting bare survival. The more we are, the less for each; fewer people mean better lives."

9. HBO personality Bill Maher: "I'm pro-choice, I'm for assisted suicide, I'm for regular suicide, I'm for whatever gets the freeway moving – that's what I'm for. It's too crowded, the planet is too crowded and we need to promote death."

10. MIT professor Penny Chisholm: "The real trick is, in terms of trying to level off at someplace lower than that 9 billion, is to get the birthrates in the developing countries to drop as fast as we can. And that will determine the level at which humans will level off on earth."

11. Julia Whitty, a columnist for Mother Jones: "The only known solution to ecological overshoot is to decelerate our population growth faster than it's decelerating now and eventually reverse it— at the same time we slow and eventually reverse the rate at which we consume the planet's resources. Success in these twin endeavors will crack our most pressing global issues: climate change, food scarcity, water supplies, immigration, health care, biodiversity loss, even war. On one front, we've already made unprecedented strides, reducing global fertility from an average 4.92 children per woman in 1950 to 2.56 today—an accomplishment of trial and sometimes brutally coercive error, but also a result of one woman at a time making her individual choices.

The speed of this childbearing revolution, swimming hard against biological programming, rates as perhaps our greatest collective feat to date."

12. Colorado State University Professor Philip Cafaro in a paper entitled "Climate Ethics and Population Policy": "Ending human population growth is almost certainly a necessary (but not sufficient) condition for preventing catastrophic global climate change. Indeed, significantly reducing current human numbers may be necessary in order to do so."

13. Professor of Biology at the University of Texas at Austin Eric R. Pianka: "I do not bear any ill will toward people. However, I am convinced that the world, including all humanity, WOULD clearly be much better off without so many of us."

14. Detroit News Columnist Nolan Finley: "Since the national attention is on birth control, here's my idea: If we want to fight poverty, reduce violent crime and bring down our embarrassing drop-out rate, we should swap contraceptives for fluoride in Michigan's drinking water.

We've got a baby problem in Michigan. Too many babies are born to immature parents who don't have the skills to raise them, too many are delivered by poor women who can't afford them, and too many are fathered by sorry layabouts who spread their seed like dandelions and then wander away from the consequences."

15. John Guillebaud, professor of family planning at University College London: "The effect on the planet of having one child less is an order of magnitude greater than all these other things we might do, such as switching off lights. An extra child is the equivalent of a lot of flights across the planet."

16. Democrat strategist Steven Rattner: "WE need death panels. Well, maybe not death panels, exactly, but unless we start allocating health care resources more prudently — rationing, by its proper name — the exploding cost of Medicare will swamp the federal budget."

17. Matthew Yglesias, a business and economics correspondent for Slate, in an article entitled "The Case for Death Panels, in One Chart": "But not only is this health care spending on the elderly the key issue in the federal budget, our disproportionate allocation of health care dollars to old people surely accounts for the remarkable lack of apparent cost effectiveness of the American health care system. When the patient is already over 80, the simple fact of the matter is that no amount of treatment is going to work miracles in terms of life expectancy or quality of life."

18. Planned Parenthood Founder Margaret Sanger: "All of our problems are the result of over breeding among the working class"

19. U.S. Supreme Court Justice Ruth Bader Ginsburg: "Frankly I had thought that at the time Roe was decided, there was concern about population growth and particularly growth in populations that we don't want to have too many of."

20. Planned Parenthood Founder Margaret Sanger: "The most merciful thing that the large family does to one of its infant members is to kill it."

21. Salon columnist Mary Elizabeth Williams in an article entitled "So What If Abortion Ends Life?": "All life is not equal. That's a difficult thing for liberals like me to talk about, lest we wind up looking like death-panel-loving, kill-your-grandma-and-your-precious-baby storm troopers. Yet a fetus can be a human life without having the same rights as the woman in whose body it resides."

22. Alberto Giubilini of Monash University in Melbourne, Australia and Francesca Minerva of the University of Melbourne in a paper published in the Journal of Medical Ethics: "[W]hen circumstances occur after birth such that they would have justified abortion, what we call after-birth abortion should be permissible. … [W]e propose to call this practice 'after-birth abortion', rather than 'infanticide,' to emphasize that the moral status of the individual killed is comparable with that of a fetus … rather than to that of a child. Therefore, we claim that killing a newborn could be ethically permissible in all the circumstances where abortion would be. Such circumstances include cases where the newborn has the potential to have an (at least) acceptable life, but the well-being of the family is at risk."

23. Nina Fedoroff, a key adviser to Hillary Clinton: "We need to continue to decrease the growth rate of the global population; the planet can't support many more people."

24. Barack Obama's primary science adviser, John P. Holdren: "A program of sterilizing women after their second or third child, despite the relatively greater difficulty of the operation than vasectomy, might be easier to implement than trying to sterilize men.

The development of a long-term sterilizing capsule that could be implanted under the skin and removed when pregnancy is desired opens additional possibilities for coercive fertility control. The capsule could be implanted at puberty and might be removable, with official permission, for a limited number of births."

25. David Brower, the first Executive Director of the Sierra Club: "Childbearing [should be] a punishable crime against society, unless the parents hold a government license … All potential parents [should be] required to use contraceptive chemicals, the government issuing antidotes to citizens chosen for childbearing."

26. Thomas Ferguson, former official in the U.S. State Department Office of Population Affairs: "There is a single theme behind all our work–we must reduce population levels. Either governments do it our way, through nice clean methods, or they will get the kinds of mess that we have in El Salvador, or in Iran or in Beirut. Population is a political problem. Once population is out of control, it requires authoritarian government, even fascism, to reduce it…"

27. Mikhail Gorbachev: "We must speak more clearly about sexuality, contraception, about abortion, about values that control population, because the ecological crisis, in short, is the population crisis. Cut the population by 90% and there aren't enough people left to do a great deal of ecological damage."

28. Jacques Cousteau: "In order to stabilize world population, we must eliminate 350,000 people per day. It is a horrible thing to say, but it is just as bad not to say it."

29. Finnish environmentalist Pentti Linkola: "If there were a button I could press, I would sacrifice myself without hesitating if it meant millions of people would die"

30. Prince Phillip, husband of Queen Elizabeth II and co-founder of the World Wildlife Fund: "In the event that I am reincarnated, I would like to return as a deadly virus, in order to contribute something to solve overpopulation." [225]

The elite relied upon their PR arms in Hollywood and New York to carry out their eugenics plan for the masses. One demographic, in particular, was disproportionately influenced by the eugenicists. White American men and women were, for all intents and purposes, neutered/spayed by brilliantly destructive PSYOPs beamed into their central nervous systems using TV, movies, teachers, professors, books and any number of trendy movements glamorizing the single lifestyle. Genocide, when effectuated by Fabian methods, doesn't offend the masse's sensibilities, even if it is YOU and YOUR genetics and bloodlines that are targeted for eradication! Collectively, these sterilization PSYOPs had their desired effect and transformed America from a reproductively self-sustaining country into a statistically certain reproductively dying country. Thank you *That Girl.* Thank you Paul Ehrlick, thank you Hollywood and New York, et al.

One of the things I have learned from dealing with halo-protected subject matter is that any discussion of them must be interrupted from time to time with a reminder to my readers that the mere mention of halo-valenced subjects, in any context other than pure reverence, will be attacked by the PC police force who brazenly declare the following:

> **"Not only are we going to engage in these manipulative psychological operations involving race, gender, religion, etc., BUT IF YOU DARE TO CALL US OUT AND EXPOSE WHAT IT IS WE ARE DOING, WE WILL ATTACH THE LABEL OF "RACIST" "HOMOPHOBE" "CONSPIRACY NUT" "ISLAMOPHOBE" "MCCARTHY-ITE" "REACTIONARY" OR ONE OF THE "E-R" SUFFIXES, E.G. HAT-ER TO YOU, USING OUR AGENTS IN THE MEDIA ENTERTAINMENT COMPLEX."**

Why undermine the father figure, you may ask? Why portray single mothers as strong, warrior-like princesses? Why promote sexual hedonism? Why portray African men as sex objects white women lust after? Why portray Southerners as racist bumpkins who are mentally challenged whose primary recreational activities include abusing women and people of other races? Why emasculate men and encourage little girls to become warrior princesses? Why was a Gay wedding ceremony inserted into the 2013 Rose Parade? Why scare the discernment-challenged masses with images of famine and bumper-to-bumper overpopulation? After all, all of the people living on earth as of 2015 would fit nicely, without overcrowding, into just one state in America, Texas. [226]

---

[225] The Truth. *30 Population Control Quotes That Show That The Elite Truly Believe That Humans Are A Plague Upon The Earth.* By: Michael Snyder, January 24, 2013.

[226] Simply Shrug. (2014), *The Over population Myth.*
http://www.simplyshrug.com/index.php?option=com_content&view=article&id=63:the-overpopulation-myth&catid=31:general&Itemid=50

So now let's take a look at just a FEW of the representative PSYOPs that illustrate my points herein. Permit me to use the literary approach used when I discussed the financial meltdown of 2008, by beginning at the end of the story.

When I work on criminal defense cases involving innocent black men accused of a sexual offense, it is immeasurably more difficult to earn an acquittal for this population because black men are presumed to be overtly sexual and predatory. This perception is arguably corroborated by crime statistics, but at the same time, this perception is the bane of black ministers and responsible black men because no matter how reserved, conservative or even prudish their behavior, black men, e.g., Justice Clarence Thomas, presidential candidate Herman Cain and countless other black men have had their characters assassinated. Moreover, black men are presumed, thanks to these same PSYOP creators, to be arrogant and think they are "superior to" other races. Where, pray tell, do these behaviors and preconceptions come from? Have black men been socially engineered to behave like this? Before I show you where all of this social engineering originated, realize that the end result of this social engineering is to harm good black men, drive a wedge between the races and to encourage white women to procreate with blacks, thus diluting the gene pool of both blacks and whites. Who, pray tell, would want such a thing, so much so that they would socially engineer it?

Stills from GEICO TV Commercial (Government Employees Insurance Company)
This commercial shows an Anglo woman ogling an African American body builder who just happens to be directing traffic while only wearing a pair of shorts. See the commercial here:
http://www.youtube.com/watch?v=M1-whbUMBJo#aid=P8lOrJ-aU0g

Subway Commercial Depicting Black Dominance and an Anglo Woman's Disgust Directed at Her Anglo Counterpart.

In this commercial, the white man exits the firehouse to notice that his Subway sandwich is missing and an empty sandwich wrapper, at which point the Anglo woman motions with her eyes that the Fire Chief has stolen the Anglo man's Subway sandwich. What happens next is the African Fire Chief brazenly acknowledges that he stole the Anglo fireman's sandwich and tauntingly dares him to say something. The end of the commercial shows the Anglo woman expressing her disgust with the Anglo man.) See the entire commercial here:
http://www.youtube.com/watch?v=AsmkvUuGzpw

Still from Vodocom Commercial "Dancing Like a White Guy"
In "Dancing Like a White Guy" an African American begins to act and move stupidly and awkwardly as other Africans in the room along with one Anglo woman laugh and point to him saying "Dancing Like a White Guy."
See the commercial here: http://www.youtube.com/watch?v=5bCaxcio6H8

263

Still from State Farm Insurance Commercial

In this TV ad a cool, calm, collected African American State Farm Agent is paired with three attractive Anglo women who conjure up a series of unattractive and flawed Anglo male stereotypes, the last of these unattractive Anglo male stereotypes named "dark side" puts his feet on the car. It is at this point that the State Farm agent enforces his dominance by saying, "Hey dark side, get your feet off the car." See the commercial here:
http://www.youtube.com/watch?v=peEMnPLqym4

Still from FedEx Commercial

In this TV ad an attractive Anglo woman is shown on vacation with her Anglo male husband/boyfriend. The Anglo man is pictured in the background ignoring the woman at which point she answers the door to find standing there an African American man who educates her about all of the benefits of FedEx delivery services. The Anglo woman actress was directed to be mesmerized, intrigued and taken with the African-American deliveryman, as her Anglo husband continues to be preoccupied. See the Commercial here:
http://www.youtube.com/watch?v=VIfgZYG-Mj8

Still from Fiat TV Commercial

*In this TV ad, Sean "P. Diddy" Combs is portrayed as a wealthy man surrounded by Anglo, Asian and a very few African American women as two hapless, stupid, bumbling, lost in the desert Anglo men prove to be too stupid to accept P. Diddy's generous and gracious help. At the end of the commercial one of the bumbling idiot Anglo men tries to pick up P. Diddy at which point Mr. Combs demonstrates his dominance by saying "Don't Do Dat (sic)."
See the Commercial here: http://www.youtube.com/watch?v=eqpeaR7P5Ck#aid=P99erA0qePA*

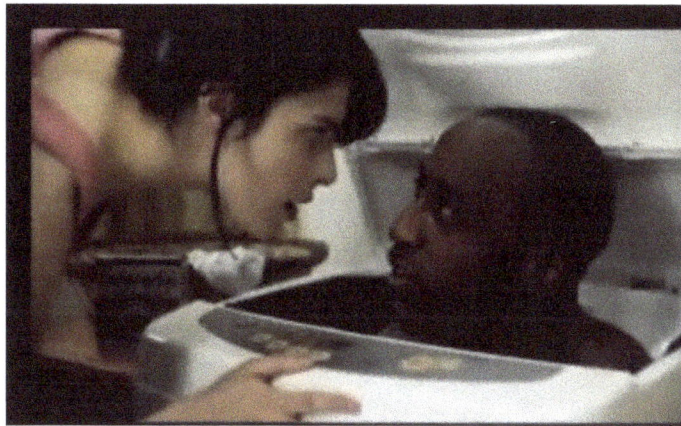

Still from Italian "Coloreria Laundry Detergent" Commercial

*This TV ad comes from Italy. The ad begins with an attractive Italian woman doing laundry, when a skinny, awkward, droopy dirty underwear wearing Italian man makes a sexual advance to her. At that point she dumps the Anglo man head first into her washing machine. After the washing machine goes through its wash cycle an African man pops out, presumably all clean and physically fit with ripping muscles. The Italian actress was told to ogle the African man and be sexually overwhelmed by him. See the Commercial here:
https://www.youtube.com/watch?v=8fyyEwBegIo*

It is not just commercials or mainstream feature films that make miscegenation central to their plot, e.g., "Jungle Fever," et al. You can also add to your list of miscegenation media children's shows. In fact, Children's networks and their parent companies have even gone so far as to recruit some of their developers and writers from the porn industry. And it is not merely the run of the mill porn industry, but one particular niche in the porn movie business. The niche I'm referencing involves the interracial escapades of a white husband (the cuckhold) whose fetish is watching his white wife have sex with a black man (the bull).[227] I don't expect my readers to know anything about this Cuckhold fetish. Suffice to say that in almost every major city in America, Cuckhold fetish nightclubs and gatherings are making money hand over fist.

Jonathan Butler is the writer and director who brought the porn world the X-rated movie "Cuckhold" in 2009. He is also the writer who has brought you the popular show broadcast on the Children's Nickelodeon Network entitled: *Bella and the Bulldogs.*

Jonathan Butler (VII)

Writer | Producer | Director

SEE RANK

Contribute to IMDb. Add a bio, trivia, and more.
Update information for Jonathan Butler »

More at IMDbPro »
☎ **Contact Info:** View manager and legal
👤 **Represent Jonathan Butler?** Add or change photos

9 news articles »

Known For

Bella and the Bulldogs (2015)   The Cuckold (2009)   Haunted Hathaways (2013)   Fanboy & Chum Chum (2009)

Filmography for Jonathan Butler (courtesy of IMDb).

---

[227] Cf: Orakwe, J. and Ebuh, G.W. *Oversized" Penile Length In The Black People; Myth Or Reality.* Tropical Journal of Medical Research Vol. 11 (1) 2007: pp. 16-18. While beyond the particular subject matter of this book, the stereotype of the black sexual male "bull" is scientifically just so much "bull," as documented by this cross cultural study corroborated by numerous other similar studies. Though seldom, if ever, discussed, this stereotype has caused tremendous anxiety in, and put a lot of sexual performance pressure on, black males who can't live up to their shadow man imaging of them. This imaging falsity is made all the worse because the average person of all races and genders assume that the myth of the black male sexual "bull," as promulgated by shadow men and their agents, must be true.

**The Stars of Nickelodeon's Bella & the Bulldogs: (left)
Brec Bessinger, (right) Coy Stewart. Writer: Jonathan Butler**

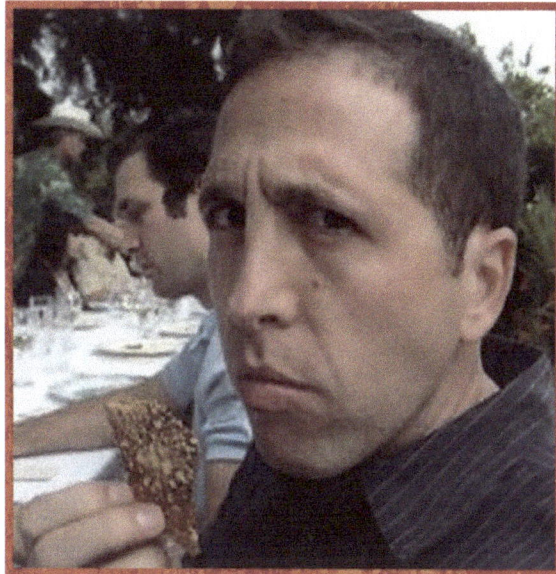

Jeffrey Bushell, Executive Producer of Bella and the Bulldogs.

One would be hard pressed to not see the obvious overlap between Mr. Butler's porn movie *Cuckhold* and Nickelodeon's children's series *Bella and the Bulldogs*. The term "Bull" (the name in the fetish world given to the black man who has sex with the white woman while her white husband watches) and **BULL**dog, as part of the name of the Nickelodeon series. The writer is the same man who wrote and directed the movie Cuckhold, after all.

It is not just that Bella, a pretty teen white girl is involved in numerous adventures with black teen boys, but that she is also a girl who happens to be a quarterback on a boy's football team. Yes, it is two for the price of one in this PSYOP thinly disguised as a tween TV show.

Viacom owns The Nickelodeon Network. Here is what Wikipedia says about Viacom:

"Viacom, Inc. (short for Video & Audio Communications) is an American global mass media company with interests primarily in, but not limited to, cinema and cable television. It is the world's sixth largest broadcasting and cable company in terms of revenue (behind Comcast, The Walt Disney Company, Twenty-First Century Fox, Inc., Time Warner, and CBS Corporation, respectively). Voting control of Viacom is held by National Amusements, Inc., a privately owned theater company controlled in turn by billionaire Sumner Redstone. Redstone also holds, via National Amusements, a controlling stake in CBS Corporation. [228]

Sumner Redstone, aka: Murray Rothstein, Owner of Nickelodeon.

I could provide the reader with hundreds of ads, TV shows and movies just like the few I have presented here, but space will not permit that and besides, the point I want to make transcends these particular content media and their subject matter.

For critics and the PC police who are undoubtedly going to do exactly what they have been programmed to do, attack anyone who exposes their master's skullduggery, I want you to read my words very, very carefully. The masterminds behind these ads, TV shows and movies ***dare anyone*** to point out their gender and racial stereotype manipulation. If anyone dares to point this out, the messenger is attacked for recognizing and calling out what creators of these brainwashing PSYOPs have done. I DIDN'T CREATE THESE ADS, SOMEONE ELSE DID!

It is none of my business who a person mates with, but I have proven conclusively that someone or someone's DOES or DO CARE about <u>promoting miscegenation</u> for white women.

What the mind control artists have consistently gotten away with is this:

The person who uncovers and calls out their gender and racial manipulation is cast as a person who is gender and racially biased. What a clever and

---

[228] a. "Global 500 2009: Industry". CNN. July 20, 2009. Retrieved May 1, 2010.

b. 2007 Results" (PDF). February 28, 2008. Retrieved May 1, 2010.

c. Siklos, Richard (February 9, 2009). "Why Disney wants DreamWorks". CNN. Retrieved May 1, 2010.

d. News Corporation – Annual Report 2007". Newscorp.com. June 30, 2007. Retrieved July 13, 2011.

devious trick! Were it not for the lack of discernment among the masses, that particular skullduggery would be laughable.

But it won't work this time. I didn't create these ads nor can the creators of this genre of psychodrama deny the empirically demonstrable patterns repeated hundreds of times in various media in the United States and the Western World. I am reminded of writer Ian Fleming's wise axiom on how to interpret repeated patterns of conduct:

"Once is happenstance. Twice is coincidence. **Three times is enemy action***"*

The actors and actresses in these ads, sitcoms and movies were performing as directed. They read the lines as written and the cinematographers, makeup artists and wardrobe managers followed the specific directions of the people behind the meta-communications designed into the ads.

My criticism of these specific PSYOPs derives NOT from the subjects chosen to socially engineer, per se, BUT the act of socially engineering ANYTHING OR ANYONE, and the harm these PSYOPs have caused to my clients and criminal defendants, politicians, schoolteachers, or a host of other targets of manipulation.

Yes, it is true, the mind control agents running the show are pushing various agenda that are purposefully designed to eradicate the traditional nuclear family and American dating and mating customs. Some of my readers may welcome that particular social engineering effort or they may take an agnostic view of this. But be advised, it would be just as easy to socially engineer behavior that would move the needle in another direction, one not consonant with your personal or political agenda. Let me repeat myself, who a person mates with is none of my business, that is why I reject social engineers who HAVE MADE IT THEIR BUSINESS to modify dating and mating habits in ways that functionally result in the genocide of particular races.

It is my hope that the masses, regardless of race, gender or ethnicity, declare a "no fly zone," so to speak, when it comes to who is permitted to fly into the airspace of their mind. Moreover, whether realized or not, the wisdom of socially engineering the destruction of traditional America, and along the way the dating and mating rituals of some of its citizens, will undoubtedly result in any number of unintended consequences and blowback. I know the shadow men behind these social engineering efforts and I have concluded that their nihilistic and soulless personalities will ultimately destroy them, right along with the masses they have targeted.

I repeat that I recognize that the performers who act in or direct these PSYOPs undoubtedly have their own *personal motivations* to participate. It may be just a job to them or the subject matter may compensate for what they experienced growing up. But nothing is produced in Hollywood or New York solely because of the "personal" motivations of the actors and actresses involved, with very, very few exceptions.

According to Marlo Thomas, and I paraphrase, she was personally motivated to promote the unattached woman ideal in *That Girl* by and through what she learned growing up with nine Lebanese brothers who embodied classic (as she describes it) misogynistic Lebanese behavior toward women. According to Marlo, she swore as a young girl coming of age that she would never be subservient to a man based upon what she experienced growing up. Marlo's personal motivations to help create *That Girl* coincidentally matched the motivations of her Hollywood producers who were serving as the PR agents of shadow men. And when all was said and done, Lebanese culture did not change, but traditional Anglo-American culture did change.

Shadow men do not recruit the masses to participate in, empower and enforce their devious plans by advertising their true motivations and intent. Can you imagine if shadow men were honest about what they intended to do with you and your fellow man? So what shadow men do, in lieu of telling the truth about what they are up to, they lie, they Trojan Horse their true agenda within comic book-like, two-dimensional motivators that fool the unwashed masses. The Torches of Freedom Campaign got women to take up smoking by praying upon their desire to be like men; a desire, I might add, that was socially engineered as the predicate PSYOP to Bernay's plot to get women to take up smoking. Linear information processing will never decipher what mind control agents are up to.

Marlo Thomas provides us with a perfect illustration of how an intelligent, talented and sincere person can serve the role of useful idiot. Thomas also illustrates the brilliance of shadow men's cloaking structures. We told you in the very first chapter that shadow men's matrix of power is so efficient at cloaking, that many of their agents genuinely have no awareness that they are merely tools used by shadow men. Shadow men's agents and operatives can virtually always assert plausible and genuine deniability when confronted with proof of their manipulative deeds. The ultimate failsafe mechanism is that people in show business who tend to be both egocentric and narcissistic, could never accept the proposition I have documented as true, that they were played for fools by men living in the shadows.

One final thought before we leave the topic of socially engineering the dating and mating habits of men and women and the assault upon the traditional American nuclear family. I am going to make an attempt to persuade those people who are so thoroughly brainwashed that they would cast aspirations at me for daring to draw my reader's attention to patterns **I had noting to do with creating or promoting**.

Any of the groups highlighted herein are merely pawns used to reorder the world to the liking of ruling shadow men. Blacks who appear in racist sitcoms, commercials or movies are simply practicing their craft. Gays offered the opportunity to be married on a Rose Parade Float are simply saying "yes" to an enticing offer made by the agents for shadow men. I mean, after all, who would turn down an opportunity to be married on a Rose Parade float? Actresses who portray warrior princesses are simply doing what they are directed to do. White actors who play uncouth, stupid, lazy and cruel fathers are simply making a living as an actor. Shadow men have pulled the wool over everyone's eyes. It's not the good hearted, intelligent and personally motivated actors, directors or grips I'm criticizing or going after when I point out racial and gender manipulation, I'M MAKING A HEARTFELT ATTEMPT TO PUT THE ONUS WHERE IT BELONGS.

Shadow men placed the American ideal of the traditional nuclear family unit in their crosshairs and targeted it for extinction. Shadow men directed their PR arms in Hollywood and New York to execute their plan using strategies right out of Edward Bernay's handbook. The shadow men in charge took aim at the father figure, casting him as a bumbling, unattractive, stupid and misogynistic character. They promoted the rejection of committed marriage in favor of a self-centered lifestyle idealizing single women as beautiful warrior princesses and/or sexual libertines who live in a world of rainbows, white wine and perpetual happiness. But like all social engineering, the law of unintended effects means that there will always be collateral casualties. And so it was in with this genre of PSYOPs. To prove my point, let's now move to the beginning of the story and take a closer look at how these social engineering PSYOPs have caused great harm to African American women and men.

Shadow men harmed African American women by casting them as "second choice" when it came to the idealized mating partner for successful African American men. African American women tell me that they have a hard time finding a black man to enter into a committed relationship with them. They tell me, along with countless other clinicians, that they see an ever more popular pattern of successful African American men who will not date within their own race. Encouraging black men to date white women is termed "the encouragement of miscegenation."

Dr. Drew Pinsky addressed this subject matter on his TV show, which aired in October of 2011. One of Dr. Drew's black female guests expressed the feelings of many black women when she said: "We're feeling rejected," and "we're tired of it."

Writer Brande Victorian, a charming and intelligent black woman reported on this particular Dr. Drew episode. Brande has thought a lot about this subject and wrote the following:

> "[I] remember when I used to feel rejected when I'd hear a black man make a comment to the tune of That's why I'm going to get a white girl," or That's why I stopped dating black girls." The idea that a white woman has something better to offer over a black woman just didn't sit well with me at all until I finally realized: That's his problem, not mine....Do I really want to procreate with a man who is more concerned with the texture of his future children's hair than the mental and spiritual qualities his partner possesses?" [229]

Miss Victorian and others in her community have been victimized by shadow men and their paid social engineers who didn't care about, or hadn't factored into their devious plot, the collateral damage that would be done to beautiful and accomplished black women like Miss Victorian by promulgating miscegenation, especially the black man/white woman model. Simply put, African American men were encouraged by the agents of shadow men to lust after white women. Miscegenation was promoted, encouraged and pushed upon the conformist masses knowing that if such behavior could be made trendy it would become popular and this particular change in the mating habits of white women would empower shadow men. As I have made mention to earlier in this book, my clients have included shadow men. I have first hand knowledge of the fact that miscegenation, with either black men or black women, among shadow men, is considered to be an abomination if engaged in by one of their own. In fact, shadow men consider miscegenation to be worse than actual genocide. So regardless what your particular views are regarding miscegenation, simply be aware that shadow men have promoted one standard for the masses and another standard, diametrically opposite, for themselves and their genome.

I knew of one shadow man who had changed his name to hide his identity. He loved black women, though he had married within his own elite group. He chose black women to be his paramours who were not easily identifiable as a black. His paramours were identified to this particular shadow man's friends as "Latinas." One of his "Latinas" retained her black identity and made the mistake of identifying herself with a famous black person. The shadow man went ballistic. He told her that he didn't really care who she dated or had sex with, but asked her why would she ruin his reputation among other shadow men by making it clear that she was not a Latina but a proud black woman?

What shadow men and their agents have done to the black family and, in particular, black women, borders on criminal. Shadow men's efforts were not limited to the promotion of miscegenation. Shadow men imaged the average black man in a particularly negative light. As a result of this negative imaging, shadow men have been able to encourage any number of destructive behaviors on the part of black men that helped to destruct the black family.

Clinically, I have worked with beautiful and accomplished black women who have been forced to deal with the consequences of various PSYOPs designed to image them "second best." In addition, black men have been shackled and harmed by devious mind control PSYOPs that rewarded them when they engaged in criminal behavior, e.g., it's fashionable to act like a thug. Rank

---

[229] Madame Noire. *Black Men Who Refuse to Date Black Women.* By Brande Victorian. October 28, 2011.

and file white men and women, along with black men and women, had little or nothing to do with these PSYOPs.

Black men are often perceived and sadly behave the way their image has been constructed in the American psyche by shadow men. As already mentioned, Herman Cain and Justice Clarence Thomas are just two high profile examples of how shadow men have blended the images of black professional men with their orchestrated negative personas. When black conservatives become a threat to shadow men, their agents invoke the negative stereotypes I have covered herein.

My experience in the criminal justice system informs me that mind control artists, by and through their social engineering of dating and mating rituals, have caused irreparable harm to *innocent* black males who find themselves in the role of defendant in a criminal court, especially when criminal sexual conduct is at issue.

Need I remind you that both conservative and liberal white male politicians have gotten away with promiscuous sexual behavior that a black man, based upon my forensic experience, could never get away with because of how mind control artists have constructed the African male's public image. And to be sure, African American men have adopted, in many instances, the roles designed for them by the men living in the shadows. So while it was the white traditional nuclear family that found itself to be the primary target of shadow men, it was the African American male and female who became just so much collateral damage.

Now I want to share with you my own clinically based, first hand assessment with regard to the current crop of shadow men running the show. Clinically, I believe that the current ruling shadow men junta is self-destructive and that unless they bridle their ambitions or another competing faction of shadow men controls their ravenous behavior, they will destruct the corpus of the entire world and may, in the process, foment an all out assault upon demographic groups wrongly perceived to be at the bottom of all of this.

Is it asking too much of the megalomaniacs who are in charge to control their own self-destructive behavior? Candidly, yes it is. Nevertheless, competing shadow men may take my words to heart and consider whether they should allow the current junta (their intramural colleagues) to bring everyone and everything down with them.

The masses may be easy pickings. But the competing shadow men who were their strongest during the 1950's and the early part of the 60's remain a potent force waiting for the right time to rise up and challenge their ravenous children who, since early childhood, have proven themselves to be dangerous and unwieldy members of the shadow man's tribe. Not all of the prior generation of shadow men's children turned out to be maniacal fiends, but grew up to be more like their parents and grand parents.

The shadow men of the 50's and early 60's revered scientific achievement. They were benevolent caretakers of the "kids" (The offspring of goats, that is, YOU) [230] and encouraged committed nuclear families, hard work, honesty and self-reliance. These benevolent shadow men took pride in their "kids" making enough money to have their own little piece of what they termed the American dream. These men had great senses of humor, were kinder and though make no mistake about it, they considered themselves to be the chosen ones; they were benevolent shadow

---

[230] The masses have no appreciation for the fact that they commonly refer to their children as "kids," which is the same name given to the offspring of goats. Shadow men NEVER refer to their children as "kids." Shadow men refer to their offspring as "children of God."

men. Someone will always be in charge. The shadow men of the previous era filled that role well and perhaps better than anyone among the masses.

Their offspring evolved into monsters of greed, selfishness and suffered from wanton megalomania. Based upon what you have learned up to this point, you may have little or no compassion for any of the shadow men, but I can assure you that they do bleed and they do feel pain.

These rulers of a half-century ago have experienced great disappointment as parents. Most of their children are nothing like them. In some instances their children have been disinherited. The act of disinheritance resulted in an unintended consequence in that these disinherited future shadow men joined forces with other disinherited shadow men to form a cabal of the worst of the worst. Hedonistic, narcissistic, maniacal, ravenous and sexually perverted monsters have assumed control. How that happened is a case study in rarified social units and privilege. Regardless, we are all the victims of this cabal, including the immediately preceding generation of shadow men.

These benevolent shadow men parents suffered, our country has been devastated and our minds no longer belong to us. Clinically, I believe that these monster children of the benevolent shadow men of the past are destructive beyond anything the earth has ever seen. While their rage and psychopathology have appeared in earlier generations of shadow men, never has their control been so consolidated and never have they had the technological wherewithal to impose their psychopathologies on so many and at the same time.

They are remaking the masses into their image as if to show their parents that they are a dying generation. Our society is devolving into nothing more than a mirror image of the psychopathologies of the monsters in charge. Dare to talk about this and every PSYOP defense mechanism kicks into high gear. A mass citizenry that has little or no frustration tolerance left will simply turn away in fear, denial or repulsion. You can always put this book down and turn on the TV and watch the latest reality TV stars cavort in your living room. After all, that is the purpose of such diversions.

The agents of the monsters in charge were chosen to reflect their master's evil spirit. Politicians today only rise to power if the monster children of the prior generation of shadow men permit their rise, with few exceptions. Their PR agents in Hollywood and New York produce media that reflect their ruler's lusts and desires. I find it fascinating that Hollywood's most popular personalities flash the same occult signs to the paparazzi and their fans as were flashed by the Phoenician/Canaanite priests in ancient times.

Satanist Aleister Crowley

Kanye West

Lady Gaga Flashes Eye of Horus Occult Symbol.

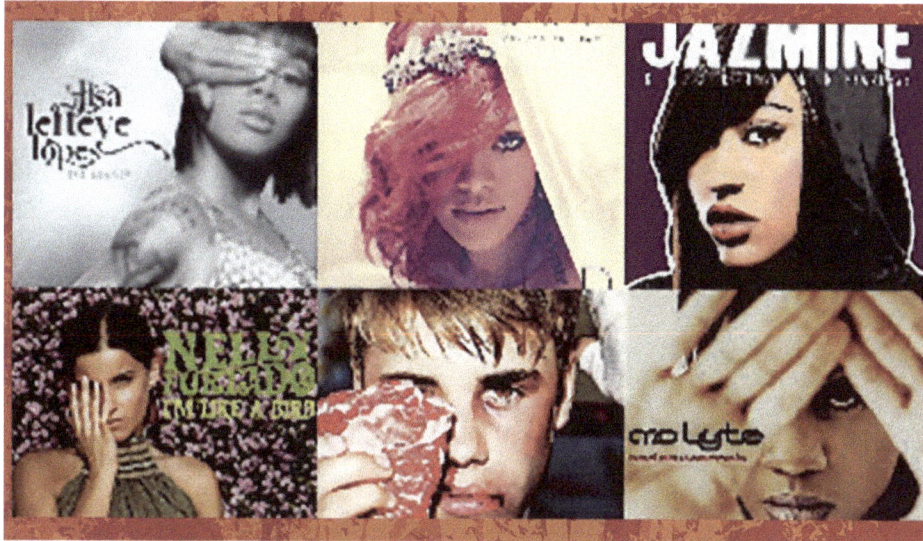

Music Stars as of 2015 Flash Eye of Horus Occult Symbol.

Various Occult Symbol Displays from Disney Artists.

The useful idiots are not only increasing in number, but they have been emboldened by the PR agent's use of them in so-called "Reality TV." Reality TV is neither "real" TV nor is it TV. It is a genre of psychological operations thinly disguised as "entertainment" that illustrates better than anything I can think of the axiom of Marshall McLuhan, "The Medium is the Message." Average people sitting like drugged prisoners watching other average people all the while the meta communications in all of these so-called reality TV programs embed themselves into the viewer's mind, that is, what is left of it. The masses are so easily infected with the PR agent's PSYOPs that they name their "kids" after these reality TV personalities. [231] [232]

For example, take a look at how the media-entertainment complex portrays Southerners. These representative images were sampled from various media and fairly represent how Hollywood and New York portray white southerners:

These people come from an area of the United States that has traditionally rejected shadow men indoctrination. This is why they have been chosen to represent to the rest of the country what being "Southern" is all about. Shadow men have been so successful at marginalizing Southerners through a barrage of PSYOPs that serious men and women who possess a Southern accent are presumed to be less intelligent and less educated than someone without a Southern accent. Universities down "south" have some of the best minds in the country. Ever consider why you NEVER see them highlighted by the media?

You might also find it interesting that some of the TV characters that conservatives and Southerners idolize do not naturally speak with a Southern accent nor do they embody the Southern values that the masses believe are deeply rooted in their conservative stars. These characters are illusory and nothing but the handiwork of shadow men's agents in Hollywood and New York.

---

[231] Mail Online. (2013), *Duck Dynasty stars spark wholesome baby name trend for 2013 as new parents opt for Korie, Si and Sadie (as Amanda and Lindsey plummet in popularity).* By, Sadie Whitelocks. December 3.
[232] Associated Press. (2012), *Most popular baby names derived from reality TV, religion.* May 14.

Some of the actors who play these roles are brilliant character actors who have convinced the masses that their made up character is who they actually are. Providing to you a name or names would do nothing but harm their reputation to the point where others may want to ruin their professional life. I do not want that.

The "useful idiots" term has always struck me as harsh, but when used as it was originally conceived to characterize the fools used to promote Italian socialism during WW II, the term seems fitting. Nevertheless, useful idiots, in their defense, always have any number of *personal* reasons for why they do what they do, but this fact only illustrates the brilliance of the useful idiot model of tyranny at the hands of the masses.

It may be 9 Lebanese brothers, it may have been some stupid and cruel policy that prevents a gay person from visiting a loved one in the hospital, it may be a woman whose father was cruel, it may be a black person not judged by their character but by their race, it may be anything and it usually is something personally significant. *But those are all incidental motivations and wouldn't amount to anything were it not for shadow men calling the shots.*

The two sources of salvation to escape this tyranny at the hands of the PSYOP masters, vis a vis the masses, derives from a select few of the unwashed masses (actual shadow men's descriptive term for the masses) defying their station in life and rising above their cognitive limitations and the brainwashing that has so effectively compromised their immune system. The second source of salvation will come from the old guard benevolent shadow men who are just as displeased and troubled over what their children have done to you AND them as are you. By fortune and chance, I became a consigliere to the old guard. By good fortune I benefited from their largesse. By virtue of my compassion I understand and want to help them. It is with their blessings, that I was permitted to tell you some of their most important secrets. They are so desperate they want and need your help.

Remember something very important, if you happen to be one of those delusional people who believe in the "collective" or the value of a socialist organization of society as a means by which the ruling elite will be eliminated, realize that someone will always be in charge. My chapter on Democracy conclusively proved my thesis in that regard. That is the nature of the world and it will never nor can it ever change. The only question is who will run the show behind the scenes? Do you want benevolent caretakers and protectors or do you want ravenous, greed frenzied narcissistic megalomaniacs who operate through and by manipulating the herd instinct of the masses? We used to have the former, now we are suffering under the latter. The old guard needs YOUR help to return to power.

Should the more benevolent shadow men see a glimmer of hope in the masses awakening from their stupor they, too, will be empowered and re-discover the hope that they can regain their lost station as ruling shadow men. If the old guard can regain control, they will take care of their offspring. Shadow men know how to do that sort of thing. But unless more than a few of the members of the masses awaken and unless those of us who still retain a semblance of free will actively roust from every perch, position of power the agents of tyranny from their quiet place of domination, we will be doomed and our country will slide into the abyss. Even though inconceivable, it can and will happen, it is just a matter of time; and the clock is running out.

If you have not noticed, permit me to draw your attention to the fact that America's Constitution remains in force. The agents of the shadow men in control have simply ignored the correction mechanisms so skillfully written into this brilliant document. For those useful idiots and proxy agents of the revolutionaries, e.g., Jeffrey Sachs, advisor to the Vatican, who glibly spout inoculations created by PhD's in think tank labs that use words and phrases like, "But times are different, we no longer ride in carriages drawn by horses so why shouldn't the Constitution change", I remind you of this: First, just know that this particular retort (life is different now) was created in a lab just like an antibiotic designed to kill a particular pathogen. Secondly, like all PSYOPs, it sounds logical until you dissect it for what it really is.

The Constitution of the United States is a document of PRINCIPLES, not a set of codes designed to regulate life as it was in 1787. Permit me to offer to you the perfect metaphor that will make this point clear if it is not already obvious to you.

The behavior of a wagon wheel made of wood and iron, circa 1787, adhered to the laws of PHYSICS in exactly the same way the behavior of a Formula One Racing wheel made of titanium adheres to the laws of PHYSICS in 2014. **The laws of physics are principles that care not about the modernity of the wheel in question.**

So it is with the Constitution of the United States. The Bill of Rights captures the same social physics that explain the behavior of tyrants and protection from them circa 18th century as it does in the 21st century. This is because though tyrants have changed their methodologies, their tendency to abuse power remains unchanged.

My prior works that have touched upon the revolution currently attacking the very fiber of America have been long on diagnosis and a little less robust on treatment. I must confess that the disease entity that is infecting America resides very deeply in the mind of man and is protected by genius level insulation and shields.

My first work on the subject: *The Progressive Virus*, confronted what the early biologists faced when they first published their belief that there may be invisible microorganisms that are infecting man and causing what the naked eye only sees as gross disease. Lots of people write about gross disease, but I was the first to track down the fundamental psychological pathogen that is actually causing the disease.

Whenever anyone speaks the truth, which is purposefully hidden by design and shielded from disclosure, that person will be subjected to any number of PSYOPs that are designed to insure that the existing propaganda-laden cognitive maps of the masses remain intact. Break into a bank and expect the alarms to go off. I've taken you deep into the bank's vault and shown YOU where the money is located.

The mid-19th Century Hungarian physician Semmelweis confronted a similar problem as I when he dared to assert that hygiene had something to do with an alarmingly high mortality rate among pregnant women at his hospital in Vienna. Dr. Semmelweis proposed that hands be washed before examining patients with a solution of chloride of lime. Using his own hygienic procedures, mortality dropped from 18 percent to only 2.5 percent. But then, as now, effectuating a positive clinical outcome isn't sufficient to create a paradigm shift among traditional, nostalgia-oriented physicians and patients, alike.

Many physicians, among them the doctors of the Academy of Paris and even the prominent Rudolph Virchow at Berlin, regarded his work unfavorably. No one would pay for his antiseptic solution, and those who did use it, were often ridiculed. Dr. Semmelweis' research was either ignored or ridiculed. Not until after Dr. Semmelweis' death was he recognized as the clinical predecessor to Joseph Lister and what we now assume as a given, antiseptic procedures. The National Case Study for the Teaching of Science published the following on the subject of Dr. Semmelweis. I'm including this information to my readers to let you know what happens to anyone who both speaks the truth and is ahead of his time:

"Despite the dramatic reduction in the mortality rate in Semmelweis' ward, his colleagues and the greater medical community greeted his findings with hostility or dismissal. Even after presenting his work on childbed fever (more technically referred to as puerperal sepsis) to the Viennese Medical Society, Semmelweis was not able to secure the teaching post he desired, and so he returned to Hungary. There, he repeated his successful hand washing attack on childbed fever at the St. Rochus hospital in Pest. In 1860, Semmelweis finally published his principal work on the subject of puerperal sepsis but this, too, was dismissed. It is believed that the years of controversy and repeated rejection of his work by the medical community caused him to suffer a mental breakdown. Semmelweis died in 1865 in an Austrian mental institution. Some believe that his own death was ironically caused by puerperal sepsis. [233]

Becoming cognizant of what is really going on must precede meaningful change. Once Dr. Semmelweis' wisdom was accepted it became du rigueur. During my hospital based internship I was taught to wash my hands both before and after patient contact. It is just what we did. None of us young interns thanked Dr. Semmelweis, but we should have.

In keeping with my metaphor, you are going to have to start washing your hands. Some people, especially conservative people, dislike change. The revolutionaries in our midst know this all too well and they bank on the fact that conservatives are likely to continue along the same path, debating the nonsense played out on cable news stages and talk radio while the real show is taking place in the shadows. They also know that progressive minded people are highly susceptible to their brilliantly designed PSYOPs. I openly acknowledge that I depend upon you to publicize and push this book to as many people as you can. Without YOU this book will be ignored.

It has long past the time for those of you who cherish your free will to bench the well intentioned, but low horsepower, pundits who are paid millions of dollars by the PR agents of shadow men to spout on stage psychodrama. Popularity means, by definition, the popular ones have the stamp of approval issued by the ruling shadow men or they simply are ineffectual or provide cover to their overlords.

Some of your political leaders WANT to help you but they are shackled because, in part, they have been blackmailed and/or threatened with bodily harm or character assassination if they dare engage the machinery of correction built into the Constitution. Many have been bought off with sex, money, acclaim and free access to their perversions. Surely, at this point in your studies, you realize that just as in the case of Pope Clement V, you can make an otherwise good and powerful man, a man of God, do your evil bidding IF you have the right kind of leverage and it is strategically

---

[233] Colyer, C. (2003), *CHILDBED FEVER: A Nineteenth-Century Mystery*. Department of Chemistry Wake Forest University, Winston-Salem, NC 27109. Published by The National Center for Case Study Teaching in Science, University at Buffalo State University of New York.

well placed and timed to perfection. If you can do that to a good man, imagine how easy it is to control a bad man.

You may shocked at the thought that good old-fashioned blackmail has compromised many of your political leader's ability to engage the corrective machinery in the Constitution. Many of your leaders are afraid because, in part, they do not trust your discernment or willingness, as a member of the public, to have their back. And why do they feel this way? Because they sense that you will be too busy watching Realty TV (conservative or liberal, it matters not), surfing the net or glued to your favorite cable news channel to stand up for them should they become a statesman and not a useful idiot figure head. I assure you, that among those few leaders who have not been compromised, there is little or no trust in the public's ability to discern the truth, much less possess the intestinal fortitude required to actually do something. Perhaps this book will change that metric.

Men and women filled with a burning desire to escape the herd instinct are everywhere. Many of these people live outside of the United States. Many European citizens find themselves on the front lines of the shadow men's revolution. They have front row seats as they watch the disintegration and destruction of their once great countries into cultures that would be more appropriately stationed in the 7th Century rather than 21st Century Europe. Never forget that this destruction was socially engineered BY DESIGN by those people who remain insulated and protected from the fruits of their labor.

The masses don't understand the basic laws of human behavior when it comes to the shadow men who rule the world. Shadow men's lives are insulated from and immune to the disastrous consequences of their social engineering efforts. The people, cultures and groups who are used by the shadow men to effectuate their organized chaos are both victims and perpetrators in this psychodrama of planned chaos.

Here is but one example of this victim/perpetrator model in order to drive this point home. Desperate and needy people are encouraged to immigrate to the countries in the crosshairs of the shadow men. They are bribed with welfare checks, citizenship papers and a reprieve from their troubled homelands that are, more often than not, in a state of chaos the result of the handiwork of the same shadow men who now encourage them to cross borders illegally. Many of these people are welcomed by the agents of shadow men and exploited for cheap labor. Shadow men's political arm uses these unfortunate souls to stuff the ballot box to insure that their professional letterhead will continue to include the salutation: "The Honorable" And again, in the absence of a reproductively self-sustaining white population, absent immigration from 3rd world countries, the country would simply die. You see how it works? Shadow men create the problem then offer a solution that kills two birds with one stone.

The naïve and good-hearted citizens of the country being invaded naturally empathize with these poor desperate souls who serve no other purpose than to destroy the culture to which they fled. The good hearted but naïve citizens who benefited from the 200-year reprieve from tyranny fought for and won by America's founders, find themselves forced to choose between their natural sympathies for the poor souls who are encouraged to invade their homeland and the destruction of their once great culture and country.

Culture is more important than any group of people in the long run. It is culture that provides the Petri dish within which good people can grow. If you destroy a proven successful culture by infusing it with ***non-assimilating*** immigrants from less successful cultures you create a citizenry that only serves the needs of shadow men and their agents at the expense of the invaded country/culture and its citizens.

The desperate *non-assimilating* immigrants, who only want a better life, would be fools to turn down citizenship and a welfare check. But, in only one short generation, these same useful idiots may very well find themselves right back at square one. This is because they will work hard to recreate the culture they left behind because their loyalties are admirably rooted to their native lands and their race. Shadow men have made intelligent discussions of race off-limits. Tribal and bloodline identity are key motivators in maintaining one's culture, whether one finds himself in his native land or the land of another tribe or bloodline. This fact is why shadow men focused their attention upon conquering white Christian America by socially engineering out white American's tribal and bloodline identity while simultaneously reinforcing those same motivators in every other tribe and race but white Americans.

Because of their huge numbers and birth rates, non-assimilating immigrants will remake some of the greatest countries on earth into the third-world hell-holes they were encouraged to leave in the first place. [234] Once they recreate their native land in their adopted country THERE WILL BE NO PLACE FOR THEM TO RUN TO NEXT TIME. THERE WILL BE NO BORDER THEY CAN CROSS THAT WILL PROMISE A BETTER LIFE NEXT TIME. This is the ruinous trick the Saturnalian Brotherhood has always played on the victim/perpetrator masses since the very beginning of time.

The masses have been so dumbed-down, so distracted, so morally and physiologically poisoned that they sit idly by watching the destruction of their own country, believing that their country is vulnerable, by law, to tyranny of the masses because it is a democracy. But that is not true and none of this organized chaos has to be. Should just a few good men and women voice the truths I have articulated herein, the organized chaos of the shadow men would crumble into an American renaissance that would then naturally spread to the European continent. It could happen first in Europe, but Americans should not wait for that.

I want you to remember this mantra: patterns, patterns and more patterns. Recall that the very first nascent shadow men rose to power by virtue of their recognition of celestial patterns. The patterns of mind control are there for you to decipher. In fact, they are hidden in plain view. These patterns are protected by a series of PSYOP shields that prevent you from seeing what is right before your very eyes. Rather than point out the patterns in explicit terms and trip the bomb's protective mantle, I am going to teach you how to perceive patterns.

Compile a listing of the men and women in charge of the on-stage production. These leaders may come from the media entertainment complex, banking, politics, factory-farms, anything. Once you have compiled that list, look carefully at the biographies of the men who comprise your list, then ask yourself these questions:

1. What are the common denominators that most if not all of these people share with one another?
2. What allegiances (politics, countries, ideologies) do these men and women share with one another?
3. Who or what do these people support with their money?
4. What do the people in one institutional category (Banking, for example) have in common with people in other important institutional categories (The Media-Entertainment Complex, for example)?

---

[234] Years before the term "hell-hole" and immigration became popularized, the author of this book publicized the term "hell-hole" to refer to unbridled immigration dynamics involving Latin America.

5. When you find common denominators ask yourself, what is the probability that the common denominators you discovered are simply chance occurrences?

Now compile another set of lists. These lists are comprised of the on-air famous people in media, politics, sports and entertainment. Now ask these questions once you have this set of lists compiled:

1. Who signs the checks for the people comprising your lists?
2. What do the check signers have in common with other check signers?
3. What do the check signers have in common with the people in your first set of lists (1 through 4)?

The answers you get may surprise you or may awaken you from your stupor. Voltaire's principle is still one of the best ways to determine who rules over you:

"To learn who rules over you, simply find out who you are not allowed to criticize."

In the final chapter of this book, I am going to provide to you a 12 Step Program designed to help free you from the mind control artists who have socially engineered your free will away. If you follow this 12 Step Program your immune system will be strengthened and you will be well on your way to cleansing your mind and regaining your free will. Before we get to our 12 Step program, however, here is how they did "it."

CHAPTER 15: THE SCIENCE BEHIND SOCIAL ENGINEERING

Social psychologists have documented, and my own clinical and forensic experience confirms, that people tend to deny or greatly underestimate their susceptibility to mind control. Even the most iconoclastic and independent minded person is often no different on key measures of susceptibility to psychological manipulation than someone who espouses the virtues of bowing before those more powerful than he.

When people do find out that they have been duped or manipulated, their first response is almost always denial. This denial is rooted to the fact that it is psychologically unpleasant to become aware of the fact that you have been victimized and played for a fool. And as if to add insult to injury, shadow men have created a virtual reality where often times the people, groups or countries you have been taught to revere and defend at all costs are the one's exploiting you and engineering your consent.

The defense mechanisms that protect the average man or woman from the truth are very powerful. For instance, as you read my thoughts on this subject, studies show that rather than apply what you learn to yourself, you will more likely apply what you learn to others. So when I write that *"the people, groups or countries YOU have been taught to revere and defend at all costs are often times the one's exploiting YOU and engineering YOUR consent,"* are not likely to make it past all of YOUR defenses.

People who deny their susceptibility to manipulation tend to be loyal to a fault. They tend to develop unquestioning loyalty to certain people, countries, and political parties. They tend to have strong likes and dislikes. Little do these honorable people realize that those exact traits were cultivated and exploited by shadow men and have been used to insure that the masses will tend to revere those who oppress them without one iota of awareness. I know that is a bitter pill to swallow, but it is true.

The scientific principles I am going to present to you were not originally developed as PSYOPs. Be aware that each model of behavior is comprised of data that would fill a good-sized library. Also, keep in mind that their original descriptor of each psychological principle included the word "theory." The principles I am presenting to you are no longer "theory" but have transitioned to well-documented fact.

The scientists who uncovered these psychological principles, in keeping with their training, first published their ideas as theories because they were presenting a newly developed set of ideas and constructs. This would be similar to what research biologists did when they first published on Polio, e.g., "A theory of viral infection." The psychological principles outlined herein run parallel to the development of nuclear technology, in that it did not take shadow men very long to take the science of nuclear fission and use it to construct a nuclear weapon.

Shadow men, by and through their agents, have weaponized psychological principles in order to use them to their benefit. Weaponized psychology, as the name implies, takes researcher's noble efforts to decipher the human condition and turn them into weapons that are used to control the masses and their intramural competitors. Surely as a nuclear bomb is the tangible result of weaponizing nuclear fission and fusion physics, so it is that PSYOPs are weaponized versions of human behavior science.

What is afoot is best described as a war on reality. The war is waged in its first phase by convincing man that his virtual reality is equal to objective reality. The next phase is to manipulate virtual reality such that man can no longer tell the difference between what is true and objective and the virtual reality he carries with him in his CNS. This virtual reality was socially engineered to serve shadow men in order to reengineer the objective world and the people who live in it.

Ever hear the old adage: "Are you going to believe me or your lying eyes?" A mid-20th century psychologist, named Muzafer Sherif, conducted studies on the underlying principle found in this adage. Years before Sherif did his research, Edward Bernays had identified something he termed the "herd instinct." Bernays learned to engineer consent by manipulating the herd instinct of the masses. Sherif set about to get to the bottom of how and why people tend to conform their thoughts, emotions and behaviors to the herd instinct.

Sherif placed a research subject in a darkened room and displayed a point of light on a screen, not unlike an eye examination where the patient sits in a darkened room and visualizes letters. Sherif set the experiment up with the research subject either sitting alone or accompanied by confederates of his choosing who had been coached to respond according to plan.

One of the tasks designed by Sherif was to simply have the research subject report how much and what kind of movement the point of light made. Sherif took advantage of something called the *Autokinetic Effect* wherein a stationary point of light projected upon a screen in a darkened room will appear to move based upon the neuro-optical physiology of the visual processing centers in the brain.

When the subject sat alone he would report his own perceptions of movement. When, on the other hand, research subjects were accompanied by Sherif's confederates, each of whom had been coached to report fluctuating amounts of movement, that differed from known standards, research subjects modified their own perceptions so that they would conform to the group consensus.

I want to stress that it was not that the research subject knew in his heart that the point of light only moved so much but conformed his stated opinion to match that of the group to avoid a conflict or having to debate the issue. No, the research subject's perceptions were actually modified by the influence of the group. Even the most stalwart subjects who resisted the effects of conformity came to doubt their perceptions and beliefs. [235]

Solomon Asch, working in the 1950's, was another early researcher who investigated how people can be controlled to deny their own perceptions by passive group pressure. The key here is the word "passive." Asch showed an unsuspecting research subject a line drawn on a card. He then showed the subject three other cards labeled "A", "B" or "C." Each of the cards had a different length of line drawn on it. The test subject, who was permitted to compare in real time the original card with the alphabet cards, was asked to identify which of the three cards most closely matched the length of the line drawn on the original card. What do think happened? Remarkably, 75% of research subjects gave an incorrect answer to at least one question because their perceptions and beliefs had been controlled, without their awareness, by the passive psychological effects of the group who knowingly gave false answers.

When it comes to perception, it is well known that by manipulating the wants of the perceiver one can modify the ease with which he can be manipulated. Many of us have experienced a naturally occurring form of this phenomenon. For instance, have you ever been expecting an important call only to swear you heard the phone ring when it did not? If you answered yes, then YOU have experienced the phenomenon I'm talking about. If you answered no, you are in denial or

---

[235] Muzafer Sherif. (Jul. - Oct., 1937), *An Experimental Approach to the Study of Attitudes. Sociometry*, Vol. 1, No. 1/2 pp. 90-98 American Sociological Association.

totally unaware. Perception and cognitive defects, both naturally occurring and engineered, can have serious consequences. One class of perception and cognitive defects involves the criminal justice system.

As of the writing of this book, *The Innocence Project* has freed 316 prisoners sentenced to death or life in prison based upon DNA evidence. The 316 people who have been freed represent ONLY the tip of the iceberg. How can this injustice happen? Is the system flawed? Actually, mankind's perceptions and cognitive processes are easily duped and confused, even in the absence of mal intent.

For example, 70% of those wrongfully convicted were the victims of faulty eyewitness testimony. This is because, in part, police investigators exacerbate naturally occurring errors in human perception and cognitive processing. As a result, these errors translate into false identifications.

Police have, in the past, provided a lineup of six faces or waist up photos and asked: "Do you recognize any of these subjects?" The photos are absent context and do not take into consideration that some people look more guilty than do other people. Think that isn't true? Well, just ask ANY casting director in Hollywood how he or she casts roles for criminals or villains. Moreover, the person being asked to identify a person in the photo lineup can't judge height or weight accurately from the photo. But the real kicker is that some police departments don't tell the person identifying the suspect from the six photos that the REAL suspect may not even be in the lineup of photos or people being shown to them.

People tasked with making an eyewitness identification of the perpetrator, when shown the standard police department's standard six suspect presentation, cognitively treat the photo presentation as a puzzle, e.g., "who looks most like the person I saw commit the crime?" Thus, subjects unconsciously scan the photos or lineup for the "closest match," concluding, that since one of the six MUST BE the perpetrator the one that looks the MOST like what she/he remembers must be the correct person. This cognitive process remains hidden to the person using it. By simply telling the identifier that the person of interest may or may not be in the photos or lineup presented, significantly reduces the incidence of misidentification. Have you ever been told you look like someone? Well, if you have, in other circumstances you may be misidentified as a criminal.

Cross-racial identification errors account for over half of the 70% of suspects wrongfully identified as the perpetrator. Misidentification is more likely to occur when people of different races ID one another. Eyewitness identification, in almost any circumstance, is an "iffy" proposition. This is especially true when police are permitted to exacerbate, knowingly or unknowingly, known flaws in human perception and cognitive organization. [236] Michael Bach has compiled a number of optical illusions and has a wonderful website that presents several optical illusions with a brief explanation of each. As you study his catalogue of optical illusions, realize that each illusion exploits a naturally occurring flaw in man's perceptual and information processing apparatus. [237]

In a more general sense, all that is required to manipulate behavior in any individual or group of human beings is to create a drive state of "want" in your target, then provide to that target a to-do-

---

[236] Dysart, J. E., Lawson, V. Z., & Rainey, A. (in press 2014). *Blind lineup administration as a prophylactic against the postidentification feedback effect.* Law and Human Behavior. doi: 10.1037/h0093921.
[237] Please see the optical illusions catalogued by Michael Bach: http://www.michaelbach.de/ot/

list, that will assuage the engineered want you helped to create within the target. This particular PSYOP works in both positive and negative drive states.

For example, mind control artists may create a positive want, e.g., a desire to eat a particular food or buy a particular car. Conversely, they may create a negative drive state, e.g., fear or dread of something or some existential threat. Once these drive states are engineered, mind control artists offer to their victims a solution or salvation from the fear they created or a product or service to satisfy their engineered wants and desires. When it comes to the drive state of fear, the salvation provided that reduces the fear is often hidden within a Trojan Horse, designed to give shadow men what they wanted all along. What shadow men want is better access to the minds of the masses by unlocking access to the masse's freedom of choice, their privacy and their rights, Constitutionally protected or otherwise, known or unrecognized.

Controllers have used fear so successfully over the years in order to take away freedom of choice and to undermine privacy that the most remarkable thing about this psychological operation is that it continues to work so well. Like a magician's trick, that no matter how many times you see it the audience is still fooled, so it is with this tried and true psychological operation. Remember this: The greater the fear, real, imagined or free floating, the greater the control and freedom the masses will happily hand over to their "protectors."

In order to cultivate mass fear, some significant frightening event must take place or be imagined to possibly take place by a large number of people. Shadow men are always on the lookout for naturally occurring disasters, upon which they can bootstrap engineered acts of salvation and offer these solutions to the frightened masses. Shadow men are notoriously impatient. As a result, they are not above engineering a frightening disaster, which then provides shadow men an opportunity to offer to the frightened masses a Trojan-Horse dose of salvation.

As we have already noted, these engineered events are termed "False Flag Events." (FFEs) I will not enter the fray on actually identifying, by name, specific "False Flag Events," that have not already been discussed. This is because FFEs are heavily protected by any number of protective mechanisms that would require that I move heaven and earth to simply make a dent in those defenses. Also, the FFEs I have in mind would be so shocking and potentially devastating to the well being of my fellow man, I have concluded that it is better at this point to maintain their cloaking.

I would be remiss were I not to remind my readers that this brief discussion of the shields protecting disclosure of FFEs provides us a teachable moment regarding those shields that protect FFEs. Paranoid commentators, plagued not only with irrational suspicions, but hobbled by a lack of intellectual rigor, have so muddied the waters when it comes to FFEs, that whoever engages the subject will immediately be lumped together with these accidental shills for shadow men. One such FFE proposal, named Operations Northwood, illustrates how the devil is always in the details when it comes to how FFEs have been treated by the media entertainment complex. Mark Rothschild, a writer for a skeptic's blog, wrote the following:

> *"One false flag operation that's long fired the imagination of conspiracy theorists never even took place. Operation Northwoods was a proposed plot by the Department of Defense to fabricate a pretext for an invasion of Cuba and overthrow of the Castro regime. Acts such as shooting down a passenger plane, sinking a US Navy ship or even attacks on Miami were suggested by the document, which was classified until 1997. The plan made it all the way to President Kennedy's desk, who wisely vetoed it. But just the existence of such a plan is enough to convince some that the US government, no matter who is in charge, is capable of brazen deception and false flag techniques*

to justify anything it wants. And of course, the conspiracy theorists add, President Kennedy was assassinated less than a year after scuttling Northwoods." [238]

Mr. Rothschild is not exactly accurate regarding his dismissive treatment of so called "conspiracy theorists" when he said that Operations Northwood never took place. Yes, he is technically correct, it never came to fruition. However, Operations Northwood was never put into action because at the last minute JFK scuttled this particular FFE. The fact that an FFE of this magnitude made it to the president's desk for consideration suggests that Operation Northwoods, and other FFEs like it, are not an anomaly.

The next psychological operation I'm going to talk about is termed Labeling Theory. This principle was originally conceived of as a purely social-psychological concept. It has evolved to incorporate many principles found in neuropsychology. Labeling theory and practice relies upon man being a symbol monger and trader. Man's CNS relates to the objective world in the form of symbols. Words hold a special place among all other symbols. Man is genetically programmed to traffic in words.

The world and the people who live in it cannot be rendered into shorthand labels without most of the meaning and complexities of whatever it is that is labeled being lost in the process. Nevertheless, mankind, as a symbol monger and trader, habitually renders complexity into shorthand labels. Labels serve to instruct human beings on how we should think, feel and behave toward whatever it is we label.

The most rudimentary of qualitative labeling are the labels "good" and "bad." To declare that something or someone is "good" or "bad" glosses over the complexities of the whole person or object labeled. We know this to be true. Nevertheless, in a complex world we often trade simplicity for a lack of precision because in many instances simplicity is all that mankind can comprehend.

The magic of Labeling theory is rooted in neuropsychology. Once something is labeled "bad" or with some other label that means "bad," our CNS filters out good qualities and actually looks for bad qualities in the person or object that has been labeled "bad." Moreover, once something has been given a negative label, our perceptions and feelings are changed forever about that person or object. It is as though once our brains have categorized something or someone as bad we lose our ability to process information accurately. In other words, once something is negatively labeled, the person, situation or object we then interact with becomes distorted, rather like looking at the world through a fun house mirror. If you substitute the label "good" for "bad" as identified above, you get the same perceptual and cognitive distortions, but only in reverse.

What is it, you may wonder, about man's CNS function, that makes him less perceptive and objectively discerning once he has labeled something? The answer, in part, has to do with the difference between "Assimilation" and "Adaptation." It may surprise you to learn that by the time you are 5 years old you will have learned about 80% of the vocabulary you will use the rest of your life. Why is this so?

The answer is related to Assimilation and Labeling theory's categorization function. Once a person or thing has been labeled with a word, it is then categorized into its own tidy cognitive pigeonhole. Once something is categorized it is defined. Once something is defined IF something new is presented to you, like a new word, for example, the tendency is to assimilate the new thing, word, what have you, into the existing category.

---

238 Rothschild, Mark. (2013), *False Flag Attacks: Myth and Reality.* Online at: http://skeptoid.com/blog/2013/01/21/false-flag-attacks-myth-and-reality/

Let me give you an example using vocabulary. If I say to you, "My, she is a garrulous person." You may ask, "What does the word 'garrulous' mean?'" I may answer you by providing a number of synonyms for the word "garrulous." I may also give to you a formal definition of the word. What most people do at that point is *unconsciously* engage their Assimilation function and squeeze the new word into an existing Label/category, e.g., "Oh, garrulous means 'talkative.'" Well, no it does not. Perhaps you can now see why most people have acquired 80% of their entire vocabulary by the time they are 5 years old. This is because when they are exposed to a new word they squeeze it (assimilate it) into an existing category where an "old" word resides. When this occurs, the "new" word is discarded. As you can see, mankind's Assimilation function begins early in life and remains fixed for the vast majority of human beings.

Let me give you a few examples of the power of Labeling theory. I want you to think of your favorite cold beverage. Picture it in your mind's eye. It may be an ice-cold beer or iced tea, a refreshing glass of lemonade, whatever is your favorite beverage. Below are a couple of photos of what many people consider refreshing drinks:

I want you to look at the images above and simply think about the ice cold drinks pictured. After you have studied these images for a few seconds or so move onto the next photos of the same beverages, but with one change:

Study these photos where the drinks are labeled "safe." When you're done studying the photos, move onto the next series of photos:

Study these photos and ask yourself this question: "If I were presented with these drinks labeled "Danger" would I drink them?"

I've actually done this study and I found that just because of the label "Danger" no one would drink the beverages. That should not be surprising.

What may be surprising to you, however, is that even when I told the test subjects that all three versions (no labels, "safe" labels, "danger" labels) of the same drinks were identical, except for their labels, and that all the drinks were absolutely safe, test subjects were still reluctant to take a sip of the drinks labeled "Danger" and more people preferred the drinks labeled "Safe" compared to the "no label" drinks. Even when I drank a sample, with a spoon, of the beverages labeled "danger," test subjects were still reluctant to take a sip of the beverage

"Danger" is a stigmatized label. It is a label attached to any number of objects and places in our environment designed to ward off an interaction with whatever it is that is labeled. We are taught beginning in kindergarten, if not earlier, that we must stay away from anything labeled with the word "DANGER."

Labels can become stigmatized using a process of operant conditioning. A stigmatized label may be used to keep you away from that to which it is affixed or, when used as a PSYOP, the attachment of a stigmatized label is used to shut down our perceptual acuity and information processing function. Just like in our cold drink experiment, once a valenced label is attached to the ice cold drinks, reason and trust go right out the window. The label, not reason or logic, defines how we will think, feel and ultimately behave toward that to which a stigmatized label has been attached.

Take a look at the next image. Which path do you want the man to take?

Labeling Theory at Work

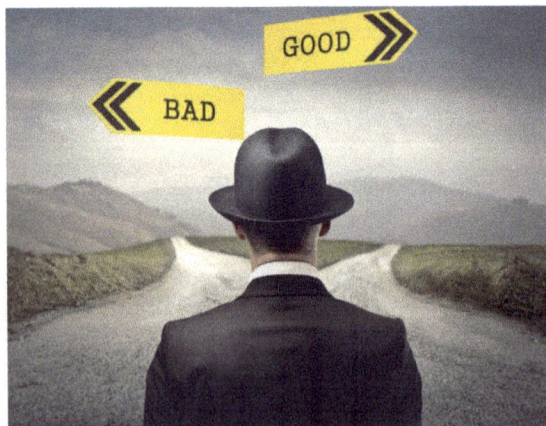

Test subjects shown this image mostly wanted the man to take the "Good" path, though they had no idea if "Good" was good or if "Bad" was bad. Next, look at this image:

Labeling Theory at Work
Which Path Do You Want the Man to Take?

Test subjects shown this image reasoned the man would take the "wrong path" because he is a "racist." Appreciate the power of the stigmatized label of "Racist" to change how you feel about someone even though all you know is that someone has attached a stigmatized label upon the man in the image.

A social science researcher by the name of Howard Becker wrote this about Labeling Theory:

"[S]ocial groups create deviance by making rules whose infraction creates deviance, and by applying those roles to particular people and labeling them as outsiders. From this point of view, deviance is not a quality of the act the person commits, but rather a consequence of the application by other of rules and sanctions to an 'offender.' The deviant is one to whom that label has been successfully applied; deviant behavior is behavior that people so label." [239]

Stigmatized labels have been strategically used by the agents of shadow men to engineer public sentiment in ways that increase shadow men's control. Stigmatized labels have the effect of altering primordial responses to people, objects, political parties, social movements, philosophies, countries, genders, authors, almost anything or anyone.

---

[239] Becker, H. (1963, revised 1973), *Outsiders*. New York: Free Press.

Valenced labels run the gamut of "halo" on one end of the continuum to "verboten" on the other. Anything that has a "halo" valence attached to it is off limits when it comes to criticism. In fact, entities with halo valences are to be revered and only spoken of in a tone of reverence. Madison Avenue uses a lot of "halo advertising." For example, advertisers will take a person to whom a halo label has been attached. That person is then paid to advertise a product. Miraculously, the glow of the halo label bathes the product in that light and, voila, the product takes on a glow all its own and is then more likely to be purchased. Even when the match up is ludicrous, for example, when a movie star advertises a drug he may or may not have taken, that drug sells.

When anyone or anything is labeled "verboten," it means that the entity labeled this way is "fair game" for criticism, attacks, repulsion and rejection. The key to remember when analyzing stigmatized labels is that because of the way man's CNS functions, stigmatized labels shut down perceptual acuity and accurate information processing, both of which are desired outcomes by mind controllers. For Labeling theory to work effectively, it relies upon people who serve as "labelers" and "enforcers." I refer to these people as the PC police.

As with everything shadow men create, their PC police serve as their agents but, for the most part, these agents have absolutely no awareness that they only exist to serve shadow men. PC policemen are comprised of known personality types. Clinically, they tend to be judgmental and angry. They are dogmatic ideologues that score extremely high on psychometric tests that gauge inflexibility and conformity. They tend to be black and white thinkers. But their most dominant characteristics include being groupies and conformists. They love all things trendy. Their identity is inextricably linked to the group for which they have appointed themselves to be the protector of in the form of judge, jury and executioner.

I am now going to share with you a representative sample of some of the most popular stigmatized labels currently in use. Remember that the agents of shadow men *routinely* use race, ethnicity, religion and sexual orientation as a cudgel to engineer consent. This is because identity is a primitive and easily manipulated classification system. They use a very clever trick to insure their success at manipulating labels by attaching a stigmatized label of the same subject matter upon any person who would dare expose their skullduggery. For example, if a reporter dares to expose their manipulation of public sentiment using the stigmatized label "racist," then the person doing the reporting is labeled a "racist." In psychology we call this projection. Expose anti-male gender manipulation and you will be labeled a "misogynist." Expose treason and you are labeled a "conspiracy nut," and so on and so forth. Once you come to understand shadow men's agent's use of projection, it is really quite stunning that it works to well and that it goes right over the heads of the masses.

Never underestimate the power of a stigmatized label attached by the media entertainment complex. Some groups are so powerful that they have their own proprietary stigmatized labels, that shut down ANY criticism, review, analysis or questioning of the group or a person who belongs to that group. Some groups are so powerful that even members of their own group dare not criticize or even gently question anything that challenges their supremacy. What these groups are asserting when they attach their highly charged stigmatized label is that they are infallible. By simply pointing out this indisputable fact, I have put myself at risk to be labeled _____. Note that I won't even use the stigmatized label because the public is so lacking in discernment that were I to use it, the group that owns the label would attach it to me in a florid display of Labeling Theory at work to shut down a threat.

An equally fascinating aspect to how labels are used by vested interests involves the absence of a stigmatized label within a patterned group. For example, look at a listing of the world's most popular religions:

Religion - Major Religions of the World Ranked by Number of Adherents

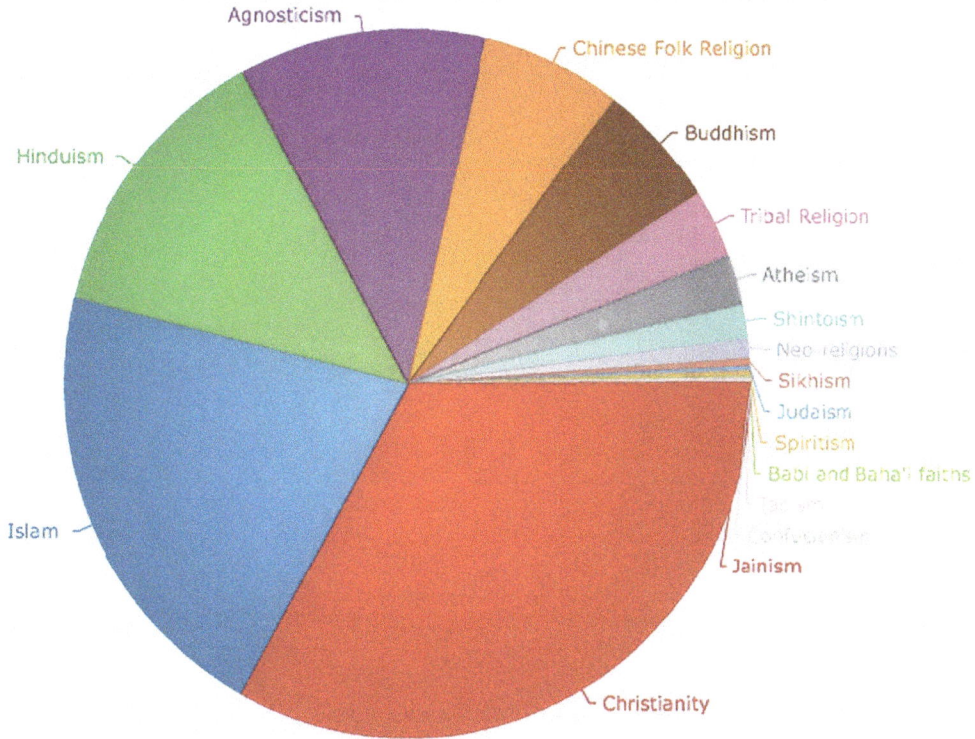

Now take a look at a listing of the five most popular religions and their matching stigmatized labels:

STIGMATIZED LABELS
Religions and their Adherents

Christians/Christianity	Christianophobe?
Muslims/Islam	Islamophobe
Buddhists/Buddhism	?
Hindus/Hinduism	?
Jews/Judaism	Antisemitic

There is no stigmatized label "Christianophobe," though why not has nothing to do with the fact that Christians are not subjected to acts of prejudice, and often times, acts of violence that result in death. Christians are certainly as much, if not more so, the object of abuse, hatred and physical assault, as are those religions that do have their own stigmatized labels.

The power of stigmatized labels depends upon four factors. The first is how easy it is to activate the application of the stigmatized label, e.g., must the violator have made a patently unfair criticism without justification or is the stigmatized label attached to *any* criticism no matter how innocuous or fact based? The second factor is related to the aggressiveness of the enforcement, e.g., is a violation enforced by a "shame on you" or is the violator made to lose his job or made to be a pariah? The third factor is related to the consistency of enforcement, e.g., is every violation met with a swift application of the stigmatized label or is the label applied sporadically? And, the last factor is dependent upon the depth and breadth of the enforcement, e.g., do selective institutions attach the stigmatized label or does every important social institution enforce violations? Ask yourself this, can you identify a label that if attached to a person, rightly or wrongly, would result in that labeled person becoming a social pariah, even going so far as to be ostracized from society? I'll leave it up to you to identify those labels because some labels are so powerful that even the mere mention of them, even in a scholarly book like this, would result in pernicious and vicious retribution.

Now take a look at the most common stigmatized labels related to gender and sexual orientation:

STIGMATIZED LABELS
Gender & Sexual Orientation

Group	Pejorative Label	Stigmatized Label
LGBT Persons	"Fags, Queers"	Homophobe
Heterosexuals	"Breeders"	None

For those of you who may not be familiar with the pejorative term "breeder," it is a term commonly used in the LGBT community to label traditional heterosexual couples. The fact that you may not have heard of this pejorative term is illustrative of the power of stigmatized labels. In the absence of a paired stigmatized label to protect the underlying group, entity, person, country or religion from criticism, the pejoratives used to criticize the underlying entity remain unknown, except to those who use the pejorative term.

The next principle is termed Attribution Theory. [240] Attribution Theory exploits one of man's most predictable information processing patterns. Everything that man perceives arouses his need to understand and explain it in terms of causation. Man is attracted to unitary causes and simple attributions because they are easy to make and satisfy his need to explain the world using linear thinking. People who lack discernment or a higher intelligence embrace single caused, literal and concrete attributions.

In the absence of actually knowing what caused some condition, event or happening, man tends to create causes, i.e., attributions. A classic example of this tendency was early man's attributions for thunder and lighting. The more creative the observer, the more elaborate were early man's attributions that explained the sounds and sights he experienced on a stormy night.

---

[240] Sanderson, Catherine (2010), *Social Psychology*. John Wiley & Sons, Inc.

Causes can be categorized by their varying degrees of complexity. There are a. Necessary Causes, b. Sufficient Causes and c. Necessary and Sufficient Causes.

1. A Necessary Cause is defined this way: If x is a necessary cause of y, then the presence of y necessarily implies the presence of x. The presence of x, however, does not imply that y will occur.

2. A Sufficient Cause is defined this way: If x is a sufficient cause of y, then the presence of x necessarily implies the presence of y. However, another cause z may alternatively cause y. Thus the presence of y does not imply the presence of x.

3. A Necessary and Sufficient Cause is defined this way: If x is both necessary and sufficient cause of y, then when x is present y will occur, though y could be caused by other necessary and sufficient factors other than x.

Causes or attributions can be proximate causes or contributory causes. Proximate causes are sometimes referred to as "But for" causes.

The masses are, for the most part, oblivious to the nature of attributions and causes. Shadow men and their agents, on the other hand, have successfully mastered the manipulation of Attribution Theory and causes. For example, the invention of the "Boogieman" is the perfectly engineered attribution for some condition, event or happening when the shadow men and their agents are the true causes of the condition, event or happening, but want to remain hidden, which is the rule, of course.

Boogiemen are relatively easy to create and can be identified by the fact that they are often covered in stigmatized labels and are modeled after stereotypical characters. Foreign leaders or countries that stand in opposition to shadow men's plans are often transformed from a real person into a caricature villain or country that is the embodiment of evil. If you want to study how the caricatured villain can be used to inflame passions in the masses, pay close attention to professional wrestling's use of archetypal villains and heroes. Keep in mind that while a few professional wrestling fans may enjoy the spectacle, fully aware of the manipulation, the vast majority of them are completely taken in by the socially engineered drama presented to them.

The world stage and the wrestling arena bear many resemblances to one another. Both dramas use stereotypical, engineered images, to inflame the masses to emotionally respond as desired by those in charge of the drama.

Bobby "The Brain" Heenan   Khosrow "The Iron Sheik" Vaziri

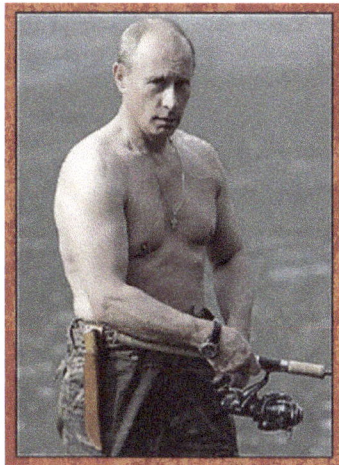

Nickolai "The Russian" Volkoff   **Joseph "The Sheik" Cabibbo**   **Vladmir "The Enemy" Putin**

Saddam Hussein was re-engineered from Hussein "The Good One" and ally of the United States into a caricature befitting a professional wrestling villain. The same re-engineering was done to Libya's late leader Muammar Gaddafi.

(Right) Saddam "The Good One" Hussein. (Left) Secretary of Defense Donald Rumsfeld.

Saddam "The Evil One" Hussein.

(Left) Mu'ammar "The Good One" Gaddafi with (Right) President Barack Obama

Mu'ammar "The Evil One" Gaddafi.

Humans "The Masses" Experiencing the Herd Instinct managed by the WWE.

It was the public relation's arm of the shadow men that transformed Saddam "The Good" Hussein into Saddam "The Evil One" Hussein and Muammar "The Good" Gaddafi into Muammar "The Evil One" Gaddafi.

Another way to manipulate Attribution Theory is to create a "Fall Guy." This person or group becomes the de facto choice for making an attribution when the real perpetrators wish to remain hidden. The art of engineering a "Fall Guy" is a well-practiced Attribution Theory manipulation in high profile assassinations. Remember, shadow men and their proxies are prolific manipulators of Attribution Theory. They relish presenting to the masses both Boogiemen and Fall Guys so that the masses never discover that they are the ones responsible (the true attribution) for acts that if understood as to who, what, why, when and how would not be tolerated by the masses. I hasten to add, however, as the masses continue to be dumbed-down and re-engineered to have even less discernment that they already lack, one day soon shadow men may be able to simply declare who they are and that they are here to commandeer what is left of man's free will.

Human beings apply Attribution Theory very differently to themselves than when they apply it to others. For example, human beings tend to attribute a job promotion offered to them as attributable to their merit or worth. But that same job promotion, when made to a co-worker of the same status as you, will likely be attributed to luck or some other attribution unrelated to merit or worth.

The more heinous the act, condition or event the stronger is the need to make an attribution to a person or group that CONFIRMS preexistent prejudices or beliefs. A good way to understand this dynamic is to reflect upon how it is used in horror films. Attribution theory is used in horror films to misdirect the audience to attribute a killing to an innocent, but suspicious, person. This manipulation of Attribution Theory in film mirrors its use in world affairs and among mind controllers everywhere. First, the director primes the audience to attribute the blame to some suspicious character. Next, the director promotes the projection of trust upon another character. This is someone you would never suspect as having the potential to do anything bad. Then the director reinforces the misdirection with a few vignettes that reinforce his original misdirection.

Finally, and only at the end of the movie, the audience is shocked to learn who really committed the killing. It is the reveal in the movie world that audiences find to be so entertaining.

The only difference between movies and world affairs is that in the real world the directors never, ever, permit the audience to learn the identity of the real killer. If a member of the audience sets about to solve the riddle and name the real shadow men killers in the real world, that person is attacked using any of a number of stigmatized labels or any of a host of other neutralizers that are, as we have learned, designed to stop that person dead in his tracks, sometimes literally, even before he can utter a complete sentence. Pretty clever, wouldn't you say, you conspiracy nut, you denier.

The next PSYOP is termed Cognitive Dissonance Theory. Leon Festinger was first to identify this psychological principle in 1957. [241] Its use as a PSYOP was recognized soon after Festinger first published his work in the late 1950's. Members of Bilderberg were ecstatic when Dr. Festinger published his work in 1957. They lost no time hiring their own mind controllers to develop Festinger's theory into a weapon for their use. Cognitive Dissonance captures man's universal need to achieve balance and equilibrium, that is, to make two things consonant with one another in his CNS. The motivation to achieve balance is so strong that ANY assertion that any two things, people, cultures or virtually anything, are different, i.e., better than the other, creates an unpleasant emotional state. Balance and equilibrium is fascinating because nature seldom, if ever, makes any two things to be identical, including snowflakes and even identical twins. In the case of identical twins, some are mono-chorionic and some are di-chorionic. It is a fact that nature both abhors a vacuum and sameness when comparing almost any two of anything. Bilderberg members plotted the dissolution of Europe's unique cultures, currency and identity into what we now call the European Union using, in part, Festinger's Cognitive Dissonance Theory. It was simply dissonant to have countries like Germany and Greece, for example, that were so dissonant with one another when it came to productivity and solvency. The EU was plotted to resolve the dissonance.

Multiculturalism is rooted in the hypnotic allure and power of convenient equilibrium. In previous writings, I have elaborated upon something I named, "convenient equilibrium." It is "convenient" because people who are wedded to convenient equilibrium only experience distress when one of their pet people, cherished beliefs or sacred cows is characterized as the lesser, the worse or the bad in a comparative context. If it is a person, place, thing or ideology that challenges their views, these same people relish the disequilibrium, thus it is a *convenient* and expedient insistence upon equilibrium.

If two things are discordant or incongruent with one another, then man unconsciously modifies his feelings or attitudes about one of the entities that is most amenable to modification in order to resolve the dissonance. Let me give you a few examples, and in the process, demonstrate how the principles we've learned thus far integrate with one another.

Let's say I'm negotiating the price of a car I really want. At some point in the negotiation I realize that I just can't afford the car and will never be able to buy it. This situation is dissonant, i.e., I want the car but I cannot have it. What occurs next is an example of how cognitive dissonance resolves the incongruity between my wants versus reality. Remarkably, more often than not, I come to feel that I never really wanted the car in the first place. And that little slight of hand the mind unconsciously pulls on itself resolves the dissonance. You see, not ever wanting the car and not being able to buy it are perfectly consonant. Do I really believe I never wanted the car? Yes. If you

---

[241] Festinger, L. (1957). *A Theory of Cognitive Dissonance*. California: Stanford University Press.

are asking yourself if this scenario about the car is similar to the "sour grapes" phenomenon, you'd be correct.

Let's use a theoretical example of something bad that can happen to nation states. Treason is an act of betrayal by an elected or appointed leader. Here is a formal definition of treason:

> treason | ˈtrēzən | noun (also high treason) the crime of betraying one's country, esp. by attempting to kill the sovereign or overthrow the government: they were convicted of treason.

Acts of treason, if recognized as such, naturally create a significant amount of cognitive dissonance. Any person, as a caretaker for the Constitution of the United States, who betrays that role, creates a cognitive dissonance in a nation's citizenry that results in a strong drive state to restore equilibrium. Presidents, for example, take an oath to uphold the Constitution while placing their hand on the Holy Bible. The mere accusation of treason creates tremendous disequilibrium or cognitive dissonance in most people. And as I have documented, the mind goes into overdrive in order to restore equilibrium. How is equilibrium restored? By altering that which is most easily modified and by changing that which is least stressful. Often times the first cognitive mechanism employed to restore consonance to a condition and/or allegation of treason is to engage the defense mechanism of denial. "It can't be true." If it can't possibly be true, the dissonance will resolve. Second, the mind will generate excuses or explanations that provide attributions for the otherwise treasonous behavior that disproves treason. Such excuses for the person guilty of treason may be incompetence, playing politics, naiveté or bad luck. By creating, then employing, these non-treasonous attributions the dissonance is resolved. Third, any person who would dare to allege treason is discredited, using Labeling theory (Conspiracy nut, Hater, Racist, Head Case, Paranoid, Misogynist, Anti-Semite, etc.). The act of attaching a stigmatized label to the accuser will resolve the dissonance because "Who could ever believe such a person?"

The underlying dynamic in all of these mental gymnastics is that to acknowledge treason, as treason, causes so much debilitating fear and anxiety in the discernment challenged masses and among politicians, as well, that is, cognitive dissonance with cherished beliefs, that these collective minds go into overdrive in order to free those minds from debilitating fear and anxiety. [242] Imagine if mind controllers knew about these tendencies? Now accept my word that they do, and have for a very long time. In fact, they rely upon these and other perceptual and cognitive defects in man to work exactly as I have described in order for their agents to engage in treasonous behavior. You see, the fault does not belong to those who commit treason or are treasonous, per se; the problem resides in the faulty nature of mankind's discernment. America's founders gave the masses and their representatives all the tools necessary to identify, roust out and then punish treason. What America's founders did not factor into their metric was the yet to be created science of weaponized psychology and a population that had been biopsychosocially gelded and dumbed-down to the point of incompetency.

The next psychological principle is Commitment. Being committed to someone or something modifies our perceptual acuity and information processing functions. Commitment is a key social indoctrination tool that makes its first formal appearance in institutions of education. Students may think that they are simply wearing school colors or merely rooting for their school's team, but what is really going on is the conditioning of malleable minds to become familiar with the good feelings associated with commitment, i.e., belonging and group conformity.

---

[242] Please refer to Aesop's Fable: "The Fox and the Grapes."

To understand commitment one must understand group identities and how they work. By asking this simple question: "Who are you?" The responder will reveal their group identity. For example, once you learn the responder's name and repeat the question, what typically follows is a long list of group identities. Popular responses include: 1. I am a man, 2. I am a woman, 3. I am an American, 4. I'm an Iowan (state identity), 5. I am a veteran, 6. I am a good person, 7. I am a European (country identity), 8. I am a progressive (political party identity), 9. I am a husband/wife, and so on and so forth. The answers given by the responder give the questioner insight into the responder's commitment and identity.

Loyalty is a behavior that measures the degree and strength of commitment. Blind loyalty is a measure of the strength of commitment. Blind loyalty is so strong that it cannot be changed, even when that to which one is blindly loyal is misguided or misplaced. Auto manufacturers have spent billions of dollars engineering blind loyalty in their customers. This engineering effort has paid off handsomely for auto manufacturers and is evidenced by the fact that even when their customers are killed because of defects, the result of cost-cutting cheapness and a wanton disregard for their customers, loyal customers keep coming back to their showroom. This is but one example of how blind commitment can promote negligence on the part of those to whom the commitment is given.

When it comes to commitment to nation states, the words of Carl Schurz, former Secretary of the Interior, who served during the latter part of the 19th century, are often quoted to support the *virtue* of blind commitment:

"My country, right or wrong."

But what many people do not realize is that this quote is not the entire quote and has been conveniently taken out of context by the PR agents for shadow men, to wit:

"My country, right or wrong; if right, to be kept right; and if wrong, to be set right."[243]

As we have thoroughly documented, commitment is a waning virtue when it comes to marriage in America. Not only are fewer people committing to marriage but when they do commit, approximately 50% of the time the commitment is not kept as evidenced by the divorce rate.

Mind control artists can undermine commitment in any number of ways. One of the most popular PSYOPs is to de-stigmatize the abrogation of commitment. For instance, in the 1950's if people lived together, without a marriage commitment, the couple was described as, "shacking up." Today, a similar couple would face no stigma for cohabiting without a marriage commitment. This last point illustrates how removing a stigmatized label can be as powerful as attaching a stigmatized label.

Another approach to undermining commitment is to popularize behaviors that are anathema to commitment. For example, as we covered in more detail earlier in this book, if my goal is the eradication of traditional marriage, PR agents in Hollywood and New York can glamorize the single lifestyle, while portraying committed relationships as boring, troubled and labor intensive. Because of man's "monkey see, monkey do" defect and mankind's compulsion to be popular and conform to that which is fashionable and trendy, it doesn't take very long to socially engineer or destroy commitment in whatever direction serves ruling shadow men's whims and fancies.

The psychological principles we have covered thus far lend themselves very nicely for use as PSYOPs in service to socially engineering thoughts, feelings and behaviors. But there is one exception and that one psychological principle is termed Reactance Theory. [244] Before I formally

---

243 Schurz, Carl, remarks in the Senate, February 29, 1872, The Congressional Globe, vol. 45, p. 1287.
244 Brehm, J. W. (1966), *A theory of psychological reactance*, New York: Academic Press.

define Reactance Theory, I am going to tell you a true story. The story is on point because, as you will learn, Reactance Theory applies to not only man, but other species as well.

During my graduate studies I had a two cats that were fast friends. I found Andy and Thomas on the street and I raised them from the time they were kittens. My apartment at the time had a 3rd floor small balcony that looked out upon a wooded area. The balcony was separated from the living room by a sliding glass door.

Like clockwork, every night at about 11:00 P.M., Andy and Thomas would do what I called "night watch." They would go out and sit on a bench and look down upon the nightlife as it scurried around in the wooded area. While Andy and Thomas were night watching, I could keep an eye on them from the living room.

One night there was a chill in the air and I went over to close the sliding glass door. As soon as I closed the door, Andy and Thomas jumped down from their perch and put their faces against the door and looked in at me. I thought to myself, "the boys must be done night watching." So I opened the door to let them in. No sooner had I cracked the door open than the brothers turned around and jumped back onto their perches and began night watching again. I said to myself, OK, I guess the brothers changed their mind. At which point I closed the door again to keep out the chill and went back to whatever it was I was doing. Once again, just like before, down they jumped and looked in at me through the closed door. I said, "Hey guys, make up your mind." I opened the door and right back on their perch they jumped. I told you this story because it is a perfect operational definition of how Reactance Theory works.

You see, human beings and, as you have learned from Andy and Thomas, other species, have an innate motivation to protect their freedom of choice. Deny the perception of freedom of choice and "reactance" is aroused which, as you saw demonstrated by Andy and Thomas, makes us do things to protect our freedom of choice.

Andy and Thomas did not want to come in from their night watch perch, but they were highly motivated to **maintain their freedom of choice to come in should they so desire, not that they wanted to come in, mind you, when they would press their little faces against the sliding glass door. Andy and Thomas simply wanted me to keep their options open and not deny them their** freedom of choice.

Reverse psychology is an elementary trigger of reactance. In a classic example of reverse psychology, if you want someone to go into a room, tell them they are forbidden to go into that room. Even though the person may have never thought about going into the forbidden room, once you tell them they can't go in, they will develop a desire to go in, all because of Reactance Theory.

Perhaps you can see how Reactance Theory is a big stumbling block to shadow men and their agents who, by constitution and design, habitually deny the masses their freedom of choice. So how do mind control artists maneuver around Reactance Theory? The answer is three fold, 1. Creeping encroachment, 2. Promise safety and security and 3. Keep your efforts hidden to deny freedom by using cloaking mechanisms. This book, *Shadow Men*, is an exposé designed, in part, to remove shadow men's cloaking mechanisms.

Reflect upon the story about the frog in the pot because it will serve you well when it comes to understanding creeping encroachment. If you place a frog in a pot of cool water and ever so slightly continually increase the temperature of the water, you will boil the frog alive. If, of the other hand, you throw the frog into a pot of boiling water he may very well jump out and escape. Shadow men continually encroach upon the masses' freedoms in incremental steps until one day they have none left.

Shadow men know that Reactance Theory is their mortal enemy. I began this book by telling you that my readers are likely to have an exaggerated need to exercise their free will. Technically, this means that my readers are likely to have a particularly strong reactance drive state mechanism. This means that not only is the mechanism strong but it also implies that their reactance triggers are "hair triggers." The Gadsden Flag, for example, was created by individuals who possessed a particularly strong reactance drive-state mechanism.

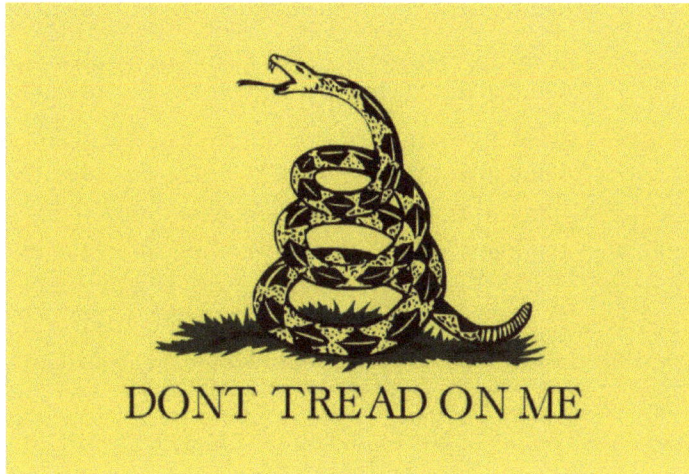

The Gadsden Flag.

The Gadsden flag is named after American General Christopher Gadsden. General Gadsden designed it in 1775 to rally the troops for the American Revolution. The Gadsden Flag has been used by the Continental Marines and any number of American patriot groups who possess a particularly strong reactance drive mechanism. General Gadsden, like most if not all of his fellow patriots, were incensed at the British who habitually denied colonists their freedoms. The Gadsden Flag may just as well have been named the "Reactance Flag."

It takes an equally strong or stronger drive state to nullify or make people hold in abeyance their reactance drive mechanism. Primitive drive states like hunger and thirst will suppress reactance, but the equalizing effect only lasts as long as it takes to satiate hunger and thirst. Greed can encourage any number of people to overcome their reactance drive state. For example, Ponzi schemes work because the marks are willing to give their life savings over to someone who promises greater wealth in return for the loss of freedom of control over their money. But Ponzi schemes eventually fail and control is lost. Of all the PSYOPs that can nullify reactance drive states, the most reliable and manageable is our old friend fear.

Nascent shadow men were the first to use fear against the masses and they and their agents are still using it today. Fear is a primitive drive state that originates in man's brain stem. Fear is as primordial as any drive state in any living creature. Flight or Fight, for example, is an autonomic nervous system mediated response to fear.

Weaponized fear is a PSYOP that is comprised of a 'one-two punch." The first punch is the creation of fear. The second part of the PSYOP is to offer salvation, if only the mark does this or that, the engineered fear will fade. As I referenced earlier, the Trojan-Horse part of this PSYOP means that the salvation component of the equation just happens to encourage victims to give up their Constitutionally protected or God given freedoms. In earlier times it was money, sex, food or an animal or human sacrifice. If you are living in other parts of the world, the process is essentially the same but in America our founders knew about this devious PSYOP and similar PSYOPs and, as a result, gave future citizens a layer of protection and wrote those protections into America's Constitution, particularly, the first 10 amendments to the Constitution known as the Bill of Rights.

Napoleon's Axiom III is related to the dynamics of fear-based PSYOPs:

> **"The greater the engineered and/or cultivated fear, the greater the encroachment of freedom intended."**

Fear generating events can be created and cultivated quite easily and without much effort or sophistication. All I have to do is to sell the masses (very easy to do) on the notion that the world is facing a horrendous natural disaster (the survival of the earth, itself, for example) unless they hand over resources, freedom, money and their peace of mind. The act of handing over resources, freedom and money provides some measure of salvation for the fearful masses. Because fear is a brainstem mediated emotion, if someone (like me) dares to question either the validity, the nature of the fear or the effectiveness of the salvation offered to ameliorate the fear, fearful men among the masses will behave irrationally, as though it is me who is causing their fear by questioning its validity and false nature. The curators of this fear will respond to those who would undermine their devious PSYOP with stigmatized labels, e.g., "denier." I trust that the reader is stunned when he/she considers the fact that this modern day strategy involving the survival of the earth, itself, is EXACTLY the same one used by the very first shadow men.

Why is modern man so easily frightened? Modern man has been conditioned, somewhat like our ancient ancestors, to fear the intangible and that which we do not understand. Intangible fears are very easily created by manipulation of the virtual world. Sources of fear in the objective world are much easier to avoid. Ancient man, for example, learned to avoid tangible fear and find a safe haven. He stayed away from watering holes at dusk, he did not lazily fish in bodies of water filled with alligators and he learned that a fire nurtured to stay lit all night kept away predators.

Intangible and amorphous fears created in the virtual world are a difference in kind when compared to tangible fears. Fear that the sun may not come up in the morning or move higher in the sky after a long winter or fear of an eclipse or rising tides that flood birthing caves, these are fears that create free floating anxiety. Fears that are amorphous, and potentially cataclysmic and that can appear suddenly are the best fears to cultivate if you are agents of shadow men.

Modern man cannot find a *certain* safe haven from terrorism, climate change, aka, global warming, unseen rogue viruses, nuclear weapons or whatever amorphous fear mind control artists choose to cultivate in the virtual world. Be assured, however, that the overseers will offer salvation that may take the form of Big Brother intrusions, carbon credits or whatever shadow men have put on their wish list. But the game is always the same; the masses are manipulated to transfer to shadow men their independence, freedoms and their material wealth.

Free floating fear is the shadow man's favorite kind of fear to cultivate because it reduces man's reactance drive state and makes him receptive to anything that will reduce the fear. Free-floating fear is defined as an amorphous, intangible, ever-present anxiety provoking state of mind. It is an existential fear. Psychotropic prescriptions and many over the counter, including illegal substances, serve as anxiety reducing medications that owe their popularity to free floating fear and anxiety, much of which has been purposefully created by the agents of shadow men.

The plan is devious, extremely effective and brilliant in a perverse sense. Cultivate free-floating fear in the masses for which no certain safe haven can ever be found. Next, offer salvation for man's free-floating fear in the form of Big-Brother or Big-Sis "protections" that result in the masses willingly giving up many of their rights guaranteed by the Constitution in trade for a *sense* of relative safety. Make available psychotropic medications that numb modern man's perceptual acuity while nullifying his reactance drive motivation. Promote and make popular recreational mind altering substances that mellow an otherwise uneasy population. Continue this pattern of fear>salvation>control, followed by more fear>more salvation>control, until the trendy masses are psychologically corralled like cattle and their survival instincts have been watered down or completely nullified through conditioning and drugs. This template for control has been around since the first nascent shadow men warned the masses that unless they did what they were told to do the winter sun may never return to its place of strength in the sky as it did last summer.

Shadow men have made it their business to psychoanalyze the masses. The Ph.D. agents of shadow men have been given unlimited resources over the years to investigate then deploy sophisticated PSYOPs in service to helping their clients achieve their goals. The contest between shadow men and the masses isn't a fair match, even though the masses have the numerical advantage. What is it about shadow men and their agents that give them such an unfair advantage in this battle of wits with the masses? The answer is to be found in neuroscience, specifically, the information processing function of the average man versus that of shadow men and, in particular, shadow men agents.

This next section may well be the most troubling to the reader because no man or woman wants to hear that they are simply not as smart as are those who control them. Think of it this way, you probably have no problem accepting the fact that you can't run the 100 meters as fast as the current Olympic record holder. You can probably accept that in a one-on-one match-up with Lebron James or the now retired Michael Jordan, that you would lose or that you would lose a boxing match with the current heavy weight champion of the world. But isn't it fascinating that the victims of shadow men are resistant to drawing the same conclusion about who would win when it comes to a contest involving intelligence? The reason people have trouble with this has to do with the fact that, as I covered in my chapter Google IQ™, at least two generations of Americans have been brainwashed to believe that intelligence has nothing to do with genetics and innate talent, but everything to do with psychology and environment. I'm sorry, the genetics and special talent that makes it possible to run the hundred meters in world record time or dunk a basketball does not stop at the neck.

You've been lied to, once again. Why lie about this subject? If I can convince the masses that they are all budding geniuses, I can exploit the fact that the vast majority of people will be average. While there is absolutely nothing wrong or bad if you are average, the person inculcated with artificially high self- esteem, who has been brainwashed that underneath all of their average performance they are really a genius, then those people will identify social injustice (since it can't be genetics) as the root cause for why they are not as rich, smart and successful as those people who possess those things.

To make this PSYOP perfect, shadow men persuaded the average man that the ONLY reason rich, smart and successful people are those things is because of their privilege or, to say it another way, because YOU, the genius who was denied his rightful place, have been exploited by those who are more successful, smart, etc. All of these dynamics have the effect of encouraging average people to give over power to shadow men and the social justice promising governments secretly controlled by shadow men.

68% of all men on earth process information in like patterns when it comes to their perceptual acuity, ability to comprehend and discernment. Statistically speaking, we label these people "average." Average is merely a statistical term that describes where 68% of the population will fit within the corpus of mankind, one standard deviation above or below the mean. **84% of all people fall within the average or below-average range of perceptual acuity, discernment and ability**

to comprehend the world around them, that is, Intelligence. This leaves 16% of all people on earth that fall in the higher range of perceptual acuity and ability to comprehend. Of those 16%, **only the top 2% include the agents of shadow men.**

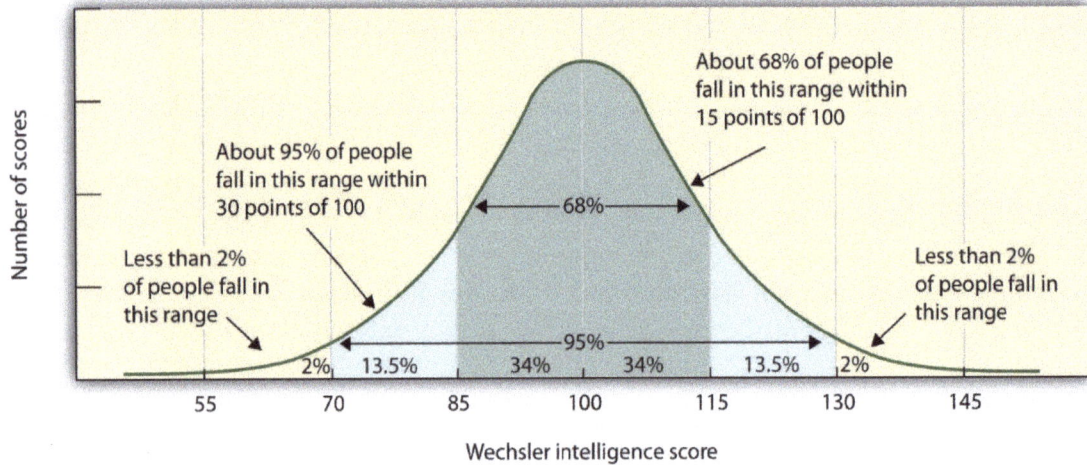

As the reader can see from the immediately preceding distribution of Wechsler deviation intelligence scores, the average or nominal IQ on the Wechsler Adult Intelligence Scale, throughout much of the 20th century, included a range from 90 to 110, with a mean of 100. But scores are changing, and not for the better. Studies have demonstrated that Western IQ's have dropped a whopping 14 points since the Victorian Era to the present (2014). [245] [246] A 14-point reduction on the Wechsler Scale amounts to a full standard deviation in diminution in IQ. In 2011 the mean IQ score had dropped from 100 to 88.5. Neuropsychologists have documented that the ability to discern patterns, comprehend metaphors and understand the overriding principles embedded into fact patterns are greatly diminished, if not utterly destroyed, when intelligence drops 14 points below 100. In the past, a 100 IQ person, that is, an average person, could be taught to discern overriding principles and constructs embedded within any communication. I know because I have done it. But today, given the lowered intelligence of the masses, concepts such as underlying principles and the discernment of patterns within the whole are simply beyond their intellectual ability. Consider for a moment that the entire Constitution of the United States is a document that articulates underlying principles. Earlier in this book we used the analogy of how the physics that regulate the behavior of an 18th century wagon wheel are exactly the same physics that govern the behavior of a Formula One Racer's wheel. With each point drop in IQ below 100, that analogy between the wagon wheel and a Formula One Racer's wheel will become harder and harder to comprehend until, at some point, it may as well be gibberish.

I ask the reader to reflect upon how shadow men's social engineering of the mating habits of the masses has resulted in the diminution of their intelligence. Whether it was the reduction in the number of children they gave birth to or who women chose to mate with or how certain cultural

---

[245] Huffington Post. *People Getting Dumber? Human Intelligence Has Declined Since Victorian Era, Research Suggests.* By: Macrina Cooper-White, May 22, 2013.
[246] Itzkoff, Seymour W. (1994), The Decline of Intelligence in America: A Strategy for Renewal. Praeger Publishers, Westport, CT.

ideologies stifle the development of intelligence, even including IQ lowering chemicals in our drinking water and food, the end result is exactly what shadow men and their agents wanted—a more supplicant, that is, dumbed down populace. For a review of some of the biopsychosocial factors involved in variations in intelligence, please see here: [247]

Shadow men and their agent's perceptual acuity and ability to comprehend represent a difference in kind when compared to how the vast majority of people perceive, discern and comprehend the world around them. To be sure, shadow men are NOT as intelligent these days when compared to their ancestors or the men and women they hire to carry out their mind control PSYOPs. With regard to the agents of shadow men, many are purposefully chosen because they are exceptionally intelligent. And as far as shadow men's ancestors, those men were exceptional, both in terms of IQ and ruthless cunning, in order to create their power and wealth from nothing.

As we have demonstrated, the intellectual chasm between shadow men's agents and the masses is growing larger. If we were to analogize perceptual acuity and comprehension to how fast an animal can run, then comparing shadow men and their agents to 84% of the population of the United States that comprise average or below average intelligence, would be like comparing a Cheetah to a groundhog in a test of speed and agility. Of all the differences in the cognitive horsepower between shadow men, their agents and the masses, one of the most important distinctions is the difference between "literal and concrete" versus "metaphoric" or non-linear thinking.

Literal and concrete thinking works well when manipulating the material world. It works well in situations where what to do and how to do it have already been figured out by someone more intelligent. Literal and concrete thinkers put things together, build things, arrange things, prepare recipes, etc.

When literal and concrete thinkers interact (not merely read from a teleprompter or follow the directions of others) with words, i.e., the virtual world, they employ their material world acuity and comprehension skills. So if I say, for example, "Shallow brooks are noisy," the literal and concrete thinker is likely to interpret that sentence as meaning: "When a brook is shallow or not very deep it tends to make more noise as the water flows." Metaphoric thinkers will interpret that same sentence in a completely different way, as: "People who lack depth tend to prattle on and on and are loud."

Let's refer to a passage in the Christian Bible that will help us to draw a clear distinction between literal and concrete versus metaphoric thinking. Keep in mind I'm drawing these cognitive distinctions between shadow men and their agents with the average man so that the reader may better understand how their overlords process information and how they have come to dominate the world. I'm going to use this passage from the Book of Mark 16: 17-18 to make a point about cognitive processing:

> *"And these signs will accompany those who believe: In my name they will cast out demons; they will speak in new tongues; they will pick up serpents with their hands; and if they drink any deadly poison, it will not hurt them; they will lay their hands on the sick, and they will recover."*

The literal and concrete thinker's perceptual acuity and information processing encourage him to interpret the word "serpents" as an actual animal, e.g., a snake. When the average man or woman reads the word "demons" he/she will most likely, without knowing it, match that word with images of demons made popular by Dante, in his classic poem, "Dante's Inferno," though the literal and

---

[247] Brighter Brains. *PreNatal & Natal IQ Factors - damaged before your born, or as you're delivered.* By: Hank Pellissier, July 16, 2013.

concrete thinker may never have read Dante's Inferno. The average person will apply his literal and concrete thinking to the rest of the passage and may take from it a mélange of foreboding mental images of drinking arsenic and/or a TV Evangelist's laying on of hands.

We know that some literal and concrete thinkers actually practice "snake handling" as they believe is encouraged by this Biblical passage. In this ritualistic practice, venomous snakes are held while the believer dances around with the snake or snakes in various poses. The person engaged in "snake handling" will often speak gibberish, or "in tongues," while dancing with the venomous snake. This deadly serious practice has resulted in numerous deaths, to wit:

> "A Kentucky pastor who co-starred in the TV show Snake Salvation has died of a snakebite. Emergency personnel received a call Saturday night that someone at a church, Full Gospel Tabernacle in Jesus Name, had suffered a snakebite, Middlesboro Police Chief Jeff Sharpe said in a statement. He said an ambulance crew went to the church, but the Rev. Jamie Coots had left. The crew went to Coots' home and found him suffering from a bite to the hand."[248]

A person who employs metaphoric perceptual acuity, comprehension and 3D discernment, when reading Mark 16: 17-18, will certainly grasp the literal and concrete meaning but will also generate a much richer and fuller understanding that was written into the passage.

For example, Mark 16: 17-18 communicates the notion that people who are close with God and doing his work will be recognizable if you pay close attention to their behavior. This passage predicts that lots of people will tell you they are Godly but you'll be able to tell the difference between posers and the Godly man or woman by the following list of cues. For one thing, Godly men have the ability to ward off evil (demons). Bad people (demons) are no match for truly righteous men. Godly men and women will talk about things and see the world in a way that at first may be unintelligible to you (tongues). Godly men and women are very powerful, so much so that if they can engage evil in battle (drink the poison) they will come out the winner. People who are suffering will get better by simply being around these Godly men and women because of their positive life force.

The metaphoric thinker's ability to comprehend the beauty, nuanced meaning and wisdom of this Biblical passage from Mark is starkly different than the literal and concrete thinker's understanding. It is the difference between chess and checkers, with the literal and concrete thinker playing checkers-and not very well at that. If you are a linear thinker, you will undoubtedly reject the above referenced 3D analysis of this particular Biblical passage that is because it is functionally invisible to you. It is not a coincidence that those who employ a literal interpretation of the Bible do not possess the cognitive ability to use non-linear thinking and information processing. Think of it this way, human beings cannot see the ultra violet (UV) spectrum of light. Imagine if all the PSYOPs I've described throughout this book were delivered within the UV spectrum. They would be invisible to you but that does not mean you will not be burned by this invisible light.

The psychological weapons so effectively used against 84% of the masses were written and designed using strategies that **can only be understood and, therefore, neutralized** using non-linear information processing and related strategies and tactics. When linear thinking people do get a sense that something is not right or "sketchy" about any given event or policy, these same people typically confront the agents of shadow men using linear thinking based retorts or counter-measures. Of course, that situation is not unlike trying to smack or catch something you cannot see.

---

[248] USA Today. (2014). *Reality show snake handler dies from snakebite.* By John Bacon. February 17.

Shadow men's PSYOPs are invariably interpreted and then countered by average men and their pundits using the only tools they have available to them, i.e., literal and concrete, linear information processing counter measures. This state of affairs is similar to the situation that occurs when checkers players are tasked with comprehending chess, they invariably apply their checkers player's way of thinking to the chessboard and chessmaster. It is a foregone conclusion who will win this battle. Even other chessmasters sometimes fail to comprehend the meaning of any one move on the chessboard taken by their opponent, that is, until the final move of checkmate is made. Then, and only then, does the chessmaster's seemingly innocuous moves reveal themselves for what they were designed to do all along. Now imagine if you are a checkers player trying to decipher then defeat a grandmaster's chess moves.

Meta-communication PSYOPs comprise a very big part of the mind control armamentarium of shadow men. Meta-communications are an ever-present part of PSYOPs and generally go right over the head of linear information processing people, i.e., 84% of all men and women. Here is a very simple example of a meta-communication.

Let's say I am a politician and I intend to deliver a speech promoting gun control legislation. The speech has been written and it has been loaded into the teleprompter. All that is required now is for the politician to read the speech. Before the speech is read, however, the politician's mind control artists construct the meta-communication components of the speech. One classic meta-communication of a gun control speech includes placing the politician in a setting where the dominant colors are red, white and blue. Behind the politician you'll likely see an audience comprised of police officers dressed in their formal "blues," with children sitting next to the police officers. Women who look like single mothers, teachers and grandmothers taken from traditional Americana stereotypes, including certain racial groups, fill the rest of the seats. This genre of speech is high drama and chocked full of meta-communication targeting gullible voters.

You can be sure that the pundits who analyze this politician's speech will limit their review to the words programmed into the politician's teleprompter, not the most important part of the drama, i.e., the meta-communication components. One of the reasons that PR agents for shadow men wouldn't dare decipher meta communication manipulation for their audience is that each and every "news" program relies upon meta communication manipulation to manage their audience's attitudes and behavior. Yes, it is true; the fox has been tasked with guarding the hen house.

Recall that the PR agents for shadow men purposefully choose pundits, cable hosts, "anchors" who are like their audience to occupy the seats of every network and cable program. They do this because program directors know that the masses feel more comfortable watching and listening to people like them. Many of the most popular pundits, network and cable hosts, for example, were recruited from the trade professions where, before becoming talk show hosts, they spent many years using linear, literal and concrete information processing strategies manipulating objects by building or putting things together, e.g., installing drywall, working as a contractor, etc. PR agents for shadow men recruit newsreaders and pundits who look most like the people who live in what the self anointed elite refer to as: the "fly over states. " Women newsreaders are often chosen because they are pretty and have nice legs and attractive breasts. The result is that political punditry and "anchoring" is often very much like the blind leading the blind or where the agents of shadow men, in the guise of political pundits, shape and mold voter's opinions while feigning objective analysis. It is not real folks. It is concocted drama where the thespians and writers actually believe they are the characters they play.

This ruse works so well that when a front man anchor is caught lying, the masses lose faith in the on air avatar, not the network executives and their shadow men owners and overlords, as though it was the "anchor" who actually generated the content that he reads from the teleprompter on the nightly news. The problem is not the veracity of the "anchor" because all he ever does, regardless of whether or not he lies or not, is pose for the camera and read what he is told to read in order to manipulate the attitudes and behavior of the masses. He is merely an image, an avatar, programmed to dupe the masses speaking and mugging his overlord's propaganda.

Almost without exception, literal and concrete thinkers perceive analyses, like what I have just presented, as a "put down" or condescending. Of course, believing that would resolve the dissonance and understandable anxiety that would follow from accepting the truth as I have presented it here. All of us need and should be thankful for people who have honed literal and concrete thinking and building skills. However, and this is the salient point, when engaging the three-dimensional chess battle between the masses and the agents of shadow men, literal and concrete acuity and comprehension is like pitting a house cat against an African lion in a death match. The masses' denial of this fact, as demonstrated by the Dunning-Kruger effect, is one of the key factors that explain why shadow men and their agents have been so successful over the years manipulating the masses. Not only are the masses ignorant of what they are ignorant of, but also, they mistake their ignorance for genius.

So, are literal and concrete thinkers doomed? The answer is not necessarily. But realize this, it will take a non-literal and concrete thinker who has not succumbed to the bribery of shadow men to free the masses from their cognitive prison. It will then take a person who WANTS to free themselves from the shackles of their own mind before things change. The vast-majority of people who know how to speak the language of shadow men work for and are loyal to shadow men. Shadow men are generous employers while the masses seldom have anything to offer those who would assist them with anything but grief. My fortune was made working for the old guard of shadow men. I doubt if I would or could have ever written this book if that was not true. I know of no other person in my situation who could or would write a book like this.

I recommend training your brain so as to disrupt its customary pattern of linear information processing. Brains have a remarkable ability to bend, adapt and form new and different types of information processing pathways. I have actually done this with literal and concrete thinkers. This book, Shadow Men is, in part, a meta-communication that has the ability to move the literal and concrete thinker to a more metaphoric modality of thinking, and thus, free the reader from his victimhood. **But brains will not change unless they are put under pressure and challenged. People will not change until and unless they have concluded, deep in their soul, that they must change or they will perish.**

Remember the distinction I made earlier between Assimilation, on the one hand, and Adaptation, on the other? Literal and concrete thinkers are habitual assimilators. This is why if you pay close attention to pundits, they always repeat the same canned phrases, questions and after watching them work for a while you'll begin to notice that one show is like all the others. That behavior is a symptom of habitual assimilation.

So how do we challenge our brains? I suggest that the reader, who desires to free themselves from the shackles of literal and concrete thinking, begin by studying Aesop's Fables. They are readily available for free on the net. If you are a literal and concrete thinker you probably think that Aesop wrote a lot about animals, he did not. Take a look at this listing of Aesop's Fables:

The Frogs & the Ox
Belling the Cat
The Town Mouse & the Country Mouse

The Fox & the Grapes
The Wolf & the Crane
The Lion & the Mouse
The Gnat & the Bull
The Plane Tree
The Owl & the Grasshopper
The Oak & the Reeds
The Crow & the Pitcher
The Two Goats
The Wild Boar & the Fox
The Heron
The Fox & the Stork
The Stag & His Reflection
The Cock & the Fox
The Fox & the Goat
The Fox & the Leopard
The Frog & the Mouse
The Wolf in Sheep's Clothing
The Eagle & the Beatle
The Mother & the Wolf
The Hare & the Tortoise
The Dog & His Reflection
The Fox & the Crow
The Ant & the Dove
The Man & the Satyr
The Hare & His Ears
The Fisherman & the Little Fish
The Wolf & the Kid
The Tortoise & the Ducks
The Young Crab & His Mother
The Dog, the Cock, & the Fox
The Eagle & the Jackdaw
The Boy & the Filberts
Hercules & the Wagoner
The Kid & the Wolf
The Bundle of Sticks
The Ass & His Driver
The Oxen & the Wheels
The Shepherd Boy & the Wolf
The Farmer & the Stork
The Sheep & the Pig
The Travelers & the Purse
The Lion & the Ass
The Frogs Who Wished for a King
The Wolf & His Shadow
The Rat & the Elephant

The Boys & the Frogs
The Ants & the Grasshopper
The Ass Carrying the Image
A Raven & a Swan
The Ass & the Load of Salt
The Lion & the Gnat
The Leap at Rhodes
The Cock & the Jewel
The Monkey & the Camel
The Ass, the Fox, & the Lion
The Birds, the Beasts, & the Bat
The Lion, the Bear, & the Fox
The Wolf & the Lamb
The Wolf & the Sheep
The Hares & the Frogs
The Travelers & the Sea
The Wolf & the Lion
The Peacock
The Mice & the Weasels
The Wolf & the Lean Dog
The Fox & the Lion
The Dog & his Master's Dinner
The Vain JackDaw & his Borrowed Feathers
The Monkey & the Dolphin
The Wolf & the Ass
The Monkey & the Cat
The Dogs & the Fox
The Dogs & the Hides
The Rabbit, the Weasel, & the Cat
The Bear & the Bees
The Dog in the Manger
The Wolf & the Goat
The Ass & the Grasshoppers
The Mule
The Cat, the Cock, & the Young Mouse
The Wolf & the Shepherd
The Peacock & the Crane
The Farmer & the Cranes
The Farmer & His Sons
The Two Pots
The Goose & the Golden Egg
The Fighting Bulls & the Frog
The Mouse & the Weasel
The Farmer & the Snake
The Sick Stag
The Goatherd & the Wild Goats

The Spendthrift & the Swallow
The Cat & the Birds
The Dog & the Oyster
The Astrologer
Three Bullocks & a Lion
Mercury & the Woodman
The Fox & the Crab
The Serpent & the Eagle
The Bull & the Goat
The Old Lion & the Fox
The Man & the Lion
The Ass & the Lap Dog
The Milkmaid & Her Pail
The Wolf & the Shepherd
The Goatherd & the Goat
The Miser
The Wolf & the House Dog
The Fox & the Hedgehog
The Bat & the Weasels
The Quack Toad
The Fox Without a Tail
The Mischievous Dog
The Rose & the Butterfly
The Cat & the Fox
The Boy and the Nettles
The Old Lion
The Fox & the Pheasants
Two Travelers & a Bear
The Porcupine & the Snakes
The Fox & the Monkey
The Flies & the Honey
The Eagle & the Kite
The Stag, the Sheep, & the Wolf
The Animals & the Plague
The Shepherd & the Lion
The Bees & Wasps, & the Hornet
The Lark & Her Young Ones
The Cat & the Old Rat
The Ass & His Shadow
The Miller, His Son, & the Ass
The Wolf, the Kid, and the Goat
The Swallow & the Crow
Jupiter & the Monkey
The Lion, the Ass, & the Fox
The Lion's Share
The Mole & His Mother

The North Wind & the Sun
The Wolves & the Sheep
The Cock & the Fox
The Ass in the Lion's Skin
The Fighting Cocks & the Eagle

Despite Aesop's chosen titles, his works have nothing to do with animals and everything to do with the study of individual and group psychology of humans. Aesop's fables are, each and everyone, masterful displays of metaphoric and non- linear thinking and reasoning. Aesop was the master of syllogisms and allegories to drive home his points. It is within the metaphoric storyline that great truths can be conveyed. After working your way through Aesop's Fables, you will begin to notice that your brain will develop an ability to see things that were never quite clear before or completely invisible to you.

Take Aesop's story about the industrious and frugal ant and the carefree, "live for today" grasshopper. Aesop captured the cultural divide between the "live for today crowd," contrasted with society's producers who generate wealth. The "live for today" crowd openly smokes marijuana, drinks alcohol, parties and spend other people's money. Recreating or recovering from recreating consumes their life. Those who generate wealth, on the other hand, have jobs and/or families, and they value work and saving for tomorrow.

Aesop captured a nuanced part of this cultural divide when he depicted the carefree grasshoppers making fun of the industrious ants. The metaphor of wintertime captures that chapter in a person's life when age, economic hardship and health issues catch up with the wasteful and carefree ingénue grasshopper. On that fateful winter day she awakens from her carefree life to find herself an older, penniless and dependent and unattractive person nobody wants to help, especially the ant she made fun of when she was a pretty, young, smart aleck grasshopper.

Metaphoric thinking permits grand meaning to be communicated using a few well-turned words. Here is but one example that illustrates this point. I'm going to describe a pattern of behavior between men and women. This pattern has to do with love and power in a relationship. First, I'll give you the literal and concrete version.

*The person who falls in love with another person invariably becomes vulnerable to that person. The
person who loves the most is the person who generally is the most vulnerable. This situation is one of
the things about love that makes falling in love a scary proposition.*

OK, that was the literal and concrete version. Now let me show you how a much shorter, poetic and metaphoric-minded writer's words can impregnate tremendous meaning into a small space:

Ah, but if we could fall into their arms without falling into their hands.

I hope that even those of you who are well-practiced literal and concrete thinkers can appreciate the difference as illustrated above, between linear and metaphoric narratives. In fact, I suspect that when those of you who are not so literal and concrete read the metaphoric version, you experienced pleasure or may have smiled. This is because the human brain, once able to experience metaphors, prefers them to any other kind of information processing.

Neuroscience has documented the fact that people wedded to certain political ideologies possess certain information processing styles. So called conservatives, for example, find themselves at a distinct *disadvantage* when it comes to being able to *counter* Bernays-like strategies and tactics used to engineer consent. This is because, in large measure, metaphoric strategies are invisible to conservative's brains. Progressive-minded citizens, on the other hand, are especially *susceptible* to the non-linear PSYOPs used by mind control artists to engineer consent to wit:

> *Political scientists and psychologists have noted that, on average, conservatives show more structured and persistent cognitive styles, whereas liberals are more responsive to informational complexity, ambiguity and novelty. We tested the hypothesis that these profiles relate to differences in general neurocognitive functioning using event-related potentials, and found that greater liberalism was associated with stronger conflict-related anterior cingulate activity, suggesting greater neurocognitive sensitivity to cues for altering a habitual response pattern.*[249]

What this study and countless others document is that when conservative politicians attempt to communicate their political thoughts to progressive voters, the conservative (literal and concrete) speakers may as well be speaking a foreign language. Is it any wonder that progressives tend to turn off or turn away from conservative ideologies? Conservative and progressives speak a different language. Once again, when the match is defined by psychological operations that use Bernays-like engineering of consent, conservative leaders and pundits will find themselves to be at a distinct disadvantage because of their failure to comprehend what is happening to them. On the other hand, progressive minded people unconsciously embrace Bernay's-like social engineering PSYOPs while scoffing at conservative critics. Perhaps now you can better understand how it is the shadow men have gotten away with so much for so long.

---

[249] David M Amodio, John T Jost, Sarah L Master & Cindy M Yee. (2007), *Neurocognitive correlates of liberalism and conservatism.* Nature Neuroscience 10, 1246 – 1247.

CHAPTER 16: NAPOLEON'S 12 STEP PLAN TO REGAINING YOUR FREE WILL

In honor of The Egyptian God Horus who marches across the sky each day in 12 steps, I am going to provide my readers with a 12 step program to awareness and improved immunity to the mind control artists who are everywhere and intent upon the destruction of our free will. Everything that I have written up till now was a preface for Napoleon's 12 Step Program that will help protect your God given freedom from the social engineers in our midst.

Each of the 12 steps has to be mastered in step-wise fashion before you can progress to the next level. Believe me, I wouldn't have created this 12 Step Program if I thought there was a more efficient way to protect you from the shadow men who never, ever, have enough of your free will and wealth to satisfy them.

STEP ONE:
I AM VULNERABLE TO MIND CONTROL AND I ADMIT THAT I HAVE BEEN BRAINWASHED WITHOUT MY AWARENESS.

You have been brainwashed and you don't even know it. No matter who you are, your mind has been programmed. Your denial or genuine belief that you are not a victim of brainwashing IS A SYMPTOM OF HAVING BEEN BRAINWASHED.

The very first thing you must do is admit, that you, like everyone else, has been poisoned to think and behave in ways that assist shadow men. "I have not escaped their hold on me but I am now ready and able to cleanse myself of their brainwashing."

COMMENTARY: This first step is more difficult to master than one might first imagine. This is because almost all people find it very difficult to admit they have been played for fools. One of the reasons this step is so difficult is because people confuse having been played for a fool to mean that you are a fool. Just because you lose doesn't mean you are a loser, see the difference?

Mastering Step One requires of the reader a fair amount of humility. It also requires the reader to give up his sense of security that comes from the false belief that he has been in control of his thoughts, feelings and behaviors.

STEP TWO:
I HAVE WITHIN ME THE POWER TO DEPROGRAM MYSELF OF THE BRAINWASHING TO WHICH I HAVE BEEN SUBJECTED.

You must challenge your most deeply held beliefs and your blind loyalties, recognizing that your loyalty to whomever and whatever was socially engineered to promote the welfare of those who rule over you, NOT for your benefit. Repeat this wisdom from Voltaire: "To learn who rules over you, simply find out who you are not allowed to criticize." Repeat this statement: "I expect to feel anxious when I dare challenge anything, anyone or any group with a hallowed label attached to it because I have been brainwashed to honor such labels since my birth." PC enforcers, who are unwitting agents of shadow men, will attach a stigmatized label on you when you free yourself of their shackles.

COMMENTARY: Others have been brainwashed and others have deprogrammed themselves of that brainwashing. If you happen to be stubborn or conservative minded or a similarly rigid personality type, you will experience a **tremendous** amount of anxiety when you begin to realize that what you thought you knew, those things of which you were are so confident, were created by shadow men to serve them. Realize that your emotional response to this realization is simply the morning sun shining on eyes that have been shut and living in the dark. Your eyes will adjust and so will you. Be patient with yourself

STEP THREE:
I SHALL NOT BOW TO POLITICALLY CORRECT SPEECH.

I shall have faith that when the politically correct speech police come after me, that means I am speaking the truth that is most harmful to evil. I shall not be afraid nor shall I submit to intimidation by the thought police. I shall consider from this day forward the thought police's gasps, anger and chastising of me to be compliments from God. If you are an American, you must remember that your founders risked life and limb to give to you freedom from the PC Police. Unless you exercise your God given rights, you may as well throw them away.

COMMENTARY: This step is very difficult for a lot of people because the PC police have cultivated your fear of them. You'll be surprised, however, at how the truth when spoken with kindness and fearless authority will make it OK to stand up and speak the truth. If you are dependent upon a paycheck from PC enforcers or if you have created a social circle that is disingenuous, you may lose acquaintances or a paycheck. Others who you thought were your friends may morph into PC enforcers once you begin to speak the truth. In trade for your loss of acquaintances and paychecks you will receive in triplicate freedom of spirit and the lifting of the psychological burden associated with being disingenuous. Choose your soul, not your social circle or your paycheck, you will feel much better and be stronger.

STEP FOUR:
I SHALL NOT, I WILL NOT, BECOME "ONE OF THE CROWD."

If I find myself swept up in the passion of whatever happens to be the focus of the media entertainment complex, no matter what it is or who it involves, I will stop, look and listen and then ask: Who wanted me to feel this way? Because I shall know that there is ALWAYS an answer to that question. I will always ask: Why this, why now?

COMMENTARY: If your goal is to be popular and if you enjoy being "trendy" then you will NEVER free yourself from the shackles of shadow men. Popularity is only that, it is popular. Truth is at a premium when compared to falsehood, though it is exponentially more important. Genuineness is not as common as is being disingenuous. No one but other disingenuous people willingly comingle with false and shallow people. By becoming genuine you will become an honored member of the *true elites*.

STEP FIVE:
I HAVE USED MY OWN VERSION OF MIND CONTROL ON OTHERS. FOR THIS, I APOLOGIZE AND PROMISE TO BE DIRECT AND ALWAYS AVOID MANIPULATION OF OTHERS.

COMMENTARY: This step requires a fair amount of self-examination. As with all of our steps it is important to keep in mind that we have all, at some point in our lives, used our own version of mind control on others. This is because we were all made in our shadow men master's images. Take inventory and be honest with yourself. Repeat these truisms: " I have learned that mind controllers have purposefully made me into their image. I have adopted their evil ways without conscious awareness but now I shall no longer be oblivious to how I have become like them. I am a child of God, not of evil." You may choose to apologize to those you have harmed in the past. If you choose not to do that, then simply change your ways and begin the process of replacing your disingenuous relationships with genuine relationships.

STEP SIX:
EVERYONE I KNOW HAS BEEN BRAINWASHED LIKE ME. THEREFORE, I SHALL BE PATIENT AND REACH OUT TO OTHER VICTIMS WHO HAVE YET TO AWAKEN FROM THEIR STUPOR.

COMMENTARY: It is easy to judge others who remain unaware. However, never forget that you were once like them in one degree or another. Human beings learn from modeling their behavior after those they admire. Be one of those people other good people admire. Allow people to learn by watching you. Always be patient but firm with those who are quiet victims or who are searching without an attitude. People who explicitly proselytize are often shunned. It is much better to set an example when interacting with others than it is to preach to them.

Repeat these truisms: "If I awakened from my stupor then my fellow man can awaken as well." We all stand upon the shoulders of those who came before us. I have stood on shoulders and I shall now provide a set of shoulders that others can stand on."

STEP SEVEN:
I RECOGNIZE THAT I MUST DO TWO THINGS: I MUST UN-PLUG AND AT THE SAME TIME PLUG-IN.

Our generation has been thrust into a battle not of our making. The most dangerous of these enemies reside within America's borders. Their weapon of choice is psychological manipulation. I shall view my digital devices and "screens," in whatever shape or form, as no different than a hypodermic needle placed into my arm. What is in the syringe or the IV bag? What are the side effects of this medicine continually pumped into my mind? Who made the social engineering content being injected into me?

COMMENTARY: Be very, very cautious of popular media. Be very, very cautious of so-called alternative media. Tune into media not as a passive viewer or listener, but as an analyst who gauges the genuineness of the presentation. If the presenter reads from a teleprompter (99.9% of the time) staged to make it look like he/she is talking to the audience, realize that this act is disingenuous and a blatant lie. In other words, the very essence of the program is built upon a lie! If your presenter has an ear-mic (99.9% use ear mics) through which the "brain" room feeds to him/her questions, corrects him/her, provides factual data, while the presenter pretends it is him or her who is so smart and knowledgeable, then realize you are being manipulated and lied to. Genuine content presented in genuine media is as rare as truth and justice. It isn't real folks!

STEP EIGHT:
DEBT IS MY MORTAL ENEMY. SOCIALLY ENGINEERED WANT IS HOW I AM MADE TO BECOME AN INDENTURED SERVANT TO MY MASTERS.

I shall live within my means. I shall not incur nor encourage debt. If I have indebted myself I will spend every waking moment pulling myself out of debt. If I absolutely need something, then I shall save for it and ask for God's help to acquire it. I shall not indebt myself to acquire my wants. I shall no longer be brainwashed to believe that my wants are synonymous with my needs.

COMMENTARY: Here is a good way to think about what you are up against. The motivational state of want and desire are engineered and fed to you through various media. So-called content is only there to fill time between the real business of virtually any media, which is to sell things to you and/or mold your attitudes and behaviors. And how do they sell things to you and mold your attitudes and behavior? They socially engineer want, desire, need, insecurity, greed, envy and pride. You are then provided solutions to these drive states in the form of a product or service or some path toward salvation.

Think that marketers don't know who you are? The products and services they advertise reveal who they think you are and what they think of you. So if the program you're watching sells to you Viagra and moustache coloring, then they view you as an aging man who wants to be virile and younger looking. If you ever wondered what the media thinks of the people watching or listening to any particular program, simply study the products they are selling to you. That will tell you everything you need to know.

STEP NINE:
I SHALL NO LONGER PROVIDE MY SERVICES TO PEOPLE WHO SUPPORT THOSE WHO WISH TO TAKE AWAY MY FREE WILL AND MANIPULATE MY MIND.

I shall withhold my services, my money, my good will and my presence to those who promote, assist or have turned a blind eye to the assaults upon my free will. I shall no longer "go along" in order to "get along."

COMMENTARY: Talk is cheap. If you really want to make a difference then you must stop supporting anything or any person that is destroying your free will. You'll know that you have mastered this step when you turn down paying customers or clients because of your principles. If you work for everyone or anyone, then you may have no principles or you may have become so indentured to shadow men and their agents, that you must bide your time. If that is the case, dream of the day when will be able to act more responsibly. Financially support, even if it hurts, people who are walking the point and walking the talk. Conversely, stop financially supporting anyone, no matter who they are, if that person espouses tolerance of intolerance. If your money makes it possible for younger people to continue to live a life of subservience to the PC Police or if the people you support ARE the PC Police, then remove that financial support. If you tend to express strong opinions, but when push comes to shove you can never reach for your checkbook, you are not being real. Put your money where your mouth is.

STEP TEN:
I SHALL SPEND MORE TIME READING THAN WATCHING, MORE TIME DOING AND LESS TIME WORRYING.

As I cleanse myself of the brainwashing I have been subjected to, I now realize that passively watching and listening to media at the expense of reading is harmful to my health and wellbeing.

COMMENTARY: Most people consume media passively. Sitting in front of various screens or plugged into headphones passively listening is potentially dangerous to your health. When you *actively* watch or listen you will find yourself continually asking questions and scanning for meaning. When you read you must engage your brain in ways that are not necessary when you fixate upon a screen. A very few presenters will force you to think. If you find an honest presenter who makes you think, tune in.

STEP ELEVEN:
I SHALL BE ON THE LOOKOUT FOR PRESSURES UPON ME TO RUSH TO JUDGMENT. WHEN EVERY MEDIA OUTLET PUSHES THE SAME STORY I

SHALL ASK MYSELF: WHO WANTS ME TO PAY ATTENTION TO THIS AT THE EXPENSE OF PAYING ATTENTION TO SOMETHING MORE IMPORTANT?

I now know that everything that is fed to me by and through the media is designed to make me look here or look there, feel this way or that way. Who benefits and who makes money and/or garners more control over me from manipulation of my mind? That is the question you must continually ask yourself.

COMMENTARY: Somebody, somewhere, wants you to think or feel something that will line their pockets or increase their power. This is the dirty little secret behind virtually all media, businesses, sellers, managers, people in general. If you can find someone, whose intent is to increase your freedom of choice, then that person is generous and secure in the power he or she has and does not want your power in addition to their power. Someone who shares real knowledge as opposed to agenda-laden opinions is the person you must search for. People like you or who are at your level of development are not going to be able to help you. Try to steer clear of ego driven media personalities. Ego manifests through grandiosity and braggadocio. These people want you around as viewers to enhance their already inflated ego. Don't oblige them.

STEP TWELVE:

I SHALL ALWAYS ASK THIS QUESTION WHEN I FEEL PRESSURED BY MY GOVERNMENT OR THE MEDIA: WHY THIS? WHY NOW?

Since the government and the people behind the media want control over my mind more than anything else, I shall jealously protect it and not give them free access to it. I'll know they are at work when something happens that angers me, makes me feel fearful, makes me want to attack the person with the "black" hat. Anytime my government or the media makes me feel something I will take back my emotional control from them. I will stop, look and *actively* listen.

COMMENTARY: Your government and its agents in the media-entertainment complex want your mind under their control. Resist, be stubborn, pause, think, avoid the knee jerk reaction and when you feel a jingoistic rush or when the "bad guys" are drawn for you like cartoon characters stop, look and actively listen and ask, why? These are the signs that the mind control artists are ramping up their efforts.

Repeat these admonitions to yourself: Since I know that I am vulnerable to the "herd instinct," I shall resist the popular crowd because I know that popularity is "socially engineered consent." I am my own person and I will not think, dress, eat, behave or do anything like the socially engineered crowd. I recognize that virtually everyone thinks they are their own person, including me, but I now realize I'm a manufactured bundle of thoughts, feelings and behaviors designed to transfer my wealth and control over to shadow men.

Good is portrayed as bad. Evil is packaged as good. If you should steer left to increase your independence and power you can be assured you will be persuaded to turn right or vice versa. A smile is just a frown turned upside down. They keep it all hidden. Overt sexuality means coldness in reality. Puffery and big talk means weakness. The people who should be in charge are cut off at the knees before you ever hear their name. Look past the preened image on your screens and judge, yes judge and emphasize character over everything else. Good is good and bad is bad. I leave you with these thoughts from a man who wanted you to know what I want you to know, so much so, that I wrote this book at my own peril.

In Chapter One of Orwell's classic *1984*, he wrote the following:

> *"Throughout recorded time, and probably since the end of the Neolithic Age, there have been three kinds of people in the world, the High, the Middle, and the Low. They have been subdivided*

*in many ways, they have borne countless different names, and their relative numbers, as well as their attitude toward one another, have varied from age to age; but **the essential structure of society has never altered.** Even after enormous upheavals and seemingly irrevocable changes, the same pattern has always reasserted itself, just as a gyroscope will always return to equilibrium, however far it is pushed one way or the other. The aims of these three groups are entirely irreconcilable....”*

In Chapter Three Orwell tells us this:

*“The essential act of war is destruction, not necessarily of human lives, but of the products of human labor. War is a way of shattering to pieces, or pouring into the stratosphere, or sinking in the depths of the sea, materials which **might otherwise be used to make the masses too comfortable, and hence, in the long run, too intelligent.** Even when weapons of war are not actually destroyed, their manufacture is still a convenient way of expending labor power without producing anything that can be consumed.”*

The 13th Step is a step you do not want to take. If you do take the 13th Step, this is your fate:

"Everybody Knows"
By: Leonard Cohen
Everybody knows that the dice are loaded
Everybody rolls with their fingers crossed
Everybody knows that the war is over
Everybody knows the good guys lost
Everybody knows the fight was fixed
The poor stay poor, the rich get rich
That's how it goes
Everybody knows

THE END

321

INDEX

H

I

www.ingramcontent.com/pod-product-compliance
Lightning Source LLC
Chambersburg PA
CBHW041428270326
41932CB00031B/3494